THE SEVENTH WIFE

Other books by Andrei Moscovit available in English:

OUR CHOICE AND HISTORY (Philosophical Library, 1985)

THE JUDGMENT DAY ARCHIVES (Mercury House, 1988)

THE SEVENTH WIFE

A NOVEL BY

ANDREI MOSCOVIT

TRANSLATED BY

ANTHONY OLCOTT

BASKERVILLE
PUBLISHERS, INC.
DALLAS • NEW YORK • DUBLIN

This book is a work of fiction. Names, characters, places and incidents are either the product of the author's imagination or are used fictitiously. Any resemblance to actual events or locales or persons, living or dead, is entirely coincidental.

BASKERVILLE Publishers, Inc.
7616 LBJ Freeway, Suite 220, Dallas TX 75251-1008

Library of Congress Cataloging-in-Publication Data

Efimov, Igor ´ Markovich
    [Sed ´maia zhena. English]
    The seventh wife : a novel / by Andrei Moscovit ; translated by
Anthony Olcott.
       p. cm.
    ISBN: 1-880909-16-2 : $23.00
    I. Title
    PG3479.7.F49S413 1994
    891.73'44--dc20   93-45939
                                       CIP

To my only wife Marina, and to our daughters Leana and Natasha with many thanks for never trying to run away from home.

TABLE OF CONTENTS

TABLE OF CONTENTS (cont.)

PART ONE

DISAPPEARANCE

1. THE CALL

THE PAIN MADE ITS
way into the gum in slow jerks, like a train in the mountains. They had
lived in the mountains almost three weeks before they were married, he
and his fifth wife, Wife #5, Jill, because she was afraid that her husband
would hire detectives and find them ("Yeah sure, you laugh, but
nowadays they know how to take pictures at night, through the windows, maybe you and I are in their movie cameras right now, in this pose
here.") and then she'd lose custody of the children to horrible Husband
#5.1, who always walked looking straight ahead, as if being forced to
walk between rows of people who were asking him for charity. That
same frozen glare, straight ahead, at some invisible point, had also
belonged to the out-of-work police sergeant to whom he had sold his
first insurance policy against Real Trouble (what did he want it for
anyway? It had already happened to him). That was a long long time
ago, in Chicago, how many years exactly he couldn't recall. Wife #2
used to love to observe that everybody who was out of work must also
be illiterate, since they couldn't read all the columns and columns of
help-wanted ads in the newspapers. His favorite answer was, "Every
good agent in my line has to remember that we aren't living in that huge
upside-down country where the word for 'insurance' is based on the
word for 'fear.' We live in America, where the people give us their
money and we give them first class confidence, with seals and stamps
and bells! Insurance!" However, all his confidence went to smithereens
when Real Trouble came to him, when the tide of unpaid bills began to
wash over his desk and he shuddered every time he saw a policeman,

and whenever he was in the charity line, meaning the unemployment office, right behind him, keeping a look-out for him or something, was always the very same black woman with a scuffle of kids—let anybody try to get custody of them!—and it seemed at times as though his heart would refuse to take its next beat, because it knew that it would stab, stab, stab with pain.

The phone rang.

Anton carefully swung his legs out from the covers, put his feet on the cold floor. Outside Mrs. Hilbram was walking her dachshund Sheba, who was balanced on four legs gathered to a single point in the middle of the lawn and was squeezing, contorting. Her tail was quivering with effort and anticipation. Mrs. Hilbram was gently lashing herself across the thigh with the other end of the leash. The night before Anton had heard an engine roar right under the window, which must mean that her husband had set off for the other end of the continent in his truck again. Why, with what load? What could he be carrying from the East Coast that they didn't have on the West Coast, in this country that was absolutely identical from one end to another, as if made from children's blocks?

The telephone rang.

It could be the credit bureau. He hadn't paid off the motorboat before Real Trouble came. A shyster had had the boat put in the name of Wife #4, in lieu of alimony. Somebody from the credit bureau had come right over to his house, the last place, and had even gnashed his teeth when he discovered that everything in the house was already taken, repossessed by the bank, that even the car in the garage was divided up into chunks for other creditors. Anton had rocked heel and toe in front of him, unshaven and unslept, holding the lapels of his pajamas as if ready to peel them off too and hand them over at the first request. The agent spoke fastidiously and made rapid notes in a notebook, sizing up the rugs and pictures that still hung on the walls, then made a jolly promise to come back within two hours with the police and a truck. The poor guy didn't know that there were others, more on the ball than he, that by noon the walls would already be bare, with big dark rectangles.

Could they have found him here, in this barn? Everything is computers now. Everything is entered, counted, registered, all the distinguishing marks are recorded, fingerprints, palm prints, teeth, the hollow of your cheek on the pillow, your footprints in the sand.

His feet were getting colder and colder on the floor. The telephone rang.

4

Of course, this could just be Mrs. Darcey, Mother-in-law #3, who was separated from him by just thirty feet of mowed grass, some violets, yammering crickets, and scrupulous ants. "Did you take your medicine yesterday? What should I make for your lunch today? Will you finish the program by Saturday? Mrs. Hilbram left her garbage bag untied on the curb again. Couldn't you talk with her and let her know that's uncouth? I cut an interesting advertisement out of the paper for you. They're looking for a consultant in seismic cybernetics. I know that you don't know anything about it, but you've got such a wonderful brain, maybe you could take some courses or something. And Susan called yesterday, she said that everything is fine with them, except that Katie announced to everyone at school that she's a 'bastard,' and now they're teasing her and making her cry. I told you and told you, a wedding is such a little thing that it really isn't too much to ask someone to do for the children's sake, even if it does support the corrupt morals of a corrupt society. There were eight letters about your last broadcast; should I bring them over? Some lady writes that all her life she's been against violence on principle, and even headed some Committee to Defend Nest and Fledglings, but when she listens to you on the radio she fantasizes about how sometime somebody will take a good hold on the gentleman's tongue with a pair of tweezers, yank it out as far as it will go, lather it up good with Era Plus, and give it a scrubbing with Brillo..."

The telephone rang.

Three brass circles hung above the telephone. For several years now the trembling needles inside them had made daily promises of storm, heat, and unbearable damp. Then there were photos of boys in wide hats. A dusty peacock feather. A little tufted rug with a map of Italy. A framed mirror. Yellow maple leaves pressed and dried in the short break between the two world wars. A bas-relief of a long-dugged African. Two duelling pistols. A poster for a movie that had broken the sound barrier.

The telephone rang.

Anton finally guessed who it must be. Old fart Simpson, the lawyer for Wife #4. He was the only one who could have sniffed out or begged out or gnawed out the number for this telephone, which he and Mother-in-law #3 were keeping a secret from everybody. He was the only one who would have had the patience to let it ring for so long. What could he be wanting? To specify adding another larcenous clause to the divorce agreement? More alimony? As if he didn't already know that there was nothing left to take, that Anton's bones were sucked bare and his last gristle gnawed. But that was undoubtedly why the perennial bachelor Simpson was the best divorce lawyer in the whole county, because he knew how to follow the doomed victim with the persistence of a wolf. He didn't just represent the interest of his clients; he punished vice. And the most terrible human vice of all was a thirst for happy change. Old man Simpson was the embodiment of just retribution for unsatisfied appetite. Sometimes it seemed that his real goal was to root up even the desire ever to marry again, or have children, or buy a house, or have money. Was it Simpson who brought the punishment for the apostasy of which we had been warned already two thousand years ago, in the sermon on that small Palestinian hill? He was so fanatical and pitiless that sometimes he worked almost for free.

The telephone rang.

Before Wife #4 was his wife, while she was still hammering away at the computer keyboard in the travel agency in Los Angeles in order to dispatch tourists to the trackless wastes of the Upside-down Country, he had got a glimpse, from behind at first, of her slightly raised, haughty shoulders, and he felt that familiar first stab in the chest, as though someone had started to blow a balloon up in there, not in the heart as poems and books promised, but always someplace a little higher, between his lungs and his trachea. He had thought then that it would be a simple thing to go straight ahead up the aisle and into the director's office without looking at her, because he had played all those games enough already, in his thirties. And that's what he did, too, except that he forgot that on the way back he would have to go down the aisle the other way, and so he let the hunched shoulders slip his mind while he was talking business and that's how he ended up face to face with her. And then they went to sit in a restaurant, probably that same day, and she behaved like a hero, pretending that this wasn't part of her work, that the director hadn't begged her to agree, to please an important guest (which is what she later admitted to him), because insurance just then was insane, you couldn't get it for love nor money, and businesses were folding right and left, offices like theirs especially, since they were sending travellers on such dangerous trips.

"You know," she explained with a shrug (padding was in fashion again then, and underneath her blouse, to his distress, there were two button-on shoulder pads), "what merciless do-gooders jurors are, how they are ready to award millions to everybody who sues, because what does it matter to them that it isn't our fault and shouldn't be our responsibility when some curious tourist in the Upside-down Country buys a meat pie on the street and eats it? Oh no, the jurors say, you are guilty because your brochures don't warn one to immediately drink a glass of vodka after that, for disinfection, the way the natives do."

And the next day, when they went to the beach and he spread cream on her back, but kept inching his hand higher, as if absent-mindedly, to run his palms over her shoulders, which she had already greased without his assistance, they continued to discuss business, how to help their office get around the dizzying costs of insurance. She still had the green of computer screen in her eyes, which didn't disappear until she came to his hotel room for the first time, when they definitely forgot about business and insurance, and her shoulders glistened under the peeling skin, ruddy as fresh pine bark under old. Apparently cream didn't help, but he couldn't decide whether to tell her about his little eccentricity, his perversion for the first few weeks. He pretended that everything was great, that he was on cloud nine each time, so that even afterwards she didn't notice anything for the longest time.

The third divorce was faster than the first two, with fewer formalities, because he and Wife #3 had never gotten around to getting married. In the beginning he rented his intended an apartment in New Jersey, seventeenth floor, right on the Hudson, so that she swore she could see his car across the water when he was coming home from work on the West Side highway and knew when to put dinner in the oven (she was still cooking then), and he loved to tease her about how many things she did with her shoulders—opening and closing doors, turning on the lights, getting the hair out of her eyes, holding the telephone to her ear—and he promised her that as soon as they made a car that you could drive by moving your shoulders he would buy it for her, and then maybe she would learn not to run into other cars at the intersections and not to run over mailboxes. It was only when they got married though that he was able to stop pretending, and in fact every time he floated off for a moment of blessed oblivion. She noticed the difference of course and it bothered her, as if he had learned how to take something from her without her permission or participation. Bit by bit she learned the games he loved best, what to give him. To make it harder for her to guess he tried never to laugh as her serious flush face hung over him. And then she would dive below, eyes shut tight. She never would have guessed though, would never have uncovered the secret, if he hadn't blurted it out himself, in a fit of passion, the time he found that damned box.

The telephone rang.

He never got excited at the sight of a bunch of letters.

He never got happy when he saw envelopes slit open by a secretary, because there could never be anything in them except inflated bills, obligating requests and insulting rejections.

The heap of incoming letters could pile up on his desk from one day to the next, but he felt something else entirely toward phone calls.

All that was exciting, lucky, victorious or new—like everything that was truly dangerous, serious, and horrible—could only be announced by the ring of the telephone, that white apparatus there on the desk, and he would try to guess from the sound of the secretary's voice what kind of surprise this next call was bringing him.

Even at times when the calls came like an on-rushing wave, such as for example after the first announcement of his great innovation, his invention of genius, which brought him fame and fortune—insurance against divorce—even then his stab of alarm didn't go away from call to call, but accumulated like needles in his fingers, which would jump all by themselves from the desk to the receiver when it began to bounce about like a tennis ball.

In those days the heap of letters on the desk rose up to the lamp-shade, but you couldn't just chuck them in the wastebasket, because a lot of them began with the words, "We were unable to reach you by telephone, so...", after which followed a list of questions: how? when? what age? for how long? how much does it cost to insure yourself against the misery of divorce?

In order to cope with the flood of clients they had to hire two new clerks, and in the evenings he would drill them on all aspects of the methodology he had worked out, but only after swearing them to secrecy, with a notarized promise not to reveal anything to the competition for a certain period. Sometimes the secretary worked until ten and spent the night on the couch in the reception area, too tired even to clean up the pizza rinds on the lamp tables.

However, when Real Trouble came and the clerks, bookkeepers, and typists began one by one to disappear from the office, and he even had to fire the secretary, the telephone became the spawn of hell, a white monster howling in the middle of the table, a greedy dragon more fearsome than any letter, heaped though they were about him. The telephone became a messenger of misery whom he would have liked to drown in the toilet.

The pain had made it to the last tooth on the right and stopped, spinning its wheels. The racket of the telephone flowed into it, falling into the same rhythm, singing along. It began to seem that if he were to kill the one, the other would rot of its own accord.

He picked up the receiver but the rattling of the lawn mower outside took over the sound vacuum, giving the pain a shove, so that it chugged onward.

"Don't lie to me, Anthony, don't you lie to me!" the receiver shrieked.

He recognized the voice of Wife #1.

"How come you don't let her pick the receiver up for thirty whole minutes? What are you two hiding there anyway? Scheming behind my back again are you? That's terrible, awful! I'm a mother, and that gives me some rights. My lawyer already knows everything anyway, so...What? I don't believe that you just came home...And anyway it's none of your business where I got your number, you son of a bitch! You should know how my heart has been aching these three days, what would it cost you to phone and at least warn me? Bring her to the phone this instant, you snake in the grass!"

"Who?"

"Golda, you stinking liar! Your daughter, you idiot. My daughter too, incidentally."

Fear was pulling a purse-string in his stomach.

"What makes you think she's here?"

"Enough of that already, all right? You've played your games, hide-and-seek is over, it's stupid already, okay?"

She began to sob, but he understood that she had believed him immediately and that all the yelling and threatening and cursing was just a part of the stage exorcism that she always set up and played out when she wanted something very badly. Or was very afraid of something.

"She disappeared three days ago. She went to her tennis lesson with her racket and gym bag, said that she was going to stop at the library after that. But she didn't go to tennis or the library. The police promised to put a bulletin out, but they let me know that they don't look for nineteen-year olds. How do you like that, anyway? The first thing I thought of was that she might have come over to your place, and you're punishing me by not calling. It took me three days to get your number."

"Did you try the college? Her girlfriends?"

"It's already the holidays there. I'm certain that she's gone to one of the girls in your harem. She always liked it better with you than in her own home. Naturally, because sweet little papa always made a two-week carnival for his baby doll, turning her head with gifts. It's a simple trick, but it never fails. Not to mention the novelty that there's always a new stepmother. And what's she got at home? She has to go to school, has to go to the doctor, has to make her bed, has to vacuum the room, has to help in the yard, has to watch the little ones. Nothing but has-tos here, aren't there?"

"Did you fight about something again?"

"I was just waiting for that. Now it's my fault, huh? Yes, if a polite request to remove somebody else's plants that I never asked for out of the greenhouse is another manifestation of parental despotism, then I confess I am a guilty despot. And if trying to make your point with too much heat is aggression, then I'm guilty of that too. Especially since the fight was entirely academic, a discussion of whether her child-genius friend from school was growing eucalyptus or marijuana in those pots. Big bushy shrubs, that's criminal already, get you four years in jail. So yes, you might say that we fought about something again the day before. That's why I want you to go today."

"Go where?"

"I want you to make the entire circuit. Start with the one that lives in Pittsburgh. Number five, I've forgotten her name. Then go to Washington. I'm almost certain that that's as far as you'll have to go. Golda always worshipped your second. That's not so dumb either, since she's got everything that I don't. Including two armpits full of hair. You'll find her at one of the two, and then you can bring her back to me in Detroit."

"Olga, you're off your nut. Pittsburgh, Detroit...I don't have enough money to make it to the corner drugstore."

"My god, what am I hearing? Who is this I'm talking to? Isn't this the famous rich insurance man, who two years ago didn't even blink at renting a private jet to fly his latest lady love to Hawaii? The one who has a dozen children and spends half his income on alimony? Why has fate so punished him that now he can't even scrape together a couple of dollars for a lousy bus ticket? What are you living on then, you poor overthrown idol?"

"Mrs. Darcey gives me everything I need. She doesn't even take any money for the cabin I live in."

When you reach the absolute bottom of humiliation, when there simply is no further that you can fall, you sense a change in your voice, you are hearing it through swamp water, but at the same time you sense an unexpected firmness in it. After all, the bottom is firm, so you can stand up, at least, lie down—stop moving.

10

"Oh, Mrs. Darcey! I can understand her. How can she ever thank her former son-in-law, who blessed her with two sets of grand-twins! Pretty soon the man's going to start reproducing by fission! But how come our progenitor here doesn't go find himself a job?"

"I'm working. I head an important section in Mrs. Darcey's business."

"Ai-yi-yi! I've heard about that too! A local radio station, that serves two whole city blocks. Every Saturday Mister Anthony Sebich is on the air with a new round of revelations. All right then, I'll send you money for the trip. But forget the bus. Rent a car and make tracks for Pittsburgh today, understood? Or Washington. Where's your closest telegraph? Hang on a sec, I'm writing. I trust that in your flight you haven't changed your name? Ladysville, New Jersey? Fitting place for you..."

He might have said that there was no point in going to Washington, because Wife #2 would never have let Golda stay with her secretly (that would be responsibility, and she didn't do responsibilities). He might have tried to explain that it would be hard for him even to get to the telegraph office, because it could be that Mrs. Darcey, Mother-in-law #3, would refuse to take him in the car (and she never trusted him with the keys), and then from the telegraph office he'd have to get himself to the rental office somehow (and the closest was five miles away). And what if Mother-in-law #3 were to announce that she needed him terribly, that until he finished the next broadcast she couldn't let him go? However, all these problems and difficulties he didn't tell Wife #1, but told himself instead, and was already thinking up clever ways around them and fishing around under the bed for his tennis shoes with one hand while trying with the other to tear his pants from the steel jaws on the coat hanger.

He could feel how he was trembling with impatience, but he couldn't understand why.

Of course it had been an eternity since he had seen his children, since he had left Ladysville, since he had gotten behind a steering wheel, gone to a roadside eatery, ordered steak rare, oozing cholesterol and carcinogens. Sometimes he took evening walks along the little main street of Ladysville, looking in the shops as they closed and imagining himself a foreigner who didn't know the language, couldn't read the signs, had not a single acquaintance, and none of the local money, but who now couldn't return to his own country because for some terrible reason it had sunk into the ground or drowned or melted into clots of mud.

He very much wanted to travel, but not because this was the first time since Real Trouble that he was able to come to the assistance of one of his children, that he was able to do something for them, for her, for Golda, for his beloved Daughter #1.1, something that all her other new fathers couldn't do, with their respectable jobs and their cars and their bank accounts and great connections and houses at the shore. For the first time in many months he felt a stab of that forgotten, elating feeling—malice. That was it, the real thing! The feeling simply flashed and disappeared, but it seemed to Anton that if he tried very hard and didn't quit, he could find the feeling again, like a wavering band on a radio receiver, like the sentence when you lose your place reading. And the malice wasn't against Wife #1 or the pain in his gums or his misplaced sock. No, it was obviously a glimmer of the big malice that he used to feel for the major enemy of his life before the catastrophe, the malice that turned out to be his spine and support, since when it disappeared he collapsed like a limp rag, a soft lump of flesh drying in the wind.

He was so anxious to be off and away that he even forgot to fear for Daughter #1.1, who had run away or been kidnapped or gotten lost.

2. MRS. DARCEY

WHEN WIFE-TO-BE
#3 took Anton to meet Mother-in-law-to-be #3 she warned him that if
it should seem to him that Mrs. Darcey was flirting with him, even
leading him on and making advances, he shouldn't take it as an illusion;
and if he should notice that she was saying something diametrically
opposed to what she had been saying fifteen minutes before, he
shouldn't think of trying to correct her, at least not if he didn't want to
make his future mother-in-law his enemy from Day One. And pray God
that he shouldn't ever say anything about the equality of the sexes, since
Mrs. Darcey was deeply convinced of the fundamental, eternal, and
unchanging superiority of women. Then they had to go a good five
miles out of the way to go to a pet store and get some kind of special
seeds for Mrs. Darcey's parrot, a box of tasties for the two cats, and a
slab of salt pork for her spaniel, who was called Sir. ("Imagine how
many male heads jerk around in the park when she yells 'Sir, Sir, come
here!'")

In the ten years since then Mrs. Darcey's menagerie had enlarged.

His neon-pink ears glistening, Mao Tse Tung, the rabbit, leapt
between Anton's legs, to hide beneath the tablecloth, and the spaniel Sir
(already Sir #2), hot in pursuit, slammed into Anton's knees. The
crocodile Nixon stirred behind the glass of his terrarium, bulging out his
billiard-ball eyes, the end of his tail dipped in the rubber-banked pond.
Mother-in-law #3 turned away from a cage of fox kits, smiled, and
waggled fingers in greeting. Elvis, the wild pigeon, swooped down
from the ceiling fixture to land on the piano.

13

Sometimes it seemed that if some murderer were to come to Mrs. Darcey to confess his just-completed crime, she would listen to him with precisely this same soft, somewhat condescending smile, encouraging him onwards, now with a lift of the eyebrow, now with a forward bend of the body, so that she would take it all in, would forgive him nothing, and would manage—without him ever noticing—to wind him up in that same two-ended rope (tight-lipped disappointment at one end, awed radiance at the other) that she was so successful in using to bundle up all the other people who clustered about her.

While Anton was recounting the telephone call of Wife #1 and the disappearance of Daughter #1.1, Mrs. Darcey kept hugging Sir to her chest, sniffling her face in his coat, as if hiding from the horrors of the world beyond the windows. However, no sooner had words like "leave" and "look for" begun to appear in his story, making plain what he was driving at, than Mother-in-law #3 threw the dog from her lap and ran to the window, which she clutched like a frightened maiden whom the fortuneteller's cards had just promised troubles, departures, journeys, and expenses.

Anton said that he didn't need money, because Wife #1 was wiring him some.

Mother-in-law #3 said that she had read in novels and seen in films such instances of profound and base ingratitude, but she had never seen the like in life, until today. Just like that, just before Saturday, he was prepared to leave, to abandon everything, not having prepared his broadcast...just when her radio station was having such difficulties!...well, she had just never expected anything like it.

Anton said that it was still four whole days until Saturday, that he wouldn't be gone long, that maybe he would even find Golda in Washington, and then he would be back the same day.

She countered: this was the more of the same thing he had told her daughter, Wife #3, before his innocent little trip to Los Angeles, where he had met that girl, the one with the shoulders like a coat rack—a trip that had lasted eight years or better, and maybe wasn't over yet.

Anton said that egotism and despotism weren't a combination that enhanced a personality much in the first place, but when you tried to cover them with a mask of injured helplessness, the result was doubly disgusting.

What was amazing, according to Mother-in-law #3, was that a masked egotist would bother to take in a beaten worthless loser, give him food and drink and a roof over his head, to say nothing of providing

14

him with a job that let the loser hang onto to some crumbs of self-esteem.

Anton said that a man who doesn't dare even to stick his nose out into the street or make a phone call, a man who doesn't have a single key in his pocket because he has nothing worth locking or unlocking, a man who has been tortured by toothache for three days already because he's too ashamed to ask for the money to go to a dentist—such a man doesn't think much about self-esteem. But that's what makes such a man so dangerous, because he wouldn't think twice about setting off on foot to the telegraph office to get the money, even though it's five whole miles there, and in the blazing sun besides.

Mother-in-law #3 said that money is money, but if he were to try to rent a car with his driver's license then his name would wing away from computer to computer, and quick as a wink land in one of the three states where he was being sought for non-payment of support, after which the Washington police would quickly be informed of the necessity of detaining a certain gentleman, who was in car license plate such-and-such.

Anton thought about what she had said. The pain in his gums had set off, jerking its way up the next slope. Sir Spaniel jumped down from the chair and came over to sit in front of him, ear cocked so that it brushed the floor.

Anton could hear a stifled sobbing.

Mother-in-law #3 studied him with a radiant, expectant look.

Then he understood that it was he who was sobbing.

The ten months of his anchorite's life in her house had been time enough for Anton to forget how dangerous it can be to want something. To really want something. The serpent head of hope slithered hissing back into its hole.

Mother-in-law #3 came over, black against the window, and sat on the rug alongside Sir. A double line of red beads wound about her black blouse like a highway at night, glimpsed through the window of the airplane as you cross the last hills into the airport. He had always had the feeling that she not only wasn't afraid of aging, but was even almost curious about each new wrinkle on her face or neck, anticipating how she might grapple with it, subduing and mastering it for the cosmetic necessities of the self-portrait which she painted afresh each morning on her triptych mirror. Once she started to talk he felt better, except that a new fear immediately flitted in, that he was so tied to her, so dependent that he had to have not just her money and her help, but her words as well. Was he really bound by the same rope that she wound about people left and right, sometimes with tears and sometimes with smiles?

"Well, perhaps I exaggerated, overdid it a little. They aren't that quick, maybe they wouldn't find you on a short trip to Washington, but that isn't the important thing, that isn't why you can't go away, it's because it would be a crying shame to interrupt the growth process. Something important has been happening to you these past months. Maybe you don't notice, but I'm outside, so I can see, that some sort of transformation is going on. Now don't tell me again that this is another of my hallucinations from church, because it's quite plain that you are being tested from on high, that right now you are like Job in the desert, though naturally I'm doing my best to make your desert as comfortable as I can, with a bathtub and a refrigerator, and I don't bother you with all sorts of advice either, like those friends of Job, and I don't let other people give advice either, even if maybe I'm doing the wrong thing, and God's going to punish me for it, so that I'll remember the Scriptures and not interfere with His doings, when He's making it so plain that He is preparing you for something special by heaping misfortune upon misfortune down upon your head, just about scraping to powder the last of His mortar and starch in you, but then look, something is being made out of that powder, isn't it, now that you've gotten the gift of speech, I mean you never had that, did you, even if I do have to admit that ever since you were little you must have had a pretty good line, or how else could you have sold a million insurance policies or gotten all your wives and non-wives, but I'm not talking about that now, I'm talking about the gift *of speech,* because it isn't just for nothing that so many people tune you in on Saturdays, you must be giving them something to take to heart, even when they get mad at you, because they get mad at you exactly because you've frightened them, woken them up a bit, I know that in myself, how sometimes I'd almost toss everything and come sit at your feet, and that's the gift that's ripening that I don't want to have stopped, you can't just jump back into the fuss and clamor of your rubbish bin a-chock with wives, and anyway, what could be the matter with her anyway, your Golda, who ran away, nobody's ever done that before? so they can't find her without your help? but what about the broadcast, which you're the only one who can get ready, you're the one and only, I mean maybe not a real prophet yet, or else how would I ever dare yell at you like this, though I must say that I don't really tell you what to think, I just worry about the outer shell, the vessel, so to say, the corruptible flesh over the incorruptible soul, and it just now occurs to me that maybe it's time to shore the flesh up a little bit, with the two incredibly fresh lobsters that it just so happens I have in my refrigerator, and why don't I just call your first wife after that myself and tell her that you can't go anywhere because you have an urgent and important job and that private detectives can find runaway children much faster anyway, and that she can easily hire one with some of the money that she has sucked out of you all these years and we have to remember to change the number of your telephone, today if possible."

Mother-in-law #3 jumped nimbly up from the carpet, bent close to Anton's face, as if trying to peer into the prison cell, and then, apparently convinced that the prisoner had gone back to the condition of complete obedience which was good for him, she dashed into the kitchen.

Anton got up and floated after her. He opened the medicine cabinet and began to rummage around, but she stopped him, popping up immediately at his side and finding the bottle of pain-killer, from which she shook tablets into her palm, forced him to open it,, clapped her hand over his mouth, and then gave him something to drink.

She was talking again, arranging things and ordering herself about— "plates here, fork on the left, knife on the right, now where can the pot-cover have gone to? To your spot, on the double! Now the glasses, no, no, not those, these, come on, I'm waiting!"

A head of lettuce squeaked under her rapid blade. The lobsters' tails flapped in mortal convulsions as they emerged from the bubbling depths, turning red as he watched. The lemon split into two golden boats, rocking gently and bumping their bows. The drawn wine cork popped free with the sound of a stolen kiss.

The first year he lived with Wife #3 Anton sometimes got the feeling that he could have gotten his wife to do virtually anything simply by somehow proving to her that her mother wouldn't like it. Even at twenty-five Susan was trying to extract herself, with curses and cries, from the wad of diapers that her mother had wound round her over the long years of her youth and adolescence.

"We have to move!" she begged Anton. "To the Dakotas or Utah or Nebraska, or the West Coast. You invent some kind of earthquake insurance and you'll be a rich man out in California in six months!"

Except she wouldn't have moved anywhere, because the diapers and ribbons held her fast, and she didn't know what to do with herself if her mother didn't telephone for two days. Not long before that Mother-in-law #3 had lost her husband, and her rage at this injustice of fate, after circling above the roofs and swimming pools of Bergamon County, suddenly flashed down upon Anton and his profession.

"So you want to get out of this just by paying some money? Just money, always money? And what about the emptiness, you have a price for that, that there's nothing can fill? How about for the shock of loneliness, eh? You know what I said to Steven when he was dying in my arms? I cursed him, that's what. I yelled at him, 'And what about me, do you think about me, damn you? Who's going to hold me, when it's my turn?' You have the responsibility to warn your clients about all this, you have to make them go to special courses where they can learn about being alone. I'd like you and Susan to sign up for courses like that, right now. They started offering courses like that at Princeton not long ago and they are quite reasonable. At the very least you should read the book PLANNED DEATH. Sure, go ahead and make fun now, but you're going to be good and sorry later that you didn't listen to me, except it's going to be too late then!"

Her husband, Father-in-law #3, developed a passion for newspapers in his final days, demanding that they bring him little local ones and big city ones and even overseas ones. Newspapers lay about in heaps in the sickroom, where he leafed through them greedily, flipping about as he looked for passages of particular importance to him, which as soon as he found he dove into. Once he called Anton over and, giggling, showed him some passage marked out with pencil. It was an obituary, relating the untimely death of Mr. Jerry Malcolm, who had died the day before in an auto accident.

"Did you know him?" Anton inquired.

"First time I hear his name."

"So what's so interesting about the item, then?"

"What do you mean, what's so interesting? Yesterday morning he came out of his house, got in his car, went merrily off in the sunshine to his work, had a martini for lunch, then later was on his way home to his wife for a quickie. Maybe he even went right past here, under my window, but not once! The whole day! Not so much as an inkling!...Ah, what's the use of trying to explain to you? You're no better. Give me the *Times*, they've usually got something about good-time guys like him too."

And he went back to passing his days wallowing in the funny tales of those who just yesterday morning thought that they would easily outlive bed-bound, mortally-ill him.

After his death Mother-in-law #3 conceived a passion for coming to visit them unannounced in their little town some thirty miles from her house, where she would ask meek permission to just sit a while in the living room. After an hour or so she would begin to talk, perhaps to confess that her long-time friend Patricia had had another party, to which once again she had not been invited.

"I understand in principal," mother-in-law #3 would say, "because who wants to have somebody at the table who might suddenly just fall silent and sit there for half an hour with her eyes glazed over? And there's who is she going to sit with too, who's going to be her partner? But when it's me the whole thing is ridiculous, because she ought to know that I'm not some kind of crazy woman who can't control herself. I'm going to a special therapy group for widows and I'm taking a seminar called 'Solitude is Freedom.' I even won a prize on the tv game show 'Who's First To Forget?' I know how to cope with my problems. Anyway people are always calling me and asking whether I don't need some help, and they all tell me not to be shy if I do, just ask for it. Now it is true that not long ago I did call Patricia to say that my refrigerator had quit working and couldn't she send Harry round to have a look, because it was Sunday, and you can't get anybody on a Sunday. She told me that Harry was away for two days, so I didn't bother to tell her that I had just seen him at the gas station about an hour before."

"The bitches!" Susan shouted, "The little hypocrites! You think it's your grief that they're afraid of? They're just afraid for their husbands! Even when daddy was alive those bastards didn't pass up a chance to give you a squeeze, and now...Anthony, you look at this woman and tell me the truth—if Harry had come over, would he have gotten as far as the refrigerator?"

Anton cast a stern glance at the abundant figure of Mother-in-law #3, with her coiffeured towers and falls, knees glittering beneath her shorts, then vowed solemnly that not only would the refrigerator have remained broken but Harry would have also wrecked the television, so as to have a reason to drop in again. He said this without hypocrisy, for even though that painful balloon that grew between his throat and his heart with such incredible ease for so many different women wasn't reacting to her, a certain something else, which Anton when he wished to be offensive privately called the odd-man-out, grew quite lively, pressing its demands.

Sometimes Susan would return from trips to her mother in tears.

"Can you imagine, I drive up without warning, and the table is set for two. How did you know I was coming, I say, and she says I didn't, so I said are you expecting somebody and she says, no, I just did it like that, just in case. Then she set a place for me, but didn't take away the other. That plate kept staring at us, the whole time we ate. And then I noticed something in her bedroom, sticking out from under the pillow. I pulled it out, and you know what? It was daddy's pajamas. Is this ever going to end?"

They did a great deal at the time to have it end, trying very hard, until one time, during a trip to the ocean that was supposed to cheer her up— with the first pair of twins, if he remembered right—when she fell into one of her trances, and they began to jibe her, and without even coming out of her funk she said to them in an angry voice from beyond the grave, "I will not try to drive him away. There are two of you, and I always have to be alone? He is my grief, all that's left of him. I'm not stopping you two from squeezing each other up there in the front, so you can just leave the two of us in peace too."

"Squeezing! Squeezing!" Twins #3.1 began squeaking in their various voices (His numbering system got a little messy when it came to the twins, but he got around it with letters A and B).

Then she came out of it and spent the rest of the day looking guiltily at them, as if she were asking their forgiveness for having told them all off and shaming herself, that she had come down from her heights for a minute, clutching her dead grief like a living man, and now she wasn't going to get another prize in these races to forget, because the game had turned out to be much longer and more difficult than she had imagined.

About three years longer. Or four, maybe? When had she first turned up with her Brinks delivery man? The Brinks man had heavy shoulders round as a watermelon and an immobile yellowish glitter in his eyes, like the reflection of the mounds of other people's gold that had passed through his hands. After that she opened a non-existent store to sell non-existent china; she ran an ad in the paper for salesgirls, and when the girls came to be interviewed she made them talk about their lives, walk up and down in front of her, turning this way and that, then undress and try on things from her closets.

After their break-up Susan had moved to Canada, taking the twins with her, so that Anton had no more reason to visit Mrs. Darcey. When they met by chance she didn't treat him with anything other than contempt and boredom, so that he had no idea why of all the hundreds of people who had passed through his life it was she who had dashed to his side when he was perishing in the abyss of Real Trouble, to pluck him up by the collar, yank him free, resuscitate him, and spirit him off to her guest cabin to dry and mend. Was it pity? Or did she remember how he had danced her court during the first year of her widowhood? Or was it just that she was happy at last to get somebody who had less will remaining to him than did a child's stuffed bunny?

He didn't refuse her. It suited him. The only problem was what she imagined, that she already knew all there was to know about loneliness and despair, that she recalled all the pathways, ridges, canyons, and watersheds, and so was able to lead another lost soul back out into green pastures. She yanked at him, tugged at him, pulled at him, but always in the wrong direction. She never understood that the pit he was in was deeper and more hopeless than hers, and he never tried to explain it to her. Instead he kept waiting to hit bottom.

They were sitting, separated by a red hillock of lobster shells, drinking brandy and eating grapes. The domestic menagerie had quieted down; the cats, dogs, and birds had settled in their accustomed edens, as if finally convinced that the Ark wouldn't leave without them. Mother-in-law #3 got up, came around the table, took Anton by a finger, pulled him after her into the bedroom.

They had done this a few times already. Not many. They didn't talk during it, and didn't kiss. Everything had to remain within the framework of treatment, of what was necessary to care for the corruptible flesh, the outer layer. Not undressing, he lay back on the bed, closed his eyes. Odd-man-out bounced around like a hound waiting for its walk. Everything else was her responsibility, unleashing, petting, taking it around its favorite spots. It was as though the two of them were in league, with perfect understanding, as if Anton had no part in it. The stories of Oedipus, Hamlet, Phaedra and Hippolyte weren't relevant to the situation at hand, because that was passion, which was hardly what you'd call this, was it? And as for crazy ideas or perversions or troubles, that was irrelevant too. He was empty, empty from the top of his head to the tip of his toes. Since Real Trouble the love-berry in his chest had never inflated once, not even to the size of bird-shot.

He opened his eyes and saw that again she had taken almost nothing off, merely undone her blouse. Her broad skirt, flung wide, covered him to the chin. Odd-man-out, the incorrigible egotist, was travelling somewhere in the darkness to the one goal he knew, heeding neither cries nor commands.

Then the woman's face began to change. Her eyes were shut just the same, and her breath plumped up the smile-puckered lips the same, but resolution had rendered her wholly alien as if the clouds had thickened and darkened, or enemy soldiers had crept into town unnoticed from every side. Once again, as he had that morning, Anton felt a jolt of fear and forgotten rage, and for a second he wanted to gird his loins again for battle with an unknown but omnipresent foe. Just at that moment odd-dog-out made its final bound with such vigor that Anton was convulsed, and forced to clutch unwillingly at the life-vest dangling above him.

The wounded and weakening conspirator was still trying to run off somewhere, now without a goal, but simply from a sense of duty. Yet for the woman these seconds were enough for the enemy forces to overtake her and carry her off to another world, and she fell back, slipped away trembling, repeating endlessly the words "a gift, a gift, a gift..."

He didn't know when she had fallen asleep. He was lying there trying to go back, to focus the rage which had flickered back to life for a moment. Leaves danced against the blinds and the freckles on the woman's back went round in circles like a necklace. He gingerly dipped his hand into her purse, which was next to the bed; he felt around, then clutched the keys in his palm. He pulled them out. The bed squeaked when he put his feet to the carpet, and the sleeping woman stirred, releasing the slipcover she had been biting. He went to the door barefoot, carrying his tennis shoes in one hand, the keys in the other. He looked back again, unconvinced that she was asleep. He was unconvinced that he had to do what he was about to do. He pushed the door handle with his elbow and backed out of the bedroom.

He didn't put on his shoes until he was in the car. The engine turned over almost without a sound. It seemed to him that the blind in the bedroom window moved, so he stomped on the gas without remembering to put the car in gear. The motor roared. The sun-warmed house swam peacefully in a sea of foliage.

He drove cautiously out into the street.

It seemed like every oncoming car slowed down and glanced suspiciously at Mrs. Darcey's automobile, an unfamiliar man behind the wheel.

The telegraph person just gave a glance at his credit card and his driver's license, then counted out the five hundred dollars that Wife #1 had sent. At the rental office though the girl noticed that his license had expired, and she shook her head.

For a moment or two he was glad. He turned and headed for the exit, sensing that tears were again springing to his eyes. Then he stopped and went back to the counter, where he counted out the deposit, and then next to it, in a separate pile, the same amount. It was impossible to tell from the girl's tense face whether she was counting the money mentally or trying to remember the telephone number for the police. He added two more bills, and then she chucked the money into the cash drawer and started filling out the papers.

He got a red and white Renault LeCar. The boy working there wiped a lump of grease off his chin, condescended to take the ten-dollar bill, and said, "Sure, no problem, everybody knows Mrs. Darcey. Take the car back and put the keys through the mail slot? You got it!"

As he was leaving town Anton saw in the distance a sign that said the speed limit was forty-five and he was going to speed up, but then the indifferent speedometer told him that he was already doing nearly sixty.

A yellow traffic light blossomed in the foliage and flew over his head.

Shields popped past, warning of the approach of the main road. Which way? South? North? The nightmare of long-ago school tests in geography began to slither from the outbuildings of his memory, but then he was saved by an arrow saying "Washington" which surfaced beyond a turn, and he breathed easily, turning the car to the right.

Within ten minutes his feet, hands, eyes fell into the groove, remembered all the moves they had to make, knitted into their familiar union for the road, and Anton relaxed. He dug out his tape recorder from his pocket, into which he began to speak his next broadcast. The words came of themselves, ridding his head of a muddled idea that had taken root long ago.

Radio Broadcast, Composed En Route to Washington
(The Idol of Life)

Once I saw a prophet on the plaza in front of the university library. He was like all the other prophets, shaking his Bible and making threats, but what he was saying was monstrous:

O, City, thou art become guilty in thy blood that thou hast shed; and hast defiled thyself with thine idols which thou hast made; and thou hast caused thy days to draw near, and art come even unto thy years: therefore have I made thee a reproach unto the heathen and a mocking to all countries.'
Listen to the words of the prophet, this Ezekiel, for you are the new idolaters. You think that you are Christians or Jews or Muslims, or atheists, but in fact you all bow before the same idol, and God is forgotten. You have made a new Calf for yourselves, and you serve it like pagans who have never heard the Word of God, nor the tongue of the prophets.

The name of this new Calf is Human Life.

Life is sacred, you say, and your eyes glisten with self-satisfaction and pride. But look around you! Can you not feel upon you the wrath of God, can you not see the retribution which He has sent for this apostasy?

Thousands, tens of thousands of comatose half-corpses fill your hospitals, joined by plumbing and wires to clever machines, human sacrifices all of them, which you have bound to the altar of this new idol. And the more clever you make your machines, the greater the number of sacrifices who will rot before this altar.

For life is sacred.

Half-demented youths with fused feet and pendulant eyeballs, their brains replaced by thin gruel, crawl among your children, dragging their transparent wires and tubes behind them, croaking and howling.

Millions of old people are condemned to lingering torment, their agony stretched out over years by you, for the sole and single purpose of appeasing your endlessly greedy Moloch. The foetus in the womb is more holy for you than the living mother, whom you are prepared to blow up with a bomb, should she attempt to rid herself of the foetus.

Life is sacred.

24

Soon we may come to the point that the death of a single sperm cell will be declared a criminal act. You will gather the sperm of masturbating lads into test tubes and save it for the eons, as if in resorts.

Millions of young people in flower are forced to labor by the sweat of their brow in order to support this cult, but should anyone try to object, to refuse to pay the inordinate taxes which go to build these medical shrines, he will immediately be clapped into prison.

The priests of this cult grow inordinately fat, the healers and appealers! It is they who force you to build ever newer machines to preserve your half-dead, it is they who have taken from you the right to begin life in dignity, and in dignity to depart from life. You however believe in this idol of life, and you submit.

You endeavor to ensnare the surrounding peoples into your faith. They look at you, so self-assured, pious and flourishing, and they believe you, and begin to be fruitful, without end or limit. The streets and hovels of the cities are jammed with the children of children, born to children from children born, and your priests and pastors demand that you feed these over-abundant peoples, who consist in half of children. You obey them in this as well, and the children of others, whom you have fed, seek new games, and at twelve take up pistols, to bathe one another in bullets.

You are astonished. "How can they do that? Kill each other? Shoot each other to death?" You are frightened, and send out your peacemakers in helmets, demanding that they do something about these irate fosterlings, but you forbid your myrmidons to use weapons. Life after all is sacred! Sometimes you even forbid them to take bullets, and then the mindless packs of young heathens fling themselves on your peacemakers, and blissfully rip them to bits.

How proud your rulers, how they strut their wealth and power before all the world! But what is there to be proud of, if any band of petty thugs can bring them to their knees? The pirates need only seize some one of you as you wander the most distant lands in frivolous search of entertainment, and what then becomes of your rulers? They babble senseless requests, begging the pirates for humanism, praying them to spare your sacred life, paying enormous ransoms, and prostrating themselves in the dust. After all, they too are idolaters of life, just as you are, and you will have no other sort of ruler.

The words of the prophet are coming to pass! I shall make you a reproach unto the heathen and a mocking to all countries, for your worship of false idols!

Yet in your madness you pay no heed and will not awake even when these now-grown fosterlings dash themselves against your borders, when your wives and children begin to fall beneath their bullets and your temples stuffed with sacred semi-corpses begin to flame, when your priests dash off to serve new rulers and new gods!

"Life is sacred!" you wail, a hex to drive away the terror of death. Cowardice is the base on which your idol rests, and egoism is the canopy above it. The mask it wears is sympathy. You are prostrate in the dust before it, not daring to raise your gaze to the furious visage of the True God, for Life is an insatiable idol. And the torments of another world await you, for your worship of it.

I listened to this prophet and my reason grew weak before the pressure of his hatred and conviction. How may such people be stopped, how may the fire of bitterness and rage be doused, how may we teach them gentleness and forgiveness? Dear listeners, who among you will find the words which will prove to such as him that life is, indeed, sacred?

3. CAITLIN

FAT DRIPPED FROM the rack of lamb, exploding on the glowing coals, to fly up in a translucent smoke, and a crust formed on the glistening ribs. Professors, grad students, and undergrads, their titles and ranks forgotten, shuffled in line toward the beer keg, wandered among the tables set on the grass. Anton hardly knew any of them. Wife #1 introduced him to her colleagues every year, but he was unable to remember their names from picnic to picnic. Anyway he had the feeling that such people regarded the acquisition of new acquaintances as a dangerous temptation now that there had opened before them that higher degree of human intercourse, the making and keeping of useful contacts and connections.

At least he knew some of the tenured members of the faculty by look, and figured that this gave him the right to ignore the visiting players, who poured through the faculty almost every year, coming anew each year from all over the country and all over the world. Somewhere in the depths of the offices dealt out to them they spun out their contractually-agreed-upon miles of spoken, written, printed, and computerized words, drank their allotted share of cocktails, and disappeared, richer by a few vital contacts and two or three lines in their resumes.

What was there to talk about with them anyway? They all studied the Upside-down Country, while—then at least—in his youth, all he knew about the place was that the train from one border to another took ten days, and he recalled the name of the town that his grandfather had left long ago, during the first Big War (which was hard to forget, since that grandfather had taken the town's name as his own). It was true that he was almost fluent in that country's roaring tongue, which the American voice-box couldn't grasp, but whenever he tried to use it, the tribe of faculty members would melt away, get as far as possible from him, smiling their reproach and misunderstanding.

That's probably why he went over to Caitlin, she was also quite alone. He glimpsed her through the shimmering haze of the lamb roast; she was tall, bushy-haired, and melancholy. Anton skirted the two students who were turning the lamb rack; as he went toward her the love-berry in his chest quivered and began slowly to swell.

She regarded him unsmiling and said, a little accusingly, that she had been invited by a girl friend on the faculty, and that she had paid her way in. He said that he had never realized that he looked like a ticket-checker, and besides nobody ever checked tickets here—thank God, since he was here as an outsider too (he kept mum about his wife)—but his way was paid too, and he had no intention of giving up his portion of lamb.

"Generally I have a problem talking to university people," she said. "They love to talk about what happened today or yesterday, and you can't talk about the most important thing, the future, with them. They are like children."

"That's what makes the students so cute. At first I thought you were one yourself. A new student."

"I think when I was in school the professors were different."

"They say that the atmosphere in the colleges has changed a lot in the last ten years, that student-coddling is epidemic. That the professors will do anything, just to get bigger classes. I read that a psychiatry professor in New York required his students to go to nude beaches, pornographic movies, and whorehouses. He called it lab work in sexual pathology."

"You see that tall fellow with the mustache? The one with 'Super-Linguist' written on his shirt?"

"I know him. He's the one who organizes the picnic every year. He buys the lamb, spits it, makes the fire. He tells good stories about shishkebabs in the Caucasus."

"I tried to tell him about the pension plan I've drawn up for myself, and you know what? It turns out that he doesn't even know what one is, and he's twice my age! How can people live like that, not worrying about the future?"

She looked at the noisy crowd with the melancholy of Cassandra, as if these were the carefree crowds going up the gangplanks into the

Titanic. Anton could feel how the love-pea in his chest was expanding steadily, already ascending the scale of fruits—cherry, plum, orange.

"I've heard rumors," he said, "that out in California there's a new company that will insure you against a sudden future drop in your pension. After all, who knows what the government will be in twenty years? They could be terrible conservatives, who would get rid of pensions entirely. The company's rates are quite reasonable."

Caitlin's face began to blush noticeably. She ran over to the trash barrel and tossed in her paper plate, scattering slices of tomato in an arc, and ran back to Anton, fishing a notebook from her purse.

"Do you remember the name of the company? Their address? Do you know anything about their reputation? Are they a solid company? I mean, judging by what you say, it seems like they're not a stupid bunch of people."

Anton studied her, melting with tenderness, unable to believe his ears, trembling from—God, don't scare her off, don't break this up!— this unexpected close brush with his dream.

"If you're interested in all this, there's a number of interesting addresses I could give you. It's my work, after all. Why don't you tell me what you already have, that will make it easier to tell you what you're missing. Health insurance, life insurance, fire and flood, those I won't even bother to ask about. I can tell that you are serious about your own fate, so you must have those. How about dental, auto-theft? Well, I can see that you've got the main bulwarks in place then, the walls are up. Now it's time to get the towers in place. What about insurance against accidental pregnancy? You're married? No? Well, no matter, none of us are fleshless angels, and we can't always keep our heads cool. What about insurance against dismissal, poisoning, kidnapping? Sure, there are companies already that will insure against that. How about something to protect you from undesirable neighbors? What if they start building an atomic reactor next to your house, or a cyanide factory or a high-security prison? Let me tell you how it works."

The university picnic went on its appointed way, powerless to interrupt them or pull them away from each other. They didn't have so much as a swallow of beer, a drop of punch, a chunk of lamb, not even so much as a hot dog. There was only the bottle of wine, which Anton at the very start of their conversation had plucked mechanically from the ice chest, to refresh their parched tongues.

Caitlin's girlfriend came over several times to ask her something serious, but Caitlin would only glance at her with shining, uncomprehending eyes, then shake her head. The face of Wife #1 floated by, then soundlessly disappeared in the stream of faces. Away! Away! Leave us in peace, go to your staterooms in your Titanic!

All of his life that he could remember Anton had fought his mysterious and primary enemy, who lived in Tomorrow, in Afterwards. Next week, next month, next year. At first the enemy had no name, just nicknames, like Trouble, Misfortune, Danger. And the attack always came from the future. The enemy's inventiveness was inexhaustible and murderous, now an open manhole cover in the street, through which seven-year old Anton fell and broke his arm, now his father getting fired, again, now his mother's illness, now their having to move to an even poorer neighborhood, now a simple piece of asphalt thrown by some unknown person which cut the brow above his right eye so badly that it dangled by a scrap of skin, and by the time he had run home the blood was pouring down his cheek, over his shirt, and under his belt.

Life divided into two uneven parts. In one part everything was clear, calm, unchanging, a bit boring, and never frightening. This was called the Past. In the other part everything was frightening, unstable, mutable, tense, inhabited by unknown dangers, dreams, and ghosts. It was there, as if in a deep thicket, that his main foe lived. At some point in his youth Anton had consciously begun to call it by a name from Russian fairy tales, Goremykal, the Miserymaker. Goremykal was black, long, swift, and faceless, with an iridescent tangled body and crocodile teeth, with octopus tentacles and two hot white eyes. He attacked soundlessly and pitilessly, to drink up the suffering he occasioned. He was more terrible than anything on earth, or more precisely, he was the very embodiment of Horror. The thin thread of on-rushing "Now" which separated the two parts of life was no defense against him; the opposite, in fact, for it was the porous border through which the dreadful Miserymaker always attacked.

By degrees Anton's fear of Goremykal had turned into hatred. He began to notice that the Miserymaker could sometimes be tricked or deceived, or noticed in time and repulsed. He began to fight the Miserymaker with what little strength he possessed. He found a way to school that was twice as long, but which went along roads that were well lit, so that the hooligans which the Miserymaker sent were afraid to show themselves. He thought up clever new places in his clothes, shoes, and book-bag where he could conceal the money that came into his hands. Quarters went into his cuffs, nickels into the peak of his cap, dollar bills into his socks, under the heel. He learned too how to toss salt over his shoulder, never to cross a threshold left leg first, to touch wood, spit when hearses went past, and pluck hairs from the top of his head so that his wishes would come true.

He looked at the Past with great interest now, studying the former tricks of the Miserymaker, trying to guess what his next moves might be. In a Wild West cowboy movie he saw how a cowboy in a saloon was able to shoot an enemy who was sneaking up him from behind without turning around, but simply by looking into the big mirror on the wall. Ever since then he loved to imagine himself as that cowboy, staring into the mirror of the past and shooting, always shooting at the Miserymaker as it slithered about behind him.

He couldn't recall when or at what age he chose his future profession, for it was so natural a continuation of his childhood war. Could he have taken up some other sort of work? Insurance for him was always something more than money, a career, success. The people who came to his office were not just clients to be squeezed for the most expensive insurance possible; no, rather they were all victims of the terrible Miserymaker, that many-headed hydra, and only Anton knew how to save them, to protect and fortify them. The mystical monstrosity shrank back before him, retreated from this man, this warrior. However, he had no close companion to whom he might recount the real and profound meaning of his victories.

He had always felt himself alone in this struggle and undervalued—until this encounter with someone who understood his major passion. Further, by an incredible happy coincidence that person also turned out to be a young and attractive woman. And she loathed the dark thickets of the Future no less than he, and was also ready to battle to the last drop of her frail human strength. His awareness of this inflated the tenderness in his chest until it pressed sweetly on his heart, like a large melon.

Within an hour, not even noticing they had done so, they let their hands roam free, stroking one another on elbow, shoulder, hair. A half-hour later they were drinking from a single glass, and moving step by step to a stand of wild sumac. Then the picnic became invisible and mute, and, transported, they kissed behind the bushes while she distractedly held her glass and he the empty and unnecessary bottle.

Then came the blank spot.

The tree trunks floated in the headlights beyond the windshield. Wife #1 drove, from time to time casting him suspicious looks. He didn't know whether she had seen them behind the bushes, and he almost didn't care. She said nothing the entire way. Then the next morning she asked with a bitter laugh, "Do you at least remember how you introduced that chubby little number that you hit it off with so famously yesterday?"

"No," he said.

"You said, 'Caitlin, this is Olga, my first wife.' Were you trying to tell me something?"

The Delaware Bridge rose before him like a ski jump. The skyline lay close above its macrame hump, thirty seconds by car to reach. There were solid railings right and left preventing a glance at the river and ships below. Every time he crossed this bridge he regretted that, and was glad, every time that he crossed this bridge, because he knew that otherwise he would have become transfixed by the distant water and would have run into the Volkswagen in front of him. Apparently the bridge designer had also known something of the tricks and traps of the black-hearted Miserymaker and so wisely had put a bulwark in his path.

Beyond the bridge they took his toll, and then he was plunged into a hopeless back-up. The cars crawled ever thicker and slower, jamming themselves in tighter and tighter. Then they stopped. The rumor went from car to car that three miles ahead a truck had overturned, blocking all three lanes.

People got out of their cars and went to the grassy shoulders.

Somebody was already sunning himself, someone else was walking a dog.

A Puerto Rican family set up a Canadian camp stove and began to make spaghetti and tomato sauce, to the blare of a stereo Sony boombox. The black girl in the Volkswagen stretched out to sleep, sticking her pale-yellow heels out the open window. The unaccustomed richness of faces and sights made Anton's head spin. He slid weakly beneath the steering wheel and closed his eyes.

How unconsciously, how naturally it had all begun with Caitlin. How easy it had been to slog through the quagmire of the first divorce, the move, the change of friends, even separation from the children, while the heavy globe of love rolled uninterrupted in his chest. And when had all that ended? When had the first crack appeared? He couldn't recall. When, even before the wedding, she had shown him her pride-and-joy, the fifty type-dense pages of wedding contract she had

. drawn up herself?

It was a document to be proud of, without question. Take for example the paragraph that forbade either of the spouses to leave the table without clearing up half of the dirty dishes. Or the paragraph that required each of them to present to the other an absolutely complete medical history, signed by a doctor, and then to agree without question to all tests, analyses, x-rays, and shots demanded by the other spouse. They contracted to send birthday and Christmas cards to one another's parents, to have a joint bank account, to go to the movies or a restaurant not less than once a week, to raise any children as Protestants, not to use suntan lotion, not to wear ear muffs, not to smoke cigars, not to snore, not to spit, not to bite his or her nails, not to get fat, to carry the garbage out by turn, to wash the car by turn, to make dinner by turn, to vacuum the apartment by turn.

Then there were the paragraphs covering all conceivable domestic specters—tussles, adventures and fallings-out which might await them in the future. If their car were to fall into water, were they obligated each to fight free on his or her own, or to wait until the other one got him or herself free? (Each on his or her own, but once he or she had broken the surface he or she had to call for help, and then dry off as fast as possible.) If one of them were to contract an incurable illness, was the other obligated to sell the house, car, and property in order to prolong the life of the invalid by whatever costly means available, or did she/he have the right to say "enough" at some point? (They contracted to stop when $20,000 remained, since life without $20,000 was the same as death.) If one of them decided to fiddle the taxes, could the other refuse? (No, because the marriage vows said "for better or for worse.") If armed bandits were to break into the home and seize one of them, and the other was able to grab a pistol (which they were obligated to have), could he/she use it in self-defense or not, in order not to put the other's one life at risk? (He/she could, provided he/she had not left the door unlocked.) If they were to hit someone with their car, were they obligated to admit who had been driving, or could they refuse to speak in court, and demand that they be tried together? (They should be tried as one, because then their lawyers would be able to tangle up the trial and stretch it out for ten years.)

And so on and so on, for fifty pages.

This vast document didn't scare Anton at all, or make him suspicious. He signed everything, laughing and touched. He regarded her as a former dancer might a clumsy deb, who nevertheless showed occasional glints of real talent. Her strategy in the war against the Miserymaker might be naive, but her energy and firmness were a lesson to anyone. Her imagination was unbounded; every week she added new paragraphs to the contract, and he signed them all.

He could have gotten suspicious, after all. He might at least have noticed that there wasn't a single clause in the contract prescribing the order of business in bed. He had simply been taken a little aback at her answer to his question, 'what sanctions await those who violate any of these clauses?' She had shot back, 'a mini-divorce,' as if it were an answer both obvious and long-pondered.

"What would that be?"

"You don't understand? A temporary halt to the marriage. For a day, two days, a week."

"Hold it, hold it. You don't take out the garbage, and I have to punish you for it with a week of abstinence?"

"You always exaggerate things awfully. But we can't be paying each other fines or locking each other in the shed. And anyway, I won't break a single one of the clauses, you can bet on that!"

"So, that means that this entire criminal code, this military regime, all this is just for me?"

She looked embarrassed and changed the subject. And he failed to add two and two, not noticing that she had already betrayed herself. And what if he had noticed? Would he have called the wedding off?

The flock on the road began to move. The sunbathers began to tug on their shirts, do up their bra straps and pull down their sleeves, heading back to their cars. The Puerto Rican children, savagely spattered with tomato sauce, tumbled down the median slope. The black woman's yellow heels stretched languorously against each other, then disappeared from the window of the Volkswagen. The glistening stainless steel milk truck roared, belched two black smoke plumes, and jerked into gear.

The cars began to move. The wind of the road began to blow between them, and they started to separate. The enormous enamelled tempters to either side again began to coax people in to eat hamburgers, to make telephone calls, to smoke big cigars, drink chocolate liqueur, ride horses, sleep in the Sheraton, play golf, buy a summer cottage, a motorboat, a television, a motorcycle. Anton again began to feel like a stranger in a new land, and wanted all of it. All the while the heartening and wary rage that Wife #1's phone call had awakened in him grew ever stronger, bringing forgotten instincts back to life. At the approach to Baltimore he recalled a bad bend in the road, let up on the gas, and went from the left lane to the center one and—right!—just beyond the struts of the bridge he glimpsed the red crab eyes of a police car, lurking in hiding. The Miserymaker gnashed its teeth and crawled off into the debris of his Kingdom of Tomorrow, to prepare new ambushes.

It was the fourth or fifth month of his second marriage before Anton began to notice that something wasn't right. More precisely, he was still so enamored until then that he wouldn't have noticed anything. However, odd-man-out began to feel angry and offended. He declared himself undervalued and ignored, that he wasn't getting what was due him by rights, and said he wasn't used to being treated this way. Wife #1 had all but worshipped him (that was a bit of an exaggeration), while this one barely even put up with him (which was a great over-simplification).

Alarmed, Anton tried to take him in hand, get him under control, but good luck! Odd-man-out announced that there was no good talking to him like that, that he wasn't some lad, he knew perfectly well how to control himself and how to respond to the desires of Anton's chosen fair ones, if there was anything they desired. This one, however, was always as pleasant, obedient, courteous, and indifferent as a bank teller. She would give out what you asked for (the money wasn't hers, after all), smile, and...have a nice day!

Anton had to agree. He tried a careful inquiry with Wife #2, who looked at him with sad incomprehension, then angrily waved him away. He began to offer her his well-worn guides to the sexual labyrinth, which he still had from college, but Wife #2 got mad, and later he found his books in the garbage. That was also the destination of the bright-colored magazines with the hundreds of photos that jostled one another for close-ups of the given object, like schoolchildren forced by a mean teacher to draw and redraw the same bunch of bananas in a vase.

Anton didn't give up, though. An acquaintance who was a psychiatrist said that everybody has some kind of bent in that area, even if they don't recognize it. All you have to do is find the bent and work on it, and then everything will go as it should.

The round-about interrogation took nearly a month, testing the ground and drawing out insignificant details. Finally, wearily, Wife #2 hinted that, yes, she wasn't worse than others, she had her kink too, but it was so stupid and shameful that she would never, ever, ever tell anyone about it, not even him. Especially not him. She'd cut her tongue out first. What the devil did she care that he was eating himself up? No, she wouldn't trade. She wasn't interested in his perversion, and besides, it was obvious anyway—an inflammation of sports vanity, that's all it was. So inflated that it became more important than closeness and pleasure. Every man had the same sickness.

He was another month besieging this wall. When at last she agreed to tell him, they were both exhausted, like racers who had had to push their conked-out car uphill.

"You're going to laugh," she kept repeating hopelessly.

"I swear I won't," he said.

"Anybody who's normal would have to laugh."

"There's nothing that I wouldn't do for you."

"I know that I'll be sorry afterwards."

"Husbands and wives shouldn't have secrets from each other."

"You'll be sorry too."

"But you know all my shameful weaknesses."

"Just remember that you forced me to do this. Really forced me."

"I love you so much that nothing I do with you could be shameful."

"Then fetch the teapot."

"Which teapot? I mean, we have two of them."

"The green one."

"Empty? Or with boiling water?"

"Warm water."

His bare feet drummed on the stairs. The teapot under the faucet seemed to expand as if made of rubber.

"Here it is. What now?"

"No, I can't..."

"Please!"

"I lie on my stomach."

"And I pour it on you?"

"You crazy? Lift my shirt up. Put the teapot there."

"It's heavy."

She was silent.

"It's not too hot?"

She was lying with her face buried in the crook of one arm.

"That's it?"

She didn't reply. He watched her quiver, the teapot rocking on the quaking hemispheres. He kept his word. He didn't laugh. He kissed her on the neck, the shoulders, the shoulder blades. It was odd-man-out that ruined everything, who seemed to have his own ideas about what was funny. Primitive ideas, like those of some vulgar gawker at a fancy-dress ball. The problem was that laughter took the use out of him.

"You see! You see!"

Wife #2 cried in his arms from the humiliation and disappointment, sobbing as if she had been spurned, insulted, scorned. The teapot, stunned by its new role, its trunk stuck out, watched them from the floor. Through her tears Wife #2 told him how this had happened the first time. She was seven, pretending with a classmate that they were on the tv program "Breakfast with Aunt Jemima." The classmate had said that they needed a stove, and she had answered that she wasn't allowed to play with the stove, so he had said that she should be the stove, and she had lain on the rug. At first they had both laughed uproariously, and then he had put the kettle on her, full of water, and suddenly she was pierced by a strange sweet feeling, from her loins to her breast. Ever since, as a youth and as a young adult, all she had to do was recall the event if she wanted to conjure up even an echo of that feeling, because apparently the one was that firmly associated with the other in her mind...

Still, later on there were some times when they came back from a party so drunk that odd-man-out lost his sense of humor, and they were able to put the teapot to its new use. Such occurrences were rare, though.

As he was going around Baltimore Anton could feel sly little ants of drowsiness creeping over him, from the back of his head towards his eyes. He turned on the radio.

"...twelve percent interest the first three years, if your balance doesn't drop below ten thousand, so if you want your money to work as hard as it can..."

"...Lord Jesus can't abandon those who keep Him in their hearts. If you walk in His Way and profess His Word and keep His Commandments, joy and peace are going to fill your hearts. Joy and peace, that's the breath of the Holy Ghost that the Gospels have promised us..."

"...Harvard sociologist Jim Goletsky has published a study examining the connection between solar activity and the growth of motiveless crimes of violence. According to his figures, the lessening of solar spot activity last year was the cause of 380 murders within the family, 205 attacks on doctors by patients, and 340 cases of arson. Professor Goletsky had the chance to make an even closer study of his subject, when one of his students shot him in the arm for a bad grade..."

"...Minnesota shepherd sued by the Society to Defend Animals. This greedy man kept his sheep in a barn, fed them special feed, supplied them with toys and dressed them in special protective coats in order to get a super-pure wool that is considerably more expensive than ordinary wool. The court ruled to forbid this sort of cruel treatment, and the sheep were turned out to pasture in an ordinary meadow. Unfortunately, the sheep's psyches had been so damaged by that point that within fifteen minutes the entire herd had dashed back into the barn for their toys..."

"...Forget everything! Drop everything! Take a week in Rio! This price includes everything! A free Brazilian breakfast! Endless sandy beaches! O, Rio, Rio, Rio, tum-de-tum-tum... So what are you waiting for?! Tarum-pump-pump..."

"...the most recent studies show that 40% of American high school graduates don't know who Hitler was, 35% can't find England on a map, 29% think that Maupassant is a fashionable section of Paris, 90% get Einstein mixed up with Eisenstein, and only 2% gave the correct answer to the question, 'On whose side did Russia enter World War II?'..."

"...yesterday, when separatists blew up another school bus. The number of casualties..."

"...in Thailand, where construction has begun on a resort and theme park next to the famous bridge over the River Kwai..."

"...in other words, you think that smell is everything?...I do. Once, I remember, I lived four months with a guy who almost didn't smell at all, and my health got just terrible...What do you mean, didn't smell?...He'd shower several times a day. My blood pressure got worse, I started having headaches, and my period got erratic...So you decided to separate?...Not immediately. A friend of his started coming around, and I got better. The friend washed about once a week, I think...Did you fall in love with him?...Come on, I didn't even like him! But his smell! You could smell him coming when he was still outside...This is very interesting. I've read about similar cases. I didn't really believe them, but now your story..."

As usual, it was impossible to stay on the most interesting program. The slowly drawled German accent spun the words farther and farther apart, until they drowned in atmospheric crackle.

Anton got his brilliant idea for insurance against Real Trouble in the first year of his marriage to Wife #2. The principal underlying it was his vague psychological hunch that inside every person there is a gambler, who loves to play, and a coward, who is afraid to lose. A client who wanted to insure against Real Trouble could pay in any amount, as long as it was more than a thousand dollars. The interest on this money would be used to buy lottery tickets, but the client wouldn't know whether any of his tickets had won. If there were winnings, these were added to the account. After a year the client could make a claim on whatever Real Trouble he wanted to—a flat tire, the death of a cat, a broken window, splitting up with his wife—and demand his money back. He never knew when he did so whether he would get his thousand back, or a great deal more.

This policy was bought by people given to a quiet dreaminess. They weren't gamblers, not people who loved the tension of battle, the cruel solemnity of victory, the sweet sadness of defeat. For his clients it was dream enough that a little happiness lay somewhere in the depths of the safes in Sebich Incorporated, waiting for them. There were many such clients, a great many. He was a dab hand at stirring other people's millions, and skimmed from them a good thick foam, without violating any laws or regulations.

Wife #2 considered it a terrible injustice that because of his large income she was not eligible to get unemployment. Not long after their wedding she quit her advertising firm, since their joint income now put them in the very highest tax bracket, and out of every two dollars earned she had had to give one back to the insatiable state, who immediately passed it off to some worthless do-nothing.

She was bored, and angry with herself for not having included a clause in the prenuptial contract forbidding inactivity. She wanted to find some new occupation for herself. She got involved in all sorts of campaigns for and against things, joined various committees, collected money to save whales, wrote the newspapers letters about injustices great and small. In the evenings she would tell Anton about her day.

"See, this one company decided to make a noodle with Mickey Mouse's picture on it, and they wanted to know what our committee thinks of it. What color should the noodle be, should it be sweet or salty, what will kids think about eating their favorite hero, those sorts of things. It's very serious market research. We spent three hours with them, and they paid me twenty five dollars."

Once he was held up at the office and returned at dusk. He was worried at the sight of a dark house, almost lost among the maple trees. Not even the porch light was on, but Wife #2's car was there.

Anton tore open the unlocked door and dashed in. She wasn't in the kitchen or dining room or bedroom. He ran into the basement, where all the lights were on. Wife #2 was hanging from a beam, her head on her shoulder, her arms along her body, palms out. He couldn't see her face through her hanging hair. Anton felt as much pain in his throat as if the Miserymaker himself had leapt on him from the ceiling, sinking all his claws deep into his flesh.

He hugged Wife #2's knees, tried to raise her, wanting to scream and not able to. Shaking he tried to remember how to perform artificial respiration, which they had been taught in school. He ran his eyes over the instrument-laden shelves, along the walls. He saw poles of some sort in the corner and dropped Wife #2's knees, to grab one. He remembered what it was for, because just two weeks ago he had been made (by the contract!) to trim the overgrown acacia. He hooked the curved blade over the stretched-out strap and pulled the rope. Wife #2's feet hit the floor, and she began to fall forward. He barely had time to grab her. He couldn't stop her, and they both collapsed onto the cold cement.

Wife #2 opened her eyes, sat up, and rubbed her scraped knee. Then she noticed the diagonal slash in the belt of parachute nylon. Her face screwed up angrily.

"Why did you do that?"

Shaking, Anton gulped the basement air and fingered the marks of the Miserymaker's teeth on his throat.

"You know that means I have to start everything all over again?"

"But why? Why? Why?"

"Because the straps have to be tested for strength. Because Jennifer and I have invented a hanging cradle and backpack for babies. What did you think, that I wanted to hang myself? You're nuts. Didn't you see that the straps were under my arm, not around my neck? Yes, I fell asleep doing the test, so what? You could have just woken me up. The Child Safety Commission requires that the straps be tested fully loaded for at least four hours. I couldn't find anything heavy in the entire house to hang in it except for myself. Have you ever seen the babies that get smashed bow-legged against the mother's breast, like frogs? Well, we've invented a sling, so that they can be cradled on the side. We got a patent already, and pretty soon this sling is going to make me more money than you do. If you don't stop your whimpering right now, I'm going to go hang myself for real, you hear me? And you won't get a penny from any of the insurance policies either, because of the dirty trick your colleagues played when they set them up—the relatives of a suicide don't get anything. Like wanting to kill yourself isn't as great a misfortune for somebody as getting hit by a runaway truck."

The sling-cradle was ready just in time to receive in its sturdy straps Daughter #2.1. And later, Son #2.2. The torments of boredom receded before the torments of worry about the children. Every new toy went through a dozen safety tests. A plastic moon vehicle went into the garbage because its wheels came off too easily and any normal child would immediately want to eat them. The rocking horse could pinch fingers, which even the newspapers had written up. And wasn't it a natural temptation for a three-year old to wind a string of Christmas lights around his neck and plug himself in? And then run off to show mommy and daddy the wonderful decoration? Knives, forks, cork-screws, scissors, and needles were locked away as if in the kingdom of the Beauty who later became famous under her first name, Sleeping. Also forbidden inside the house were plastic bags (the children would pull them over their heads and suffocate), cigarettes (they'd eat them), lighter fluid (they'd drink it), meat cleavers (don't even think about it!). Their childless neighbors got an expensive gift from them, a leather recliner that opened at the push of a lever. ("What do you mean, you didn't read about it? A five-year old girl was playing in a recliner like this and pushed on the lever. I can't even tell you what happened then, the way she was mangled.") When the papers wrote up a gas leak at some factory, the children were immediately bought little gas masks.

Anton took little part in this war for safety, but he supported it with all his heart and was astonished by Wife #2 and her talent for anticipat-ing and stopping up the crannies through which the Miserymaker might slither into their lives. One look at the children was enough for him to grow so weak with tenderness that he lost all will to fight. This tender wave was nothing like the love-lump that inflated in his breast when he met women. It splashed much lower, washing in, washing out, flowing down his legs and tickling the soles of feet like sand that the surf washes out from beneath them, little by little. The wave washed him somewhere far down the ladder of evolution, to the level of the birds, and he only wanted one thing, that the two shining pairs of eyes would stare eternally up at him from the nest of their bed, that their stubby little teeth would continue to glisten in their pink murk and would greedily snatch strawberries and cookies and tangerine slices from his fingers.

When he had to cut their fingernails and toenails, translucent as petals, he broke into a cold sweat. It was as hard to endure this tenderness for any length of time as it was to hold a razor blade near your open eye. He wanted the children to grow up as fast as possible, so that this tenderness would cease to be so sharp and naked.

He couldn't defend himself from terror for the children even behind the beautiful printing of the insurance policies. As if he could have touched the money if something were to happen to them! And what good would money do anyway? This was the sole branch of his professional activities in which he was always unsuccessful; he almost never succeeded in selling insurance for a baby. Sometimes his voice betrayed him, sometimes the look on his face, and people didn't buy.

Yet the thought of the children could never hold him when he decided on divorce. Did he unconsciously want to divorce the children as well, to purge them from his life, to nail this dangerous chink shut? On the other hand, didn't this tenderness come back around through some labyrinthine course to inform his monstrous perversion, to be admitted to none, shared with none, not to be read in even the most shameless of magazines?

Mr. and Mrs. Fichter (which was the name that Wife #2 and his children now bore) asked door-to-door salesmen and evangelists not to disturb them, and guests who had dogs or cats to leave them at home or in their cars, and warned the garbage men not to look at the contents of their trash bags, as that was an actionable invasion of privacy. This last phrase on the sign was more freshly-painted than the others; apparently there had been such an invasion recently.

Anton hadn't been here in about three years. Bigger now, the children were sent to him for the Christmas vacations by plane or bus. He saw that there had been a second veranda added to the house, with glass here and there, and a bent, Chinese-style roof. If Golda was really hiding there, would the owners admit it? They might lock her in a bedroom and pretend a sacred innocence.

Anton's finger froze over the doorbell. He could see a corner of the living room through the window. A televised dealer in Japanese motorcycles was enticing an empty couch.

He backed down from the porch and on tip-toe went around the glassed-in veranda. Behind the house watery stalks from a sprinkler were watering a little garden. Off to one side, out of reach of the spray, a girl about five years old was swinging; an enormous inflatable mattress big enough to sleep four was spread on the grass beneath the swings. No amount of centrifugal force could have thrown the girl beyond its yielding edge.

Anton couldn't remember the girl's name, nor when she was born, nor even her numeration (#2.2.2 or #2.2.1?). He couldn't remember how many children Wife #2 had had with her new husband. Even so he could feel a dangerous wave of tenderness washing down him uncontrollably, beginning to suck the sand from beneath his feet. The girl looked at him without alarm, then sort of smiled, or made some sort of grimace with her lips, sucking first the upper one, then the lower, and then spat them both out with an audible pop. Then through all this inflatable silence, the rustle of the water drops falling on summer leaves, the poor little domesticated rainbow, the creaking of the swing-set, a terrible inhuman roar exploded over Anton's right ear, easily pierced his head through, threading its way through all the painful places in his brain, turned out the lights in his eyes, and jerked him backwards onto the grass.

When he came to he saw the frightened faces of Wife #2 and Husband #2.2 leaning over him. Wife #2 turned away the hand with the hose, and the spray of water ceased to lash his face. Husband #2.2, Mr. Fichter, Gordon, was on his knees, still squeezing the portable siren in his hand.

"Golly I'm sorry, sport, I'm real sorry...we weren't expecting anybody, and then Caitlin says, there's somebody in the backyard, sneaking up on Betsy. I grab my .38 first, but then I look and see that it used to be family, so I think, let's give him a thrill. But golly, you dropped like a shot! I'm real sorry..."

The little Betsy was bouncing on the air mattress, kicking her legs in the air with exultation, and shrieking, "Again! Do it again! I want you to do it again!"

"Betsy, be quiet!" Wife #2 shouted. "Uncle Anthony could be deaf for life. Anthony, can you hear me? You could go deaf! He hears, Gordon, he hears! Boy, you're lucky, Gordon. If he had gone deaf, can you imagine the suit he would have had against us? Can you imagine it? And you call yourself a lawyer!"

"Suit? What suit? I could quash a suit like that with my little finger. Was there trespassing? There was. Was there an action threatening to the life of a child? Beyond doubt. The jurors would all be on my side. Self-defense, pure and simple, and without a weapon at that. Believe me, sport, nothing would have come of your suit, so don't be upset.

Anyway, what wind blew you our way? Why didn't you call, or knock at the front door at least?"

"Anthony probably wanted to see the children," Wife #2 said. "He suddenly remembered that it had been more than a year since he's seen them and he decided to come visit. Things like that happen, I've read about it. Paternal feelings can flare up at the most unexpected moments."

"But the folks took the kids for the month."

"Some people are still capable of doing something spontaneous. Something strikes them, the mood hits them, and they jump in the car and go. And then they don't think about it for years again. They call it 'let your feelings be your guide.' Any feelings except duty, of course. It's a comfortable way to live, because you can forget about birthdays, not worry about their grades, never think about their health, their homework. Feelings don't say anything about those, of course."

"We were just sitting down to eat, sport. Join us... No, no, I won't take no for an answer. Otherwise I'm calling the police and having you up for criminal trespass. Then we'll go roll a few balls this evening. There's a great place near here, no broads, no dancing. Just elbow and eye, eye and shoulder, eye and arm... and bingo! For club members only, and their guests. Then we'll go to the pool and the sauna and the Jacuzzi, wherever the hell we want!"

They went inside. Anton was led upstairs, forced to take off his wet jacket and shirt, and given a pair of Gordon's pajamas. He was left alone for a moment, remembered his mission, and set off to investigate the second story. A nursery with bars on the window. Master bedroom. Guest room. Rooms for the older kids, with shiny computers and stereos. One door was locked. He stood at it, listening, then called softly, "Golda! Golda, it's me. If you don't want me to, I won't tell anyone you're here. I'd be the only one to know."

Nobody answered.

"...Even so I can't imagine what possessed you, sport. To walk away from the business at a time like that! All right, so there had been some bad luck, all right, you lost your wife, but that's not the end of the world. Especially for you. There were wives before her, and there'll be wives after. You might at least take a peek out of your hole and see what's going on around you. Do you have any idea how wide open things are now? No matter what happens, no matter what kind of disaster, you can always turn up somebody with a big fat wallet who's responsible for it. I mean even before that was true, you didn't need a very big brain to find somebody. But there didn't use to be this...this niceness. Everywhere, a flood of niceness. Flaming damn sympathy. Runaway, boundless charity. Look, let me give you a simple quiz, okay? A pissed-off teacher, a psychopath, wanders into the school that he got fired from, he whips out his .38 and starts firing right and left. Two dead, five wounded. Who's at fault?"

Husband #2.2 froze for a moment, his forkful of rosy ham dangling in the air.

"Right. The school district. Why? Because they didn't anticipate the psychopath would do that, because they had offended him, because they didn't put a guard on the school, and...this is the main one..because their budget runs to tens of millions and they have insurance against civil judgments. The relatives sue them, jury selection begins, and now suddenly everything depends on me. That's where the main trick to being a lawyer comes in! Believe me, I'm damn good at this by now, because I see through a fellow. If you've got any kind of spark of intelligence, if you've got even a glimmer of intelligence in your eyes, I reject you. Same thing if you can talk normally, or smile ironically or you're well dressed or, God forbid, if you've got some sort of higher degree. No, what I need's the types that can't put two words together, who stare straight ahead—slackjawed and dull-eyed—the ones that just nod and say I'm sorry all the time, they're my stock in trade. With a squad of jurors like that I can topple mountains! I can make them feel so sorry that they're in tears, turn them around so that the school district is going to have to go to seven figures to pay me off."

"I don't know why but I never get called for jury duty," Wife #2 said. "Our neighbor has already been called up twice. She never went, she got out of it. But I'd like to go, and I never get called."

"I'd reject you, you can be sure of that. You'd flunk my niceness test. Really, now I come to jury selection for that sort of case with a bunch of rubber dollies. Ones that come apart. The court permits it. So in front of a prospective juror I break off one of the arms, or tear off a leg. If the prospective juror doesn't get upset, then I boot him out. He winces or gets upset, then I leave him in. What I need, understand, is just double-nice types."

"Listen," Anton said, apropos of nothing, "my Golda hasn't come round your place recently, has she? I haven't heard anything from her in ages."

The Fichters glanced at each other, thought for a second, then shook their heads firmly and went back to the conversation.

"And where's the school district going to run to, after they get hit for five million or so? To you, of course, the insurance guys. And you don't have to do a thing, just raise the rates and rake the money in. It's a panic, that's what it is! Some drunk falls asleep with a lit cigarette in his motel, burns to death, and who's got to pay? The motel of course! Why aren't there automatic sprinklers in every room? Another drunk runs into you and cripples you, but who's going to pay for it, when he doesn't have two nickels to rub together? There's one lawyer turned up who had the bright idea to sue the restaurant where the guy had tanked up. And he won! The story I love best though is how a bum in New York tried to kill himself by throwing himself under a subway train, except he didn't die, but lost both legs instead. And what do you think, he sues the subway. Why? Because the drivers brake too slow. And the subway authorities were scared of a trial, and so they settled. Six hundred thousand! Nope, sport, I don't get it and I probably never will. It's just like walking away from the table when the damn ball keeps dropping on your number!"

"They're always warning us that there's going to be a drought," Wife #2 said. "They say that the water level in the reservoirs has dropped, that they are a million cubic feet short."

"A billion," said Husband #2.2.

"I don't understand whether that's a lot or a little. The radio is always full of their percents and gallons and barrels...million, billion, I can't picture it."

"I'm a three-sport man. Swimming, auto, and slalom," Husband #2.2 said.

"Finally one tv man turned up who had the brains to say that what we needed to fill up the reservoirs was seven cloudbursts..."

"If the snow is just a light layer, then you've got to lighten up on the turns. And the soles of your feet have to be flexible all the time, not stiff, like you're dancing..."

"Seven cloudbursts, now that I can understand. That's a lot. So it's a real drought. I'm trying to save water. I make sure to turn the taps all the way off, and when I take a shower I bring the plants into the shower with me, so that I don't waste a drop. I've been counting the rains, and we still need two. Of course, it's not entirely clear what's considered a cloudburst and what isn't. Today is the first day that they've allowed lawn-watering."

"Listen, sport, I hope you'll excuse us if we go up to the bedroom for a half hour?"

"Gordon!"

"What? I told another big secret? Anthony doesn't know what we do alone?"

"For Christ's sake, don't pay any attention to me!" Anton said.

"See, sport here understands. He knows that there's people who find it very difficult to change the plans once they're made. Especially since he came without any warning. You can find something to keep you busy for a half hour, can't you sport?"

"I could do something around the house, like wash the dishes for example. Without wasting water."

"Cut the grass out front instead. Anyway that usually takes a whole hour. Caitlin, what do you think, does Anthony have an hour or not?"

Wife #2 didn't answer, but looked out the window as if trying to understand how the same world could contain the radiance of leaf and water alongside the unending human vulgarity.

"The thing of it is, sometimes she's awful slow to stoke up, and you never know in advance. Anyway, what am I telling you for? So don't get uptight, just watch the tv or something, look at a magazine. Don't bother about Betsy, she can swing for hours."

Husband and wife got up from the table and went upstairs. Wife #2 tried to keep her look of thoughtful distance. "I'm not here at all, no I'm not, do what you want, say what you want, I shall always be among the leaves, under the splash of the water, in a wreath of flowers."

"Hey," Anton yelled after them, "you forgot the teapot!"

"Teapot?" A note of interest popped into Husband #2.2's voice.

Wife #2 grabbed him by the sunburned arm and pulled him after her, shooting Anton a withering glance. "I never never am going to forget that and I'm never going to forgive you, you traitor!"

Upstairs Anton heard the rattle of keys and the click of a lock unlocking. He remembered that after the children were born their house too had had a room set up with a lock, where everything sharp was kept. And anything that might hurt any children unborn too, that was kept in the room as well. So one way or another it was clear that Golda wasn't in the locked room. Anton went to the phone.

As he dialed he couldn't help hearing the noises from upstairs. His ear was still ringing from the experience with the siren, so it was hard to catch the irregular squeaks, shrieks, and rustlings—the sounds of an orchestra settling down before the start of a play, and you're stuck out in the lobby in front of the ticket window where the sign says "Sold Out."

Husband #1.3 answered.

"Special agent Sebich reporting," Anton said. "No trace of subject in Washington. Departing for Pittsburgh."

"Listen, old man, forget about Pittsburgh. Things have turned out badly."

The voice of Wife #1 broke onto the phone.

"Anthony, it's what I was afraid of! She's been kidnapped! They're asking a ransom for her! Half a million, can you imagine?! They say that they were paid four hundred thousand for the kidnapping. Some rich Arab wanted to marry our daughter. Bride-napping! Except if we want her back, we have to spit in the Arab's eye, and pay more..."

"It's a lie, it's all a lie, don't believe a word..."

"It's like some movie. They're some heartless, brainless punks that couldn't write the screenplay themselves, they're doing everything the way they saw it on the screen. And if the movie ended with the hostage being killed, then they'll kill her."

"I'll fly up there," Anton muttered. "Settle down and wait for me, everything's going to be okay. The airport is close to here, and I've still got some money. I'll be right there, don't get upset."

"As soon as I heard that son of bitch's voice, I knew what kind he is, we had one like him in school. He shut my finger in the door once and then laughed. And half a million! They know that we don't have that kind of money. Probably they are counting on you. They can't know that you're in a hole up to your ears now..."

"Maybe they found out about grandpa Kozulin? Did you phone him?"

"I'd rather die than take even a dollar from my father. And you, you have to tell them immediately that you're totally bankrupt, you hear?"

"Of course, I'll tell them everything immediately. At least the mystery is over, right? If they call again, say that I'm flying in. Say that her father will be there any minute. Say that in our family it's the father who takes care of kidnappings, that they have to deal with him. And if anything happens to the girl, they're dead. Tell them that, that they can consider themselves dead meat."

He threw down the receiver, dashed upstairs stumbling and stuttering like a late will-call for the uppermost seats in the house, grabbed his dried jacket, shouted, "Good-bye! I've got to fly to Detroit! An adagio can become an allegro, you know! Thanks for supper!" Then he ran outside to Le Car, which was sheltering in the chilly shadows at the side of the road.

4. OLGA

WIFE #1 ENTERED
his life to the sound of tennis balls. He was a junior, just back from
summer vacation, in a new dormitory. He was standing in the middle of
the room trying to decide where to put the egg-timer (three minutes of
sand, so as to keep track of himself and not go broke with long-distance
telephone bills), when under the window he heard a female voice
panting over and over, "Yes... yes... again... marvelous... yes, yes...
don't stop... great!... you're great!... again... yes... oh... yes, again,
again..."

He felt himself blush, hot. He knew that discreet people are well-
regarded, and tactless ones are disgusting, but knew too that right now
there was no stopping himself, and he would have to be disgusting for
a minute or two. He squatted down and duck-walked to the window.
Poking his head above the window sill no higher than his nose, he
looked out, to learn that the irregular pounding noise and female voice
ascending to ecstasy were no extraneous noise or snatched pleasure. A
short girl was in the middle of a tennis court, her tan legs firmly planted;
she was taking ball after ball from a hopper, which with a flash of the
racket she was hitting over the net to her pupil, now to the right, now to
the left. Her pupil, panting through a gaping mouth and dripping sweat,
was constantly tangling himself up in his own calves, his heels, his
knees.

"Yes...yes...again...great...well done...again...yes, oh yes!"

Later he found out that she was taking Slavic languages. That she
was a year ahead of him. That her father, like his grandparents, had

emigrated ages ago from the Upside-down Land and become filthy rich making dog- and cat-food, but that they didn't give their daughter any money because she wouldn't do a single thing that they wanted her to. So she had to earn money giving tennis lessons.

Anton tried to sign up for lessons with her, but the line of people wanting her proved to be too long. Someone introduced them in the library, but he wasn't sure whether he had made any impression. She was always dashing up and down the halls, always surrounded by a suite, sometimes large, sometimes small; she was always humming, in a hurry, dashing off. He tried to catch her eye, shrugging off the faces surrounding her like so many tennis balls headed for out-of-bounds and thus not worth lifting the racket for.

He was awakened every morning by her panting voice outside his window. "Yes...again...yes...terrific!...yes, yes, yes!" He would lie there for a while, eyes closed, pretending that she was talking to him. Then he would leap out of bed, jump in the shower, jam his sopping head into a shirt—the cold wet streak clung to his spine for quite some time—and leave the dorm, looking indifferent. Yes, students do exist who love to get up early. Who don't have to hurry anywhere, because they have done everything they had to the night before. Who don't need breakfast or a morning jog along the paths, but who do adore watching the sun-sparkles creeping over the pseudo-gothic wall, the clever squirrels working the edges of the lawns, the chirping of the birds in the thickets. And what's this we have here? A tennis match? Practice? Why, I guess we could hang out here by the courts a little while...

Her ankles, embraced by blue-striped socks. Her calves, with the rippling double muscle. Her knees, always bending, always far apart. Her hidden talent, under the floating white unnecessary little skirt. Her round Bobbsey twins bouncing about under her tee-shirt, trying to get in the way of the game, too stupid to know that there was no place for them in the game, too stupid to know how lucky they were, that in the ancient, pre-Slavic days of the Amazons they wouldn't get to live in pairs, that one of them, the right one, would have been cauterized in childhood, so as not to interfere with the swing of the spear-throwing arm. Her arms, thin and powerful as the cables of a catapult, rocketing the ball across the net with such power that the two-hundred pound hulk at the other end of the court was just about split into fifths trying to reach them. Her black curls, bound up by a white ribbon. And, finally, her face, finely and tenderly chiselled, with a delicately up-turned nose, mouth pursed in a half-smile between her suggestively shouted commands. Her face, which made the love-berry in his throat grow to the size of a fairy-tale turnip which man, woman, boy, girl, dog, cat, and mouse couldn't pluck out of him, and which prevented him from drawing so much as a breath.

The courts were closed in November, and life become empty. Sometimes he ran into her as she made short dashes from one classroom to another, amid the falling snowflakes. For a second she would slow, with a momentary flash of a greeting smile, but he always muffed his moment. Even if he had something ready in advance he still didn't have time enough to use the second he was allotted before she was gone.

Once he forced himself to shout to her, almost trotting after her, "Tomorrow. One. Cafe Dominique. Lunch."

"Okay!" she shouted over her shoulder.

But she didn't come.

They ran into each other three days later.

"Did something come up?"

"When?"

"You didn't come to the Dominique."

"Ah, that's right. I didn't come. I was sorry about it later, though."

"Maybe we can try again?"

"When?"

"Tomorrow. Same place, same time."

"Great! I'll be there!"

The surge of students carried them apart. She waved her mitten to him over their heads.

And again she didn't come.

He was astounded. And furious. He felt robbed. The next time that he saw her in the crowd he crept up behind her and whispered in her ear, "Is this a game? You enjoying this? And does the kitty cat have a lot of mice like me to play with?"

She looked at him uncomprehendingly and distantly. When she tried to brush him off haughtily, she had to toss her head so far back it looked unnatural.

"Didn't your mama ever teach you that it's not good to break your promises?"

"I couldn't come. I got held up."

"It happens. But generally people telephone later and explain what happened."

"That would be like apologizing. I hate apologizing. Mama taught me to apologize for a run in my stocking, for not doing my homework, for sneezing, and for picking my nose. Hey, you there, in the last row! You hear my fart? Okay, so I apologize! That make things better? It doesn't stink anymore?"

He couldn't help giggling.

"To be perfectly honest, I hate promises too," she said. "We can't change anything about yesterday, right? So why should we deprive ourselves of freedom where some of it still lives, in tomorrow?"

He decided that she was just making fun of him. After all, she was the star. Famous. She was making the revolution. Everybody was making the revolution then, but she was way out in front of everybody else. If for example everybody was trying to overthrow the bad government in some far-off country, her group was already trying to overthrow the government that would come to power when the old one was overthrown. And if everybody else came to a demonstration to demand the end of the war and getting the troops out, then she would be carrying a sign protesting a war that hadn't even begun yet and getting the troops out of places they hadn't yet been sent into. When everybody else was signing petitions against tests of nuclear weapons, bacteriological weapons, lasers, firearms, and even clubs and knives, and hanging posters in the windows of the dorms, she had sneaked up and slapped a bumper sticker on the trunk of a police patrol car, and the cops couldn't figure out why the students outside were laughing and pointing at them.

Anton also signed petitions, demonstrated, and carried signs. Once he even spent a nocturnal half hour hanging over a highway bridge with a bucket and brush, painting "Down With..." in enormous letters (the rest of the slogan was being painted by somebody he didn't know and whom he couldn't see in the darkness, and then he never did find out what had been there, because the police had already painted over the whole thing by the next morning). He did all of this without passion, however,, more out of fear of being counted as a reactionary, meaning one of the damned, because not to take part in the overthrowing of bad governments and the ending of wars in far-off countries was just as dangerous in those years as trying to cross the freeway on foot, at rush hour.

Olga was a different story. This was her world, her natural element. In this world promises weren't kept, the property of others deserved no respect, pardon wasn't begged, gratitude was neither asked nor given, aid was given only to those far away, not those close, parents weren't obeyed, homework wasn't done, seed wasn't sown, harvests weren't reaped, but people somehow winged from day to day, becoming as they did the objects of envious admiration. Everything in that world was alien to Anton, because it was precisely there, in its thick and tangled shrubbery that Miserymakers both great and large proliferated madly, there that they found such cozy hidey-holes that no arrow, no matter how true, could find them out and paralyze them, not for a day, and not for an hour.

So why was it, one wonders, that he felt such a sharp shock of happy brotherhood to all the world when she fluttered for a moment out of those jungles and froze, for a moment, before him, with her nose perked up and her thin expectant smile? Why was he so powerless to wipe her from his memory and submit to the come-hither glances of Sarah Kappelbaum, who was hopefulness, faithfulness, and reliability incarnate? Why was it that sometimes all the other people seemed like locked doors to him, and only she was unlocked and about to burst open?

In the spring, just before the Easter vacation, there was a phone call. She didn't say who she was, just "It's me," but he understood at once, recognizing her even though he hadn't seen her or spoken with her for almost two months. She announced that her work was all done (all the governments had been overthrown? all the wars were ended?), that they could leave whenever he wanted, even tomorrow (for where? why?), that it was almost a day's drive to her parents' house so he had better check his car and fill it up, and that she would pay for the gas. He listened to her excited, slightly panting voice, asked no questions, and thought with a tremble of what excuse he might give for delaying his trip to his father in Iowa—sickness? car accident? a make-up exam?—which he had promised for so long, all the details of which had been long ago worked out, including presents, dinners in his honor, and visits by other relatives.

The next morning at the appointed hour he was in the car, trembling slightly, and trying not to look at the law building that she was supposed to come out of. Supposed to? She? No, that was the whole thing. He didn't know whether or not she would come, but he did know that if she were to pop out from behind the columns right now it would absolutely not be because she was bound by her past promises to come, and not because of some string of plans and designs peculiar to her, which he didn't know, but because she was as always free as a bird, obligated to no one for anything, able even now, as she had appeared from the completely opposite side, scattering pigeons, to think suddenly of something, shake her head, and go back the way she had come, or, now already come up to the car, the handle in her hand and smiling at him, to suddenly change her mind and fly away, trailing her sailcloth bag in the wind behind her, but able too to open the door and sit trustingly down beside him on the sun-warmed seat. Who would believe the tale of the bird that came to rest in his car?

The stewardess bent across Anton, brushed him with something soft (whatever could it be?), said sorry. His neighbor by the window took the little bottle of whiskey from her hand, shook out the last drops into a glass with ice, swallowed greedily. He was visibly nervous the entire way. The ice cubes rattled in the glass.

"Sometimes I think about how terrible it must be to be a surgeon," the man said. "They see right through us. We'll be talking to them about something and they look at us and they're sizing us up, thinking 'Okay, pal, your liver's about to go. About time to change the kidneys. Gall bladder too, you've probably got a goodsized rockpile in there already."

He wiped his forehead and neck with the little napkin, but a minute later he was covered in sweat again. His swollen eyelids blinked guiltily behind the lenses of his eyeglasses. "When I buy the ticket myself I always take a seat in the tail of the plane, or in the nose. But this one the company bought, and they've stuck me right in the middle. And next to a window, too."

"We can switch if you'd like," Anton said. "I even prefer the window seat."

"It won't help. I understand that it isn't where the seat is that's the problem, it's knowing too much. How is it in the Bible? He that increaseth knowledge increaseth sorrow? I'm an engineer, see. My specialty is those babies there, roaring away outside the window. Every time I've got to fly, I see their guts in front of my eyes. They're so delicate, so vulnerable."

"That so? From the outside they look so solid and reliable."

"Oh, if only I could switch off all this dangerous knowledge during the flight, forget it, get out of my head that drum and its little steel flanges, that have to turn so incredibly fast. Little steel flanges, hundreds of them. Think of a porcupine. If even one of them comes off, they'll take out the engine, and the wing, and this window. Slice through them all like a sword. How about if a bird gets sucked into the engine during take-off or landing? There've been cases of that. At that speed the bird's body is like a bullet, shatters so you can't even find bones. Don't get the idea that I'm just trying to scare you, either..."

"It's all right, it's okay," Anton said. "I've always wanted to find out what's inside of those things. It's very interesting."

"Forget it, I've got to forget it! Those scorching drums! They're called burn chambers. That's where the fuel goes. To these fuel injectors. If you only knew how little the holes are in the fuel injectors. Smaller than the eye of a needle! So that's what I'm always imagining, how some little piece of dirt comes flowing in with the kerosene, gets to the fuel injector, and plugs one of the holes. One hole, two holes, three...and that's it. The engine dies. You don't have to take a bomb on board a plane, all you have to do is throw a handful of dirt in the fuel tanks and the plane is as good as destroyed."

"How come terrorists haven't figured that out yet?"

"Who says they haven't? How many crashes have there been already that no one can figure out the causes for? The worst part though is at the end, where there's this rotating disc. Hotter than hell, and hellish centrifugal force too. One little crack in the casting and goodbye Charlie. That's where we're sitting today, right across from that disc. That's it out there, rotating like crazy and just waiting to fly all to hell. And it's not like the other passengers will survive because they're in the front or the back, but just to sit like this, looking down the cannon barrel and knowing all this...there's no mechanics' bible that tells them when it's time to revolve and when it's time to refrain from revolving, and go all to hell. Miss! Miss, please, another bottle, if you would."

Anton had never been afraid to fly. He knew of course that it was no easy job for The Miserymaker to break through the high stockade of computer calculations, numbers checked and rechecked, high insurance premiums, endless inspections and tests. Not like that first trip with Olga to see her parents; that was genuinely dangerous, because he rarely even looked at the road. It was incredibly difficult and he couldn't do it for long, to take his eyes off...she was right there! Alongside him, for so long!...the face turned toward him with its sharp, avian...did birds have upturned beaks?...nose, the crossed, tanned tennis knees.

She talked about her family. Her mother she might have been able live with, because some glimmer of human feeling remained, but her father, he was a completely hopeless monster. He was ten when they brought him to America, but he had somehow managed to make up for those ten years, to soak up the most horrible American sins. Where had they come from? It wasn't quite Russia, but somewhere right next to it.

One of those little northern countries that Russia was always seizing and releasing again. His parents, though, were Russian, and he had an older brother who still lived there. On a bit of that northern land that Russia had seized again, at the end of the last war. It's awfully hard to study the history of a country where the borders are always going in and out. Not like America, where everything always gets fatter and bigger and wider and richer, decade after decade. Annex that, buy this, steal that, conquer this.

So anyway, the Kozulin family had come...great timing!...right at the height of the Depression. They were incredibly poor. They tried first one thing, then another, did some speculating, lost everything, started again from nothing. There were people who had capitalism in the blood, like a poison. No matter what their class origin is. It was either there or it wasn't. Marx was wrong on that score. Take him for an example, or Engels, or Lenin. Where had they gotten such correct revolutionary views, coming from an exploitational background? And besides, almost all the revolutionaries had had horrible backgrounds. It wasn't an accident that they were killed right after the revolution. "And when the revolution comes here, it's going to cost me dear too," she said. "But that's right, that's as it should be. Justice has been hanging around with that bandage on her eyes long enough. Let her take it off and see who it is she's dealing with."

Finally the Kozulins got into something, dog and cat food. They were just starting to get on their feet a little, and another blow. The war. The father was drafted into the Navy and sent to take Studebakers and powdered eggs to the Russians, so that he was back home again. He walked around Murmansk and Arkhangelsk some. He even got promoted out of being a midshipman to become a military translator, made some money in some deals with the Russians. When he came back the business was about to go toes up, the competition was killing. The cats would only eat sturgeon and the dogs would only eat fillet after a grumble. "Listen, I think that gas tanker behind is kind of mad. Do you always drive in both lanes?"

So anyway, the father came back, and bang! It hit him. Their family forgets about July Fourth, doesn't bother about Labor Day, mixes St. Patrick's Day up with St. Valentine's Day, but they keep a holy reverence for the day that he had his great idea! Simple as the wheel, as brilliant as the perfect square. A brainstorm, a flash of genius. "He realized that adding one word to the labels of his cans would make all the difference. One little word, and not in very big letters at that. And boom! Pirgoroy Pet Food started selling like hot cakes. Can you guess what the word was?"

Anton couldn't, of course. He just turned his head, to her shining face, to the bumper of the car in front, to the ribbon in her hair, to the road divide, twisting the car right and left to avoid the passing, honking, angry trucks.

"Kosher! That's the one word, they just started putting it on every label. Kosher...kosher...kosher. That's what started the whole thing! And it wasn't just Jews that stampeded to buy it. Because if you aren't Jewish, but love your cat anyway, why would you begrudge an extra nickel for her? And everyone knows that Jews don't follow their eating rules for nothing, the rules have been proven by the millennia! Oh, some people got upset of course, some people protested. There were committees that came to check, but of course they set aside one little line where everything was done strictly according to the laws, just like the rabbi they invited to help told them to. And as for how many cans come from that building and how many from the other buildings, just try to check! And the cats just lick their chops and the doggies wag their tails. You laugh, but just think how I felt in school when they use to call me 'Kosher Kozulin, Kosher Kozulin.' How about the smell that seemed to hang everywhere, fish leavings and meat scraps? I was always convinced that even my schoolbooks were perfumed with "Eau de gnawed bone" or "Rêve des chiennes." I used to wrap everything in plastic bags and tried never to breath through my nose. It was only when I got sent to prep school in Connecticut that I learned how to breath normally."

A horrid childhood. It was enough just to recall the horde of relatives who descended on holidays ("God, how I'd have loved sometime to serve them 'Kitty Delight' or 'Mixed Seaside.'") Or having to write Christmas and other cards to each of them, off a list ("For God's sake don't get their patronymics mixed up!") Or the trips with the whole family to the Russian church, a hundred miles away, where you had to stand for hours listening to their droning. Or a mother who thought that there was nothing more dangerous in the entire world than wet sneakers and dirty hands. Or a father who always knew everything, was impenetrably correct, and was eternally reproaching you with his inquisitorial look. Or giving you explanations that were more crushing than an Iron Maiden.

When at last she had to pause for a breath, Anton took advantage of it to ask why then were they going to visit such awful people?

She said that she needed money dreadfully and there simply wasn't anyplace else that she could turn to get it.

He asked why her parents should give her any money if she never told them anything, didn't go to church anymore, never wrote Christmas cards with the proper patronymics, but was always making revolution, taunting the police, and overturning governments far and near.

She said that everything was going to be different now, because she was going to tell them that she was getting married and needed money to pay for the wedding, a double bed, and a washing machine.

"What will you say when they ask who you're going to marry?"

She smiled thoughtfully.

"I'LL TELL THEM I'M MARRYING YOU."

Anton's jaw dropped and he stared at her proud, upturned face. She took his chin in her hand and turned his face forward. "The road, the road, keep your eye on the road. We've got a long ways to go yet."

However, he no longer wished to go anywhere. He wanted to hang a U over the dividing strip and go back. He wanted to chuck her out of the car. It was with the greatest of difficulty that he managed to hold on until the next exit, where within five minutes they were in a roadside MacDonald's, indifferently wiping french fries in ketchup.

"What's with you? What got into you? Why did that upset you so bad? I thought you'd get a kick out of an idea that horrible, but you..."

"Because I hate lying."

"You won't have to. I'll do all the talking. All you have to do is nod and smile. You'll see, they'll like you. You're quiet, reliable, predictable. Talk Russian with them a little and they'll just melt. Anyway, it's a duty to trick the capitalists. I mean, they got all their money by tricking people, right? 'Come on and suck your kosher bones clean,' right? And it's not like they're going to put a knife to your throat, marry our daughter or die, you scoundrel! I'll spin them a story you could cut a pair of pants out of, about how we've already found an apartment but have to have a deposit, that our friends are making the wedding, so that they shouldn't think there's going to be anything for the relatives in it, that we aren't going to let them do folk dances and balalaikas around us, waving fronds or whatever it is. And the honeymoon is going to be in Canada? Okay? And la-de-da and blah-blah-blah..."

"You're good at that stuff."

"At what?"

"Lying like a trooper."

"For your information, I never lie."

"Ha. Tell me another one."

"I never lie about the past. Once in a while I do about what there is ahead."

"What's the difference?"

"Because I never know what lies ahead. Neither do you. Nobody does. You can say whatever you feel like about the future."

"But why me?"

"About the past you can choose not to say something, you can hide something. But I don't want to hide anything from you. You've probably seen that tall Argentine around, Ramon. Ramon Mortadero— should have been the name of the guy who killed Trotsky. But he's the other way, almost a Trotskyist himself. We were a thing, he and I. It's funnier in Russian, a romance with Ramon. But that's all in the past, way way back, almost two months now. Just a little trace of it left, that it would take a microscope to see right now. But it gets bigger every day. I should have listened to what my parents said, that you should never drink during the important moments of life. But Argentines never worry about things like that. We're Catholics, they say, we can't use anything. And now I have to have money for the operation, pronto."

"Okay, but I still don't understand why out of all your friends who have cars..."

"You know I can't force you to do this. Do what you want. When we go back out on the highway, see how you feel. Turn east, and we'll be heading toward that aroma of 'Rapture of Chicken' and 'Doggie Deli,' turn west and we'll go back to the university and forget the whole thing. I'll work it out somehow, I know a lot of ways to get money, so don't you think I won't be fine. For example, right now I could go over to their manager and tell him that I broke a tooth on their damn butter, and swallowed it too, and they should pay me three hundred dollars as compensation. You think they won't pay it? They'll pay just to get rid of me, so as not to get involved. You wouldn't happen to have a busted tooth would you? Wouldn't you know it, all mine are fine."

She wouldn't look at him, but kept drawing question marks in the ketchup with her finger. Then she put parallel french fries between them, so that it became the formula for a question equals a question. Satisfied, she licked her finger.

"At least answer me, damn it," he kept on. "I just want to know, how come out of all your friends that have cars you had to, god damn it, choose ME for this little adventure of yours?"

"You know my friends, any one of them would be enough to make my mother faint and my father run to call the cops. They not only wouldn't give me any money, they'd disinherit me. And anyway, none of them would have agreed to just get in the car like that, with no warning or anything, and take off for hell in a hand basket. Nope, none of them would have come."

She erased the other ketchup formulae on the tray and began a new one. $O + A = 0$.

"Because there isn't a single one of my friends who is in love with me. Not a single one. Except you."

And that short final 'except you' rammed a fuzzy tennis ball into his throat, choking him so completely that they could have called over the manager and demanded compensation for him choking to death, except that he got up and took her hand. She followed him obediently but puzzled to the car, and they went out to the highway, where he turned to the east, for Cleveland, for Buffalo, dashing faster and faster for the kingdom of "Bow-Wow Bones" and "Meow-meow Kitty Kidneys" and "Salmon Supper-Sippers."

Anton had never met Husband #1.3, who turned out to be meticulous and perceptive, meeting him at the airport by holding up a big photo of Golda.

"Olga couldn't come. Somebody has to stay by the phone. I told her, let me do it, after all it's your former family that's flying in, not mine, but she said, I'm half blind from fear and anger, I'll drive into the first lamppost I come to, or run over all the old ladies. The nerves in your family are damn weak, you know?"

He sounded like a dissatisfied customer who had long ago misplaced the warranty and is pretty sure that the defective goods won't be taken back, but wants you to at least make some partial compensation. You must have some sort of conscience, right? He was wearing an outdoor jacket that seemed to have been sewn together out of nothing but pockets, with buttons, zippers, hooks, padlocks, chains of brass rings, and puffy circles of something stuck together like cockleburrs.

The daisy chain of automobiles wound its slow way down the levels of the airport garage. In the chinks between the concrete beams could be seen snatches of overcast sky, against which the commonplace miracle of a plane taking off was displayed with thundering minute-to-minute monotony.

"In fact, things have been heading this way for quite a while," Husband #1.3 said. "Not kidnapping necessarily, but something criminal. The people she runs with are all bums, dopeheads, cut-throats and undiscovered geniuses. Well-read sons-of-bitches though, just say something to one of them like okay kids, enough fooling around, time to give a little thought to the future, and they'll slice right into you, hit you in the face with a quote from like Hobsek Shylock or say you're just like some Snopes Popes or Karatai Karamazov or something. Kind of make you sorry you said anything, you know? But having to lock all the doors in the house when Golda's friends are over, what about that? How can I not lock up, when the first time they came over they drank up my entire collection of old wines, and then tried to give me money! Twenty bucks! I could've cried. What is it with you, damned bloodsucking winos, you couldn't run round to the store? They won't sell us any, they tell me. 'Your underlings, capitalist hirelings, the state legislature set the drinking age at 21. They can send us overseas to die in some stupid war at 18, but let us have a drink before we go, unh-unh!'"

Finally the car got to the cashier, ducked under wooden guillotine and moved out onto the highway.

"But I've never said anything to Golda, don't think that I have. Whenever she and Olga get into it, I always try to get between them, a buffer like, or a cushion, so that they sink their claws into me instead. I'm the new boy in the family, of course, just three years, but even in the first year I could see. Naturally it's wonderful when a woman is unpredictable, eccentric, passionate. Jump up of a sudden in the middle of summer and demand to go skiing, so you've got to drop everything and take her to like Alaska, or Australia. But when she makes her daughter like that too, then there's going to be no peace in the family. All of a sudden she wants to go to a restaurant—right now! this minute!—goes in the closet and sees that her daughter all of a sudden has jammed herself into her favorite dress and gone out dancing somewhere. She comes out in the morning to go to work, looks around, the car is gone. The daughter got it first, again. And I'm not even going to mention staying over at some girlfriend's and not calling, because she does that all the time. That's what we were figuring this time too, that she's just out running around someplace. We weren't even especially worried after the first night, until the next day, when her friends began to call, asking where she was. That's when we figured out that something was wrong. And then this phone call today. To listen to the guy, he'd have to be a psychotic, absolutely. Out of control, absolutely unpredictable. Half a million the guy wants, and if he feels like it, he'll let her go, or sell her to the Arabs, or shoot her. Shoot himself too, maybe. And won't take boo from anybody."

Suddenly the car began to slow down, pulled over to the right, stopped on the shoulder. Husband #1.3 turned to Anton.

"This is where we turn, but if we want to report this to the police, we have to go another mile and get off there. The real question is, do we want to do that? I'm an outsider, of course, but if I was the mother or the father, I wouldn't drag things out anymore. What do you think?"

"What about Olga?"

"She's dead against, afraid. But that psychopath could do bad things even if the police don't get involved. I heard how the guy talks."

The trucks speeding by pounded the car with fists of solid air. On the right, under the dark shrubs, the love calls of the frogs changed unnoticed from courting calls to cursing calls. The rusty balance arm in Anton's soul dipped left, then right beneath the weight of the monstrous moist terrors which had plopped down into the scale's dusty pans, each side up, down, up, down, finding which was heavier.

"Okay," he said, "let's go to the police."

Husband #1.3 sighed with relief.

They drove the extra mile and got off at State Street, which cut right through the city, south to north. The little antique shop still stood by the first traffic light, but jostling after it were high-rise department stores, hotels, movie theaters, and banks. Twenty years ago none of this had been here, just a stand of maple trees and a weedlot and the glitter of water in the little alleys, and the little store, struggling to entice travellers with the charm of its outmoded objects, while he had driven past with the girl who had come to roost in his machine from parts unknown and for god knows how long. Moreover, was it to him she had meant to fly?

When he had finished filling out the report, the duty officer couldn't help reaching out and sticking his finger through a ring that was bouncing around on the chest of Husband #1.3

"For the love of God, what in the hell's that?"

"Opens a special bait pocket, water-proof, for live bait. Worms, grubs, minnows. But if you want to, you can put anything liquid in there, like gin, or soup, or gasoline. Not a drop gets through."

The duty man shook his head enviously, took another glance at the report.

"Not a pretty picture, gentlemen. Tomorrow morning we'll begin asking her friends, but for now, the only thing we can do is hook up to your telephone and wait. If he phones tonight, let us know immediately, and we'll try to trace the call. You think you can keep him talking? We'd have to have at least ten minutes or so. Dicker with him, tell him you're broke, make him let the girl come to the phone. Remember too that we have to inform the Bureau about this. Kidnapping is their territory."

They were already on the way out when the duty man shouted after them, "Just don't think about paying him even a dollar! We hate when they do that."

Wife #1 threw herself at him with so much excitement that for a second Anton had the hope that Golda had returned, been found, been released, and that it was all over. But then he saw the glass in her hand, the open bottle, the melting ice cubes on the rug. She offered her cheek to one of the men, her lips to the other, then dragged both of them over to a little table.

"No, nobody called, but I found this incredible article, it's just amazing, that right now...The hand of fate, really...just a second, I'll read it to you, and you'll see what...It's about frozen embryos...foetuses in deep freeze...It's very very new, but the method has already been tested... They take an egg from the mother or from a donor, fertilize it in a test tube, and then stick it in a freezer. One, two, three, a dozen if you want. Just in case. It's not a regular freezer, like the one in a kitchen, of course, it's a special one, in a clinic, about three hundred degrees below zero. And that solves all the problems! Now you don't have to worry about your children. They can get themselves drowned or run away or crack themselves up in cars or get dreadful fatal illnesses or shoot themselves or let themselves get kidnapped, and it won't matter a wit to us. Just go down to the clinic, spread wide for the doctor, they put the little frozen pea in the proper place, and nine months later you get a brand-new baby in exchange. Of course, this is so new that there's a whole bunch of unforeseen problems cropping up... Imagine for example a case where..."

It wasn't precisely that she had filled out over the years since Anton had last seen her, rather that she had become tense everywhere—hands, cheeks, thighs, neck, stomach—and then forgot to relax... She had a new short haircut, with a tuft over the brow. You might have thought that the hair stylist was working not from a fashion magazine but from an ornithology text, the chapter on peacocks. She was running in circles about the tight space of the living room, while Husband #1.3 watched her from the middle, summoning with a finger, talking to her.

"Olya, Olya, settle down, please, go get some sleep, you're up two days straight already. Anthony and I will stay up, it's after one already, and you know what might happen, he'll call and then we'll have to do something, make a decision, and you won't be able to..."

"No, just a second, listen, there's more, about this one wealthy couple that couldn't have babies normally, so they paid for about five of these little embryos in test tubes, froze them, and then went to Brazil for a vacation, to get ready for the implantation, and then, poor devils, they were killed in a plane crash. And then when their heirs got together to divide up the estate, the lawyer said, nope, sorry, I've got these five test tubes with direct legal heirs in them. The others were in a panic, of course. What heirs!? Those are bastard icicles! We'll just chuck them into the Jacuzzi, make Good Humors out of them! Put them in a glass and drink to the dear departed! Chuck them in a soup pot! Make tomato aspic with them! Nope, says the lawyer, can't do that. We've just opened up a competition, and have quite a number of volunteer mommies signed up already, who are willing to raise our heirs for us. That's what I'm going to do too, I decided. I'm going to put my name in. I wrote their address down. I might be over forty, but I can still do that, and I've got an awful lot of experience, and I just lost my own daughter, so I should get some kind of special consideration, if frozen embryos are worth so much fuss, I mean there must be something left over for the living, you'll let me, won't you, Anthony...I mean Harvey, Anthony's got nothing to do with it, we blew our time, didn't put anything away, although he was always against taking on other people's children, but those were warm ones he was talking about so he probably wouldn't have had anything against frozen ones, because he was a great guy, Anthony, I have to tell you about him sometime, how he was always trying to make everything nice and safe, and he tried so damn hard that his safety could make your bones crunch and blood pour out from under your nails, but that was in the past, we've got other things on our hands today, today..."

Finally she let them take her upstairs to the bedroom, where she fell face down on the bed. They gingerly removed her shoes and covered her with a blanket. She was quiet. They were leaving the room when they heard her say, in a firm tone, "But why, why, why? Why out of all wanderers did it have to be her?" For a moment Anton wondered whether she wasn't parodying him, what he had said twenty years before.

Andrei Moscovit

When Anton woke up the curtains were already light, flapping upturned saxophones, keyboards, horns, drums, and violin notes. He remembered that he had been put in the empty room of Son #1.2. Husband #1.3 had laid down in the living room, near the telephone. It was quiet in the house. The walls were covered with posters of ecstatic singers, wildly flailing guitars, eye closed under the spotlights. There was room though too for family photos. Golda with her brothers and cousins. Grandma and grandpa Kozulin. The room's owner, in a square cap with a tassel hanging in front of his nose. Wife #1 next to a smoking lamb roast. Could that have been taken at the same picnic where he and Wife-to-be #2 had first kissed, behind the bushes and off-camera?

Anton looked for a picture of himself, didn't find one. He tried to think whether any of his ten children would have found room on a wall for a picture of their father. Maybe Daughter #5.1...She had wept bitterly when she found out that he was leaving. How old would she be now?

He looked back at the old Kozulins. The nourisher of millions of dogs and cats stood straight, not at all like an old man, theatrically spreading his legs; the condescending smile on his lips made it easy to guess that the camera was being held by one of the grandchildren. For some reason Wife #1 hadn't inherited either his height or his Scandinavian ruddiness. The black curls, low-slung build, and bird-like manners all came from the mother. Tartar genes running about in her, no doubt.

Anton would never forget the slightly guilty heartiness with which Father-in-law-to-be #1 greeted him that first time, when he came with Olga. They were teasing Anton because he happened to come into the house in just one sandal (the left one), forgetting the other in the car, because he liked to feel the pedals with his bare sole. But Mr. Kozulin silenced the teasers, saying that tactful hosts would never have let on they had noticed, but instead would immediately have taken off their own right shoes or slippers, "Like this!," and would have pretended that everything was normal, that this was a new fashion, to limp on the right leg. There was nothing frightening in his appearance, and he would steal tender, melancholy glances at his daughter. Mrs. Kozulin's face shone with expectation, as if the theater curtain was about to go up in front of her at any moment, and it didn't even matter what the play would be, because she would take anything, everything as true.

"Which should we do first, have dinner or take a spin on the lake in the motorboat?"

"The spin, the spin, while it's still light!"

The sailboats were heading towards them, coming back in after weaving their loops and circles and cosines and sines, repeating their mathematical proof of the vanity and pointlessness of all movement through space. The sun, still hot and dangerous, was descending over Canada, which lay invisible below the horizon. Seagulls were hopelessly intent in their pursuit of a gilded Egyptian grain ship.

Mr. Kozulin showed them his empire. No, you couldn't see the dog food factory itself from here, it's over there, beyond those hills. But over there, to the northeast, those are the stacks of the fish-processing plant that he had just bought, and over there, the other way, was his slaughterhouse. It wasn't actually his slaughterhouse yet, but they were working very closely together. This stretch of Lake Erie was extremely clean, because neither the processing plant nor the slaughterhouse discharged much waste at all. Everything could be used, transformed into "Sup-sup for puss-puss" or the new flavor, "Finicky Friend."

Anton quietly pointed the binoculars downward, towards the nose of the boat, and the deck chairs that skimmed over the waves. Olga's beach wrap was flapping, giving glimpses of the sunburned hummock of her tummy, topped by its tender crater. Mrs. Kozulin was leaning over her daughter, asking her about something and, periodically, picking up her hand and feeling the girl's cheek.

Did Mr. Kozulin miss Russia? To tell the truth, no. He was ten when they left, after all. And it wasn't even Russia they left, but Finland. It would be interesting to take a trip to have a look, but for some reason they wouldn't give him a visa. They refused him every time he applied. In fact, he had an idea why. During the war he had been involved in some things with the comrade commissars up in Arkhangelsk. They were absolutely normal honest deals, but with their upside-down laws you could have been shot for them. Those comrade commissars had become big deals now, and probably didn't really enjoy the idea of a witness to the sins of their youth coming over. Kind of a laugh, really, because if he had wanted to ruin them he could have told the story to the American newspapers. But what was the point of him doing that?

"Olga, though, she went last year, with a student group. What, she didn't tell you? Oh, it made a big impression on her. She had the chance to look at everything, but like daughters everywhere, she only noticed the things that made her parents out to be big liars and story-tellers.

Everything I ever told her was wrong, I lied about everything. Nothing is upside down there, and the people are terrific, two legs like the rest of us, and it isn't life in a prison camp at all, and the food is marvelous and the rivers all go where they ought to go and the trees have leaves just like they should and the trains are always on time, and even the cats and dogs manage to get by somehow without stupid canned pet food and they don't seem upset by that at all. Naturally I didn't argue, I just listened and kept nodding my head. What are you going to do? Of course, it has to be that I make her mad, really mad. Ever since she was little, as long as she can remember, I'm always right. Who can stand something like that? Ah, dear Anthony, please misplace your sandal more often, give them a chance to laugh at you, to limp and stumble a bit. The girl has to make her own way, so why should it be so important how she chooses to do it? On the other hand, can you imagine, she managed to get through and visit my brother!"

Mr. Kozulin's Scandinavian profile floated against the rosy clouds, slicing the evening air with all its jags of chin and nose and forehead and bill of cap.

"My brother's the sore spot with me. He's eight years older than I am. You don't have any brothers? Then you couldn't understand how you can worship an older brother. The idea was that he would finish his degree in Finland and then follow us. He was studying to become a doctor, and had a fellowship, and we knew that medical school in America would cost the earth. The war caught him though, the Russians captured him. He almost died. They let him go after the war, but the village he had lived in became part of Russia and everybody living in it was declared a Russian citizen. So of course it was already impossible to leave. However, my brother didn't even try to leave. He considered himself still to be a citizen of Finland and didn't want to make any requests of the Russian authorities. Of the occupiers, that is. He was a terrible idealist! Still is, for that matter. He works as a doctor, but also considers himself to be a great unacknowledged artist. He doesn't draw anything but suitcases though, leather ones, wooden ones, ones with locks, ones with clasps. Nobody wants his pictures, but he wouldn't leave without them for the world, and the customs laws won't permit any kinds of pictures out. Your pictures have no artistic value, they tell him, but they are property of value and therefore are the property of the government. It's a kind of hopeless closed circle. The artist is the hostage to his own paintings forever, because without them he can never achieve immortality—I guess that's what one of their poets said.

One of our poets, I mean."

During this speech the very end of Mr. Kozulin's nose violated the severe sharpness of his profile, bobbing up and down above his upper lip when it touched the lower lip to make the P and B sounds, the V and F. The more human features this succorer of all the hungry of the earth acquired, the more depressed Anton got as he thought about the unprincipled way he was going to cheat and defraud his host. He hid himself behind the binoculars for longer and longer.

"It could be that sooner or later I'm going to be able to go there and visit my brother, but I know my heart will break. My dream is to manage to get him over here. So he could live the rest of his life here with us, drawing his suitcases. I'd even set him up with a one-man show, and a full-color catalog and get him into the encyclopedias. It was the dream of my entire childhood to be able to do something for my older brother, but how can I do it?"

Finally Mr. Kozulin noticed the sour wrinkles on Anton's face, noticed too where the binoculars were pointed, and his tempting daughter, who was sprawled obliviously in the deck chair.

"I'm glad that Olya has a friend like you. I worry about her a lot. I can't even give her money, because all the money that we've tried to send her she gives to some kind of revolutionary maniacs or the 'Lilies of the Field' commune or some class of welders, who call themselves sculptors. She even started studying what used to be my native land only so she could prove to me that I don't know anything about the place. So, believe me," he said suddenly, concealing his voice and his sympathy in the roar of the engine, "Believe me, I've been loving her for twenty years already, and I know what a hard job that is. But there are minutes...you never know when they're going to come, you just got to be patient and wait."

Could she have heard what he said? Could she have suddenly submitted to this infectious love on some inexplicable whim? Or did she just get into the role herself, later, as she was describing their wedding plans over dinner? No, no, of course they would finish college and get their degrees, and there would be no children until then, it wouldn't be easy at first, but they both knew how to make an extra buck or so on the side, isn't that right, Anthony? And if the parents should feel like helping them, well, that would be very nice of them, but was it really necessary? What did he, Anthony, think? Had she gotten so into the role that she couldn't get out of it, and that was the only reason why she showed up in his room at one in the morning? And sat on the bed, to say that she couldn't bear his face any more, contorted with Shakespearean sorrow, that he had almost wrecked the entire presentation, and the main thing, that she was sick to death of the fact that he simply could not understand the proper connection between "was" and "will be." Couldn't he understand that "was" doesn't necessarily have to govern "will be," that things can be the other way around, that "will be" can turn everything into "was," make the miraculous disgusting, a beloved hated, the truth a lie, or vice-versa?

"You still don't understand? You need a for instance? Okay, if you want, we can make everything that I was inventing at dinner today come true, all right? No kidding, everything, down to the tiniest detail! You want that? That make it easier on you? I mean I didn't say anything about love, did I? I don't even know what that is, really, but everything else is easy to do, and who knows, maybe your love will be enough for the both of us, we'll get married and spawn a few kids and then crawl out of bed at the crack of dawn every blessed day at the same damn time to drag ourselves to some good honest job and hate each other because someone set the alarm clock wrong and because we always say the same things (because where would anybody get new things to say, day after day?) and because of a busted headlight on the car and a misplaced credit card and because someone feels guilty or jealous for no reason? Is that what you want, you miserable barefoot little coachman?"

And he, poor fool that he was, at first shook his head proudly—No! No, by god, it's going to take more than bare hands to get me!—even though he wanted to shout Yes! Yes! Yes!, but he still didn't believe that you could just take her at her word like that, enmesh her in a web of verisimilitude, catch her in the game she had begun. And while she was flinging aside her robe and diving under the blankets beside him and searching for him with her hands (but no matter where she reached it seemed like all she found was odd-man-out), during all this he still didn't believe, and it was only when he heard the familiar "Oh yes, again...again...good, good, harder...don't stop...again...yes! yes! yes!," only then did he believe and begin vaguely to understand how she managed to live on that slender thread between "was" and "will be," not as people do, plunging only ahead, but sometimes going this way, sometimes that. But all this insight...

Husband #1.3 tore into the room holding a portable telephone like a fishing rod cast out into the electronic waves, with the antenna straight ahead.

"It's him! He's calling collect, the son of a bitch, so it's on my bill! Talk to him! Say whatever you want, but make it long! Keep the fucker on the hook, don't let him wriggle off!"

Numbly Anton took the receiver in both hands.

5. THE KIDNAPPER

"**M**R. SEBICH? LOOK, would you mind telling me why it's always got to be me? Why am I the one who's got to do everything? I mean, I think we've both got an interest here. You should have a little sense of fairness about this at least. I've got the last part worked out. It's a terrific plan. You drive out to the lake shore, untie the right boat, put the bag with the money in it, and turn on the motor. That's it, nothing more. Radio control takes over after that. You hear me? You thinking about what I'm telling you? So then I drive the boat over to where I am, put Golda in it, and send the boat back to you. We never meet, we never see each other. But how about before that, how you get to the shore at the right spot, you want me to tell you that?"

The kidnapper's voice was young, with a slight accent. Mexican? Cuban? Every word rang with the irritation of someone who was constantly being distracted from important affairs to look after some one else's whims and caprices. And at the same time he scattered his words about so fast that it was as if he wasn't certain that anybody would bother to hear him out.

"If you give me the name of the lake and the address of where I'm supposed to go, I could come out in the car," Anton said.

"In a car! Will you listen to the guy? And how am I going to know that you aren't tricking me? That you aren't bringing the police with you? You want me to just trust you now, all of a sudden? No sir, you give me some kind of guarantee, you do the work of figuring that one out..."

"Well, how about...we could use those portable radios, walkie-

72

talkies. Radio stores sell them in pairs. One for you, one for me. You send over one of your friends, let's say, and he puts a walkie-talkie in my car..."

"Right, and the police are watching your car the whole time, and they pick my buddy up..."

"That's true."

"Think, Mr. Sebich, think."

"I'm a little nervous."

"You think maybe I'm not nervous? You ever think what it'd be like, doing all this? You think this is something I do every day, huh? Kidnapping for special orders, that's what I do for a living. But this returning the person, it makes for all kinds of complications. And the only reason I'm trying to work them out is because I feel sorry for your daughter. She asked me not to take her away from her home. That's worth something, isn't it? So you have a good think, Mr. Sebich. Together the two of us can dream up something that will work, right?"

"Okay, we won't do the walkie-talkie. How about a plain envelope? With an address inside, of somewhere halfway to your lake. Your partner goes to a restaurant, maybe Cafe Olga, you know it? No, no, it's got nothing to do with Golda's mother, it's just a coincidence. He'll take a seat by the window on State Street, glue the envelope on the underside, without anybody noticing. Then he can leave. The police can't arrest everybody who sits at the table, can they? I'll come an hour later, get the envelope, and go to where you tell me. Your partner can follow me, and if he's satisfied that there's no one tailing me, he can give me the second half of the directions."

"Getting better, I have to admit."

"Except we can't get that much money together."

"Now they start, dickering down how much they love her. Second rate goods, right? All the prices going up, but this goes down? What, you don't understand that I'm going to have to give back the front money, and even then my customer is going to be very unhappy? Tell you what, let's have an auction. This free free world of yours, that's the favorite game, right? So you bring me fifty grand, and my other customer gives me sixty. You up him fifteen, but the customer throws in another five... The law of the market, right, supply and demand, the holy of holies, right? If you win, you're a lucky guy—lose, and we're sending your daughter to a mysterious overseas lover-boy, put her in wedlock or lock her in a harem, eh?"

"What's your name?"

"Pedro. Or Pablo. It's not your business, anyway, so don't confuse me."

"I was just going to tell you, but...well, I don't know, maybe you've already heard, about the new law in this state. Absolutely barbarous, really. At first I couldn't even believe it, but they say that it was in the papers."

"What are you hinting around about?"

"Oh, don't think I'm trying to scare you. We'll do whatever you tell us to. But this law...well, it only seems fair to me that you should know about it."

"Okay, so don't drag things out, tell me."

"They call it 'picture-window prison.' See, they know that the death penalty won't ever get through the legislature, so that's why they dreamed up this amendment. Somebody who's convicted for murder, say, they put him in this cell that has a little opening in the ceiling. It's covered with a grill but doesn't have glass, so it's for ventilation, except that outside, in the room above, it's set up so that anybody who wants to can come to that window. The visitor might be just some curious gawker, but maybe it's a relative of the dead person, or maybe just some crazy person. You know what they figure with this, don't you?"

"Clever, clever...cruel and unusual punishment, right?"

"Can you imagine what the prisoner feels like? Waiting day after day, wondering when the shot's going to come. Lie down to sleep and watch the hole above your head, never knowing whether you're going to wake up again. The relatives of a victim can be so vengeful, you know?"

"You know what? I think you're trying to scare me."

"No, really I'm not, it's just that kidnapping is one of the crimes that comes under the 'picture-window prison' law."

"I figured that out already. But that's not the right way to go about this, because we've got a serious job ahead of us, we should work together, become partners. You've got a huge responsibility, you know? One false step, and... Even when Golda's already in the boat heading back to you, if I should see any police, anything might happen. An explosion and a cloud of steam. Why should I leave a witness, right? It all depends on you, my friend."

"I understand. No police. But could I at least talk to her?"

"Fat chance."

"But how will I know that you have her? That she's alive and well?"

"What if I tell you that on the bottom of her left foot there is a birthmark shaped like a maple leaf? And that when she was little her mother forgot her when she fell asleep in a bus station, she told me that herself."

"Okay, now I can see..."

"All right then, the Cafe Olga, five o'clock. I have to have time to get everything ready. It's going to take you about an hour to drive, because I'm going to wind you all around. And please, I'm begging you, don't do anything stupid, because sometimes I get the feeling that your daughter's life is worth more to us than it is to you."

The receiver clicked, buzzed, became a shriek. Anton continued to sit, pressing it to his ear. Husband #1.3 came into the room, trailing the wire from another phone.

"She was hanging around that type too," he said, "and he really could blow her up without blinking an eye."

The phone rang again.

"Mr. Sebich? This is Sergeant Barnes. Not a bad job of chin-wagging there, but he's no fool. He called from a booth."

"Where?"

"In Brighton, from a Sunoco station. That's a half hour north of here."

"Can't you send somebody up there? Or notify the local police?"

"You think he's hanging around the booth waiting for us? Besides, he told you, no police."

"What now then?"

"Do what he told you to. Go to the Cafe Olga at five. He's undoubtedly going to be watching you, but so will we."

"I don't like that."

"He talked about a boat. That means that the exchange is going to be on the lake. We'll have enough time to get everything ready on the shore."

"I can name twenty lakes within a half hour of the Olga. Which one of them are you planning to set up your ambush at?"

"Let's just agree that everybody's going to do what he's supposed to, okay? You do your part, we do ours."

"It's my daughter he's blowing up, not yours."

"Nobody's blowing anybody up. We'll put a canister of gas in the bag with the money, odorless and colorless. When he opens the suitcase, it sprays him in the face, and that's that. Acts instantly."

"He might have partners. They could act instantly too. I mean without thinking about it. There wouldn't be enough gas for every-

75

body."

"You want us to help you or not?"

"Of course I want you to, but can't you at least..."

"No, I can't. You'll just have to rely on us. By the by, that law that you were telling him about, what state passed it? No state, so far? You made it up? You got it from one of your radio shows? Quite an idea, why don't you send us a copy of the text? I'm sure the boss would be very interested. It was a very very effective piece of work. We'll use you again, we need guys like you."

Husband #1.3 carefully removed the fishing pole-receiver from Anton's frozen hand, shut it off. They sat side by side in silence, like passengers entering a train, forced unwillingly to accept that they would be relying wholly on others, the invisible engineers who would be driving them along invisible rails, slowing down and speeding up whenever they felt like it, and all they could do was hope to God that they would be taken unharmed to where they were going. If only they knew where that was.

Anton was thinking that he hadn't seen the Miserymaker so close to him, face to face, since Real Trouble. "Ah-ha, you thought that you didn't have anything left to take, and you let your guard down," sneered the familiar teasing grin. "Did you forget that nobody gets away from me alive? Every life, even one as miserable as yours, is a pain. They're different lengths, widths, colors, like a nice big bouquet of wild flowers, blossoms of pain big and small, wrapped round in leaves of fear."

"There was one time," Husband #1.3 was saying, "when Golda's gang got to giving me such a hard time that I went to a bar and got drunk. One of the mechanics from my printing plants was there, Charlie Sirtaki, a Greek. I said to him, Charlie, tell me the truth, am I blood-sucker or not? Am I a real and proper exploiter of the working classes, or are there skinflints worse than me? He says to me, you know Harvey, we've been wanting to have that out with you for quite some time. Your grip's no good, you don't know how to get us by the throat, or anywhere else. If things go on the way they are, we're going to ruin the printing plant for you, and put ourselves out of work. There's probably a night school somewhere that gives classes in how to be a better exploiter. You should go brush up, because otherwise things are going to be bad."

"You know, I think I'm going to go to Brighton," Anton said.

"You're nuts," said Husband #1.3.

"Don't say anything to Olya when she wakes up, okay? Or Sergeant Barnes either."

"You're going to screw things up. You'll scare them off, or worse, you'll make them panic."

"Most likely of all is that I won't find anything when I get there. I mean he's right, they're not going to hang around the telephone booth waiting."

"Watch out, or your daughter's sunk."

"There's lots of time, right? I mean, I can't just sit around until evening with my hands in my lap. And anyway I don't believe that their tranquilizing gas would work. They probably just want to try out one of their new toys."

"Looks like Olga wasn't lying about you."

"Which car can I take, the Dodge or the Toyota?"

"She said that there's like a wall inside of you, like that one in China, and once you go behind it, no words in the world will bring you back outside."

"Once, when she was little, Golda locked herself in the toilet. She did something to the lock so that she couldn't open it. And we'd stepped out somewhere for a minute. She made such a racket shouting and banging that the neighbors heard and came running over, to break down the door. She just can't stand being locked up."

"All right, take the Toyota. The keys are in the ashtray. The window on the right side doesn't roll down, and the horn doesn't work. Otherwise, it runs great. Or it will get you there, anyway. If you find anything out, you'll phone?"

Two columns bore the Sunoco sign so high into the sky that it was as if the builders had wanted to make its immaculate plastic inaccessible even to pigeons and crows. If the long-ago days of the dirigible were ever to return, they could be moored right to this heavenly wharf, drop their hoses, and fill up on gas and helium. "You are fully aware that you are living on top of a bomb?" Anton usually said when he was trying to sell insurance to gas station owners. "Or a barrel of poison? I'm not just talking about fire, you might not notice anything for a long long time but if there's even a tiny little crack in a weld under the ground there, the gas could be seeping into the soil and poisoning everything around here. There was a case like that in Long Island recently, and the neighbors got two million out of the owners in court."

The attendant finished washing off the corpses of the beetles, horseflies, and gnats which had stuck to the windshield during the brief drive to Brighton, and then stood waiting patiently.

"Top up the oil too," Anton said, "and it wouldn't hurt to check the radiator, either."

The attendant looked to be about sixty, gray hairs pushing out from beneath the Sunoco cap with its bent visor. Was he busted, widowed, broke, a drunk? He moved with emphatic quickness, almost hopping, as if trying to demonstrate that this teenager's job was no problem for him, entirely within his powers.

"You know Brighton pretty well, do you?" Anton asked, counting out the money.

"I've lived here twenty years, mister," said the ancient teenager, suspiciously studying the extra five Anton had tipped him.

"You know, I've got myself stuck here like a damn fool. I saw an ad in the paper, and called the fellow. We arranged to meet, I wrote down the address and his name, and then I went and left the paper at home."

"That happens, mister. And thanks."

"I really don't want to just turn around, you know. The guy is named Pedro, or Pablo. He's from someplace in South America."

"There's a bunch of them moved here in the last few years, whole damn flock of them. Don't bother to look for work, any of them, just go right onto the welfare."

"I was going to buy a boat motor from him, he said something about working with radio stuff too. Short-wave receivers and transmitters."

"There is one fellow here who's a whiz with radios, but he said his name is Armando. The boss uses him sometimes, if somebody's radio is on the fritz. A short little guy, and always sniffing, like. Seems like I even saw him here today."

"I wonder, maybe it might be him. I mean, I've never seen the guy, just talked to him on the phone. You wouldn't know where he lives, would you?"

"I gave him a ride home once, let me think for a minute here... Kind of think you do this: go out this road, then take a left at your second turn. In a couple, three blocks you'll see a flower store. There's like a driveway goes back of it, then dead-ends. There's a three-story old dump there's got people living in it. A year ago anyway that's where he was living."

"Thanks a million."

"You better make him test the motor while you're there, at least in the tub or a barrel or something. These immigrants are a no-good lot. If you don't like the motor, come on back here, and I'll put you on to somebody who's got good merchandise to sell."

"You bet."

"If us Americans don't stick together, they'll be squeezing us off into Canada or something, you know?"

At first the house gave the impression that it was woven over with scaffolding, but then it become obvious this was just a maze of fire ladders, that seemed to lead not only to all the doors on the second and third floors, but to all the windows as well. The names next to the door bells were all worn off or painted over or crossed out or illegible. To be on the safe side Anton took out one of his old business cards: "Sebich Incorporated, Insuring Against Troubles Past and Future." He knocked at the front door; no one answered.

He chose one of the outside fire ladders at random. From the ground it was impossible to figure where it led to. The sun-warped wooden railings bristled with thousands of invisible splinters. When he got to the second floor, he heard voices. A man, talking so fast that he seemed to be trying to stuff up all the cracks and crannies in space and time, leave whoever he was talking to not the thinnest of hairline cracks through which might be slid an objection. A woman answered quietly, whinily, without hope of waiting until there was a pause, her response therefore floating above and around the machine gun hail of words.

"It's me again it's always me it's me didn't listen me didn't do it right me that fucked it up me that has to do this has to do that but no, don't ever listen to me, when's somebody going to owe me something for every damn thing they did to me took away everything I had used what they took from me to buy their houses and yachts and servants and dogs and horses and leather coats and Sony room-size tvs and discos and resorts and hunting lodges and all this damn Hollywood Disney Caribbean shit!" screamed the man.

Anton recognized Pablo-Pedro.

What the female voice was saying couldn't be understood, because the words were drowned in sobs.

"That's not following the rules," Anton thought for a moment. "You can't keep kidnapping victims in the same house you live in. None of the movies do that."

He crawled over the bannister and jumped onto the little wooden balcony on the third floor. A needle of fear was silently stitching through his chest, leaving long painful stitches along his left side. The female wailing was ear-piercing. He ran along the rickety, gaping boards and shouldered in the door. The door wasn't locked, and he nearly fell, then stood on the threshold and raised his hands. His business card was still trembling in his hand, like a tiny flag of surrender.

"I'm alone, absolutely alone, there's nobody with me, not on the ground and not in the car, so let's talk this over calmly, the money is okay, money's just one of those things that comes, today you don't have any, tomorrow you do," he murmured.

Pedro-Pablo backed into a corner and took a pistol from a coat hanging on the wall. He aimed the pistol at the new arrival. The barrel went up and down, and Anton could feel the dull end of the firing trajectory in his forehead, then his gut, then in odd-man-out. The room looked like a radio shop after a robbery, or an explosion.

"I knew it, I thought so. It's all a trick, isn't it, all cute stuff?" Pedro-Pablo squeezed out. "But I warned you, didn't I. Did I warn you or didn't I, that there shouldn't be any tricks? Come on, one step, one more. Close the door. Okay, Lin Chan, give me a pillow, I'll shoot him through the pillow. Otherwise the neighbors will complain again that we're making noise."

Anton finally decided to turn his head. A weeping Chinese girl was watching him from the other corner of the room. Long strips of paper scrawled over with hieroglyphics flowed every which way on the bench in front of her.

"Don't listen to him, Mr. Sebich, please. Don't be afraid, he won't shoot. There's no bullets. I took them all out and hid them. It's terrible, anybody can buy a pistol, any little kid. It's a dangerous country, guns get them worked up. Worse than drugs, and the wives have to watch out for them—be careful all the time."

"Wife? You're no wife to me!" Pablo-Pedro shouted. "I'm divorced from you eight times already you tricked me into it for money lied to me with no conscience at all you made like you're from Red China not stinking Hong Kong that's false advertising that's illegal you could go to jail for that in our rotting empire give me the bullets right now or I'm going to rip up all your proofs and manuscripts I'll force you to starve along with the rest of progressive humanity."

"I don't understand. Mister Sebich, this is false advertising? Explain, for your famous Christ's sake. Just five years in the country. Don't understand, who paid whom money? You me? Me you? My whole family paid, saved up ten thousand dollars. American dollars.

Three years it took. I had to get married in America. I bought you, I've got the right to take the goods back. Question is where. He's missing a kidney. No one warned me about that. He's got a picture of Che Guevara on his back. Three colors. He couldn't even remember my name. We went to get married and he couldn't remember my name. He doesn't know the name of his own bride."

"The deal was that we get divorced after a year!"

"Impossible, and you know it. Immigration authorities, arrests, arrests, arrests. It's five years for a phony marriage. I'd get deported, and you'd get another sentence. You want that? Two years for rubber checks wasn't enough? You're already doing time. That's the truth, Mr. Sebich. You're visiting a convict right now."

Pedro-Pablo hitched his pants up proudly and pointed to a little box fixed to his ankle.

"They're doing an experiment with him right now, the very latest invention. It's not quite your 'prison with windows' but it's close. If he takes the box off, it rings a bell at the police station. And if he goes more than five miles from the station too. In olden times they would fix a cannon ball to your leg. I've read about that. Now it's a radio transmitter. So they don't have to pay for a cell, or food in prison. You have to make your own living, find yourself a job. But no more than five miles from home. And what happens if you couldn't find it in fifty miles? That's none of their worry."

"But how was he going to go to the lake, work the radio-controlled boat, get the ransom?"

"The lake isn't far off, we walk there to go swimming, and nothing happens, the police don't come around. And I was supposed to be the one who took the envelope to the Cafe Olga, then follow you. Give you the orders. It's not a bad plan. His head works, sometimes at least. But he's too greedy. He doesn't understand rich people, he doesn't want to understand their problems. He doesn't understand money any bigger than a thousand, beyond that it all runs together. Twenty thousand, fifty thousand, he can't tell the difference."

"Where's Golda?" Anton bellowed, surprising even himself. "What have you done with my daughter?"

"Good God, not so loud, Mr. Sebich, good God! The neighbors are always angry, they've got their problems, and we've got ours. Who's got more? Who knows. But they complain to the landlady. We don't. They want us out of here, but where can we go? Rents keep going up. I proofread all day, ten hours a day, twelve, fifteen, but still it isn't enough. And him, all he's got is schemes, schemes, schemes. Going to get rich! One big strike, all in one day! I begged him, kidnapping isn't reliable, don't get involved. But would he listen to me? Not if Golda tells him something, she's like a voice from on high to him."

"Golda talked him into kidnapping her?"

"Not completely. At first she wanted to take out life insurance with us as the beneficiaries, then disappear. That's how it ought to have been, but it didn't work out. Need more time. She said that her father would have set her up. You, that is. But you aren't in the business any more."

"Why did she have to disappear?"

"She showed up here a week ago. Said that she had to leave immediately. That she was in some kind of trouble. And that she wanted us to make some money on it. Her running away. She was very sorry for us. What am I telling you? She always wanted to help. The insulted and injured. And in that sense we are the very bottom of the most insulted. Of people that she knows. It's society that insults us. But we make it worse for each other, so it's twice as bad. But nobody kidnapped anybody. Pablo-Pedro dreamed up the kidnapping after she had left. I said to him that he should ask for twenty thousand—you would have paid twenty thousand, right? But he wanted you to spring for a half million. Greed, and now he's lost."

Weak, without will, without anger or thought, Anton slumped down onto a mattress pushed against the wall.

"Where did she go?"

"I'll tell you, Mr. Sebich, I'll tell you everything I know, but just one thing, one condition. That you won't tell the police. Please, please, please don't. Promise you won't. I mean, who thought all this up? Your daughter did. Insurance fraud. That's a crime. Pablo couldn't have thought it up on his own. She egged him on. To the deception and the extortion. That's very bad, a person could get three years for that. And only if he'd been absolutely excellent until then. If there weren't any other crimes. She had others, but she hadn't been arrested. She always got out of things. She is very white and doesn't talk with a funny accent. So he's looking at least at five years. Though maybe that would be good for me, very good. Five years I would be out of danger, beyond his schemes and pistols. I could just wait calmly until I get my citizenship papers. I could proofread just five hours a day. Why am I trying so hard?"

"Golda was too arrested!" Pablo-Pedro-Armando shouted. "The Coast Guard arrested her."

"Aha, as if I didn't know about that. He's talking about the visit of the cruiser crew, when the students and sailors met. The whole town was filled with young men. Good looking ones. All in white. Golda had five or six hanging around, in the Dominique Cafe. Your Golda asks, which one of you pushes the button? Which button, they ask. The one that fires the rockets, she says. So they pointed him out and she poured Italian sauce all over him. His white uniform. As a protest. They threw her out. They took her by the arms and lead her away. The boy cried."

"Doesn't matter, it's an arrest! All the same, he's an aggressor! I would have poured boiling water on him, not sauce."

"He's in love with Golda, so he forgives her everything. She's absolutely fearless. The FBI is following her, and she's in contact with the Russians. She's even been in their embassy, she went to Washington. She's a hero, priceless. Twenty thousand is too little, make it a hundred. Two hundred, a half million. Why not a million even?"

Lord, nothing's changed here, Anton thought, nothing at all. The antique store, the Cafe Dominique, the protests, the sound of balls on the tennis courts, the crewcut little sailors that fill the streets once a year. Like people out of the old films, all in black and white, and good and evil, and brave and cowardly. They dock to check whether or not the carefree strolling crowds are worth defending out there somewhere in the high seas, with all their armored cruisers and their zippy rockets and their thin wrists sticking out below their white sleeves.

"What trips to the embassy? What Russians? You know them personally?"

"There's a lot of Russians here, teaching and studying. Cultural exchange. Exchange of information. Other things too. Things that aren't supposed to be exchanged. But it's hard to draw the line. A certain photograph. A blueprint. A xerox copy. They all want to make extra money. It's better than narcotics, after all. And the Russians pay. Then the things have to be sent on, but not by mail. They don't trust the mail. That's what they're used to. So Golda kept making trips to Washington. To your second wife. They asked her to take things, once, another time. At first she didn't know, they said it was letters home, to their children. Then she began to guess, and got afraid. But they convinced her that it was the last time. But there was another, and another. And if she refused, then they would turn her in. But then an American got arrested here."

"A Hawaiian, not an American," Pedro-Pablo butted in.

"There's a difference?"

"Hawaii is an occupied country. When the time comes, we'll liberate it."

"All right, so he was a Hawaiian. And then one of the Russians disappeared, went home to be ill. Another Russian told her that she had to leave too. Because the Hawaiian knew her. That's called a cut-out. And all the cut-outs had to leave immediately. But she didn't want to leave. Really didn't want to. But she said that there was no choice. We don't know where she went. Pablo thinks Havana, but that's what he'd love. 'My beloved is in Havana.' But I think she went farther, like to Prague, or all the way to Moscow."

Hmm, I wonder if you could insure against children running away, Anton wondered, out of habit. Say to age eighteen. There'd be a market, of course, but the problem would be what it always is, to protect yourself against fraud. Parents could send their child off in secret to some aunt out in the Dakotas and then say that the child had run off. But what about paying the insurance out monthly, instead of in a lump sum? Over ten years, say. And not to the parents, but to a private detective who looks for missing people? As soon as the child is found, payments stop. Then frauds would have to give up their children for real to make any money. Would there be people like that? On the other hand though, what about the little wiseacres who would tell mom and dad that they were going away for good to where the folks would never find them, so why shouldn't they all make some money out of it?

"All right, I won't tell the police," Anton said, "but I don't want you to tell anybody either. There's no reason why Golda's mother should know that the girl is in any danger. She just had to leave and that's all. Her so-called friends decided to take advantage of the situation by setting up a little joke. Twenty thousand, half a million, what's the difference? They just wanted to get a firm price on parental love today."

"My parents wouldn't ever have paid," the Chinese girl said. "They'd have been delighted. Otherwise they're going to have to marry me off. Pay a dowry. That's big money. Getting married in America, that's something else. Expensive too, of course. But that's like putting it in the bank. Big interest later. They'll all be able to come here, to get away from the Reds. Maybe they won't though, the Reds are already here. Look at me, I came before them. And who did I marry? A Red."

"You know perfectly well that I'm not a Red," Pablo-Pedro shouted. "We are the Levellers of the Way, like it says in the Bible. 'Every valley shall be filled and every mountain and hill shall be brought low.' Luke three, fifth verse. Levelling, that's our holy book. And not just levelling rights and property, either. That's just the first step. We're going to take it farther. Surgical equality, that's our goal. No more tall and short, pretty and ugly, muscle-bound and scrawny..."

Anton went to the door.

"Wait a minute, Mr. Sebich," the Chinese girl got up from behind her bench and came over to him. "I want to show you something."

She ran to the refrigerator and proudly flung it open. The web of empty wire shelves and their shadows filled the entire space. Only at the very bottom was the whiteness broken by a bottle of dried-up ketchup and a leaf-like curl of dead cheese.

Anton wavered. The Chinese girl looked at him with black and innocent eyes. The insulted and injured no longer wished to sing beneath windows, sell matches, or read palms. She suddenly puffed out her jeans-tight tummy, pushed a hand in a pocket, and then threw whatever she had pulled out in the direction of her fictive husband. He caught the glittering cartridge in mid-air, stuck it adroitly into the clip, then slid the clip into the pistol, then pointed the barrel at Anton again. He was glowing and panting so heavily that it was as if he had been held under water for a long time, without oxygen, and only just now had he finally been let go, returned to normal life, a life in which an undemanding sort of fellow needed so little to feel himself a man, just a trifle like keeping some other fellow in the sights of your gun.

Anton piled the remains of his easily-gained dollars on the top of a dismantled radio. The dollars had rained down on him without warning just yesterday, but even so he didn't feel any relief. He was sorry to lose the money. Along with the other emotions his instinct of ownership had apparently also awakened. As he was leaving the den of these young pirates he couldn't restrain himself, and slammed the door viciously.

He stopped at the Sunoco station and telephoned. He was strangely excited. Having depended for scant seconds from a complicated chain of firing cap, firing pin, spring, hammer, and the finger of a hysterical boy, life had acquired some kind of new sheen and value. He was filled with a new flood of readiness to battle with the Miserymaker. He remembered that the phone was tapped and so gave no detailed explanations, but just said that he had pretty good news and that he was coming home. Then he added that they would also have to call the Agency.

"No, old man, we won't have to," Husband #1.3 said, "because they are already here. Two very polite gentlemen. So hurry home, you hear?"

6. A SCHEME

THE DENTIST ASKED his questions ("Is this where it hurts? Does it pull or jerk? How about here?"), then waited expectantly and pleasantly, forgetting each time to take his tools and fingers out of the patient's mouth. Anton obediently bugged out his eyes, winked, and blinked. It would have been rude to say nothing, but he couldn't figure out how to start talking without biting the dentist's finger. He was flooded with respectful gratitude to this man who with his needles and cotton wool had managed in five minutes to rid him of three days' worth of pain. The dentist was an old acquaintance who had known him even when he was in college, and so had agreed to see him in the evening, after hours.

A bird-feeder was rocking outside. Chickadees hopped down onto it periodically, but then would notice the glistening hell of the dentist's office and fly off in repulsion. That Anton could see, none of them ever succeeded in getting any seed.

"It'll be about ten minutes while I develop the x-rays," the dentist said. "You want a magazine or something? There's a tv out in the waiting room."

Anton shook his head. What did he want with a tv? The last two days had left him with a mountain of mixed-up scenes to remember, develop, and sort through. The men from the Agency had in fact proven to be very tactful and apparently well-disposed. They repeated several times that Golda Kozulin-Chichikov's parents had nothing to worry about, that she wasn't being accused of anything herself, personally, that she was wanted just as a witness. Apparently even that had frightened her, and she had preferred this sudden disappearance. No wonder; today a lot of times it was more dangerous to be a witness than it was to be a criminal. In her case there was no big threat here, but there... Of course, there never was any kidnapping. Someone had just decided to take advantage of her disappearing act to make a little money. At first they hadn't known where she was, because they hadn't had a round-the-clock watch on her. Then it turned out that she had flown to Helsinki. That was where it was easiest to visit the Upside-down Land on a tourist visa. They were guessing that she had been told to take advantage of that loophole, but they weren't sure. The day before yesterday, however, she had telephoned the American Embassy. In Moscow.

She hadn't given her name, just said that she was an American and asked them to tell her parents that she was all right. So they wouldn't worry. She gave them her mother's telephone number. That's how they found out who she was. Incidentally, why had she taken such an odd name? Was this Chichikov a relative of some sort? No? An ancestor of some sort then? Maybe she thought so? Anyway, they were sure she was in Moscow, though the Russians said "Nyet." The embassy had made an official inquiry, and the official answer had come that morning: "Miss Golda Kozulin or Chichikov has not crossed the Soviet border. Nor has anyone under her name." However, the embassy was sure that it was a local call. They taped it. Do you want to listen?

Golda's voice had been recorded with some kind of low constant ringing, as if the line had had to run through all the coins rattling down into Moscow's public telephones.

"Please tell my parents that everything is fine. The dormitory is sunny and comfortable. They shouldn't worry, and tell them I'm sorry, things just worked out like this. I had to leave suddenly, without any warning... And tell them not to forget me either, I'll remember them forever and ever. I'll write when I can. The ice cream here is very good. I love them and think about them. I don't know what's going to happen to me. Here's their telephone number."

She had only sobbed once, at the word "ice cream." In general she had been trying to speak clearly and calmly, but without success. The words had come with unnatural slowness. That was how she talked when her throat hurt and swollen glands clutched at her every word, like customs men digging for bribes.

Wife #1 asked them to play the tape from the beginning again. The agents told her they could give her the tape, they had a copy of it.

"Where?" Wife #1 screamed. "In your secret files? In the file you're keeping on her? You've got files on everybody, haven't you? All of us, right? You have our voices and our faiths and our fingerprints and specimens of our hair? You see what you made our daughter do, with your tailing her? Did you hear her voice?"

The senior agent looked out the window and waved his hat, then said that it wasn't true that they had a file on everybody, on very few in fact, but that they did know a thing or two about what university professor Olga Kozulin was up to. It was no secret that for twenty years now she had been telling her students how unjust everything is here and how wonderful everything is there, in the Upside-down Land, which made Professor's Kozulin's anger a little strange. She should have been happy that her daughter had finally ended up in such a marvelous, just, and safe country.

"So okay then, that means that you know everything about me too? You've got me in the bag too then, huh? You're going to control every step I take, everything I do? I have to get your permission? To go to Moscow, for instance? Am I allowed to go visit my daughter? Please, I'd like to go tomorrow. You won't take me off the airplane?"

"Godspeed, you don't need our permission, as you know perfectly well. You're going to need a visa from them, though, and they aren't going to give you one."

"Says you! I've been to Moscow hundreds of times!"

"That was before, things are different now. As soon as they said that your daughter isn't there, that's the story they'll stick with, and none of her relatives will get visas."

"Why?"

"They might tell you that the workers of their country have asked them not to admit any foreigners whose names begin with 'Koz' this year. Or maybe that they think you have some new virus that they don't have vaccines for yet. The usual formula though is 'not necessary.' 'We have decided that your visit to our country at the present time is not necessary.' Makes us a little envious even, the work's so easy for them."

"I'm flying to Washington tomorrow, to their embassy, and the day after that I'm going to send you a post card from Moscow, so you can put that in my file too!"

"Well, we'll see. The main thing is, let us know if you hear anything about your daughter. And tell her that she's got nothing to be afraid of here. Her professors have exaggerated how bloodthirsty we are, we only eat little kids on Tuesdays, and the rest of the week we live on lettuce and parsley."

When the agents had gone Anton told Wife #1 about his visit to the den of thieves in Brighton. Things were beginning to make sense now, and the picture was clearing up, but were they to be happy or sad? Which was worse to think about, Golda with a gun to her head, but close, here in the country, or Golda alive and safe, but beyond thrice-thirty seas and thrice-thirty borders bound round with barbed wire? Maybe for a long time, maybe forever.

Finally they decided they had better tell the Kozulin grandparents about what had happened.

Which drove grandfather Kozulin into an incredible excitement, in which only one thing wasn't quite clear—was he angry, frightened, or glad?

He shouted that he was flying there immediately. That this was the hand of fate. That he knew how to get the prodigal daughter back. That he had a great plan. He was leaving Cleveland on the first plane, and nobody was to do anything until he got there!

Not do anything? That put an end to Wife #1's indecision; her stubborn instincts of childhood kicked in and she immediately went upstairs to start packing. Husband #1.3 had to make an urgent trip to do something at his print shop, and he wanted to take Anton with him ("You haven't seen our new press yet, have you?"), but then he noticed Anton's swollen cheek, the throbbing and moaning that Anton simply couldn't keep hidden any longer. "How come you put up with this so long? You don't have any money? What are you, nuts? Here's a blank check, you go to the dentist right now!"

It looked as though his children had finally had the luck to get a good stepfather this time. The one before, Husband #1.2, Ronald Ironhand, had been a health nut. When he was around the children had something to do every minute of every day, on a schedule; they knew when they had to take cold baths and when they had to run and swim and sun and work out on the exercise bicycle, row, lift weights, break boards and watermelons with the side of their hands, kick each other in the stomach, do squats and pushups.

The main obstacle to health was held to be conversation. Talking at the table, and laughing even more so, distracted a person from the correct absorption of calories and also could lead to accidental choking (one in every hundred Americans once in his or her life got a poorly chewed piece of food stuck in the throat). Talking while skiing interfered with the breathing; while shooting baskets made the aim worse (that's right! They'd done studies, and talkative people were only three-quarters as good at aiming). Before it could go in the refrigerator, every item of food had to be registered on a computer, and the computer would quickly indicate how much fat was in it, how much sugar, vitamins, carbohydrate, cholesterol, cellulose. If some vital ingredient was low, then another trip was made to the store to make it up. The children when they came to visit Anton on holidays were as brown, silent, and impenetrable as walnuts.

This Ronald had hung around them while they were in the university, and in the first years they were married. Oddly, her marriage did nothing to lower Wife #1 in the eyes of her friends; anyone else they would never have forgiven, would have called a renegade, a traitor to the enemy camp. Not her though. She remained as she had been, absolutely secure on her throne; in this as in everything else, she had simply gone farther than anyone else, to the point where she had made revolution against revolution. This stage was foretold in their sacred writings (the negation of negation), so that her wedding was considered to be the most extravagant and daring act of the year.

Anton made no attempt to compete with her or catch up to her. Even when he was trying to convince her to have the Argentine Ramon's child, this was no grand gesture or attempt to paint himself with the brush of their blessed dogma, which he then understood as the attempt to make a gradual transition to reproduction through pollination. Did his voice here perhaps squeak, or break, or strain, a presentiment of what he still only vaguely guessed at, because there was nothing with which he might compare it? Not very likely. It was simply that thinking about the future little person whom no one yet had seen and who had seen no one filled him with an unfamiliar excitement. This was a living sign of whatever lay ahead, in the dark woods of the future, of the possibility that more than just the Miserymaker wound among the thickets. Yet she refused out of hand. To bear the child of a man who had permitted himself to praise Prince Kropotkin and to doubt the primacy of matter and the laws of evolution? Never!

Would she have agreed to bear Golda had she known what was going on in Anton's head? As a rule he kept quiet, his puppy-dog ideas on a short leash, letting them gnaw and tug at the slippers only when he was alone with them. This was no difficulty to him. What was truly exhausting, what took all of his time, strength, and nerves, was the eternal war she conducted with things, a battle to the bitter end.

At first it had seemed to him that now, with his help, she would win this war easily. The first room that they had rented after their marriage had almost no room in it for her enemy. Anton tried patiently to explain to Wife #1 a truth long ago known to all and only recently discovered for himself, that if something is always returned to the same place that it was taken from, then there is a high degree of likelihood that in the future it will be there again, when the need for it arises.

Wife #1 would listen with distaste, her face bored and sour. The scum of petty concerns had the obligation to know its proper place, which was outside the threshold of consciousness, at the service entrance for deliverymen and garbagemen, who could be permitted no farther than the kitchen. It seemed that she found debasing even the idea that some low-life lost button could force her to get up, walk across the room, open a cupboard, get out a box, open it, take out a spool of thread, and then—after some minor fiddling of needle-threading, button-sewing, thread-tying and biting-off—to do the same thing, save in the opposite order, to put a thing back where it came from, shutting one box, then another. And to remember to do all this? To permit such banal, insignificant thoughts into her head? No, to submit willingly to all this was the same for her as to submit willingly to prison or to becoming a slave. She defended herself against this with desperate conviction.

Soon though Anton understood that persuasion would put nothing right in this regard, that her attitude was set so deeply into her that no bathyspheres of argument could descend to them. He decided then that the only salvation was to take everything upon himself. After all, when he had lived alone he had coped with rebellious material objects, keeping them in peaceful submission. How could he fail now to control the enemy, simply because it had doubled in number? Now as he pushed his cart along the aisles of the market he had to keep a list of food and other needed items in mind that was twice as long as it had been before, as well as to avert his eyes when the cashier packed up the monthly packets of tampons. And to turn his own back to hide his wife's underwear when he moved it from the washer to the dryer. And to make meals for two, and clean up for two, and to pick up the pantyhose tossed into corners, empty twice as many ashtrays, fix two bicycles instead of one (the female dented again), and to return a double-size pile of books to the library.

Did any of this mean anything to her? Maybe. Sometimes. But it didn't bring them any closer. Relieved of minor cares, she could fly the farther from him, into the past and into the future, to leap from one of these boundless oceans to another and back barely bothering to stop for a second on the thin string of the present, which increasingly became for him his only place of residence. The excavations at Troy, flights to Mars, the sermons of Thomas Munser, the Great Barrier Reef in Australia, the transition from feudalism to capitalism (which was irreversible, was it not?), the formation of crystals, laser weapons, the controversy over Sakhalin Island, Byron's romantic dalliances, the sound of the carillons in Rostov, Marx vs. Bakunin, and the Pharisees vs. the Sanhedrins, what could he know of any of this when he didn't have time even to read the headlines in the newspaper? By degrees his face became a mask of eternal preoccupation, and even his eternal enemy, the Miserymaker, was pushed somewhere to the side by the clamoring crowds of tiny gnawing "have-tos."

Nor was it enough that his wife refused to be his ally in the battle against things; very often she behaved like a turncoat, a fifth-columnist. Very quickly she learned all the places where he kept his notebooks, scissors, combs, toothpaste, dictionaries, razor blades, gum erasers, into which she constantly conducted raids. He tried hiding them in different places, but then would forget himself where it was he had put them, which would put him into a fruitless frenzy. Next he tried buying everything by tens, dozens, boxes, and pounds; he conducted experiments—how long did it take for a box of pens to disappear, or a dozen coat hangers, a box of light bulbs, a bundle of notebooks, ten can openers. It sometimes seemed to him that she must have some secret place outside the home, an altar on which she sacrificed all these innocent objects as an offering to the god of indifferent wastrels which she worshipped.

When all the same need or desire forced her to take up some small task she tried to accord it precisely the seconds of attention which in her view it deserved. "All right then, I'll iron the blouse since we're going to the concert today, but there's no way that you're going to make me think about what my hands are doing, about irons and cords and ironing boards and water for the steamer and an ironing pad for the table."

And the objects, as if able to feel her contempt, repaid her in kind. Can openers would skitter from the edge of the can and cut her wrist, light bulbs would leap from her fingers an inch away from the socket and shatter on the floor, keys would break in the locks, lighters would flare up and scorch her eyebrows, and the iron would scorch the varnish of the table.

Sometimes Anton grew so weary from this exhausting and hopeless war that he could feel his brain shrinking to the dimensions of two or three absolute immediate tasks. But what was it he really wanted from her anyway? That she should return pencils to where she had gotten them, that she should learn to make the scrambled eggs? Or was it something else, and more important, that he wanted? That she should stop flying off into her eternal was-will be-sometime-maybe, escaping at no matter what cost from the here-and-now? But if that was the case, then why out of all the other girls, who respected the here and now even more than he did and who were just as pretty and more accessible, why did it have to be that his heart grew warm only for this migratory tormentor, this dangerous perpetual nomad? And what otherworldly breath was it that inflated the loveberry in his throat each time that she came to his bed from the shower, freeing herself from the bondage of things as she came, hurling towel, shower cap, slippers, belt, comb, and robe about the room, which with only the remnants of his darkening consciousness he understood he would have to pick up the next morning and so push back the chaos one more time, so that she would have a place to land—always, always for just a moment—and bestow upon him bitter happiness, and upon odd-man-out his greedy pleasure, in her brief descent to the thin filament of "now" as it wafted through the cosmos.

The dentist came back and showed him the x-rays. Black and white cliffs, crevasses, foothills. And the tunnels where the pain hid and from which it crawled forth. Stitching all this up would require considerably more time than the dentist had thought at first. Did Anton have the time? "Sure, whatever it takes." He could go back to Mrs. Darcey's cabin tomorrow, whereas he absolutely did not have the strength to free Golda from the forests, swamps, and dormitories of the Upside-down Land. Let someone else do it, someone who had not been hit by Real Trouble. And besides, did she even have to be freed? Maybe the girl would even like it there, maybe it was just what she needed. The knowledge that she was so far away chilled and hardened his eternal worry about her, like his gums as the anesthetic took hold.

How they had prepared for Golda's birth! Buying a crib, repapering a room, reading the necessary articles in the medical encyclopedia, interrogating friends and acquaintances who were parents about the dangers that newborns faced in this world—all this Anton could take upon himself. He could not, though, give birth. Wife #1 would have to give birth herself, and he couldn't believe that she would, because that would require that for ten hours, maybe twenty, she would have to stop flitting about, frozen in the "now" she loathed, in the grip of unfamiliar pain. He was afraid for her. There was no more room in his throat for the love-bladder, as if it had been moved to Wife #1's belly and was growing there. Sometimes he wanted her to spare him the approaching horrors by giving birth elsewhere, faraway, on the fly, in the past or the future, so that the baby would appear in the crib with a flapping of stork wings.

The birth was easy. Golda with a single lunge cleared the threshold separating fish from animal, gulped down the dry, burning air, and howled, then shut her tiny toothless mouth, emitted a few bubbles, and calmed down. Wife #1 lay exhausted and sweaty, as pleased with herself as if she had just won this interesting secret prize in a difficult tennis match.

It was later that the horrors began. No medical handbooks or guides, nowhere in Dr. Spock (though maybe he had just missed it) were the torments of nursing discussed. At every feeding Anton had to go to all the neighbors—left and right, up and down— to warn them, apologize, and ask them not to call the police when his wife began to shriek. No one was knifing her or beating her or raping her; breast feeding was terribly painful.

"So why not use a bottle? The formulas they sell now are wonderful."

Because his wife refused, that's why. She said that breast milk conveyed the most important information that the child needed for its future life. That the child had no need to suffer all the diseases that she had suffered, and that there was also no need to repeat all her errors and mistakes. Wife #1 would hook her feet under the tv stand, take out her breast, and as soon as Golda fastened her toothless gums to an inflamed nipple, would begin to howl and shriek.

"She's going to be an impossible little sadist!" Anton begged her to stop. "All her life the child will associate the pleasures of eating with the shrieks of a tortured victim. Come on, stop this! Look at the wonderful formula I've made in this bottle, try it yourself!"

Wife #1 would shake her head, weep, howl. The two-month old torturer would calmly pump in her necessary and unnecessary milk information. The neighbors on the right side had turned up Wagner full-force, and the ones downstairs would go out for bicycle rides.

There were no such torments with Daniel, Son #1.2. He ate without fuss, slept like the dead, and would smile even at his own fingers. He did though eat up a ton of time; having a second child in their situation was like loading a piano onto a boat that was already sunk to the gunwales. To lighten the boat they threw the last ballast overboard—going to the movies, seeing friends, swimming, evenings at the Dominique. The 1440 minutes that made up every day were sliced into tiny portions and doled out as if by ration card, for only the most dire of needs. Even Wife #1 was forced to take some account of this blockade economy.

It was only the children who weren't troubled. Their unconcern and the cult of their "wannas" seemed at times a conscious and savored form of banditry. At every moment of the day their desires were always different and always at odds; they each wanted to sleep, eat, go for a walk, fly a kite, pet somebody's doggie, watch television, draw on the walls, or cut the pictures out of their parents' textbooks at different times. Even their microbes and viruses became an unpredictable leapfrog, since they would without fail get sick separately, one after the other. They lost their clothes, broke dishes, and knocked over the flower vases always at that precise last moment when it still would have been possible to fling them in the car and hustle them off to the latest in a series of student babysitters and still not be late for work.

Nightmares woke the children on different nights, in turn, showing the parents no mercy. Wife #1 the next day would make some career-fatal slip for a new professor (confusing Vasilii Rosanov and Vasilii Temnyi, for example), while Anton, who had just been taken on trial with an insurance firm, could just barely drag himself to lunchtime, when he would drag himself to the car park and lay out on the scorching back seat and rest like a lump of rising dough. He would fall asleep in a second, lacking the strength even to undo his shoelaces. "Anthony's cooked in a necktie," his fellow workers would tease him when he returned.

They probably wouldn't have made it through those first years if it hadn't been for the Morrisons. The Morrisons had burst over them unexpectedly, as if dropped from the skies by a rescue helicopter. They moved into the house next door, and were twice as old as they, without children. Mrs. Morrison didn't work. She said that she would take Daniel and Golda at any time, any time, she repeated, insisting that they understood she meant it. Three in the morning even.

The Morrisons did everything. They took the children to the eye doctors, the barbers, the pediatrician, the orthopedists, the photo studio, the chiropractors, and the fortunetellers. They showed them the zoo, the puppet theater, the swimming pool, the aquarium, the street market, the car races, the beach. They bought them electronic toys and expensive clothes. They sighed when the parents took the children on their days off. They taught the children to say "Please" and "Thank you" and "Pleased to meet you" and "Come again." They were irreplaceable, saintly. They were also sneaky and dangerous, as things turned out, no more than prettily painted Miserymakers.

Anton remembered how a vague alarm had stirred within him all that day, but he couldn't understand where the worry was slithering out from, and what it was threatening. It was only when Wife #1 kissed him a third time, in front of people—a crowd of them had come out of the restaurant, old friends and new, and Ronald Ironhand was circling ever closer then too—that Anton felt something was definitely wrong. Once they were at home, in the living room, she pushed him into a chair, jumped into his lap, and began to whisper urgently and tenderly in his ear, even though the house was empty, because the kids were at the Morrisons.

"You know, I've really perked up this last year. Our neighbors, they're like some sort of blessing from heaven, I can't imagine how we'll ever repay them. Have you noticed though, there's days every month when they won't take them? They're always begging us to leave the kids, and suddenly they won't take them, and always for the stupidest of reasons...I never used to understand that, what the deal was, but then I figured it out...I understood that she's still hoping, even though she's forty-three she's still hoping...and she told me that's what it is, that these days are set aside for trying, two weeks after her period. You read to me yourself how that's the best chance for impregnation, except that it doesn't matter, nothing comes of it, no matter what they try. She told me recently how much money they've wasted on doctors and all sorts of charlatans, one of them made her stand on her head for a half hour after every time they...I imagine that the Russian word for copulation is probably like from population, and not from co-optation, right? And they can't adopt, the line for kids is years long, and they're absolutely desperate...."

He didn't want to hear any more; he had trouble enough of his own. He didn't like her wheedling tone and her conspiratorial whisper. He tried to toss her off his knees, but she held the back of the chair firmly.

"Hold it a second, I'm not done. I'm trying to tell you how incredibly awful it is to look at them whenever we pick up the kids, their begging eyes. It's so unjust. We've got two and are going to have more, and they don't have any. It's not our fault, of course, but then there is something that we could do, I mean are we really going to do just for ourselves all our lives, raking it in and raking it in? I'd love to be able to help them, we're always shouting about equality and justice, but when it really comes down to sharing with a friend..."

He finally pulled himself free, chucking her off his lap. He was shaking with anger and disgust, sensing how he was ready to strike her, hard and to hurt, with his fist.

"Share? What are you hinting at? That we should share the children with them? Give them one of ours? You've gone loony with your equality! You're a terrorist, a monster!"

"What are you taking it like that for? Turning everything around..."

"You ought to have a guillotine, then you could really get on with it? You'd make everybody equal as can be, just like that! You'd set it up on the plaza in front of the library, where the Mormon boys preach, and there'd you be alongside, 'Hey, come on, all you tall ones and short ones, you fat ones and thin ones, we're going to make you all equal, we're going to even out the way to Him!'"

"That's not what I was...I never even thought about anything like..."

"It's not going to happen! You're never going to get your way on this! There's always going to be stupid ones and smart, handsome and ugly, tall and short, healthy and sick, childless and with children, bald ones and hairy ones..."

"Already there's a number of people doing this, and in some states there's laws now..."

"...lucky and unlucky, good singers and bad singers, sharp-eyed and nearly-blind..."

"And here you were boasting about how you're not jealous, so that there won't be anything hard in this for you, and anyway we're going to do it so that nobody will know, I've got everything figured out. During the birth you go to another state, and then you tell everyone that the baby was born dead, and who's going to know?"

"I can't stand to hear this nonsense anymore! Why don't you just spit out whatever it is that you've got in mind?"

"To have a baby. I want to have a baby, a little baby. For them. With Mr. Morrison. Apparently everything works with him. I want to have a baby by him. But I really need your permission on this. No, what I need is...what I need is that you should want this as much as I do."

When Anton got back from the dentist, the newly-arrived Kozulin senior had just finished listening to the tape of his granddaughter's telephone call, and was stubbing out tears at the corners of his eyes. The thin ribbon of voice had flown across the ocean and was now winding about the room as if hung from electronic clothespins. Kozulin had gone gray and stooped (how long was it since they had seen each other? Fifteen years or so?), but his chiselled Varangian's profile wanted as much as before to be cleaving the sea air out in the open, without all this cowering behind slabs of glass.

"Olya, Harvey, Anthony, don't be done, we'll free her! It's amazing how much you can tell from a voice. If she'd only been able to get a letter to the Embassy, it could be we wouldn't know anything. The intonation though, that's more important than any words. At least we know the main thing now, that she doesn't want to stay there. It was a mistake that she got there in the first place, because she was spooked, panicked, and now she's tired of it. We have to help her, and we will."

"I'm already packed," said Wife #1. "I'm flying to Washington tomorrow, and from there to Moscow."

"Listen, dear heart, you aren't going to be flying anywhere. Our guests from the Agency have already explained things to you correctly. You've been knocked out of the game before the game even began. You're a spent shell, a trumped card, an exposed film."

"I have friends in the consulate, and in the embassy too."

"They're going to smile at you and offer you vodka with red caviar, but they won't issue you a visa."

"So who's going to go then, you?"

"No, they won't give me a visa either. I've tried lots of times, as you know. They won't let Harvey in either, he's too close a relative. Anyway, there's no point in going over there. What are you going to do, fly over and demand, 'Hand over our Golda!'? 'How many times do we have to tell you, she isn't here!' That's what they're going to say. They'll just stick whoever we send in the madhouse if he tries to insist on anything. No, there's no way we'll get anything by going at it straight. When he kidnapped Europa, Zeus turned himself into a bull and swam up calmly through the waves. You can learn a thing or two from the celestials, and we ought to take at least two elements from that story, the transformation and the sea voyage. There's absolutely no point in flying there. We have to go by boat."

"'...said the old sea wolf'? What's the difference between a sea liner and an airliner? Or did you have something else in mind? A submarine maybe, or a trawler, or a mine-layer, or an aircraft carrier? Maybe you're suddenly a bit nostalgic for your old war days, huh?"

Her father's inappropriate liveliness and gaiety apparently was offending Wife #1, upsetting her. She reached under the glass of the coffee table, got out the phone book.

"If whoever we send finds Golda and she agrees to come back with him, he's not going to be able to just go up and buy a ticket. That's not how they do things in the Upside-down Land. They can ask you for your passport there when you're trying to buy bread, so we're going to have to take a third element from the gods, too—kidnapping. And for a kidnapping we're going to need a ship."

"Why not a balloon then? Or a carriage with a false bottom, or a flying carpet, or a genie from a bottle?"

"Because I don't have a carriage or a carpet or a balloon, but I do have a boat. You've seen my Babylonia. It's not much, but it's a wholly reliable motor yacht. Last year we took her out on Lake Ontario and she handled beautifully. Ronald Ironhand couldn't deal with you, but the yacht responded beautifully to him, like a pet dog. He's an excellent navigator, and I'm delighted with him. A summertime Atlantic crossing would be nothing for him. So all we have to think about is captain and crew."

"Hello, Pan American? I need a ticket to Moscow and back, from Detroit, with a stop in Washington for a day, perhaps two...Yes, tomorrow morning, if possible...And then I'm going to need a second ticket, from Moscow to Detroit...yes, I'm going to go there alone, but I'll be coming back with another person...I'll take care of the visas. That's my business...my credit card number is..."

"I won't try to talk you out of this," grandpa Kozulin said. "It's even better this way. It would look suspicious if her mother didn't fly in to try to get her daughter out. You can be our smoke screen, our distraction. And while you're doing that we'll get together our rescue operation. The main thing now is to find a captain. He has to be somebody who's brave, educated, able to convince, with a talent for transformation, a certain love for risk, and, if possible, somebody who believes in equality and justice. The authorities in the Upside-down Land should trust this man, and be interested in him. He has to have a mission too, some reason to be making the trip. That part I'll do. I've had something worked out for a long time, for other reasons. But the captain, the emissary, the fellow I've been looking for some many years, who I couldn't find no matter how hard I tried, now by some quirk of fate or chance, or maybe some gift of providence, is sitting right here in this room with us."

Wife #1 and Husband #1.3, who had unwillingly been drawn into Kozulin's happy excitement, turned their heads in the direction he was looking, so all of them were staring at Anton. Who shuddered in his chair and then said, surprising even himself, "I keep wondering, what dormitory is this that she talked about on the phone? I've read that in China for example the graduate student dormitories have rooms that are separated by walls with windows. But the windows don't have any glass, they're just rectangular holes. The students put flowers and twigs in vases in them, and you can hear everything that's said for several rooms. But then China has its own weirdnesses..."

Wife #1 turned to her father.

"So this is some kind of deal that you cooked up a long time ago? But why did you have to get Golda involved? The girl got herself tangled up and got scared. You should be thinking about how to free her, not about how to make little deals because of her. This rescue operation of yours is only going to cause her new problems."

"Who's talking about Golda? What's she got to do with any of this? She's an independent grownup person who left on her own to visit an exotic country. The Pirgoroy firm has no connection with her whatsoever. We are on a long-planned advertising and business trip. By modest count the Upside-down Land has a hundred million dogs and two hundred million cats. That's an enormous market that's just waiting to be conquered. The people who live in the Upside-down Land love their pets as much as we love ours. And this opens up a virgin field for friendship between peoples. In sports after all there's always an element of battle, of enmity. Here's there's just love. At joint dog shows there'll be nothing but radiant souls, so that you won't even need a common language. Dogs don't need translators, and cats understand each other from the first meow. We'll set up new voluntary associations and get them involved in our voyage. 'NO WAR FOR CATS! DOGS WANT PEACE!' This is an enormous project, and the fate of one crazy little girl isn't going to influence how it goes at all."

"I can't tell you all the details of my plan right now, those I'm only going to tell the captain. Anthony my friend, before you say yes or no, let me tell you the details—as a secret—of what it is I've planned. Olya, where could we talk in private here? Upstairs, in Daniel's room? And don't look at me so mad and hateful. You believe in materialism and don't accept signs from fate, but Anthony and I, we believe. This couldn't have come together so perfectly if it weren't for the interference of higher powers. And it's not just that Anthony is completely perfect for my plan in every way, or that it was the Upside-down Land that his beloved daughter ran away to—after all, she could have run away to Cuba or Ethiopia, places I couldn't use even if you gave them to me for Christmas. On top of everything else it all happened right now, when the perfect captain and emissary stumbles on us at the precise moment of his life when he has absolutely nothing to lose! Come on, Anthony, let's go upstairs. I'm right behind you, after I grab a bottle and some glasses. This is going to be a long talk, so we'll be needing them."

Radio Broadcast from the Shores of Lake Erie
(The Rotation Clinic)

One time, before my Real Trouble, I had an elegant customer visit my insurance office. She said she was a lawyer representing a flourishing clinic in the next state, which had the curious name of Rotation Clinic. She wanted to buy malpractice insurance against patients who might be dissatisfied with their treatment. Clinics and hospitals can't function without this insurance, of course. Why had she not approached an insurance company in her own state? Because she had been told that our prices would be about ten percent lower.

I promised to draw up the necessary papers and asked her to come again in two weeks. Naturally I investigated the Rotation Clinic. Everything suggested it was flourishing. A small group of physicians worked there, but they all had excellent reputations. The clinic was in an expensive mountain resort town and was surrounded by beautiful grounds. The telephone operators always answered very sweetly that they were distressed to have to say that there were no empty places and there was at least a two-month wait. There was only one detail which was disturbing: rumor had it that up to one third of the patients who entered the clinic died. However, none of the surviving relatives had ever sued them. The doctors explained this melancholy statistic by saying that they weren't afraid to take on even the worst and most hopeless of cases.

I drew up the necessary papers, but the lady lawyer never came back. Her phone was always answered by a taped voice, on a machine. Then, a week later, a scandal broke out in the next state. The papers had front-page headlines about a police raid on the Rotation Clinic, and all the doctors were arrested. It turned out that this clinic serviced suicides, guaranteeing those who desired it an easy and painless exit from this world. The prices were incredibly high. As you can imagine, patients of this sort don't worry about money. However, even if you didn't have a penny to your name they might accept you for the clinic and send you off quietly into the land of the shades for nothing, because another source of income for this criminal band was the sale of organs from the suicides for transplanting into people who weren't of the opinion that they had supped fully of this transitory world. As you might imagine, there was no competition with the Rotation Clinic for the freshness of their product, so the prices for organs was also very high.

The court discovered horrible things. There were instances when the suicide changed his mind and he announced that maybe he wouldn't kill himself after all and was ready to give life another try. They would say, of course, why hurry, all the roads are open to you. They couldn't release a patient with so unsettled a psyche, however—one who couldn't bring even something that simple to an end. Sooner or later the patient would begin to talk. Therefore as a parting gift they would give him a little shot, ostensibly of vitamins, and the person would get no farther than the gates of the beautiful grounds.

On occasion the relatives would bring an old relative they could no longer endure, a man who had been seized by the pettiest old person's egoism, giving no thought to the peace of those about him, who couldn't even imagine doing without his petty old man's pleasures. They were given a paper to sign that they would have no complaints against the doctors who would try to cure the extremely grave but so far undiagnosed illness from which this too-long-lived patient was suffering.

Of course the clinic preferred patients who had no importunate relatives. But if the relatives should happen to sense that something was a bit off ("So young? What do you mean his heart couldn't bear the operation? What operation?"), they were faced with a dilemma, whether to remain silent or to sue the clinic, prove the death a suicide, and lose the insurance settlement.

The criminal medical group was done in by chance. Or by vanity, really—the attempt to improve their product. They removed one young suicide's kidneys, liver, and stomach before he was completely dead, and by some incredible confluence of biological circumstances the patient came to in the morgue. He didn't remember what had happened to him. He found a shirt and some pants, got dressed, and slipped unnoticed out of the clinic. He was a little upset by the unusual lightness in his gut, but decided that he was simply hungry. He went to a pizzeria and ate a half pizza, before he got really ill. The ambulance took him off the street and fetched him to the city hospital.

Naturally the doctors were astonished when they discovered their patient lacked so many vital organs. In his delirium he said the word Rotation several times. They phoned there, but the people at the clinic equivocated, saying that there had been a misunderstanding. Bring the *young man back and we will try to get his kidneys back from Arizona and his liver from Vermont, and if we're not able to get his stomach back from the sheik in Saudi Arabia, then we'll think up something. Then the biological marvel ended, the sick man who had been condemned to linger a bit at the exit from this transitory world finally died, and the criminal gang was rounded up.*

It looked as though nothing might save the doctors of the Rotation Clinic from their just retribution, but their woman lawyer found a simple, but very effective approach. One after another she showed the jurors people from each of the lines which ached to get into the Rotation. The television interviews were each about ten minutes long. At first she showed the line of would-be suicides—tormented, despairing, tortured by misery or incurable disease, praying for surcease. Then she showed those waiting for transplants—trembling with the desire to live, all their hopes on the operation which would save them, the quick transplant for a failed heart, eye, kidney, all of them surrounded by loving relatives who prayed for the return to life of their loved ones.

"The doctors who sit before you now were the last hope for these unhappy people," the clever lawyer said. "Yes, they did do something that our laws currently prohibit, but isn't what we see here rather a prevision of new and marvelous times to come, when death will retreat even farther in the face of science? Is it really so difficult for us to imagine two people sewn into one, literally living with a single heart? A single liver? Or breathing with the lungs of one and cleansing the blood with the kidneys of another? Is this not the debut of the future society, in which any of the organs of the human body may be acquired as easily and freely as new batteries for a transistor radio? But there remains the question, where are these organs to be obtained? Auto accidents are not going to suffice. Sooner or later everyone is going to understand that all these marvelous healthy livers, kidneys, and hearts which now are being wasted by people who drown themselves, set fire to themselves, hang themselves so that they twist uselessly in their attics for days, all these should be and must be used for transplants. All that is necessary is that the disillusioned be permitted a hygienic, productive, and estimable way of doing what they are going to do anyway, but in horrible conditions, with pain, dirt, and nervous torment for their loved ones."

"So who are these doctors who sit before you in the dock?" shouted the alluring lady at the end of her speech, "Are they criminals or fearless pioneers of progress? If you are to find them guilty, will you not find yourselves in the annals of history alongside those who condemned

Socrates, Galileo, John Brown, and Dreyfus?"

At which the jurors shuddered, unable to come to a verdict. A mistrial had to be declared, and a new trial was continually put off. As far as I am aware, there still has been no new trial.

What do you think, dear radio audience? What verdict would you have brought against the doctors of the Rotation Clinic? Against doctors who had taken it upon themselves to satisfy the great demand for their unusual goods and services?

7. SETTING SAIL

THE FLAG SNAPPED and furled in the wind. The dog's head portrayed on it strained forward, chasing after a tumbling can of dog food. Delivery boys scurried up and down the gangplanks. The Chinese girl Lin Chan was dressed in a white cook's hat and was checking boxes of bottles and bags of provisions, checking things off on her list. Pablo-Pedro, wrench and brush in hand, was moving along the right side of the Babylonia, tightening loose screws in the handrails and netting, painting over little spots.

It had only been a joke, a gag, when Anton had tossed out their names in discussing possibilities for the crew. However Kozulin, an unpredictable adventurer, immediately warmed to the idea and went himself to Brighton to talk with them, convincing the piratical pair to sign on that same day ("They know and love Golda, for one thing. For another they are representatives of the insulted and injured peoples, so that they'll get a warm reception in the Upside-down Land. For three, Pablo-Pedro was in the Marines, so that he knows something about the pirating business, which could come in very handy. And besides, they have absolutely nothing to lose.") Kozulin had brought them in his own car. The prisoner's transmitter had been unbuckled and removed from Pablo-Pedro's ankle at the edge of the five-mile zone, then thrown into the lake. ("A runaway prisoner on board, with fresh traces of his shackles on his leg, that's great! Got a real style!")

Ronald Ironhand, the navigator, was pitiless in preparing them for the voyage. Every morning before daybreak they had to weigh anchor and plow around in Lake Erie until long after dark. Even at night the dance of the sun on the waves would remain, drifting across shut eyelids as if on a screen, and the handles of the helm would rock against a background of polished brass tubing. Dials quivered and fingers did too. The wooden planks underfoot trembled, and so too did the heart, sweetly, anticipating and fearing.

At the waterside cafe which had been set up for their farewell luncheon the waitresses opened oysters with hooked knives. The four propeller screws that turned overhead strained valiantly to lift the dining room up above the earth. The people who had come to see them off crowded the dance floor, glasses in hand. They were waiting for the old Kozulins, who had telephoned to say that they would be a half hour late.

Mrs. Darcey, Mother-in-law #3, smiled sadly at Anton and let go of the sleeve of his newish captain's uniform.

"This isn't at all what you need, you know."

"I'm not doing it for pleasure..."

"The radio-prophet business is so big right now, you could make a real name for yourself, you might start getting offers from other stations..."

"We've already agreed, I'm going to send you broadcasts every week."

"It makes me sick even to think that other stations might get you away from me. But I understand that our little town is too small for someone of your talent..."

"It'll sound terrific: 'From our overseas correspondent, specially for the people of Ladysville.'"

"In the future you might even have had a television program..."

"Golda was able get another message to us. This was a real scream, a cry for help."

"Yes, yes, I heard it. Are you going to go through Montreal? If you want, I can try to talk Susan into letting you see the kids. After all, it's a dangerous expedition you're taking on, and a father has a right..."

"Try. But I doubt it will work. You know your daughter."

Mother-in-law #3 looked at him with silent reproach. Men are so irresponsible. With no warning at all they suddenly decide to leave, decide to die. Men are unpredictable. The lariats of words and phrases slither from them like watches from your wrist, like rings from withered fingers. You think that they are there, they're yours, close at hand, wholly obedient—there for you to use!—and then suddenly you have nothing in your hand, just the empty leash. It is such a sad thing.

The new communique—shriek, summons, lament—from Golda had come to them this time wrapped in the words of others, in another's voice. A strange woman called from Philadelphia, said her name was Mrs. Glendale, and that she had just returned from a tour of Moscow. Yes, everything was marvelous there except for the trip they had to take to that grave place in their main square, because she had a terror of corpses, and they made her go right up against this corpse in a glass case. Other important dead people were walled up in a wall alongside, but this wasn't very reliable, since they later might find errors of some sort in their life and take them back out of the wall. Their group had already finished their tour and bought all their souvenirs, had left their hotel for the bus to take them to the airport, when this girl ran up to her on the street and at first Mrs. Glendale had just thought that she was collector of badges and other souvenirs, but as soon as she spoke she understood that this was an American, in a big hurry; she stuffed a note with a telephone number in her hand, spoke in a scattered way, but asked her to call and just tell her parents that she was being sent to work, to harvest ("I forget what they call that thing that's like half plantation and half farm") for a few months. She mentioned maybe in Pskov. But then two young men ran up and literally dragged her off.

"Now it's true that they were smiling and trying to make it look like they were playing with the girl, but I could see how scared she was, and I didn't like that, so on the bus, to be on the safe side, I copied the number into my address book and tore the paper into teeny-tiny bits. I know that in cases like this you're supposed to eat the paper, but I didn't have any tomato juice to wash it down with, I don't drink any other sort, and then at the airport I was invited into the office of the main customs official and they asked me questions for the longest time, what had the girl given me or asked me to do, but I lied and said that she was looking for somebody named Jerry Newcastle, from Seattle, and I told her that there was nobody in the group by that name, but that there was another group coming behind ours, and they kept me for almost an hour, which was the other very unpleasant part of Moscow, even worse really than the visit to the dead man, but since you say this is important news, then I'm very glad that I was able to help a fellow American and that this was all for something, because our group was very unhappy with me, because on account of me the flight was delayed for a long time."

This story absolutely flattened Wife #1. She was already downcast by her failure in Washington; her father had proven correct (as ever, and as unbearably as ever!). The consulate had told her that her request for a visa would be considered in the usual order, meaning over three months, and this they had said not even offering her a chair, to say nothing of red caviar already, and then there was this call from Mrs. Glendale...

She stood between her two former husbands, a tiny, tufted, beaten thing, as if her feathers were matted, wings sticky from an oil spill, touching and touching again her little black crest of a hat. It was clear again how much she had filled out and flattened from life on this earth. "Yes, I've become hideous," her face seemed to say, "but the hideousness is from sorrow, and the sorrow comes from you having achieved your end, from forcing me to descend into your swamp, a place where children are kidnapped and sent off to do heavy labor. So now take from me what you will, get from me what you want, and what you deserve..."

It was just this face, and tone, and look, just such a descent into the sink of intended ugliness—the last weapon in the struggle for freedom of flight—which had broken over Anton fifteen years before, when he had refused to have a child for the benefit of the Morrisons.

Mr. Morrison worked in the library, and also speculated in houses and land. He was lanky, gray, and slightly humped, and loved to say that he would have stood straight long ago, if it weren't for the taxes he had to bear. The more houses he sold, the heavier the burden of taxes. One time they all went to the beach together, and Anton noticed a tattoo on the librarian's chest. Over the curly gray underbrush, like an arc over a dusty park, was written "Sin lieth at the door. And unto thee shall be his desire, and thou shalt rule over him" (Gen. 4:7). If anything had scared off the future children of the Morrisons, it seemed this inscription would have done so. The idea that Wife #1 would have to bury her face in this thicket, or at least read that grim inscription five times...ten? How many times would it take?...filled Anton with quivers.

"You're an uneducated savage! A fool!" Wife #1 shouted. "A stupid and ordinary jealous idiot! You really think that I would ask you for permission to get into bed with another man? You mean you've never heard about artificial insemination?"

He had heard about it. He had read about it. He tried to imagine how it was done. They would be put in rooms side by side. Or maybe even in separate little cabins. The spermatozoa's path through the universe of rooms had to be made as short as possible. Mr. Morrison would be given a picture magazine to read. Probably one that had been well-read, with the corners dog-eared. Or would they be so well-off that they could permit themselves several subscriptions? Probably they would have an entire bookshelf of erotica, to any taste. Once Anton had seen a news stand with three competing journals side by side, one for fans of tiny, walnut-sized breasts, one for lovers of enormous, melon-sized breasts, and one for fans of pendulous flabby breasts, like summer squash grown on a fence. No doubt each of the magazines had its subscribers. There were all sorts of customers, so the clinics probably had to be ready to satisfy any requests. Maybe they would even have a nurse trained to do stripteases?

Wife #1 no longer insisted, or asked, or complained. She simply began to wither quietly. She would sit for hours on end at her desk, head in hands over her school work, open always to one and the same page. "Bazarov possessed a strong character and from time to time wished also to possess Odintsova..." Or she would lie with her back to the cluttered room, which had been given over utterly to the triumph of things. The Morrisons almost never showed themselves. In the evenings Anton would pick the children up there and take them to eat at a pizzeria which had enormous mechanical figures which played guitars and danced and said happy birthday to the customers and handed out prizes and embraced those who dared and asked you to come again. The children begged him to let them spend the night there, with these incredible fur-covered dancers, and not take them home to their mother, who no longer knew how to talk or smile or fly.

It had been unwise of him to have fastened on that trip... The firm wanted to send somebody down to their Texas division. "But it's for four weeks. You're sure that after a week you're not going to ask to come back? You've got a family, children..." He was sure. He ached to get out of the house. Leaving, he told Wife #1, "You have a month. Decide for yourself. But I don't want to know anything. I'm never going to want that, no matter what you do to me."

The tenth day in Houston he got drunk. The bar was decorated with pictures of race car drivers leaning out of their cars, and they were shaky on the ground from too little speed. All of the customers at the bar would turn their heads toward the television like parade-watchers when there was a roar from the screen. Then he wandered around the night streets carrying his overheated lighter in his hand, because girls in short leather skirts would ask him for a light at almost every corner. Then he sat on the bed in his room and one of the girls hastily undressed in the corner—she apparently thought that he was just about to go to sleep, but he wasn't tired at all, not a smidgeon, he just wanted to try to make out the title of her book; he had chosen her because she had a book in her hands. Now she opened the book, which turned out to be a box, and dumped a heap of condoms out on the table, rolled the money around a bankroll, and hid it in a plastic replica of odd-man-out, and then came at him bearing a little plastic cap in her wide-open fingers—he was always amazed at how small the bit at the end was, they couldn't really think that there would be enough space for all his brave little fellows?—but this time neither the end bit nor the hat itself proved necessary, because odd-man-out demonstrated not the slightest shred of interest, no matter how the two of them tried to talk him into it. He simply shook his head on his soft neck and strained, without permission, to fulfill his other functions, which at the moment seemed considerably more important to him. The girl dressed and left with a proud and offended look, while inexperienced Anton did not know whether under the circumstances he had the right to ask for part of his money back.

In the middle of the night he leapt up, awakened by a simple idea that would solve the whole problem. He grabbed the telephone, dialed, and began shouting, not even letting Wife #1 fully awaken.

"I've got it! It's so simple! Why didn't we think of it earlier... Why do you have to do it with Mr. Morrison? Why don't I do it with Mrs. Morrison? That's a lot simpler and quicker. She's no beauty of course, and not a spring chicken either, but better I should suffer nine minutes than you should suffer nine months. What? The hell with fallopian tubes. My little fellows can get their way through any cut off, break down any barriers, even go around, if they have to! You know them too, right? So let's put together a special drop team and get on with it! You're saying no without even thinking it through. So this means that all that talk about generosity was just camouflage? And you just really wanted to have a go at the gay life? So how's the insemination going? Is Mr. Morrison pleased with you? Or are you going to have to do some coupling anyway?"

Wife #1 called him a bad name and threw the receiver down.

However, when he flew back, she came to meet him at the airport. Just one look at her put odd-man-out into such a state that Anton had to run to her and hide the uprising hooligan in a short hug of greeting, then sit down on a chair, where he waited a half hour in the lobby before he was permitted to go any further, to the car.

"The poor, poor fellow," Wife #1 said, glancing at him touched and amused, "he doesn't know that he's going to have to wait a couple more days...Yes, it worked out poorly...yesterday it began...you see how it is?...the poor Morrisons...nothing came of it. But that's the end of it with them. You see, I had to at least try..."

Now he understood not only her but—or so it seemed to him—he began to guess as well the secrets of odd-man-out. It was now that the proposition first flashed before him that his unpredictable roly-poly was mixed up in the production of children. That he was ready to take it up alone or in a group, seriously or as a joke, with his wife or his wife's girlfriend, but if for any reason the production of children was excluded as a possibility, then this little pervert was prepared to go on strike at any moment!

Oh, the Morrisons, the Morrisons, with their unfulfilled, tormenting dream! Why had they passed so close in their life, like the iceberg next to the Titanic, to strike somewhere in the unseen depths of their solid and happy little world? For the gash remained, and it would have done its work even if there had not occurred soon after, behind the branches of the flowering sumac, in the smoke of smoldering lamb, that meeting with Caitlin at the picnic.

Right after the Kozulins stepped from the limousine there appeared two workers in overalls who pulled out a long roll. The journalists tossed aside their glasses with drinks and dashed to the doors of the cafe, digging out their cameras and tape recorders and pens and television cameras as they ran. The workers with the roll on their shoulders went up the gangplank to the yacht, put the roll down on the deck, and began to unwind it. The focussed lenses caught the huge shining eyes and silky brow of a red spaniel—at the lip of an opened can—just at the moment when the advertising banner unfurled over the side of the Babylonia like soft paint rollers on long sticks.

"Put the cat's head on the left side," old Kozulin ordered, "but closer to the rear. The demands of symmetry are no law for us. Put the dish of veal balls and the name Pirgoroy on top of the cabin. We have to give a thought for those who will be taking pictures from helicopters. Incidentally dear friends, write this down in your notebooks, the advertising agency assured me that these signs are made of special plastic that will stand up to gales and salt spray and burning sun. If so much as a corner rips off, they're going to give me my money back."

Kozulin resembled an old admiral called out of exile—for the umpteenth time!—to save his motherland from the enemy. Or perhaps to conquer the last overseas island without which the empire would fall. At the meal he said, "You probably all know that our trip even before it begins has become the object of evil inventions, hostile intrigues, jokes that border on slander, slander beyond the boundaries of the believable. The vulgar press and the corridors of the clubhouses and tee-off areas of golf courses are full of people industriously spreading rumors that under cover of trade and advertising we are preparing to gather espionage materials (I'd like to know about what? The number of fleas on the upside down kitties?). Or that the cans of food are very handy for transporting diamonds and drugs. Or that we are intending to conduct anti-propaganda, secretly convincing people that peace between these two great countries is as impossible as peace between dogs and cats.

"We have not attempted to discover who is spreading these rumors. (Our competitors? Political radicals? People who love scandals in the newspapers?) In the course of my long life I have become convinced that as a phenomenon of human frailty slander accords only to phenomena of human rectitude and worth. Be proud that you are slandered! Go bravely forward, for you are on the right path!

"So what is the goal of this voyage?

"The answer to that question is as difficult as the answer to the question why seven hundred years ago Marco Polo set off from his native Venice, heading for the rising sun. He could have made profits without leaving Europe, and with considerably less risk. He went because he was tormented by a wall, a wall of ignorance and misunderstanding which eternally divided East from West. He wanted to open the eyes of each to the other, while at the same time opening his own eyes to the entire world. He knew too that in this world there is no language more universal than the language of trade.

"Trade is not considered an exalted activity. Or at least not so exalted as killing. A soldier always enjoys higher status than does a merchant. For many people trade is an argument, a conflict, a quarrel. It is not everyone who can acknowledge that the market is the cathedral of freedom. It is no accident that, throughout the world, trade fairs are gay and festive occasions, for it is only there that a purchaser of maximum freedom will encounter a seller of maximum freedom, and they may effect the mystery of free exchange of goods. It is not for nothing that English uses the same word 'fair' for a market, for beauty, and for justice!

"So we wish our captain, this new Marco Polo, this missionary of free enterprise, a safe journey to distant shores, so that he may offer the inhabitants of those far-off places living proof of how much they have lost by destroying the temples of freedom. We also wish that he shall return home safely, and that perhaps he may also open our eyes. Perhaps he will learn something to explain how this suicidal delusion, this burning thirst to destroy the free and happy market, was able to seize millions of people. We see how this delusion slithers its way about the world, and who is to say that we are not the next to suffer?"

In the mad crush of farewell handshakes, hugs, and speeches, Mrs. Kozulin led Anton off to the side, clutching a small parcel to her chest. Her eternal readiness for the lifting of the curtain had faded a bit with the years, but she still looked him in the face with hope—after all, somewhere there still have to be good plays, don't there?—about us, but with a happy ending.

"Antosha, God only knows whether we'll see each other again...but you've always been like family for me, like a son. You're the only one I could ask to do this...because you're the only one I trust. So here, a little jar and a box, they were blessed in church. Swear to God and the Son too that you will bring me some water from the Neva and some dirt from the Summer Garden. Or if you can't, then at least from the Tauride Garden. It's for my grave. It'll make it a lot easier for me to last until the end if I can be put to rest in Petersburg soil, even if it is just a pinch. A lot of our friends have already gone there, but I couldn't bring myself to ask any of them. I look at them and think, they'll forget, or won't do it, and then when they get home they'll just dig up some dirt from the lawn and take the water out of the tap. And then I'll spend the rest of my life torturing myself about it. But you'd never deceive me, so I can be confident with you. Just make sure you come back safe and in one piece, as they say here."

Anton took her parcel, kissed her, hugged her to the buttons of his uniform. Wife #1 pushed her mother away and flung her arms around his neck, hanging there for a minute, feet off the ground, which started up the odd-man-out for no reason. Then she smiled sadly, nodded her head, and moved off into the crowd: Mrs. Darcey, Harvey, Daniel (Son #1.2, who had flown in from California to beg to be taken along, and only was dissuaded with the greatest of difficulty—by being promised a trip to Alaska instead) and some unknown well-wishers, relatives of relatives, correspondents. He and old Kozulin had gone over the last details the night before, the necessary telephone numbers and addresses committed to memory, all contingencies and forkings of the deep and devious plan gone over, like a matryoshka doll with seven insides, save that inside the final one was a dangerous, reclusive, and smoky genie. Now all that remained to be done was a click of the champagne glasses for the photographers, a handshake, and then they were off, up the carpeted gangplank to the ship.

Which was precisely the moment that a police car flew into the lot, destroying the solemnity and pleasant sadness of the farewell, hurting the ears with the pitiless baying siren, starting up all the old fears and new ("What have I done?"). Two patrolmen got out of the front seat, while out of the back seat, long-haired, heavy-browed, glasses pushed up on his head, stepped the prophet of distribution and confiscation of property, the financial Nemesis, the pitiless defender of abandoned wives and unborn children, the lawyer Simpson.

"That's him," Simpson said, and went straight for Anton, following his pitilessly pointed finger. "Don't pay any attention to the captain's uniform, that's a masquerade. The fingerprints will show you that he's the one."

The policemen, tapping their nightsticks, moved toward him. Pedro-Pablo pulled his forage cap down to his nose and backed up the gangway, to disappear into the hold of Babylonia.

The policemen were stopped by grandfather Kozulin.

"Fred, David, what's going on? Where did you get that guy?"

"I don't know where he came from, Mr. Kozulin, sir. He showed up at the station and said that he has to arrest an alimony-skipper. He said there's warrants in three states."

"Did he show you any papers? A warrant signed by a local judge?"

"He doesn't have anything. He says he just flew in from New York and hasn't had time to do the papers yet. He promised that tomorrow he would make a proper legal presentation. The sergeant ordered us to come check it out."

While this was going on Simpson came up alongside Anton, drumming his fingers on his briefcase, dancing nearer and nearer, licking his lips.

"Whose yacht is this, Mr. Sebich? Looks like it would be worth scads of money. Out on the ocean, a million at least. Here, inland, probably cheaper though, huh? But even so it will easily cover what you owe for the year. I don't know whether there will be enough left for the rest of your ex-wives, but my client will get what she's owed, anyway."

"The yacht is mine," Kozulin said, "so don't go drooling over her, because you'll choke on her. Mr. Sebich is working for me as her captain. I ask you to step back from him and stop spoiling our little ceremony."

"Damn New Yorkers," one of the policemen grumbled, "always sticking their noses in where nobody asked them."

"Got the whole damn East Coast in their mitts and think that they can give orders here too," the other agreed.

"Fred, David, you know me, right? Would I have taken somebody I didn't know to work for me? I've known Mr. Sebich twenty years already. I'll vouch for him completely."

"You know how many wives and children he has abandoned without means of support?" Simpson barked.

"If they don't have the means of support, then how could they have hired such an expensive noisemaker as you? To make things short, if you have some claim against Mr. Sebich, go see my attorney tomorrow. For the time being, you can disappear, because you've already spoiled our little festival here."

"No way! I demand that the yacht be impounded immediately, until ownership of the yacht is established. And as for this phony captain, he should be taken to court immediately."

"Fred, David, I'm amazed," Kozulin said. "This is an obvious intrusion into my private life. It's an obvious disturbance of the peace, and you're still standing there thinking about something."

"He's right, pal. You've made your noise, and now that's enough," Fred said, taking Simpson's elbow.

"That's how it is? That's enough? Are you going to do your duty or not?"

Silently the policeman squeezed Simpson from both sides and began to push him back toward the car.

"Hey! What are you doing? Hey! I'll call the DA! You're going to lose your badges! Hey!"

"Fred, seems kind of like he's threatening us, doesn't it? And us in the line of duty and all."

"These New Yorkers have got a hell of a nerve, haven't they?"

They twisted Simpson's arm up behind his back and shoved him into the back seat. The last words that he shouted came to Anton as clots of sounds that only with difficulty—and maybe a guess? or a presentiment that these would be the sounds?—he was able to turn back into words.

"Nothing...for this man...never...not a cent...not a handkerchief...to own...I'm going to...he can't...forever!...as per paragraph 185..."

The shore was getting farther away.

The houses, trees, billboards all grew smaller. The fluttering flags waved above the cafe roof like a flock of colorful birds, arranging themselves for migration. A truck drove slowly along the shore. Painted on its sides was the sailboat which had come to these shores three hundred and fifty years before. A blue and white mail jeep drove by with the day's supply of letters, newspapers, bills, checks, campaign promises, advertisements, and appeals for charity. The horns in the band glistened with sun and the sounds of the march grew fainter.

Earthly life floated ever farther and farther away, while water flowed easily into the space of parting.

"Sailing away, departing," Anton thought, "this is like a shot of non-existence, a little dose of death, that lets you take a peek back and so convince yourself that life can go on without you."

"This man will own nothing."

However the itch of anticipation, and a hearty anger, and the readiness to grapple with the ever-young Miserymaker, and hope all returned to the forgotten crannies of his soul, like blood rushes burning back into frostbitten fingers, to push away and silence Simpson's gloomy prophecy.

Ronald's iron hands gripped the helm and the prow of the Babylonia turned toward the east.

PART TWO

THE VOYAGE

Radio Broadcast Inspired by the Sight of Canadian Shores
(The Angry Canadian)

Once when travelling through Canada on business I met an ex-American who had resettled in Canada about twenty years before. He was still very angry with his former homeland. He held that we, the Americans, did not wish to see our mistakes, and when people pointed them out to us would only smile politely and say that the comment was very interesting, but right now we had to hurry home and pay the babysitter. I asked what our major mistakes were and he answered that we were nuts about politics, that that was our major failing.

"You can't get away from political arguments in America," he said, "and nobody wants to admit how senseless they are. But they're senseless for sure, because all of our political views are just going to be reflections of our fears. Some people fear terrorists more than anything, and others are afraid of pacifists. For others it's communists, imperialists for others, negroes for some, Zionists for others, immigrants for some, smugglers for others, homosexuals for another group, and repeat offenders for yet another. Some people are horrified that we are headed for anarchy, and others are convinced we are headed for totalitarianism. What can you argue about here? Nobody would argue with a man who's afraid of heights or snakes or enclosed spaces or water or airplanes or fire or cars or lightning or earthquakes. Every person is condemned to live his life with the fears to which he is born, and no one has ever succeeded in curing him or convincing him otherwise or making him over into someone else.

"What you have to do is consider the specific problems and the ways they can be fixed," he said. "I tried to do that, but nobody wanted to listen. That's why I left. What are the problems? Well, for example, there are traffic problems. Every day cars collide and get wrecked and people are crippled or killed, and nobody ever takes any responsibility for it, because everybody pays money to the auto insurance companies. Who naturally raise their prices all the time, as you know yourself. So then the criminal driver gets behind the wheel again and takes to the road. What should be done? The cars should be branded, the way they used to brand criminals in the

old days. You would see some car with a big green circle in front and behind and you'd know immediately that this car had run into someone and then tried to drive off. A yellow circle would mean DWI, and a red that somebody had been killed or crippled. Everyone would keep a bigger distance from these branded cars, and the number of accidents would drop considerably.

"Another concrete problem is that in all of America, for all its incredible riches, you can't find a single cheap restaurant that serves boiled food. Fried meat, fried fish, fried chicken, everything is fried. Or covered in pepper or drowning in vinegar. Why? You'll never guess why. Go into any drugstore and the reason will immediately become obvious, from the endless shelves of medicines for heartburn. You stuff yourself with fried peppery meat and then gallop off to the drugstore to buy a bottle of Alka-Seltzer or a packet of Rolaids, and your dollars continue happily on into the coffers of the pharmaceutical giants. They are the ones who make sure that there's no restaurant where a person might find a normal boiled dinner. They are making billions from our heartburn, and so just try and do something to stop it.

"A third problem is how everyone complains about the high cost of health care. Can't people see that the main reason for this is free health care for the poor and the old? Our lawmakers have never been poor or old, so they don't understand that millions of these people get up every morning with one and the same question: how in the world to kill the day. They have money enough for food, they have a roof over their heads, but what do they have to fill the time? Still in their beds they investigate how they feel, the creaking of their joints, the movement of gases in their large intestines, the roar in their ears, and they decide that they should see a doctor. It's free, after all. And somebody will listen to you carefully, ask you questions, feel you, shine lights on you. For an hour, maybe even for two you will become the center of caring attention, and so will be spared from boredom and loneliness. As for the bill that the doctor will make up for his procedures—who cares? It's not the patient who's going to be paying, is it?

"I've known those sorts of old people. My parents were like that. I've seen how a good half of the state budget is wasted on nothing. I could have saved the treasury hundreds of billions. I wrote to legislators and journalists to suggest they introduce a small, nominal payment for doctors' visits. No more than what it costs to go to a movie, even. The sort of money that even the poorest person could come up with, except that then the person would have to choose. Nine out of ten would go to the movie, of course, which is why the doctors saw me as an enemy. But why did everyone else *turn their backs, and not want even to listen to me?*

"All right, I'll admit that there's a political dimension to this. The votes of poor voters and all that. But how about a wholly economic problem then? The average mouth size of the average American? That's right, nobody's working on trying to enlarge that, are they? Even though there's a huge possibility for economic growth there. Take a look at this tiny little mouth here, and then look at a double hamburger. You could easily make a triple burger, or quadruple!! Imagine five patties, one on top of the other, lettuce dripping down the sides, hunks of tomato and onion and pickle sticking out all over. Beautiful sight, wouldn't it be? Wouldn't all of our farmers that are going broke pick up from that increased demand for beef and pork? Wouldn't business pick up for all those combine companies and grain silos and fertilizer traders and contract harvesters? But this isn't going to happen, because your average American is too lazy to stretch his mouth just a bit wider, and none of the research doctors want to work on this problem, don't want to work out some way of enlarging the jaw.

"There are a lot of problems! How much good you could do for people, if only they would stop blathering about politics and start working on the simple and necessary things!"

I said that it was probably hard for somebody with such a wealth of ideas to find people to talk to. He agreed that that was true, and that because he had no audience, he had worried his wife with his speeches until finally she had left him. He couldn't complain about being lonely, though—he'd learned his lesson. He'd worked out a special method of being with people near and far, and now his house was filled with guests every day. Yes, people came in a steady stream—friends, neighbors, co-workers, old lovers and new, business partners and drop-ins. It is about this method that I would like to tell you more, dear radio audience, because it seemed to me to be the most interesting of all of my angry Canadian's ideas.

"In the first place," he said, "you absolutely always have to have food in the house. And you can't try to get by just with baloney and cheese and crackers. You have to keep the fridge stocked with frozen crab legs and sour tomatoes and roast beef and lox and three or four kinds of herring, olives, chicken filets that fry up real quick, shrimp salad, ham, beer, smoked turkey, chocolate cookies. Never ask a visitor whether he would like to eat; your first question should always be the same thing, 'How's things now?' Even if you can't remember the visitor's name right away, even if you have no idea of what ails or alarms him, he'll immediately think that you are asking him about whatever is most important, for him and his life. He'll believe that for the past few days the only thing you've thought about is his problems, and he'll start talking about them warmly, as if you were his brother.

"That's when you put food on the table, not making a fuss of it. Drinks too, of course. This isn't hospitality, you were just getting ready to eat yourself. And it's nothing to get a second plate. As you set the table you answer, and say how amazing things are, and how horrible. If you know that the guest likes to take pictures, ask to see his latest. If he writes, ask if he wouldn't happen to have something of his most recent work with him, that he could leave for you to read. You have to be careful with musicians though, they might happen to have their violin or saxophone out in the car and then they'll want to play something for you. That always takes a lot of time and can put off the other guests.

"Usually the arrival of another guest, or a third one, is always a bit of a problem. Never bring the new guests directly into the room where the first guest is. Spend at least five minutes alone with the new guest and ask that magic 'How are things now?' It's only after he's had a chance to answer that you take him in to be with the person who was there first, so you can introduce them. They should be relaxed by now, and can be distracted from themselves for a moment, pay attention to eating. You can put out fruit, make coffee. If more guests come, then you can be alone with them too, for longer even now, because the others are set up all right. When you introduce the new person to the company, exchange looks and hints about how the new one has just told you such an amazing, such an important thing...and always keep your eye on the table. Even if one of the guests doesn't touch anything, that's no problem. Somewhere in his unconsciousness even a fleeting thought of you must be connected with something tasty, so as to evoke a pleasant salivation.

When people begin to leave, see each of them off, and insist that they keep you abreast of whatever it was they told you about today. If you follow my method point for point, I assure you—not every time, of course, there's no absolute guarantee here, even a rocket launch for some rocket that they've spent years getting ready, even that can go wrong, right?— but the probability is incredibly high that someone among those leaving, even if it's maybe only one out of ten, will suddenly remember and turn around to ask, 'And you, how's it with you? Again you didn't say anything about yourself. How's the wife and kids?'

"God forbid that you should let down here. God forbid that you should give into that happy wobble of the heart and yelp out, 'My life sucks and I'm dog tired and my wife ran off with somebody else and my kids won't even pick up the phone when I call!' Just nod in an embarrassed way, smile mysteriously, and say, 'What's the point in talking about me?' Then ask them to come back whenever they can.

"If you master my method, you're never going to be lonely ever again. That I can guarantee you. If the method fails to work for you, call me at this number, and drop by. I'll greet you with my happy, 'How are things now?' and we'll talk over what has to be done."

Dear radio audience! Write us and we will help you get in touch with the angry Canadian, a remarkable generator of unappreciated ideas!

8. MONTREAL

ANTON HELD THE
wheel with one hand, flipped through the ship's log with the other.
Ronald's handwriting was simple, the letters as round and smooth as
vitamin pills, scattered out and arranged on the page in lines of
absolutely equal length.

14 J u n e.
Going through Welland Canal. Lake Erie is be-
hind us, 570 feet above sea level. Ahead is Lake
Ontario, 245 feet above sea level. This difference
in altitude created Niagara Falls. It is to the right.
We have neither seen nor heard it. That is too bad.

15 J u n e.
We are passing by the north shore of Lake Ontario.
We have already passed Toronto, Oshava and Coburg.
There has been conflict on board. Sailor Pablo-Pedro
struck his wife in the face, the cook Lin Chan. His
opinion is that she is making the Chinese dish *pork
lo-mein* incorrectly. The captain ordered me to lock
Pablo-Pedro in the hold with the cat food for two
hours. Pablo-Pedro is afraid of the dark.

16 J u n e.
We are rounding St. Lawrence Park. Its other name

is the Thousand Islands. The tourist season is from
June to October. Sailor Pablo-Pedro taught me how
to play communist poker. The rules are the same as
for poker except that the winner doesn't get the
money of the losers, but instead has to throw it
overboard. The idea is to learn to get pleasure not
from winning but from the opponent's loss. It is a
strange sensation.

17 J u n e.
We are entering the St. Lawrence River. America
is on the right, Canada on the left. We have 750
miles of river and bay ahead of us. The water is
absolutely clear. This is the only large river in North
America that flows from west to east. Its width is
from one to three miles. The captain and I talked
about women for a long while. Including our former
wife. I learned a lot that was new to me.

Anton closed the journal and looked at the river instead. The
Canadian waves squeezed up against the American ones, then washed
back again. The gulls ran their smuggling lines from shore to shore. The
sunny morning lassitude dissolved the boundaries between sky and
water, earth and tree, living and dead, past and future.

It was still about four hours to Montreal. They would stop there for
a day, take on food and fuel supplies, and give interviews to the local
papers. They would have to make sure that the photographers got good
big shots of the Pirgoroy ads on the sides of the yacht. In the afternoon
he would have a few free hours, and come what may, he was going to
go to St. Luke Street. Wife #3 couldn't refuse him something so small,
to see his children before he left. After all, it was a dangerous voyage
he had before him, and there was no guarantee that he would be
returning whole and safe.

He had not seen the twins since she left for Canada. How long ago
was that? Eight years? In the pictures that she sent to Mother-in-law #3
the older children already looked as tall as their mother. True, that
wasn't such a trick. His first meeting with Wife-to-be #3 had amazed
him, she had been so small. Wife #2 had spoken of the up-coming visit
of her school chum with such excitement that Anton had begun to
imagine someone who was at least bigger than Caitlin herself.

"Susan Darcey was the most important friend of my youth," Wife #2 said. "There's so many things that she opened my eyes to! I'm terribly glad that she's agreed to come visit us. But please, I'm begging you, go easy with her. She's so easy to hurt. It takes some time to get to know her better and then you'll fall in love with her."

Susan Darcey was scarcely taller than the suitcases which the taxi driver brought in. A contemptuous smile flitted about her lips. Her fingers spread a packet of money into a green fan. The driver didn't look at her. He put down a second pair of suitcases in a way that left Susan boxed in a square, as if inside a watchtower.

Anton rushed up to help.

"Why didn't you call? We'd have met you at the airport! I can get away from the office whenever I like."

"Don't touch them!" Susan shrieked. "I'll do it myself! I can do it just fine myself. Who said he should touch them?"

"Just imagine," she went on, looking at the door which the taxi driver had just slammed shut, "he asked where my parents were. He wouldn't believe that I had flown in alone. He said that he had never seen such a little kid travelling with four suitcases before. I asked him whether he wasn't trying to corrupt a minor. He started apologizing, and then I told him that I suffer from pituitary gland disease, that I can't be driven quickly. I said that if he tried to go faster than forty miles an hour, I'd sue him. Which he believed, the idiot. We crawled along so slowly that everyone was looking at us. I hope he lost at least twenty dollars taking me. Hey, where are you taking that? I told you not to touch it! I've got an expensive camera in that green bag, and the yellow bag has the main lights, they'll break if you breathe on them. There's probably nothing in there now as it is except glass dust."

Susan was a photographer. Magazines and ad agencies ordered her work. She was able to come visit only because a local firm here in Chicago had invited her and paid for the ticket. It used to be that inexpensive slaves were shipped in from Africa, now they are summoned by telephone from New Jersey. Progress!

At supper the girlfriends began picking over the bones of old acquaintances.

"Cindy Robinson? I'll tell you about Cindy Robinson! She married that hairdresser that worked in the salon near the bank, and had two kids by him, who they tried to starve to death. That's right, to death! How did it come out? The kids went next door and cleaned out the neighbor's refrigerator, that's how. They ate all the ice cream and baloney and grapes. The neighbor had a burglar alarm and the cops were there in ten minutes. The kids were picked up at the scene of the crime. The papers wrote it up, and the kids even got into the record books, as the youngest burglars. Two and three years old..."

"Tom Godzillo? Okay, you want to hear about Tom Godzillo? He fell in love with Patsy Gluck, and asked her to marry him. You have to remember Patsy Gluck! She's the one whose skirt was always slipping down, and I gave her men's suspenders for her birthday, remember? She refused Tom at first, and let me tell you about suffering! He came to me to pour his heart out. He said he was going to kill himself. He got drunk and then went driving around the neighborhood, looking to die. Cats, raccoons, squirrels, skunks, they all died, but not Tom. Finally Patsy said yes and there was a crazy week, all the plans being made for the future and everything. But then there was this unhappy circumstance, that poor Patsy couldn't have kids. For some reason or other kids would be the death of her. Naturally the question came up whether the groom oughtn't to have a simple little operation before the wedding. Nowadays its absolutely safe and simple, in and out in a day. But all of a sudden our crazy lover starts to scratch his head and wonder. Second thoughts, right? See, he'd always been dreaming of reproduction, wanted to have little ones like himself. Bland, vain, commonplace little egoists like himself. So there was no wedding. I tell you, men are such hypocrites! All that sighing under the moon and the fashions of passions, but the first time that you ask them to give just a little bit..."

Wife #2 nodded sympathetically, giggled, sighed, and wanted to hear more and more. Not because she was interested in the friends of her youth either. Susan's stories drew her for some other reason, excited her like a shoot-'em-up movie. The world was filled with sinful, cruel, and dangerously pitiful people, who stole up on every side, and in the middle was brave little Susan, scattering acid remarks right and left. And the listener stood alongside, in the firing zone, but at the same time, in safety, because you were a spared member of the select, you rejoiced that the bullet-words weren't aimed at you and loved her for that.

"You wouldn't recognize our town. There's no way of knowing what goes up faster, the prices or cheating. Sometimes when I just can't take it anymore, I try to fight it. Let me tell you the story about the coupons from the telephone book. I bought a used car recently, and the very next day the tail pipe falls off. I call the store and demand a new one. They laugh. But that's dishonest, I tell them, and they laugh harder. So that's when I figured out how to get even, if you can believe it. The store had put coupons in the phone book, come in with the coupon and get $100 off. I went round to forty of my friends, cut the coupons out of forty books and went to the store. I found a car for four thousand, and when the salesman asked me how I wanted to pay, I said cash. I was wearing dark glasses and had gone to another guy so that they wouldn't recognize me, and while he was filling out the papers he just about melted into puddles of friendliness. But then when I put my coupons down in front of him, you should have seen his face! The way they all ran around and made a fuss! They started shouting how any idiot could see that it was one coupon per car, but then I said I was going to sue them for false advertising. Maybe I still will, even. But they were scared to death."

On Susan's lips "That's dishonest" was the most horrible of accusations. It was not good which battled with evil in this world, not light with dark, wit with stupidity, but only honesty with dishonesty, truth with lie. The newspapers, films, etiquette, traffic laws, people's actions (especially men's), politicians' promises, and weather reports were all lies. If truth survived at all, it was only as some tender shoots, some alpine edelweiss, in a tiny number of the righteous—which included you and me—on account of whom the city might be spared.

Oddly this sad condition of the world afforded Susan enormous pleasure. Every tidbit about some new victory of lies, of the latest movement of the armies of deceit, brought a triumphant smile to her lips. She enjoyed seeing that her contempt had received so full and firm a confirmation and justification. And vice-versa, if some deceit proved upon examination to have been true, then she would scowl and get upset. Not for long, though, because life and people were most generous to her, and soon would toss her some new affirmation that she could be free to despise with a pure heart.

Her friend's visit livened Wife #2 up, her boredom was forgotten. She took Susan to work at the agency and brought her home at night. She lugged the heavy suitcases of lights and tripods. One of the rooms in the house was made into a darkroom, where they sat at night, developing and printing the day's snaps.

One day they came to Anton's office very excited. They started going room to room, paying no attention to the secretaries, talking softly between themselves. From time to time Susan would put her camera to her eye, focus.

"Look at that bookcase," Wife #2 said, "the top shelves are very high. If you make him stretch for the books, you'd get an interesting foreshortening."

"I like the light from that window," Susan said. "It comes in in uneven layers and trembles, like yogurt."

"What's this you're up to?" Anton asked.

"Susan got a new assignment! You should congratulate her. From a magazine this time, the editors liked her idea. This isn't some ad, it's a whole cycle of serious art shots. Except everything has to be done right now, hurry-hurry. She's got to hand the photos in Monday, and today's Friday already. So you have to help us."

Anton decided to ignore that "us" and tried instead to understand the idea of the cycle. "Unadorned Men"—what did that mean? A man at his desk, a man talking on the phone, a man at the bookcase, a man at the computer? All right then, in a normal working environment. Who'd be interested in that? Ah, there's one other little detail? The man would have no clothes on? Just a tie around his bare neck? So the idea is, the emperor is naked?

They laughed and put their hands over each other's mouths. Almost everything was set already. They had caught an agent right at the end of the day, and he had gotten hold of an actor who had agreed to pose. Not for much money either, really. So all that was left was the tiny detail, that they needed a place to do this. A normal business office, nothing fancy. But all the offices were already closed for the weekend, so what could they do? That's when they had thought, why not use his office?

"You're nuts!"

Anton ran over to his office door and hastily shut it.

"In my office? To publish? To put it all in a pornographic magazine? What if one of my clients sees it? Or the press gets wind of it? Then there'd be such a scandal that in two days I'd be ruined."

Susan looked out the window, toying with the camera on its strap and smiling contemptuously. Wife #2 sat in a chair and clutched her hands to her eyes, as if trying to recover from a shameful discovery.

"What are you talking about? What pornography? This cycle is being done for a woman's art magazine. I hope you've heard of the Venus de Milo and the painting *Déjeuner sur l'herbe* and Michelangelo? Or are the words "nature revealed" always going to be connected in your mind with the cover of *Playboy*?"

"Forget it, Caitlin," Susan said sharply. "I told you it would be useless. He's typical."

"Anthony, I'm astonished at you. Everything else aside, how can you think that anybody would be able to recognize your office from the pictures? This model of conformity and tastelessness that is indistinguishable from millions of offices just exactly like it, how could anybody's brain ever connect the pictures precisely with the insurance office of Sebich Incorporated, room number 2735 on the 27th floor of one of Chicago's fifty major skyscrapers? So maybe then you'll be happy to know that the magazine that ordered the "Unadorned Men" cycle of pictures from Susan is printed in Canada, and has almost no circulation in the states?"

Anton held out for about fifteen minutes more, then gave up. In the end, life cannot consist entirely of the predictable, of routines, keeping contracts. Every now and again you also have to have wild extravagances and some shaking up and adventures and unpredictability. Who might have expected that a taste for risky enterprises might suddenly have awakened in Wife #2? He shouldn't get angry at the tiny visiting photo-adventurist; he ought to thank her.

The next day he took Susan to the office himself, helped her set up and arrange the lights, showed her where the sockets and light switches were. When he got back home he ceded to the kids' requests and sat down to help them do a puzzle. An old-fashioned castle was repulsing an attack. They already had done the towers with waving flags, and could make out the commandant's hat and the crenellations of the walls. Son #2.1 was digging through the heaps of cardboard curlicues, looking for the haunches and heads of horses. Daughter #2.2 was concentrating on blue pieces, bits of sky, storm surf, the castle's windows.

At some point during this Wife #2 came upstairs, her face worried.

"Susan called, almost in tears. The actor still hasn't shown up, and nobody is answering at his phone."

"Probably stuck in traffic somewhere. The traffic is impossible on Saturdays."

"They just have to take Susan's cycle, they have to. Right now in her life that's what she really needs, a little success."

"Everything will be all right. What are you doing?"

"With this?" She looked down at the open razor blade in her hand. "I was finally getting down to working on the rosebeds. The children have been running around the garden a lot lately, so that they get right up close to the bushes. Naturally I can't cut off all the thorns, but I could at least get the big ones."

Another hour went by. The battle for the castle was filling in. The assault ladders groaned beneath the weight of the attackers, and from a jolly little grove on the right poked new cannons, already wreathed in smoke.

Wife #2 appeared again, and beckoned Anton with a finger. He had not seen her so upset and worried in a long time.

"Susan's in tears," she said once they were out in the corridor. "The bastard never did show up. She says that if she were home, in New Jersey, she could find somebody in fifteen minutes, one of her acquaintances, but here in Chicago she doesn't know anybody. I don't recall Susan Darcey ever crying."

"Yes, it's bad luck for her."

"She asked me whether I'd mind if she asked you to pose."

"ME?"

"Why not?"

"But I've never studied acting. I've never even been in amateur productions."

"The acting abilities of that bastard were not the part of him we were most interested in. And you've got everything else that he had. I'd bet yours isn't worse than his, either."

"Come on, you know that flattery doesn't work with me."

"In the first place, flattery does work with you. And in the second place, she says that she can make you up so that nobody would ever be able to recognize you. And anyway she says that the face of the person in the photographs is not the most important thing here."

"So what did you say? I'd be kind of interested in hearing that."

"I said that of course I wouldn't mind. The whole question is whether or not you'll agree. That you had a terribly puritanical upbringing and that sometimes your hypocrisy will show up in the most unexpected place, like a birthmark."

"You think you'd be able to pose in your birthday suit in front of some strange man?"

"No, but that's because I'm a hypocrite too. Worse than you, even."

"I'd have to agree with that, if you figure how many months went into learning the secret of the teapot..."

"Listen, you're making some huge sacrifice out of this. If you can't do it, just say so. I just really really want to help Susan. I've always wanted to help her, but she's such a proud little thing."

"You going to come with me?"

"Why?"

"I don't know why. It would make things easier."

"Susan might think that I've come to keep an eye on you two. She would absolutely scorch me with contempt."

"I've gotten fat this year."

"This isn't a beauty contest. And anyway, somebody has to stay with the children."

"Well, maybe it'll be fun. It might open up a new career for me."

"I'd be incredibly grateful."

"But you'll remember that I asked you to come along?"

"I'm putting the roast in the oven, and everything will be ready by the time you get back."

"Help the kids finish the puzzle. Bring up the final reserves and the battle's done."

"Be nice to her, okay? No jokes, especially about her profession."

He waved goodbye and went downstairs, the car keys in his pocket. In the dining room he sneaked a slug of whiskey, then went out the side door and crossed over to the car, past the fresh-clipped rosebushes. He tried to keep his face set in the look of an orderly being sent off to fulfill some general's idiotic orders. He could feel how hard it was for him to breath.

On that day throughout the city of Montreal the usual stream of fires, crashes, demonstrations for and against, murders, robberies, and political scandals had apparently gone dry, leaving a heavy silence. No sooner had the Babylonia pulled up to the docks of Montreal than a flock of starving correspondents and cameraman descended upon them.

"How's the voyage going, Mr. Sebich?"

"Did you get your Russian visas yet?"

"You got any plans to test Pirgoroy's products on the pets there?"

"Aren't you afraid that while you're on the boat your competitors will fly to Moscow and get control of the market before you?"

The tv cameras whirred. Microphones slithered in from all sides. The tiny crew of the Babylonia—just three of them, in white jackets and hats—stood behind the captain, smiling stony smiles. There was a pyramid of pet food tins on a table in front of Anton.

"We think that the Russians will definitely be interested in Pirogoroy's new products. No, production began a year ago, before we thought about a trip to the Upside-down Land. We just asked ourselves the question, how would a dog owner feel if he had suddenly become a committed vegetarian, whether for moral or dietetic reasons? It would be a terrible struggle in his heart, wouldn't it? He would have to feed his four-legged friend the meat products which he himself believed could only bring harm. Vegetarian dog food is just the thing for people in that situation..."

While this was going on a crowd of gawkers gathered on the pier. An elderly couple, interested in everything else in the world save each other, just as it is impossible to be interested in one's own shoulder, ear, or the back of one's head, pushed far forward. Bent beneath the weight of his boombox some both-end candle-burner pushed in, fringed hair, fringed cut-offs, face thoughtful, neglected, pimply. Two children were hugging their mother's knee and feeding each other bright-colored ice creams. Their raspberry green tongues licked circles around the hard cold balls, then ducked back into their mouths, loaded with sweet booty.

"...sparing no expense, the Pirgoroy firm makes a tasty and nutritious mixture of twenty different grasses for vegetarian dogs. No, we don't go out into the fields with a scythe, like some Leo Tolstoy, and we don't rake our own hay. Science has come to our aid here too! Our scientists caught wild rabbits and opened their stomachs, so that the contents could determine what kinds of grass animals like best. That's what we used to make the mixture from. Naturally we add vitamins and calcium and iron and aspirin and antibiotics..."

The old couple were tired of watching the dock groaning beneath the correspondents. They bent over the children and pretended that they wanted to take away their ice creams. Howling, the children hid behind their mother's skirt. The mother took off the visor which had hidden her face in a plastic green shadow. She smiled. She looked nothing like Wife #3. He had been mistaken.

Susan didn't come out to meet him at the door of the office. She was sitting at his desk, like a boss waiting for an underling to come take orders. Her face was as displeased as if he were the careless, tardy, no-show actor, who had broken all promises and was a dishonest, terrible person, and not at all as if he were her savior, who had graciously agreed to help her, at the difficult cost of overcoming his hypocritical prejudices.

"There's not a single mirror here. Just in the toilet. But that one's too high. I'll have to stand on a chair."

When she stood on the chair, their heads were on the same level. Her touch was rapid, like the flutter of fishes' lips under water. She glued false eyebrows over his own, giving them a pitiless mephistophelian cast. She brushed his hair back and sprinkled it with a reddish spray. She stuck a boxer's mouthpiece into his mouth and ordered him to put it between his teeth and gums. A ticklish mustache appeared under his nose. He was unrecognizable, crafty, evil, and impenetrable.

"You can get undressed right here. I'll get the cameras ready. Remember what I asked though, the necktie on your bare neck. Please."

Undressed, he stopped in front of the mirror, thought that in essence she was probably right. What other than contempt did these drooping shoulders deserve, this curly triangle on his chest, this white-fleshed belly hung from his ribs like a half-empty oat bag from the muzzle of a horse? Under the makeup his face was that of a stranger, but she had been able to see something true about him and to sketch it in this caricatured mask. Of course, this was him, the lover of pleasure, who moved through life in little jumps, from one pleasure to another, hip-hop, from tuft to tuft—whatever is the highest hummock, that's the one I'll jump to— with no goal and no meaning. A sucker for flattery, and knowing how to flatter as well. A coward, goggling every minute at the shadow of the Miserymaker over his shoulder. An idler who has feared real work all his life and so has fastened onto this simple craft, which allows him to grow fat on the miseries and fears of others. A skinflint, who just yesterday had refused to buy a two hundred dollar racket for Golda (Wife #1 had telephoned to remind him that the girl had finished the first grade with all As), buying off his conscience with a pocket tape recorder. A hypocrite, who asked his father about his health on the telephone but immediately forgot the whole list of diseases—which were different every week—that the lonely old man suffered from. A spineless uxorious lickspittle, who had let himself be dragged into this stupid game of dress-up.

In the confined space of the toilet the air grew thick with contempt, became hot. In his memory Anton went through all the television comedians that he could remember, hoping to steal some wisecrack from one of them that would do for his exit, and cover him like a fig leaf. He could remember nothing. And anyway, he felt sure that the little snapster would never abandon her medicinal parched business-like manner for anything, no matter what jokes he stole. He made a big sigh and went out silent and obedient like a patient, studying the blue and white stripes of the despicable tie on his equally despicable naked stomach.

"It would be best if you paid no attention to me whatever," Susan said. "Just pretend that it's Monday morning and you've come to work and started doing something. Get out the file you'd look at and start looking at the papers in it."

Her tone had become almost friendly, almost jolly, but Anton already knew her well enough to understand what had brought on this improvement of mood. In his person the world had given her yet another confirmation of its insignificance, which had livened her up.

Obediently he went to the wall of steel file cabinets, opened one, got out Mrs. Turkinson's file. The company that had sold her home insurance wanted to raise her payments just a bit and were looking for reasons they might give for doing so. He had driven by Mrs. Turkinson's home yesterday and had noticed that the sidewalk in front of it was buckled and crumbling. Monday he had been going to write the company a letter and point that out, because anybody passing by who happened to stumble on the up-turned corner of a slab and then break a leg would have the right to sue Mrs. Turkinson for healthy money, which the insurance company would have to pay. So the company would have to put a choice to Mrs. Turkinson, either she should fix the sidewalk (which would go a thousand or better), or else jack up her monthly payments to cover the greater risk. The advice was sly and precisely calculated (because who can lay out a thousand all at once?), sharp as a fishhook, and Anton loathed himself for giving it, with all his heart.

With half an ear he listened to the clicking and whirring of the electronic camera. The burning cones of light slithered about his naked skin. Susan circled him, shoes off, now climbing on a chair, a table, cramming her back into a corner, throwing herself on the floor.

Suddenly everything grew quiet, and the lights went out.

He looked up from Mrs. Turkinson's file.

The contempt on Susan's face, passed as it was through the lens of the camera, seemed to have been gathered to a point, bouncing off an invisible mirror in the distance and breaking into two burning points, which were her eyes.

"Aren't you ashamed of yourself?"

"What happened?" Anton asked.

"I might have expected something of the sort from a hired actor, but from a civilized man, the husband of my best girlfriend..."

Anton looked himself up, then down, and discovered the cause of Susan's anger.

Odd-man-out, proud and alone, was fiercely refusing to submit to the flood of contemptuous self-condemnation, to efface himself and disappear.

He stood like the last Spartan at Thermopylae, like Malakhov Hill, like the last anti-aircraft gun of a sinking aircraft carrier, still ready to fire. He was flinging contemptuous challenges to all his enemies, defending his besmirched worth, like a flagstaff ready and begging for a flag.

"Well *do* something!" Susan shouted.

"What can I do?"

"How should I know? Take a cold shower!"

"There's no shower in the office."

"Just don't tell me that it's got nothing to do with you, all right? You had to have been thinking about something along those lines, something dirty. About me, probably."

"I was only thinking about Mrs. Turkinson."

"Who's that?"

"She's eighty-two."

"Pervert! My God, what's Caitlin going to think? She'll think that I was working you up."

"How's she going to find out?"

"I'll tell her, of course. I'm going to phone her right now."

"Good idea. If a wild animal gets out of the cage, who's the first person to call? The zookeeper, right?"

"Even if I don't say anything to her, she'll be able to tell from how I act that something's wrong."

"We'll tell her that your camera broke and we had to end the session."

"Sure! Isn't that just like a man? To grab hold of the first lie that floats by? You can't really think that just to cover for you I'm going to debase myself by lying?"

"I was only trying to help. For which you repay me by ruining things with my wife. That's your honesty that you're so proud of?"

"Caitlin will understand. But this is so unprofessional!"

"Maybe we could just wait a bit? Sooner or later he's got to settle down."

"Do you know that for a fact? This has happened to you before?"

"Lots of times. The worst time was when he got excited during an econ exam. One of the girls in the room started to fix her bra straps, and that was that. It doesn't take much with him."

"But I didn't do anything like that, did I?"

"I don't know. You did take your slippers off."

"Okay, so now you're trying to make me the guilty one."

"Nobody's guilty. Things happen in life, and then they pass. You have to give everything time. Patience, a little."

"It doesn't matter, because I can't take it anymore. Three hours of pointless waiting this morning, and now this... My nerves are ringing like a bell. I can't work. Couldn't you take him away somewhere, tell him that the photo session is over? Tell him that he flunked the interview, and won't be in the picture?"

The excited soldier boy wasn't volunteering to go back into his foxhole, and so had to be led by force. Dressed now, Anton was helping Susan gather and pack the lamps, but tried to keep his back to her the whole time. It was only when they got back to the house that he could stand upright again and look Wife #2 straight into her inquiring eyes.

Susan quickly took her friend by the hand and went back into the kitchen. The tribunal met for about fifteen minutes. Anton took up a newspaper but couldn't make out why the shooting in Beirut had begun this time. He wanted to be forgiven. He wanted everything to be as it had been yesterday.

The women came out into the dining room, each carrying a pot. They smiled mysteriously through the steam. They were the most tender, the most faithful of girlfriends in the world, for which the entire contemptible world—including even men, including even the worst of men—received a temporary and conditional right to exist.

The correspondents, who were getting ready to leave the Babylonia, had one more pleasant surprise coming. A taxi pulled up and out came a pair of handmade iguana-skin shoes, then a handmade briefcase painted by the master artisans of Palekh, then a jogging suit custom-made by a Japanese designer, followed by the rest of Admiral Kozulin. The cameras again began whirring and the microphones raised their snaky heads.

"Yes, yes, I just got in and I'm going right back...but something's come up, that I've got to tell the captain and crew about...oh, quite the opposite, everything is very positive...The Russians are showing more and more interest in our trip...They now realize that our intentions are quite friendly, and that there's no other motive. Well, of course they have a little contempt for our western drive for advertising, but you and

I know that advertising is our bread and butter, right? Yours and mine, both, right?"

Seeing the correspondents off, Kozulin said that he wanted to talk with each of the crew members alone. He went from cabin to cabin, and his briefcase got lighter and lighter. When he got to Anton he pulled out two parcels—the last, apparently.

"I don't want you to open these packages ahead of time. This is for when—and if—you find Golda, and this is for when you meet my brother. You'll find detailed instructions inside. Make sure you hide these well, because the Russian customs people are very thorough. How's the voyage going? How's the mood?"

"Everything's fine."

"The crew obeys its orders?"

"Ronald laid out the duties and keeps order."

"We've been able to neutralize that lawyer Simpson for the time being, but he's going to try to grab you in Europe. It's going to be harder for us to protect you there."

"My fourth wife is the only one that I didn't have children with, but thanks to Simpson she was able to get the biggest settlement of all."

"I get the impression that he doesn't work that hard just on account of his clients. There's something more serious in it. I've got someone finding out what it is he's got against you. We'll know eventually. Doesn't one of your exes live here in Montreal? The fifth, I think?"

"Third."

"You going to visit her?"

"I don't know yet."

"Old flames sometimes flare up stronger than you'd think."

"I don't want to talk about it."

"I've heard that she hasn't let you see your kids."

"Instead of that, let me tell you about an idea I've had: tinned cat food for travellers."

"They say that she's got her own photo studio here in Montreal, and that it's doing pretty well. True, they also say its got something to do with pornography..."

"They'd really be just ordinary tins, but the traveller wouldn't take them with him, but instead would leave them in a special refrigerator..."

"She's even a dual citizen, US and Canada..."

"There are millions of single cat owners who would like to go away somewhere, on business or vacation, but they can't leave their little kitties..."

"Whoever marries her could become a Canadian and stay here..."

"So we would offer them a refrigerator with a simple timing mechanism..."

"And Canadian lawyers are awfully good at protecting their citizens from other lawyers..."

"Once a day this refrigerator would open automatically and spit out a can. Or twice a day, depending on how hungry the cat is..."

"So if you've got some idea about taking advantage of this and staying here, then I'd have to tell you that it would be a hard blow against all my plans..."

"The traveller would put the necessary number of cans in the refrigerator...three, five, seven...and then could go away with a song in his heart..."

"And I'd have to take measures."

"And when he came back he'd find a row of empty cans and a happy kitty, licking her chops."

"Measures I sincerely would not like to take against the father of my grandchildren."

"What in the devil are you talking about!? Staying?" Anton shouted. "I'm not even sure that she'll want to talk with me."

"Well, that's good," Kozulin said, going to the door of the cabin. "And as for that refrigerator for travellers, it's an interesting idea. If anything comes of it, I promise you a share of the profits."

The days remaining until Susan's departure passed in heavy, unbearable twitting.

At first she wanted to leave immediately, the next day, but Wife #2 talked her out of it, that it would be stupid, that nothing had happened, absolutely nothing. That their relations weren't spoiled at all, that men really can't control themselves, that they are really the weaker sex, if they don't even have control over all the moveable parts of their bodies. The job with the magazine might come to nothing, but she should at least finish the job for the firm that had flown her out there.

During this time Wife #2 somehow became the head of the house. Susan and Anton were quiet, as if in disgrace, fallen sinners. Anton worked late a lot at the office, and when home locked himself up in his home office. He had more work than he could handle. Insurance against Real Trouble was getting increasingly popular, and customers were stampeding in. The real truth though was something else, that often he was unable to play with the kids or be with the women as they watched television, because the mutiny was continuing.

The odd-man-out was showing every sign of turning wild. Like a beaten dog who remembers his attacker for many long years and who leaps up, hackles stiff, at his tormentor's merest appearance, he would stand and almost howl at just the sound of Susan's footsteps outside the door, at the waft of her perfume, from the sight of the camera bouncing on its strap against her stomach, the sound of the water falling on her in the shower in the morning. There was no arguing with him either. "Stop it, you idiot, it hurts!" Anton was ready to shout. He knew though that the answer he would get was "It's me being hurt, it's me!" Odd-man-out was infused with a vindictiveness, some cruel decisiveness. It seemed as though he was not content with having destroyed the creation of the photo-cycle "Unadorned man," but wanted to seize his offender by the throat, by the heart, by the very crux of things, and smash through the wall of contempt, to prove...

It was just a day or two before her departure that Anton understood what was happening. The three (or four?) of them were sitting by the fireplace, drinking cognac, and in the half-light, in a soft chair, legs crossed, it was possible for a moment to hold back the wild rebel and even to smile when talking to Wife #2's best friend, who had flung a leg over the arm of the couch. He could even study the pattern of her stocking, lit by the light of the burning logs, falling through the pattern of her fingers. Then she noticed his glance, put her legs down, and hid them beneath her skirt.

And then he got it.

It was just that the love-berry had fooled him this time, that was all. When he hadn't felt it in its usual place, in his throat, he had imagined that the berry was drowsing innocently beneath the chilly snow of domestic routine. In fact though the berry had long ago run off from its usual pit or rut—why not? People say that even the kidneys can set off on some sort of wandering in us—to settle carelessly in the throat of odd-man-out, where it swelled as it willed, driving the poor old thing half nuts, driving it to the point of frenzy.

At about two in the morning he was suddenly awakened by the insomniacal rebel. He got up quietly and went out into the corridor. He went past the staircase to the first floor, past the kids' room, to the bathroom. Then he went a few steps farther and stopped in front of the guest room. He stroked the brass knob of the door handle. His touch seemed to set off sparks between the brass and his palm, which flowed and bubbled somewhere into handle and set off some invisible motor, winding in invisible, soundless cables, pulleys, reducing wheels until the doorknob, without so much as an "Open, sesame!" clicked and began to turn of its own accord.

The door opened.

Releasing a flood of darkness thick with contempt. The door opened wider. He closed his eyes, then opened them, wider. In the doorway, her nightshirt tied with a belt, her hair tangled in the lace of the collar, her face full of confusion, stood Susan. The incomprehension was directed not at him, but at her own hand. What did you do, my hand, who gave you the permission, the leave to so suddenly open the door in the middle of the night?

He stepped into the bedroom. She stepped back. He took another step. She raised her hand to him, then took his pajamas and pulled him to her, but the mutineer did his best to shove her away. Then she got up on a chair, pulled him to her again, and stood a little akimbo, so that the mutineer would have a place to go. Now he didn't interfere with a real embrace. Anton could feel the entire despised world flying away beneath their feet. Because of some inexplicable whim Susan Darcey had decided to single him out, to draw him up to her level, to pardon him or commute his sentence and to make him—for a second? a minute? an hour?—the choice of her heart.

Up there on high it was as terrifying as at the porthole of an airliner in flight. The earth below was frightening, with the sharp roofs over its sleeping, unforgiven, and unexalted mundane citizens. He had to hold on quite tightly, but to what? To this tiny, tender, and vulnerable little body which he suddenly found in his arms? This body itself needed defending and support, the only hard things in it the two little shoulder blades beneath the skittering nylon, and the two hummocks that crushed against his chest.

They stood, not moving. They stood so long that even an antediluvian squeeze box camera of a hundred years ago could have photographed them embracing without even a magnesium flash, using just the light from the open door.

Then even that light went out.

Anton looked around and saw the daguerreotype silhouette of Wife #2 against the doorway. Seized by a momentary panic, he opened his arms and would have plunged back down into the thick of the sharp-pointed earthly roofs, had it not been for Susan. She held tight to his neck and stared at the sleepy, distraught face of her friend.

Wife #2 began to rub the wall with her hand, fumbling for the light switch. Light poured into the room like some pitiless fixative, transforming the transitory weave of light rays, movements, emotions and shadows into the frozen fact of a photo-document. Wife #2 made a few steps forward. Susan frowned, but her arms didn't open. Anton stood, flew, fell, floated, dissolved. Wife #2 came right up to them, grabbed Susan by the waist, and laid her cheek on Susan's shoulder. Then she took Anton's hand and put it in hers. The immobile scene lost the last molecules of its light-reactive layer, and the black-and-white of awkwardness grew stronger. The poor rebel, with no idea of how to behave in this situation, which was threatening to transform him from odd-man-out into the fourth corner of a triangle, was crestfallen, deflated, withdrew to be forgotten. The frozen moment was as unlike reality as Mephistopheles in the opera, when he crawls out of his trapdoor.

Anton decided not to call, but to just show up, without a warning. Susan hadn't given anyone, not even her mother, the address of her house; all they had was the address of her studio, which was in the northern part of the city. Outside the taxi window, monuments floated by—to Nelson, Queen Victoria, Edward VII—but everywhere the English signs were jostled and shoved by French, and the staircases stretched up to the doors on the second floor just as they did in Marseilles, and the main cathedral did its best to mirror Notre Dame in Paris, with all its towers and flying buttresses. The shards of the French Empire glistened everywhere through the shards of the British Empire, often seeming better preserved and more solid. The taxi driver answered all of Anton's questions with guttural French grunts.

A cafe, an electronics store, a small print shop, a wine store, a huge supermarket, a car repair shop...all of this stretched around what once had been a market square, now choked with ranks of cars. The photo studio had a few copies of a pink Renoir and in the corner, a small sign that said "Intimate portraits. Portraits intimes." The young narrow-faced assistant who smiled at Anton from behind her desk tossed him an inquiring "Oui?"

"I would like..."

An invisible English Channel stretched across the assistant's smile and she went to English.

"You have an appointment now?"

"I was passing through, I'm just here today, but friends in Cleveland gave the place a very strong recommendation..."

"You want just one portrait, or a whole selection? Postcards? A calendar maybe? I know that men don't often order calendars... It's not done for some reason, but they like it afterwards."

"Maybe you've got some samples? And how about the prices?"

She pointed to a little table by the window. He took the calendar that was on the top. An inscription in a curly-cue half circle glittered in gilt, "A mon cher Marcel de Jeannette". On the first page the somewhat bony Jeannette was photographed bare in a fox jacket, one shoulder slipped off for the January frost to kiss. For February she was getting ready to go skiing, half-dressed—in sweater, hat and gloves—and was now back to the lens, on tiptoe, looking in a closet for the rest of her clothes. March's weather remained off-camera because Jeannette was taking a bath and revealing certain intimate glittering scraps of herself to Marcel's gaze through the mounds of bubbles. April was warmer, warm enough that Jeannette could go out on the balcony in a flowing transparent nightgown. When he got to May somebody's hand came over Anton's shoulder and slammed the calendar shut.

"Hi, Susan," he said, not turning his head.

"What do you want? I forbade you ever to get in front of my face again. That was the only condition I ever set."

"I'm passing through, just here today..."

"I don't have time for you. Not today, not tomorrow, not the day after. And especially not now."

"A half hour?"

"NO!"

"I'm really sorry, Miss Darcey, for God's sake I am. I thought that the gentleman just wanted to..."

"It's nothing, Nicole, nothing. You couldn't have known. The gentleman is leaving right now."

"I'm not going anywhere. I'm going to sit and wait. And if you can't find a half-hour for me, I'll sit here all day, and follow you home after work. Then I'll finally find out where you live and where you're hiding my children. Then I'll see them and tell them about how their mother..."

"That's blackmail. I'm phoning the police. Nicole is my witness, you tried to blackmail me."

"Go ahead and phone. And I'll phone the newspapers, and my kids will learn the truth about their parents at least..."

She studied him with fastidious pity. The way people look at a raccoon run over on the highway. Her temples were a little peppered with gray. Then her wicked squint disappeared and it even seemed for

145

a moment as if she might smile. He understood that he had confirmed her worst expectations and so had given her a moment's pleasure.

"All right, but just a half hour. Nicole, ask Madam Contrassier to dress and wait. Tell her that I couldn't find a proper shawl in the closet and so I had to go home to get it..."

They cut across the market square and went into the cafe. Wife #3 nodded at acquaintances, waved at the owner. The waitress tidied a table in the corner for them. A cupola could be seen in the distance, on the slope of a hill. Could this be the famous Cathedral of St. Joseph, with the staircase of a hundred steps? That repentant sinners mounted on their knees? Or maybe it wasn't sinners, but sick people who wanted cures?

"Mother wrote that you looked like a dug-up corpse. And what do we discover? That once again the old lady is lying, for absolutely no good reason."

"It's the sea life. Of course I don't have to scale the masts or man the windlasses, but the sun and the wind...you should have seen me a month or so ago."

"Where's the trip to? I mean I know where you're going, I read about it. But what's the point?"

"Advertising, in part, market research in part. It's a long story. Tell me about yourself instead. I can see that things aren't so sweet for you either, that you've got to do whatever you can to make a living."

"Meaning?"

"You were always against pornography."

"You never did understand what that word means."

"How should I understand it?"

"Pornography is dehumanization. It's when a naked body is presented to the eyes of a stranger, or many strangers. Our calendars are only made in single copies, from one lover to another—generally wives giving their husbands presents. You see the difference?"

"Ah, in that case...I didn't think of that, I'm sorry..."

"Anyway, as I understand it, you can finally take it easy. When I heard that my mother had put you in that cabin, I was almost sorry for you. That cabin was always a punishment for us in the family, for dad and for me. But then I understand that you were just an enlargement for her menagerie. I hope she's feeding you well, and changes your kitty litter every day?"

"Stop it. You always underestimate your mother, and that upsets her. She misses the grandchildren a lot."

"If she misses them, any day she wants she can come up and visit them. I'd save money on baby-sitters."

"How are the kids? Where are they now? Do they know anything about your work? How are they anyway?"

"Healthy. Growing. The little ones copying the nasty things the older ones did when they get to the same age. They had their birthday not long ago and I knew even before they did it that they would feel compelled to put pepper in the punch that was for the guests. And they did. Later I even understood that they didn't even want to, but couldn't not do it."

"What do you say when they ask about their father?"

"That he left us and doesn't want to see us."

"But that's not true!"

"How come? You wanted to get them for the holidays, like toys. Is that what you mean? But all those 'I-want-tos' of yours, the big ones and the little one, fight from morning 'til night. Then one of them wins, and you do something that makes it clear which of the 'I-want-tos' is strongest. The fact that all those other 'I-want-tos' continue to live on, that they aren't killed off in battle but continue to chirp away, that doesn't mean much. You can't explain that to little kids, it's too complicated. When they grow up, they'll understand it themselves, in all the details."

"Let me see them. Just for a little."

"No way."

"But how come?"

"Because you are a sinful, dangerous, perfidious, and incorrigible man."

"Me?"

"You are an incurable tempter. You are capable of making them fall in love with you after ten minutes and then you'll break their hearts forever by leaving them. I can't permit that."

"You remember our first trip to the sea? In Virginia, in September? How that one time we left the restaurant and went out onto the pier, and there was that Mexican family with the fat mother, how she was ordering everyone about as they looked for crabs, with lanterns, and how the crabs, while the traps were being raised from the water to the gunwales, the crabs waved their claws like crazy and tried to turn onto their bellies again, as if all they had to do was flip onto their fronts and life would be normal again, and they could go back to scaring things that were bigger than they were and eating the things that were smaller, and how we went out to the very end of the pier and hugged and do you remember what you told me then?"

"It's always words with you, isn't it? Always words..."

"You said, never, never, don't for anything ever believe me if I say there was ever anything more important or better than you in my life."

"That's all?"

"That's how I remember it."

"Oh, of course. Remember what's convenient and forget what isn't. Did I or did I not add right after that how sorry I was I had said it? Because even then I knew none of that was going to be for very long. You're an eternal nomad, greedy, nearsighted, and insatiable. Nomads don't build houses. One morning I was going to wake up and see nothing but the stone ring and matted grass from your tent, the smoldering coals and the bits of pottery. I could sense that with every fiber of my being, by instinct. Sometimes I think that even my anomaly, this two sets of twins, wasn't by accident. As if my body knew better than I did that you weren't for long, and hurried to get as much as it could."

"You still think that it was all my fault?"

"Fault? Is it the nomad's fault that nature drives him from pasture to pasture? Even if someone talks him into leaving his tents or his tepee or his cart and teaches him how to build a house, the nomad remains true to himself. Yes, he says to himself, I like that idea, building a house together, but your boards are always going to be your boards, and my bricks and boards, those are mine. And you can't break him of it. He's convinced of his right of possession, which is what he calls freedom. So that when something catches his eye he picks up his bricks and boards and he leaves, and he could care less about the fact that what he leaves behind isn't half a house, it's the ruins of a house."

"Catches his eye? What was it then that caught his eye?"

"I don't know, and what does it matter anyway? Has there ever been a time in your life when something swam past your nose and you didn't grab it with your pincers?"

"No, you couldn't say that I learned your lessons badly. You hammered your housebuilding lessons into me pretty hard, and I was starting to get straight As. There was just one snag, what should I use to hold the bricks and boards together? In theory what holds them together is emotion. Preferably strong emotion. Preferably shared emotion. Love? No, you knew that you didn't have enough of that to patch up a porch, so you wanted to use what you had more than enough of. You wanted me to share your strongest and most beloved emotion.

Your contempt. Including your contempt for me. I mean you wanted me to have contempt for the entire world, including for myself. That was the stern stuff you wanted to put foundation, walls, and roof together with..."

"Now that's a lie..."

"And I tried to do it. May the God of potties and diapers be my witness, I tried. And I almost succeeded. I almost despised our town, our neighbors, my ex-wives, your dying father and his happiness at the funeral announcements of people who had gotten to be dead before him, and your widowed mother and her menagerie, and of course myself too! But I guess that the fatigue of it all built up. I just couldn't do it! And then I met a woman I could rest with. Who was almost in awe of me. And life, and herself. And I felt an immediate relief. Even soldiers are given occasional home leave, even prisoners in the strictest of prisons are given a little time in the exercise yard. Not me though. Wasn't it you who threw the kids in the car and left, without even saying where you were going? Who cut the knot while it was still fleshy, not even giving the condemned man a final word? Who left a note full of swear words on the refrigerator door, instead of a farewell note? And after all that you can tell me that it was me who took my bricks and boards, that it was me who left and destroyed the home?"

"Trust. You killed the trust. Why won't you understand once and for all that in everything that you've said..."

"I only understand one thing, that instead of a house what you built was a tower of contempt and that you want to spend the rest of your life locked up behind its walls. The windows are shuttered, the doors are boarded up, the drawbridge is up, and there's no way some magical knight in shining armor is going to get at you in there. Because somebody ripped all the pages about pain out of your textbooks. About pain's power to knit things together. There's no stronger mortar that sympathy. But that's not for you. A complaint, a groan, a begging for mercy, that's all for your contempt. It's taboo, and you despise whoever uses them, whoever builds a house using such mortar. Damn it, if just once you had shown that something that I said or did hurt you! But no! Never. All you ever did was cause pain and take pleasure in other people's pain and never admit you felt any!"

He said all this without looking at her, face to the window, looking at the wooded slope around the cathedral, trying to make out the miracle-working stairs up to it through the foliage, and so he didn't understand immediately the source of the choking mewling sound. The sound grew, became higher, thinner, more penetrating. He turned toward her and saw her furrowed brow, her squinched-up eyes, her palms dug into her cheeks, and her mouth, deformed by sobs and crying.

It had grown still in the cafe. The owner hastened over, screened her from the room with his body, bent to say softly, "Has something happened? Are you not well? Do you want to go into my office?"

"It's nothing, Albert, it's passing already. I'm incredibly embarrassed, excuse me...we'd better go outside for some air..."

Watching the distant, foggy cupola, he crossed the market square with her beneath a thieving misty rain. He wanted to go down on his knees and crawl up the wet stone stairs to the cathedral... for forgiveness? For condemnation? For healing? They got into her car and spoke without thinking, choosing ready phrases at random from the charges and counter-charges that had built up between them, boiling soundlessly away all these years. Every reproach, accusation, sarcasm flew with such deadly power that it was hard to imagine a wall which might withstand such a blow, repel it. Immediately though the smoky enemy murk would emit an answering salvo that would strike painfully below the heart, so that they had to dig ever deeper, into the most airless of storage vaults, for new rounds of verbal shot that they could fire and fire and fire, not aiming, in the vain hope that the enemy would die away or surrender or begin to sob.

Without quitting the battle or falling still Anton suddenly remembered with great clarity the night of their first innocent adultery, that sleepy embrace in which they had been discovered by Wife #2. And how he had had gone obediently after his wife and fallen into a deep and defensive sleep, and how when he woke up he saw her over him with sheaves of paper in hand. She had not been able to sleep the rest of the night and had spent it writing a letter. She wanted him to read it. After he read the letter, everything would fall into place.

He started to read.

> "Dear Susan, What happened last night opened my eyes for me. I am not at all angry, because neither you nor Anthony is guilty of a thing. You both acted involuntarily. He was my unwilling...involuntary emissary, a part of me, my alter ego. I infected him with my feelings for you. That was me who embraced you, with his arms. My feelings proved so strong that they were able to overcome even the eternal and quite

strong anger that your sarcasm and pride always provoke in him. Recently he said that the amount of arrogance which we are allotted is probably figured for some sort of average person, since it simply doesn't fit into small women and so is constantly slopping out. He has also complained that there is some strong smell about you, that makes him think of locker rooms. And still my feeling proved stronger than that, stronger than all the negative fields, strong enough to get him out of bed and send him to you, the way the moon leads the lunatic to the edge of his roof.

Remember our senior year? How much I wanted you to come to my birthday, but you said that you had already promised that mousy little Patsy Robinson and I even wanted to change the date..."

That was followed by stories from school that now were seen in a new light which required long and detailed re-examination. Wife #2 sat cross-legged on her half of the bed, watching her husband's face, fishing for hints of his feelings but listening only to her own.

"I'd like you to stay in our house another month, two months, six months. We have to understand what it is that's happening to us, to test ourselves. You were always so bold, above all sorts of prejudices and conventions. You'll see that I'm not so chicken myself. If we have the guts to let our feelings have their way..."

The letter, in a birthday-card envelope, was left next to Susan's plate the next morning. Cinnamon pancakes sizzled on the griddle, moon craters bubbling here and there on their surface. Wife #2 watched the staircase impatiently. Then she went upstairs. A minute later she was down, her face ravaged by insult.

"She's gone! How do you like that? Her things, her suitcases, all gone, and no letter. She left. I don't know what to say. What could she have been thinking of? Why did she do that? And what about my letter? No, we've got to get her back. The airport...Anthony, you've got to get her back...we have to go the airport right now... But what if she's already left? God, how cruel she is! Go get her in New Jersey, you hear me?

Where's the flight schedule? And be sure and give her my letter. Then she'll see everything and understand...I'll wrap breakfast up for you... You can't waste a minute..."

He tried to talk sense, tried to prove that all this was for the best. That their life would go back to its normal rut and that they would forget about the extravagant detonators of all embellishment. That even their prenuptial contract had no clause about one partner being the intermediary for the other to explain tangled emotions to a third party. Wife #2 wouldn't back down though. She demanded angrily that he set off in pursuit, a hunter making his setter keep after the snipe. Yet in spite of all the evidence she insisted "I'm lost and done for, done for..."

So he obeyed. He went to the airport with the letter, where he was told that Miss Darcey had already left. He bought a ticket for the next flight. He flew to Jersey, went to the little town of Westfield. And handed her the letter. And they laughed, both of them. They had no choice but to laugh. And he never ever went back to Chicago.

It was quiet in the car. Exhausted by battle, all powder shot and all hatred spent, the enemies sat spent inside a well-lit cage of rushing wind. Then without a word they turned to one another and silently embraced.

Oh, Susan, oh, Wife #3! Why did it have to be that we wanted the impossible of each other? Why did no one warn us that we couldn't change each other with words, but only wound one another?

Oh, Anthony, oh my one and only husband, oh father of my children, why wasn't the passion we had enough for you, why did you want more and more and more?

Because my whole life I chased after the same thing, after new fields of love. I could lose an enormous field already conquered while chasing after some insignificant little meadow. But wasn't that how I found you? Without that how ever would we have found one another? At first weren't you just that sort of briefly glimpsed sunny meadow right alongside me?

How can you love a field that isn't yours, that belongs to someone else? I will never understand that. You infected me, you drew me into the sin of betrayal, the sin of theft, for which sin I am now punished.

I always departed unpunished, the entire field mine. Because I always continue to love all of you. That doesn't excuse me, though.

I am building a home, always, my whole life. It's my house. If you destroy it, I'll build a new one. I can live alone, with the children. I don't need anyone anymore.

I stand in front of your home. The door is closed. Oh, how I'd like to go inside. Back inside. Oh, how am I to find the words that will open the door?

You are before my home. You are tired, alone, tormented. You have tramped through other fields, burned other meadows. But you are still the dangerous destroyer that you were. Oh, how am I to find the strength to lock the door in your face?

Oh, how I would love to learn no longer to love! Then I would be afraid of losing you.

Oh, how I would love to learn to forgive, then I would be terrified of remaining alone...

He was the first to leave the embrace and to creep backwards through the narrow portal. He went through the rain to a telephone, to call a taxi.

The Babylonia was supposed to leave in ninety minutes. He thought he had time to stop in an office supply store, to buy paper and tape cassettes, enough to last the long voyage across the ocean.

(The Proper Peoples)

A few years ago I went to visit my daughter in Michigan, for a graduation party. Young faces under black mortarboards, bobbing tassels, blue medieval robes, the air thick with hopes, forebodings, belief in success to come, all of this stirred up a bittersweet memory of my own youth. I was charmed by the farewell and valedictory speeches of the masters and thought about how the banalities pronounced at times such as these have a certain ineluctable charm.

Then a woman stepped up to the podium whose name had been printed in the program in much larger letters than everyone else's. It was said that the administration had invited this famous participant in many international commissions, congresses, meetings in order to have her speak about the organization she had recently founded, "For the Proper Behavior of Nations."

There is no way that what this woman said could be called banal.

"Imagine that you have invited guests for dinner," the speaker began. "And suddenly you find that among them there is a man whose health is seriously imperiled. Worse, the man loves to draw attention to himself by telling stories about his ailments. You are disturbed to see that he has loosened his tie and undone his collar so as to show the people about him at the table the new rash which has broken out on his neck. Then he opens his mouth very wide, so as to show the sore that has appeared under his tongue. Then he pulls off his shirt and lets everyone see the catheters that run from his stomach and the bottle that is catching some stinking fluid from an ailing liver. Then he begins to lay out his x-rays of the tumor on his kidney, then lets people feel the humps on a poorly knit broken finger, then remarks on his urinalysis and stool samples.

"Would you put up with a guest like that? Would you ever invite him to your house again?

"I don't think so. Because propriety is an absolutely necessary condition of normal human relations. We demand that the people about us observe the proprieties. We don't want people to insist that we look at the tooth

they have had removed or their gangrenous foot, or the sarcoma on their shoulder.

"So why then is it that we don't demand the same thing of the nations which are about us?

"When our television screens show us demonstrators falling under bullets or buses which have plunged over cliffs or the fly-covered faces of exhausted mothers or blood-soaked murdered parliamentarians, do we not feel a painful impulse in our breast? After that aren't we left with the sensation that someone uninvited has burst improperly into our lives, into our comfortable home, to upset us and to deprive us of the possibility to savor life and pursue happiness, the things which our Constitution promised us?

"No, we shouldn't accuse our journalists or our tv and film cameramen for gathering such torturous scenes all over the world and then waving them in our faces. Would we make accusations against our eyes because they had seen all nasty sores on our improper guest? Of course not. Journalists do what they are meant to do just as our eyes and ears do what they are meant to. The responsibility must lie entirely upon the improper peoples which permit journalists to view their wounds.

"Recall how many years the peoples of Southeast Asia tormented us with the spectacle of their misery. How we suffered at the sight of napalm-burned children, burning villages, homeless old people wandering the streets, animals howling from hunger. And how the manners of these people have improved in the last ten years! They have withdrawn modestly from our sight and our tv screens, they have covered over their sores. Naturally we know that life isn't sweet there, that the disease is getting worse and that tens of thousands are trying to run away and drown in the ocean trying. But our lenses don't catch their gasping mouths, which is the main thing. That is what I would call propriety.

"They say that all of the residents of the cities were chased out into the bare fields there, that millions died of hunger. They say that millions were helped to die by having little blue plastic bags placed on their heads and the strings pulled tight. However our televisions—our eyes—have not once bothered us with this repulsive spectacle.

"The most numerous people on earth conducted themselves most worthily, in a cultivated way, befitting their traditions of thousands of years. And how disgusting was the California professor who tried to tell us about the abortions in the eighth month which he witnessed there. His American colleagues were right to shame and expel this improper person from their midst. Unfortunately of late there has been some tendency to

open the doors a little wider to our journalists, to make a show of the difficult and unpleasant moments of life. We may hope, however, that there will come an end to this.

"In the age of television and radio we must reexamine the idea of intrusion into the home and private life. The legless donkey herder who stepped on a mine in some far-away mountains and who is shown on my television screen upsets me as much as if he had broken down my own door. For that reason I have the right to take defensive action.

"I shall always respect the Albanians. Who has ever seen a suffering or starving Albanian on his screen? No one. The African countries are much better behaved too. Its only in the south that our journalists are still allowed to roam around almost free and stick their pitiless lenses into the scars and burns (let us recall only the burning auto tires, put about the necks of living people!). We may hope that soon there will be an end to this and the whole continent will become a model of propriety."

The speaker offered a detailed survey of other countries and continents, comparing each to the other. At the very end she drifted a bit from her subject and spoke of a minority people who are champions of propriety. For political reasons or perhaps because of some other reasons of propriety, she did not name the people. She said only that they lived in a valley surrounded by mountains. Life there was good, peaceful, and plentiful, so that this people had nothing to hide. Its propriety lay in another direction, for if residents of this nation heard that somewhere else among another people there had been some act of cruelty, they immediately asked their government to break off all relations with that country, so that—God forbid—they would bear no guilt for the acts of evil.

In recent years the idea of not resisting evil with force had sunk ever deeper into the consciousness of this people. Monuments to Tolstoy and Gandhi are everywhere. Unfortunately their neighbors abuse this attitude and gather in bands to descend from the surrounding mountains to rob and kill. The proper people offer no resistance to the attackers. Instead they fight this evil in their own way by redefining the criteria of defeat or victory in these battles. For them it isn't a question of how to defend themselves against bandits (this they hold to be as impossible as defending themselves against tornadoes and hurricanes), but of how to make it so that bandits kill and rob them without having any moral grounds on which to do so.

This is no easy or simple matter. If any of the residents of this country permits himself to hang a strong lock on his door or put sturdy shutters on his window everybody condemns this as something which will offend the *attackers and provoke them to justified fury. If any one among them buys a pistol or a gun or even a bow and arrow, he is an outcast. They say that there was one man who shot at the car his attackers drove, but no one remembers his name, because he was immediately driven out in shame, and all of the bandits' victims who had died over the following five years had died without the slightest sense of being in the right, which was very hard on them.*

"And so," the speaker concluded, "the growth of collective and individual propriety in international relations is the main goal of the organization which I have founded. It seems to me that for young people just entering life this opens up broad vistas for fruitful and ennobling careers."

She was applauded for some time. I confess that I too was infected with her conviction and slapped my hands together a time or two. But then the attraction of the banal came to the fore, and I stopped.

And you, dear listeners? Do you think that what our world most lacks is propriety? Or do you think that there are other and more pressing problems?

9. BOARDING

A WAVE...

A wave...
A wave...
A wave...
A wave...
A wave...
A wave...
And another wave...and another...and another...

It seemed as though they had prepared for all the dangers and difficulties of their long sea voyage save one—boredom. Cranking the helm left and right, Anton tried to imagine other ships which had sailed these waters. The Viking longboats. The Spanish galleons, taking soldiers in one direction, gold and silver in the other. The slavers' corvettes. The pilgrims' schooners, them praying in the hold, in a circle about their prophet, sitting on barrels of gunpowder and wheat. The pirate brigs. English frigates which conquered half the globe, only to be conquered themselves by a puff of steam concealed in a steel cylinder. The steamships full of immigrants, wallowing to the gunwales with their loads of new words: 'kielbasa' and 'mafia' and 'pogrom' and 'cinematographer.' The German U-boats. American convoys of Studebakers for the Russians. Kon-Tiki. Arab oil tankers.

This age-old carnival of vessels bounded about on the waves, circling, growing denser. Anton shook his head, rubbed his eyes. The compass arrow had already crawled a few points astray and returned to where it should be reluctantly, like a child whose game in the dangerous next block over has been interrupted.

Voices floated up from the crew's mess below. "Raise two...Pass...Another five...a flush...what you got?...two pair..." This was followed by a shriek of joy and the drumbeat of hands on the table. Anton saw Pablo-Pedro come up on the deck, walking backwards, glowing, shaking dollar bills. He held them up against the porthole of the mess, leered in at the faces of the losers. Then he tossed the dollars to the winds. His joy was obviously overplayed; money lost its magic in the middle of the ocean. It wasn't much of a trick to part with money out here. At 52 degrees north, 45 degrees west even communist poker was no help against boredom.

A few minutes later Ronald Ironhand came up to the wheelhouse. It was still a half hour until his watch. Anton could feel how the skin at the back of his neck was tensing in painful anticipation; what was Ironhand going to start? Running in place, shadow-boxing with dumb-bells, skipping rope? When he was exercising Ronald never brushed against him, but even so the sensation was unpleasant. Couldn't a man regard at least the thin layer of space about himself as his own? Particularly when all around were millions of cubic meters of emptiness? It was true that today was rather cold on the deck. Not long ago Anton had learned the navigator's secret and now he wasn't anxious to meet his eye.

"Our little couple has gone to bed again," Ronald said. "I never use to notice that the walls between the cabins were so thin. You know anything about sound insulation?"

"There are inflatable mattresses in the hold."

"Sometimes it seems like they're still quarreling even when they're making love."

"I see you lost again."

"Yup. But it's for the best. When he wins Pablo-Pedro stops hating me, for an hour or two anyway. Yesterday he even talked with me almost nicely. He said that sometimes a weakness comes upon him and he begins to feel sorry for the exploiters. Because they're doomed. I told him that my people were lumbermen in Montana, and that I've been living on salary my whole life. So how come I've got to be counted as one of the exploiters? For your size, he says. People over six foot tall automatically belong to the class of oppressors. And we aren't going to waste a lot of words talking to them, he says. Probably he can't forgive me being the one who locks him in the storeroom, but I only do it because you order me to. You, though, he likes."

Anton threw a quick glance at the navigator's face. Poor Ronald.

Even back in college he was always the one who couldn't get a football ticket or a girl at the dance or a seat in the car or a bottle of beer at the party.

"Yeah, the sailor we got is no treat. This little joke of Admiral Kozulin's is going to come out of our hide yet."

"Day before yesterday he was almost eloquent. He was describing how much my biceps disgust him. And my straight nose. And my light-colored hair. And broad shoulders. My teeth are just begging to be beat in with a baseball bat. He'd like to make me use my sweat-suit to grease the engine with. The fact that I never swear he takes as sick hypocrisy. I never drink, smoke, or shoot up, and he says that's because I'm a coward and afraid to live a little. If he sees Lin Chan bump me with her hip one more time he's going to pour hot soup on me. On me, notice, not on her. I can't remember when I was last the object of such strong feelings."

What's true is true—Ronald wasn't a person who inspired strong feelings. He was always somewhere about, handy, ready to help, to smile, to lend you his apartment, to vanish in good time. He never bothered anyone with stories about what annoyed him or what he really cared about. If on occasion he relaxed a bit over a glass of wine, it was hard to follow what he said without an anatomy text in hand. "Yesterday I spent the whole day working on my quadriceps femoris... Massage, dynamic and static loosening up, vibration loading... There are these ancient Japanese exercises that judo experts use... To stretch out the ligaments of the gluteus medius. Somebody promised to get me a video cassette. If you want, I can tell you when I get it... Incidentally, you might want to pay some attention to your externus abdominis... I mean I don't think you want to completely lose all the fat, because that's just trying for an effect, that's an extreme for show-offs. The muscle layers have to have a fatty layer for insulation and for nourishment. And as for the obliquus externus..."

But you had to admit that Ronald rarely got carried away in one of those monologues. He understood and had come to terms with the fact that his friends were unable to share his major passion in life. The mysterious movements of fluids and forces within their own flesh did not enchant these people, who were greedy animals. They forced everything from their flesh that they could, then paid attention to their flesh only when its exhaustion and torment forced them to take a break from their pursuit of pleasure. Or in labor. They burned off their field, sowed a few chance seeds, gathered a few pitiful harvests, and moved on, the day after, next month, next week. Susan was right, absolutely right; they were a band of nomads, prehistoric Neanderthals.

This bothered Ronald, but he didn't try to make them see it was wrong. If a person is blind to a miracle, what can you do? To the miracle of the blood, flowing in rivers beneath the skin, right here, almost out in the open, the miracle of inhaling and exhaling, the miracle of smooth joints, slithering one against the other, the miracle of dilating and contracting pupils, the mystery of how the vertebrae are joined. Ronald wasn't looking for people to agree with him; he was prepared to perform his rituals and worship alone. After all, to be a prophet demands confrontation, and Ronald could not endure confrontation of any sort.

When he was in college the football coaches and the basketball coaches and the boxing coaches were always after him, slapping him admiringly, like a horse, trying to get him to come to them. He always shook his head and left. Even the competitions in which the sportsmen didn't touch each other but rather, say, raced side by side, pedalling bicycles or leaning over glistening oars, even they held something that put him off. Even games that separated the opponents with a net lacked the purity that he needed. Only where the body struggled one on one with the forces of nature—with gravity and inertia and the weight of air and the resistance of water—only in this fight could he forget himself wholeheartedly. He lifted weights, threw the javelin, did long jump and high jump, wrung himself on the horizontal bar, swam and dived, but always alone. Whenever he would have had to compete, he would disappear or get sick or avoid it, and finally the coaches just gave up on him.

And women? Why were they always leaving him? He was so handsome, masculine, reliable. He loved to pick them up and run along the edge of the surf, raising a cloud of spray. But they left him. Commitment, love, devotion, that wasn't what they wanted after all. Amenable statutes of accusation, a quiet terror... If they really thirsted for constancy and devotion then Ronald Ironhand would have been their ideal. Poor guy. Apparently all that he had had in his life was those three years with Olga. Poor, poor Husband #1.2, who had lived alone ever since.

Anton had heard about their wedding. What Wife #1 hadn't dreamed up! She had out-done herself. And they had found a with-it priest who was willing to participate, and Ronald had agreed to everything too. A wedding on water! They had rented all the boats on the lake for guests. Bride and groom were in bathing suits, with rubber caps; they swam breast-stroke at the head of the procession. The priest waited for them at the dock. "Ronald, do you take this wet woman as your wife, to love more than your morning run?" "I do." "And you Olga, do you take this snorting man, and promise to forgive his ignorance of Slavic languages?" "I do." When they came to kiss-the-bride, they did it under water. The blasphemous priest took a step forward and, just as he was, in his cassock, also disappeared under water. The guests rocked tirelessly in their boats. The elder Kozulins refused to take any part in this debauch.

Later, when the children came to him on the vacations, Anton timorously inquired about their new father. "He doesn't mistreat you? He helps you with your homework?" The children weren't complaining. They got a little tired of the endless flexing and exercising, but on the whole they liked it. Life was like non-stop sports camp, and the question of what they were training for never arose. Training was good in and of itself, and had no need of a goal to justify it. Apparently the only one who knew the purpose was the heavenly Head Trainer, who had sent us to this world.

On one occasion nine-year old Golda, thoughtful, said of her stepfather, "You know, dad, I don't think he's afraid of *yesterday* at all." Anton knew at once what she meant, because he too had noticed this oddity about Ronald. When they were still students even. When everybody was sitting around bored and trying to figure out how to kill the evening ahead, he would suggest they go see the exact same movie that they had all watched the evening before. "What, are you making fun of us? You couldn't think up anything more clever than that?" He would shield himself from the barrage of paper cups and jesting blows, and would smile, but it was clear that he really didn't understand why cups and blows came. Why not go again? It was a great film, and they had all laughed so hard yesterday—why not do it again?

He was like that in everything. He could finish reading the last page of a book he liked, then flip the book around and start to read it from the beginning again. On the entire campus there was no better audience for jokes than Ronald. He could guffaw heartily at the exact same joke a dozen times in a row. He was always astonished in the cafeteria when his friends shoved away dishes they had grown tired of. Ham and peas! So what if it's the third time or the fifth or the tenth? What's the difference? It still tastes good, doesn't it?

Supposedly there are deviations—incredibly rare, one in a million—when a person has no sensation of pain. Couldn't it be a variation just as rare that had happened to iron-handed Ronald? Maybe fate had spared him, had forgotten to curse his birth with the curse visited upon everyone else—some more so, some less, but still everybody, every normal person—that is, the torment of boredom? But if that was the case, was that a curse or a blessing? If nothing ever gets stale, not your street, not your work, not the view from your window, not your wife's voice, or the records on the shelf—if you can continue loving that street, that work, that wife, that music to the end of time—isn't that a gift from heaven? So what did everybody want from this good-tempered strongman, why did they make fun of him? Why could no one take him as he was? Oh, ye insatiable overthrowers of far-off states, oh, ye composers of novelty, oh, ye inventors of floating weddings and unusual insurance policies! Are you not devoured by envy? Isn't that why you drive the poor fellow away, because he isn't afraid of repetition, that he is able to enjoy the hundred millionth sun-verdant white-foaming, smoothly sliced wave as much as he did the first, while you, the damned and insatiable, begin to go nuts after ten?

"I keep trying to imagine when we actually find Golda in the Upside-down Land," Ronald said. "I can't tell you what this expedition means to me. The whole three years that we lived together I never stopped worrying about her. I felt like I couldn't give her what she needed. I didn't even know what that was, still don't. She'd always corner me with her 'why? why?' Generally I'd end up having to say, because that's how things are in this world. So once she answered, 'You don't have another world then?'"

"Golda always spoke very warmly about you," Anton said. "It was usually her mother she was mad at. She was really upset when you split up. She kept doing exercises, trying to keep up the program you had designed for her. She used to say that the best way to forget about yourself was to get dead tired. For some reason that was what was most important to her, to learn how to forget herself. It didn't work though. She had to have a coach, someone who would work her and work her and work her. She couldn't make herself work like that."

"She's a great girl. This is true, what you're saying? She wasn't mad at me?"

"She never said anything but good things. She used to say that you should have kids of your own as quickly as you could. She never could understand why you didn't remarry."

"That right? I don't understand myself why I didn't. I kept putting it off, somehow. And to tell the truth, I was afraid. Our laws are always on the woman's side. Fathers don't have any rights at all. Whenever there's a divorce they give the children to the mother. If I got so attached to your kids, what would have happened if they tried to take my own kids away from me? I can't even bear to think about it. You'd have to be an insensitive idiot to marry and have children in this day and age."

"Thank you very much."

"Oh, excuse me, for Christ's sake. I didn't mean... It's true, I always thought that you kept getting married precisely because you were afraid of ending up without any children. Because they kept taking yours away. I always admired your courage and persistence. How many is it you have in all so far?"

"Ten of my own and two that belong to other people. To tell you the truth though, nobody ever took anything away from me. I was always the one who did the leaving. The only wife who left me had no kids."

"That was your third one?"

"No, the fourth, but don't apologize. I mix them up myself sometimes. So you see how it is, you and I went completely different ways, but we've both run aground in the same place. You might say our voyage is an expedition of failed fathers. How long is it to the end of my watch?"

"Four minutes. It won't bother you if I do some push-ups, will it? After that long poker game the pectoralis major gets to be like wood, and the rectus abdomini wants to move around too."

"Of course, by all means. You have enough room behind me there? You don't want to joke around with your pectoralises, do you?"

The tree roots hung over the undercut bank. The breeze played in the tree tops, tugging and testing their tenacity. If it found a weak spot, it dug in and began to press without letting up. The tree couldn't resist and crashed down into the water. Blinded ants dashed up and down the upturned roots. The river flowed between the branches, seeking new prey.

The rowboats had to go around the trees in the water. Sometimes the people in the boats grabbed wet branches and hung on, dangling in the stream. Anton listened to their cries and laughter, but every time they noticed Anton looking at them, they fell silent. Kayaks went by, and rubber rafts, and little fishing boats, and every time the people in them fell silent and began nervously to watch the shore.

Anton couldn't figure out what was frightening them. He was alone, peaceful and unarmed, in a good temper. Apparently his car was still somewhere on the shore. Apparently he had gone down to the river to look for a bridge. He remembered that there use to be a wooden bridge somewhere in this stretch. Maybe it was knocked out by ice? He wanted to ask the people floating by whether they could see the bridge, but their glowering faces dissuaded him. What was it they saw on the shore, that he couldn't see?

Suddenly the ground began silently to shake beneath his feet. An enormous slab of the root-woven sand began to turn, to get up on its haunches. The people in the boats tugged at their oars, trying to row aside as quickly as possible, to get out of the way of the branch-covered tree trunk. As he fell Anton saw boulders in the water, coming at him faster and faster. He didn't know whether to put out his hands in front of him or to try to shield his head. The ground continued to shake. Using all his strength he pushed away from it with his legs, trying to fling his body over the boulders, into the strip of clear water.

And he woke up.

Ronald's worried face hung over him in the narrow space of the cabin. His iron fists stopped shaking Anton's shoulder, then rubbed guiltily one against the other.

"Captain, there's a ship of some sort to starboard. I think you ought to have a look."

Anton followed him up to the wheelhouse. The Babylonia, throbbing quietly, was slithering through the gentle waves. Above the horizon the Celestial Sketcher was stubbornly experimenting with pinks in the oddest combinations. All efforts by the heavenly hosts to break through to the briny deep had been beaten back for the day. The last bubbles escaping from captivity streamed upwards to the surface. Aqueous oxygen was once again separated from atmospheric oxygen by the thinnest of boundaries, greenish, rippling, and impenetrable.

The ship which had been spotted to starboard seemed not to be moving, without lights. It seemed to be a fishing trawler, and a fairly large one. What kind of fish could have enticed it so far from land?

"It looks completely abandoned," Anton said.

Ronald silently passed him the binoculars.

The gunwales of the trawler, lit by the setting sun, came very close, filling both eyepieces. It was a picture in an oval frame, suitable to hang on the walls of the ship's cabin. In one place the railing was broken and twisted upwards, as if someone had tried to fish the ship fast out of the water with a great hook. The flagstaff on the stern was empty. Forward, like a concussed skull, there was a ragged hole, puncturing an inscription of six hieroglyphics right in the middle. However, the hole was high above the water line, and not dangerous. For a moment Anton thought that a shadow had scudded along the deck on the left side of the oval frame. The familiar needle of an impending encounter with the Miserymaker jabbed him in the throat. He adjusted the focus, and just then made out the shape of a person.

It seemed as though the person had been trying to climb up a ladder to the upper deck, but at the last moment had lacked the strength and fallen face down. An arm hung motionless through the railing, and then Anton understood that this was a woman.

"I tried to raise them on the radio, but no answer. I tried flags, same thing," Ronald said.

"Maybe the loud hailer?"

"We'd have to get closer for that."

"It could be there's nobody alive there."

"We'll see."

"We couldn't just go on by? Like we didn't see it? There's something about that ship that I really don't like. It's obviously Asian, like the Flying Dutchman, only from Vietnam. What brought it out here in the Atlantic?"

"We can't leave disaster victims without assistance. The laws of the sea make that a crime. We could get sued for it if anybody saw us."

"So what can they do to us? Sentence us to a hundred lashes? Keelhaul us? There could be some sort of horrible illness on board there."

"You're the captain, you've got to make the decision. I'm going to get a little closer though. It's almost calm now, we could almost come alongside."

The becalmed boat drew nearer. The dirty spotlights were clearly visible now, the streaks of rust on the superstructure, the hanging shreds of netting.

Ronald shut the engine off. The Babylonia silently moved on the remaining kilogrammeters of inertia. And then, in the sudden silence, they clearly heard crying. A child crying.

"The devil!" Anton said, almost relieved. "Belly up and a bottle of rum! That's just what we need to get stuck with! Why did you ever wake me? We could have gone on by, and that would have been that."

"Maybe we ought to send out an SOS? Tell about the ship in distress and give its coordinates?"

"First have to find out what the distress is."

"You know, you're probably right about disease. It's pretty likely. I'll run down to the galley for some rubber gloves."

The strip of water between the ships grew narrower. Anton switched the engines on again and began to maneuver carefully. Reverse engines, forward, reverse again... Ronald stood on the prow, holding a boarding ladder ready. The black lenses of the spotlights reflected the white wheel-house of the Babylonia, the flag with the dog's head.

The child's crying was broken from time to time by coughing. The woman's hanging arm was either waving to the rescuers or rocking in the breeze. The hooks of the ladder came even with the gunwale rails of the trawler. Ronald turned a lever, made the bottom rung of the ladder fast, and it suddenly looked like a gangplank. Then he went back to the stern, threw a grappling hook onto the deck of the other ship, pulled it tight, and made the rope fast. Babylonia bumped softly against the old tires that hung over the side of the trawler. The engine went silent.

Anton was the first to grab the ladder. Above there was the stench of rotting fish. The child's cry was ear-piercing. He thought that the child would have to be put in the aft cabin, so that he wouldn't keep them awake between watches. But what if this was a little infant? What would they feed it? And what if it needed a doctor? Where were they going to get one? Ronald had had some first-aid courses, and that was the extent of it. True, they had brought a medical handbook with them, titled *Symptoms*. "If you have a persistent cough, this could be: a) pneumonia (if accompanied by a high fever); b) a heart attack; c) emphysema (chest pains, fever, general lassitude); d) an aneurism; e) measles (spiking fever, inflamed eyes that are light sensitive, a red rash on the body. In one case out of a thousand this can become encephalitis, with fatal results, so the patient must be kept in absolutely strict quarantine)," and so on...

Anton's head was above the railing. He threw a quick glance about the deck, then froze. The wood quivered under his feet as if wishing to leave. His head spun, and he closed his eyes. The Miserymaker had not appeared so close to him, and so suddenly, for quite some time.

Human bodies were scattered about the whole deck.

They were in filthy rags, starved, blackened. Men, women, children. The stench covered the trawler like an enormous jellyfish. The little breeze wasn't strong enough to rip its tentacles from the railings, the masts, the rusty hawsers. Anton crawled over the railing, then put a hand back to help Ronald, who was following. Ronald gasped at the sight of the floating cemetery, froze for a moment. The Celestial Sketcher gently and dreamily added some green to the pinks.

One of the bodies suddenly moved, raised to its elbows, crawled toward them. A Vietnamese? A Cambodian? An Indian? White, black, yellow? Man, woman, child?

"Human uniqueness ends at the level of the skeleton," Anton thought. "Pedro-Pablo would be pleased at that. In bone structure at least we are all equals."

The slant of the eyelids, the color of skin and hair, the shape of the lip, all that became undecipherable and unimportant. Hunger had gnawed out the details, leaving only the hardened, wizened essence. A human being. Or had been at one time. Now all that was left was eyes. Clouded ones.

"Boat people," Ronald whispered. "I've read about them...they pay their last pennies for this. The captains promise to take them to America, to Australia, Canada, and then at night they disappear with the whole crew. The passengers drift. People say they start to eat each other. First the children, then the old people."

"We have to radio the authorities right now."

"Which authorities? We're in neutral waters. Nobody wants anything to do with these poor wretches. And look for yourself, what could be done with them?"

His reserves of strength exhausted, the person who had been crawling toward them once again flopped down on the rough boards. Ronald touched him with a rubber finger, lifted his eye lid.

"He's like a dead man. We should check the others. Maybe there's people alive inside, in the cabins? They could help us."

"Let's start with the kid."

Stepping carefully over the bodies they went toward the sound of the crying. One of the doors opened for a second and immediately slammed shut. Had it been the wind, or the waves rocking, or a hand? Some of the scattered bodies opened eyes at the sound of footsteps, began to moan, scrabbling at the deck with incredibly long fingernails. It was as if life would fly off from these shapeless lumps, then return, like flies to filth, trying to figure out whether there was anything there to live off, or whether it had all been sucked dry.

They went around the superstructure, climbing over the windlasses and hawsers. In the stern there was an old net spread out, with holes here and there. The child, pinned under the mother's body, lay in the middle and cried without stopping. At their approach the mother suddenly got up on all fours, looked back, and snarled. Black Asiatic curls, a withered breast, but somewhere inside, it seemed, there still lurked a reserve of fuel for energy, two or three rice kernels' worth. Flailing her knees and elbows rapidly, her rear end humped up like a dog's, she ran away from them, disappearing around the corner of the superstructure.

Anton and Ronald approached the crying infant, who was lying in its own filth. Absolutely naked, with the face of a five-month old old man. The out-sized head had no desire to perish with the rest of the body, and so dishonorably was absorbing the last of the nourishment. Bending over it, Anton tried to make out whether the abdomen was covered in a rash, as the medical handbook had promised.

He was deafened by an explosion.

More exactly, that was what it had seemed to them to be, in the first second. But then they immediately understood that this was simply an engine starting up. It seemed that somewhere in the depths of the trawler there were still hands moving, able to reach a button, and there were still a few cups of gas, able to ignite and move the rusty pistons.

The corners of the net on the deck of the trawler rose like cobras to the piper. Ronald was the first to understand what was happening and flung himself to the side.

Too late.

The net rose before them like a wall, and then flung itself back over Anton. The extended cables hastily hauled the edges of the trawl net upwards, towards the boom of the crane. The motor roared, the windlasses squeaked, and tumbling about, tangling up in one another, poking limbs out the holes, both representatives of the Pirgoroy firm hung high above the deck. Somewhere around their feet the large-headed humanoid bait shrieked desperately. Anton was turned on his side, his face pressed against the knots of the netting. The rosy horizon, suddenly stood on end, revolved slowly before his eyes, the masts of the Babylonia, the deck of the trawler. And the deck was no longer lifeless.

The deck was rapidly filling with people.

They were crawling out of two open hatchways, running from the doors of the superstructure. They were also thin and dirty, but still not as starved as the near-corpses scattered about the deck, although it seemed as though those too had come to life a bit, to take part in the general running about.

There was some silent harmony and purpose in this running, which was directed by a few men, taller than the others, and wearing conical Chinese straw hats. These waved sticks and stretches of cable, now directing, now driving the runners. The crowd parted to let through people bearing heavy rolled-up nets. They were unwound and thrown overboard, to become rope ladders, which clattered down onto the Babylonia. The horde streamed down, boarding the other vessel.

Anton watched in helpless despair how the treasures that they had accumulated with such difficulty before their departure floated above the filthy, shaggy heads, passed from hand to hand, to disappear into the holds of the trawler. Sleeping bags, batteries, crates of bottled water, fuel cans, the barometer, the primus stove, chocolate cookies, the radio, a harpoon, lifesavers, spare lines, boxes of calculators and phonograph records (gifts for the upside-down people), an inflatable raft, chronometers with the guts still dangling, a hand winch, bottles of gin and whiskey, rubber boots, a broom, propane tanks...

The pain in his upside-down leg stretched upward like a vine, intertwined with the pain of the outrage which had settled in his throat. Yes, precisely, he rattled with the bitterest sense of outrage at these dangerously poor, these thankless starving people who had come so slyly back to life, in such thoughtless greed. The last time he had felt anything remotely similar was when he found in the purse of Wife #4 those diabolical pills with which people had learned to poison unconceived children, and this after all their discussions and even arguments about what color they would paint the nursery, what kind of insurance they would get for the child, where they would move, to be near the best schools! But these people! How had they known, how had they guessed what would surely lure him—them—into the open net?

The thicket of dark skeletal hands worked without halt, passing things overhead, over the gunwales, up the rope ladders, and into the holds. In went fire extinguishers, buckets, dog food and cat food, electric cable, oars, an air pump, a tape recorder, fishing tackle, engine oil, a clock, boxes of medicines, a teapot, spaghetti, a lock and chain, a generator, a saw and ax, smoked hams, signal flags, a flare pistol, jam jars, lanterns, flippers and masks, an aqualung, books and magazines, dried fruit, toothpaste and soap, sacks of flour, sunflower oil, towels and pillows and candles and blankets...

Something heavy splashed into the water. The overseers in the straw hats immediately flung themselves at the guilty parties, sticks flashing.

"The sextant!" Ronald suddenly cried in a thin voice, "At least leave the sextant! You don't even know how to use it!"

Better he had stayed quiet! They had been forgotten, it seemed. Now scores of grinning excited faces swarmed up at them. The crane operator, invisible in his booth, couldn't pass up such a moment. He once again cut in the motor of the winch and the net with its unheard-of catch began to lower into the ocean off the stern, to the laughter and whistles of the pirates.

"What a prophetic watery dream that was," Anton thought. "From now on I'm going to believe in dreams. Sometimes they have something important to say about the Miserymaker's plans..."

And then he knew that they had no more 'from now on' remaining to them. That the sensation-starved boat people simply could not refuse themselves this great a pleasure. Human sacrifice was probably the only thing that could still tingle the nerves of these starving people.

The rosy water approached with gathering speed.

The horde dashed to the gunwale of the trawler, leaned out over the railing, frozen in anticipation.

In his former life, the life before Real Trouble, his profession often brought Anthony Sebich into contact with people on the edge of death, old people who had been ill for ages. They had horrified him. Their stumbling tongues, watery eyes, baggy, empty skin, wafting filth, their groans, their hands clutching the sheets all made him think of the Lethe and Styx in flood, high water in the kingdom of the dead, slopping over into our world, washing over us without warning and carrying these old people away with it, half-drowned corpses before the eyes of the living. And every time he used to say to himself, 'If you're ever in a flaming plane crash, remember this horror and try to have time to be glad that yours was a quick clean death.'

But now it had come, direct, sunny, transparent, and no thoughts of deathly ill old people helped.

He was not ready.

He thrashed, punched, struggled.

He shouted something.

It seemed to him that somewhere in the depths of his memory, in one of the languages he knew there was hidden a password, a secret word, which might have stopped the ratchet of the winch from turning.

The water splashed up, unexpectedly cold on his stomach. He had time to grab a full breath. Oh, if only leukocytes and erythrocytes weren't so greedy! Oh, if only they knew how in emergencies to dispense the oxygen as carefully as they do bread in a besieged city! But no, they rebel almost immediately, demanding more and more, splitting the temples, rupturing the aorta, bulging out the eyes...

The net-wrapped human ball splashed up into the air, several meters, and once again went down. The crowd groaned in admiration. Anton convulsively gulped air. The parting circle of air and waters was thicker and thicker with greens and pinks.

Then something happened. There was a thump, not of blood in the ears, but outside, in the air. And the downward movement of the net stopped with a loud blow. And Anton, who had never heard it before, deafened and half-dead, suddenly recognized this sound, this blessed sound that he had secretly waited for, the noise that ripped out old stitches and sewed life back in new ones, the sound that brought back hope.

The crack of an automatic weapon firing.

The glass of the cabin where the crane operator was hiding disintegrated.

The net hung a meter above the water, revolving slowly.

The crack splashed again, echoing off the gunwales, muffled by the screams and groans of the wounded.

The boat people scrambled shrieking up the rope sides of the trawler.

A pistol shot from the stern of the Babylonia. Another. Another.

Straw hats dashed along the ship's side, waving sticks and slashing the ropes and ladders.

A cloud of smoke belched from the trawler's stack.

They began to throw flaming oily rags onto the deck of the Babylonia from the windows of the superstructure.

The wound-up lines stopped the net, and before they began to turn again in the opposite direction, Anton saw the rapidly widening strip of water between the two ships.

The gun fired again.

Now he could also hear the passing whistle of the slugs. They were whizzing past quite close. Anton thought that Pedro-Pablo had gone mad and was now shooting right at them. By that time though the buzz-saw of gunfire had already done its work; the lines had been cut in several places and could not hold. They ripped, and the now-open net dumped its whole catch into the ocean.

Not the ocean of death, after all, but of freedom.

His hands and legs milled of their own, bringing him closer with every stroke to his dear gunwales of salvation, and his lungs gulped in all the oxygen above the water, oxygen in such incomparable abundance. Then, already clinging to an iron stanchion, already half out of the water, Anton looked back, finally remembered, and shouted the password which would have saved them, which turned out to be the foulest of Russian swear words.

Framed by its rejuvenated lights the trawler beat into the evening shadows like a spider. The plundered, looted, and ravaged Babylonia rocked amidst the floating corpses. From somewhere Ronald emerged snorting. He was swimming on his side, with one arm, and in the other was holding the quietly howling boat baby, born between water and air, who perhaps had never even seen land.

It was only at morning light that they could really understand the dimensions of the disaster. The doors of the empty cupboards flapped desultorily in the galley. Wires curled from the walls. The diesel was frozen in the dark of the engine room; the pirates had somehow drained the fuel tank almost to the bottom. All the instruments which might have sent or received radio waves had disappeared. All the lamp bulbs had disappeared. Even if they had been left there was nothing to drive electrons round their filaments. A packet of margarine which had miraculously survived was melting in puddles on the bottom of the hot refrigerator. Lin Chan was squatting down, carefully trying to bail it into plastic cups.

They decided to begin by searching for food and drink. After an hour there was a small heap on the table in the wardroom: a packet of noodles, two jars of jam, a box of prunes (which Pedro-Pablo had kept in his cabin under his pillow), three boxes of crackers, a bottle of Perrier, and a head of lettuce. They carefully bailed out the fresh water from the toilet tank, and the little glass bottle with the remnants of ground pepper was immediately tossed overboard; just looking at it made your throat dry and thirsty.

Then they had a council of war. Should they stay on the Babylonia and wait for help? Or try to make a raft? Or maybe they should rig up a sail out of a sheet? But the yacht was too big, no sheet could budge it. And Ronald had once proposed that they should lay in some real sails, but no one had listened, because they were worried about space. Anyway, the sails would also have been stolen by the omnivorous sea pirates.

Pablo-Pedro was sitting silent and gloomy, taking no part in the discussion. It seemed that he could not believe that the triumph of victory had passed and that it was now time to return to the unbearable trivia of existence. His fingers kept squeezing the gun's trigger, as though this were some sort of universal tool for resolving all of life's difficulties, to warm and nourish, to shape all necessary things, and to steer the ship to a safe harbor. No one had dared to ask where he had gotten the gun. His contemptuous expression seemed to say everything: 'No sooner do I go to sleep, than you get the ship into *that* mess! Well, now you made it, so you can fix it, without me!'

Ronald's left hand was bandaged. When they were tumbling about in the net he had either dislocated or broken his middle finger. Anton had gotten away with a raw cheek.

The sea-going orphan sobbed beyond the cabin door. He couldn't get a moistened cracker down his throat; it came back up as a mush on his lips. There was no milk. In the half hour of the attack they had been flung back into a pre-electrical, pre-canned, pre-wire age, into the age of cavemen.

Fear slid down upon them slowly, like a glacier.

A rising west wind rocked the dead Babylonia from wave to wave, driving it farther and farther into the sunny yolk that was swelling above the ocean.

Radio Broadcast Composed in the Middle of the Heartless Atlantic Ocean
(The Creator's Error)

Once I took my vacation at the shore, in Maine. (Oh, how I would love to be transported there now, to be again in a warm room, two steps away from my beloved restaurant!) From the window of my room a small island was visible, with just a single house on it. I was told that some sort of solitary eccentric lived there. Sometimes he would come over in a boat to buy groceries. The locals tried not to talk with him, but just waved, said hello, and ran off. That was because he always talked about just one thing, and they already knew by heart what he was going to say. It was like a broken record. So the solitary islander would snare inexperienced tourists in the restaurant or on the beach and force them to listen to his harangue.

I was one of the ones he cornered.

"So you say He made some mistakes in creation," he began, plonking his gin down next to mine (although of course I hadn't said anything of the sort). "But I'm prepared to prove to you that He went step by step and always upwards, and that each time He found the best solution. If you look at things real close, there's not a place, not a single place that you'll find so much as a single cock-up, not one single misstep.

"Oh, at first glance maybe it seems that He's just playing around, and cold-bloodedly gives His new creations the old ones to eat. Today He makes the beautiful little krill to float in the ocean, and then tomorrow He makes whales, to eat the krill by the billions. Today He makes the little fishes, gamboling under the ice, and tomorrow He sets His new toy on them, the seals, and then the day after He lets polar bears eat the seals, and then about a million years later these tailless monkeys start shooting at the bears.

"Take a closer look, though, and you'll see how carefully each of the creatures is separated from the others, how carefully the pens in time and space are constructed for every creature. The walls of these pens are made of the invisible and invincible, born of the intersection of time and space, of a material which we call speed. A lion can never run down a healthy

gazelle and a cat can always make it to the tree in front of a dog, but a squirrel can always scramble away from the cat to a higher and skinnier branch, and the swallow always avoids the falcon and the badger makes it to his set ahead of the fox. But if a creature is too slow, then He builds around it a wall of pure unadulterated time. He multiplies them to infinity, like the crabs in the depths of the ocean or the caterpillars on the leaves or the worms in the thick of the earth, the lemmings in the moss. Hey, you swift squid, nimble titmouse, tireless mole, eternally hungry wolf, just try to eat all the crabs and caterpillars and worms and lemmings! You can't do it; they multiply faster than you eat.

"Some people say that the extinct dinosaurs and pterodactyls and the other creatures which have vanished from the face of the earth are just the endless succession of His failures and mistakes. And that even today many species continue to disappear and that He can't prolong their life even for a couple-three centuries. But how do we know that He wants to prolong life for eternity? Have you ever seen a child who loved all his toys the same, identically and forever? If he gets tired of one, he throws it out and lets it disappear to the basement with the other junk. Sure, some animals disappear before our eyes, but what do you find a failure about the Bengal tiger, the bald eagle, the manatee, the buffalo, the snow leopard? And our frantic efforts to save them, isn't that a reflection of our admiration? Aren't we like poor kids jumping on the toys discarded by a wealthy household, taking them home to glue and paint and sew up again?

"Of course, He did have problems, serious ones. And most likely solving them took a good deal of time. When He went from sessile plants to animals that move around in space, they had to be taught how to look for and find themselves food. He gave them the torments of hunger and the sweetness of repletion. They ran off joyously to find themselves food. Egoism became the synonym for the ability of any animal to live. Eat everything you can get your teeth on, or your claws or your feelers. The female praying mantis eats the male right after fertilization, and sometimes the female pike doesn't even wait until the male deposits his milk on the eggs, and the big crocodile eats the little crocodile, and doesn't even bother with one of its famous tears.

"But then the two tasks came into conflict; they had to eat but also reproduce. Following the Creator's plan, the animals ate everything that came in their way, leaving nothing for their descendants to eat. Often they also ate the descendants, if the descendants weren't quick about it. Entire species died off that we know nothing about. Yet gradually though He began to be drawn to more complex creations. To creations that could

react faster to the various moves of His game, to changes of heat and cold, dark and light, and the most important thing, to the appearance of new creations. That is they had to know how to teach one another, the older to teach the younger. How can you leave the younger alongside the older, if the older are going to eat them?

"That's when He thought up His most elegant move. I figure that He's secretly kind of proud of it even today, and rightly so, too. I can't see anything more admirably clever in all of creation.

"He invented love.

"Love for your own puppies or kittens or ducklings or cubs or children or chickens or dolphins. Love for other creatures of your species. Love in general.

"I figure that was when he chucked out the ichthyosaurs and pterodactyls and brontasauruses and other simple-minded stomach-stuffers. He just wasn't interested in them, so He let them disappear in the dust. After that He was mostly busy just with those who had managed to grasp the charge of love He had sent. Meaning the birds and mammals. And people, later.

"How quick everything started to turn over for Him! Once, creating a new animal took millions of years, but now? Even 200,000 years ago there weren't any of the domestic animals. All the cows and chickens and pigs and goats and llamas and camels and even domestic bees, all these were created out of the ferment of a loving system of 'you feed me, I feed you,' all this gathered around man because of love.

"Naturally He set us apart, and naturally He loves us specially. Because we're the only creation that can value and admire His creation. That was the reason He gave us the ability to imitate Him, meaning to create.

"However, there's one question, one puzzling thing He didn't finish, that I can't figure out how to explain, so far. No, I'm not criticizing Him, mind, it's that because of my human frailty and stupidity I can't imagine how He's going to cope with it. We have to believe that He's capable even of solving the insoluble, because otherwise his marvelous, bare-skinned, two-legged find is going to perish, is going to devour and destroy itself.

"I'll say it again, we can't, we dare not charge Him with the torment of unrequited love.

"It's just our lack of understanding to imagine that it wouldn't have been easy for Him to set things up so that the love of the lover would immediately stimulate an answering love in the loved, just as a tongue of flame makes warmth, like a ray of light makes a reflection. We shouldn't fear unrequited love, and when we are choking in pain, we must believe that *He will think up a solution, soon, very soon, in a few score thousand years.*

"*Yes, unrequited love torments us, like unsatisfied hunger. But maybe we are the ones who are at fault? Because we are always wanting the love of this one woman, this one friend, this one child, our own. Maybe by punishing us with unrequited love, He is teaching us to love everyone? Or perhaps He is a little jealous and wants us to direct our love to Him? Or could it be that this imperfection, the senseless, irrational torment of unrequited love, makes us interesting to Him? And when He fixes that too, when He overcomes it and we start to love calmly and reciprocally, guaranteed, even-steven, I love her, she loves me, maybe then He'll get bored with us and chuck us out the way He chucked out hundreds of His other creations?*"

Dear radio listeners, if I am able to return to you alive, I am anxious, as always, to hear your answers to the questions asked me by the solitary islander, an uninvited defender of the Creator.

10. ADRIFT

ONCE WHEN HE GOT home from the office Anton saw that Wife #5 had a bandage over her eyes. Yes, her eyes absolutely had to rest, that was what the doctor said. No, she didn't need glasses, the retina was just tired. It was a fairly rare disease, but the doctor promised that within a week everything would be better. It was just that she had to have absolute rest, with no irritation of the retina. And vitamins. She had already bought the necessary vitamins. Would he get her the green box from the table next to the buffet? The kids and he would have to get along without her services for a whole week, and even to help her do everything. What did he think, would that be terribly hard for everybody?

The children thought it was great. Especially the older ones, from her first marriage. They led their mother on walks, dialed the telephone for her, poured her coffee, wiped her mouth with a napkin, tugged at her, scolded her for being careless, and warned of dire consequences. The exchange of roles turned their life into an exciting show. They learned to prepare supper, to look after the younger ones, to run the washing machine, cut the grass, run the vacuum.

Wife #5 insisted that the bandage couldn't be taken off even at night, because someone might have left on the light in the bathroom and then God alone knows what would happen to the retina if it should suddenly get zapped by a ray of light. Anton got used even to that. Odd-man-out was a little confused at first—after all, he had never before had anything to do with blind women, who could operate only by touch. But then he even seemed to come to like it, and like the children began to get into the carnival spirit of the whole thing.

It was only Anton who was still upset. What could have happened with a retina to make it fear the thing for which it was created, a ray of light? He had never heard of such a thing. The week passed, but the bandage stayed on the eyes of Wife #5. Anton decided to go see the oculist and have a good talk with him. Maybe she needed some sort of medicine besides extra vitamins? He went without saying anything about it to Wife #5, and came out of the offices incensed. It turned out that the oculist had absolutely no idea about any of it. According to her records, Wife #5 hadn't had her eyes tested in more than two years.

So why did she have to make all this up? What was she trying to get? A vacation from housework, like a leave? But couldn't she have talked about that openly, discussed it, come to an agreement? Naturally he would have let her go for a week to Aunt Clarence's or the Bahamas or even to Europe. They might have hired a woman to come in to watch the children and take care of the house instead of her. How could she make him get this upset?

Wife #5 didn't try to justify what she had done. Tears leaked from beneath her bandage. She sat on the bed, head down, listening silently to his scolding and yelling, quivering every time he shouted "But *why?*"

"Because I wanted to," she finally forced herself to say, "it was something I wanted a lot. And you wouldn't have let me. You would have laughed. And told our friends! I know that it sounds really weird, but I just had to try to find out what...to feel myself...HOW BLIND PEOPLE LIVE."

Wife #5 was absolutely totally different from his previous wives. Unlike Wife #4 she was always thinking about everything under the sun except herself. Unlike Wife #3 she had contempt for no one on earth, except herself. Unlike Wife #2 she did not believe in the possibility of finding safety in this world. Unlike Wife #1 she was not in constant rebellion against the "have-tos" and "got-tos" that encircle every person, but rather lived in complete and uncomplaining slavery to them.

She was prepared at any moment to leap up and gallop toward the first "have-to" that appeared, as if she had been shouted at or whipped. Actually, the word "first" here is not quite right, because the various "have-tos" hadn't discussed things among themselves and hadn't set up a polite queue. They all shouted at her at once, like snarling guests in a residence hotel, who couldn't share the single serving girl. Running to answer the shout of "have to water the flowers" Wife #5 might suddenly be seized by "have to telephone Aunt Clarence," but then even before she got to the telephone she would stop rooted by the shout of "have to get the fish out of the freezer," but as soon as she grabbed the freezer handle, she would suddenly get fogged over by the thought "have to pay the overdue electric bill." Her face was always distorted by tense expectation, and her eyes swam with the rainbow-hued stingy soapy bubble of fear.

Every now and again friends would bring her bits of papers with the telephone numbers of psychotherapists, who had just recently cured some friend of a similar kind of irrational fear. Or an exaggerated guilty conscience. Oh, how our parents and teachers poured those guilt feelings into us, like an extra supply, just in case, to guarantee themselves a comfortable old age. It would be very difficult to pump that guilt back out without professional help.

She agreed and took the papers, phoned around, but she had no luck, because all of the psychotherapists turned out to be weird themselves. One told her that treatment would only work if she would try—yes, you heard what I said—if she tried to seduce him. Another, a woman, went into raptures from her nightmares, even envied them, asked about them in minute detail, saying that she had never heard anything so spontaneous in all her life, so creative and unpredictable. Another one, every time she got upset about something, told her a similar incident from his own life, explained how much more painful and burdensome everything was, then said, but look, he hadn't fallen to bits, he was still working and leading a full, normal life.

True, she soon found out that there was nothing normal about his life, because he admitted that he was slowly slipping into deep deep debt, that his grown children refused to see him, that his patients wrote complaints about him to the psychiatric journals, that he drank alone at night, which was the only way he could hope to fall asleep even as early as three. She was sorry for him, brought him bouillon to sober up. She tried to reconcile another psychotherapist with his wife. She liked worrying about them precisely because nobody made her do it. Apparently that even had some healing effect, because for a short time she cheered up. But here too all of her "I would like to" feelings were transformed—by people? fate? herself?—into gnawing "I have to"s. It was as though she carried about her some sort of magnetic field which could infuse each approaching desire with weight.

It was Wife #5 whom Anton most often recalled in the morning, when he woke up in the stuffy, rocking cabin. It seemed to him that she was the only person in the world who might have gotten some pleasure from the disaster that had befallen them, perhaps even some happiness. Because there was no "have to" persistent enough to drown out—even in her, of that he was sure—the two mighty "I wants" which filled their souls. I Want to Eat. I Want to Drink. Eat and Drink. Drink. Eat.

Ronald had hidden the ship's log in the safe, so it had survived, which allowed them to keep a record with the only pen which remained, a ballpoint that had been in Lin Chan's notebook.

1 J u l y.

The third day of drifting. This morning we finished the last of the water. The only hope now is
rain, but there isn't a cloud in the sky. It is hot even
at night. Every thought is of water. The food is ending
too. We are trying to catch fish. I took all the pins
out of Lin Chan's clothes. For a long time I wondered how to bend them. We don't have a hammer
or pincers or pliers. The captain found the answer.
He stuck the sharp end of the pin in the handle of
the stove. He pressed on it, and the pin broke. The
next one he held over the flame. It bent properly.
Now we have hooks. Lin Chan had some strong threads
for line. There is no bait though. We decorated the
hooks with pieces of tinfoil. We looked over the
side all evening. You can see fish. But they don't
pay any attention to our tinfoil lures. I would very
much like a drink.

2 J u l y.

Fourth day adrift. Hot as ever. The captain said
that he has an idea. Maybe we can get a little water.
To do it though we have to take the cover off the
engine. Alas, this is impossible. We have no tools.
Pablo-Pedro said that he would take it off. But he
wanted a reward for doing it. He said he should get
the first water. We didn't believe him. We all went
down to the engine room. Pablo-Pedro put his cheek
to the engine cover. He bit a nut. There was a creak.
We thought that he would lose all his teeth. But no,

the nut moved. Now it could be moved by hand. He
went on to the next. He undid sixteen nuts. The gun
and his teeth, those are his weapons. But the gun is
totally out of bullets. He also broke one tooth. He
deserves his reward. But will he get it? Toward evening
we saw a ship. A tanker headed west. We pulled off
our shirts, waved them, shouted. But the tanker didn't
slow down. Then we soaked the rags in what remained of the engine oil and set it on fire. There
was a column of smoke. Still the tanker didn't stop.
Probably they didn't notice us. And if they had noticed
us? They might have thought it was smoke from a
stack. And we were simply drunk and dancing on
deck. In the evening the captain and I tried to fish.
Nothing again. Pablo-Pedro suddenly came over to
us. He got the captain a clean towel. Got out a knife.
Then he slashed himself on the forearm, then again.
He cut a thin slice of skin and flesh from his arm
(before we could stop him). He baited my hook with
it. He hung his arm over the side so that the blood
trickled down into the water. Fish began to seethe
in the bloody cloud. It wasn't a minute before a
good-sized mackerel took my hook. Victory! Now
we had bait. We cut the fish into chunks and put it
on the hooks. By nightfall we had caught a dozen
fish, of different kinds. Everyone sang Pablo-Pedro's
praises over dinner. He sat at the head of the table,
his arm bandaged. He was very proud of himself.
For me, though, he is a puzzle. He has no respect
for his own body. I envy him. I fear him. I loathe
him, a little.

3 J u l y.

The captain's idea worked. But not completely.
Dew really did gather overnight on the engine cover
when we left it on deck. There was about a half cup
in a puddle in the bottom. But when Pablo-Pedro
tried to drink it up with a tube he immediately spat
it out. It tasted of oil. We have to wash and scrape
the cover all day. But now we have a lot of fish. We

fished all morning. I showed everyone how to make cuts on the fish's back and squeeze out the juice. The thirst is intense. People drank the juice without protest. Even the "sea orphan" drank a few spoonfuls. The captain ripped the telephone line out of the wall. This made a strong fishing line for the strongest of the hooks. We baited it with a flying fish. Soon we caught a dorado. This fish has a sharp, hook-shaped bone behind its gills. I have read that savages who had no iron used that as a fishhook. We tried tying the bone hook to a thread and soon we caught a pretty good mackerel. We have to fish all day. It is not easy to feed and water four people with nothing but fish. Four and a half, even. I am beginning to understand Eskimos.

Anton first met Wife-to-be #5 in the lawyer's waiting room. He remembered her because several times he found her looking at him sadly, above the magazine stand, the secretary's typewriter, looking only at him, almost at the point of shamelessness. When he went into the lawyer's office, he asked who that had been.

"It's a tough case," the lawyer waved his hand dismissively. "Her husband left her with two kids after ten years of marriage. Ran off with a girl from the bank, that he'd had an affair with for five years. A black girl, matter of fact. And now he's trying to take the house and the kids away. I keep telling her that she has to be real careful, that in these wild times even an adulterous husband can turn out to be a winner, if you give him something to latch on to. It just goes in one ear and out the other. All she really wants is that the settlement should have one point in it, a long answer from him in writing to the question 'why?'"

Still, that first meeting had been so fleeting that Anton soon forgot about her. His own divorce proceedings were taking all his strength. He was still in shock. He had proven wholly unprepared for the role of the one who is left. Oh, how he now understood the wives he had left! A wave of sympathy for them washed through his heart, leaving a painful salt trace, followed by a flood of guilt, and then a wave of anger at all those who leave others, which of course flowed into the wave of anger at Wife #4, who had had the gall to give him such a blow. Okay, he deserved it, okay, it was revenge. But still! After grappling with

Simpson, his lawyer would return frayed, debased, ready to capitulate on all points. Anton had to squeeze the last dregs of will from himself to impart them to him and send him back into battle.

He next saw the abandoned woman at the airport. She did not recognize him or else simply did not notice him in the crowd of arrivals. To be on the safe side he nodded to her as he went past. Something did strike him as odd about the way she stood, something about her glassy, glittery eyes. He turned about carefully and began to watch. She was staring at two middle-aged friends who were embracing in the middle of the entry. Brothers, maybe, from Athens, or Barcelona. Naples. Beirut. Tangiers. Tel-Aviv. Cairo. In any event that sort of passion, those piratical mustaches, that tenderness, that indifference to the convenience of other people, who were having to squeeze past them, could only have grown up along the shores of the Mediterranean.

She stared at them, hands locked on her chest, the way people stare at some beloved singer, who is dragging out the last note of a beloved aria. Ready to leap up, explode into mad applause, rush toward the stage with flowers. Anton really was expecting her to run over to them, squeeze into their embrace. She would be their sister, niece, daughter. But no, she just watched them and then went back to looking at the crowd. She was plainly paying no attention to the singles streaming past, met by no one. But then she saw a grandmother toward whom was rushing, arms flung wide, a five-year old grandson, and the woman once again clasped her hands on her bosom, froze.

Anton shrugged and went on. He drove away a momentary puzzlement, as if he were driving away a wasp, not touching him, trying not to stumble on the sting that was concealed within this puzzlement. A week later though he was in the same airport, at the same gate, now in the role of someone meeting. Awkward thirteen-year old Golda was coming towards him with a soldier's kit bag on her shoulder ("Okay, it's horrible! Okay, it's filthy, but nobody else has one like it!"). Her smile from beneath her gloomy curls was an unexpected, undeserved present. And as they walked, hugging each other, he suddenly stumbled again on the admiring look of the abandoned woman, who was standing in her accustomed spot, devoting to them alone the besotted joy of stranger's reunions. He was unprepared and did not shrug it off in time. He understood why she came to the airport and pity soaked into him, somewhere quite close to the long-inert berry of love, which might have been stored in a freezer.

That year Golda was absolutely unbearable. Her enchanting smiles would be replaced by derisive sneers as quickly as a traffic light changes. She refused to wash her hands, brush her teeth, make her bed, say 'please,' pick up her dishes, iron, answer the telephone politely, or visit the relatives. And better nobody should touch her, because then she might fall into bottomless depression. She was already going to the school psychiatrist, who suspected that the cause of all this was her parents' divorce. It was they who had dealt the girl this blow, so they should keep their mouths shut about it now. The psychiatrist also explained to her that with girls the process of adolescence frequently was quite painful. Science had proven that between thirteen and seventeen girls have to be disgusting, capricious, unpleasant, egotistical, and spoiling to fight. And she was prepared to use these golden years in a way that would give her what to remember in her dust-dull adulthood—like the one you are suffering through now, dad. And maybe she wouldn't stop when she was seventeen, either. It was the first time that Anton was happy when her vacation ended.

Once he was alone again, the first thing he did was to phone the lawyer and asked how things were going with the client whose husband had run out with the black cashier. "The same," the lawyer replied. Reluctantly he gave him her telephone number. He learned her name was Jill. He phoned, said who he was. He said that he had seen her a couple of times at the airport. And in the office of their lawyer. Did she remember him too? Really? He confessed that he was also going through a divorce right now. So they would have what to talk about. If she would agree to have dinner with him. And she did.

> 4 J u l y.
>
> I slept poorly because of pain in my finger. We are trying to determine where we are drifting to. We write down the time every day at which the sun reaches it zenith. Following my directions the captain rigged up something like a sextant. From a wooden ruler and a pot cover. There isn't much good in it though. We are continually rocked. It seems that wind and current are carrying us to the south. From time to time we escape the heat by swimming over the side. Today Lin Chan swam all of three meters away from the side. And then there was a sudden squall. It began to carry the Babylonia away from

her. So fast that Lin Chan couldn't catch us. I grabbed
hold of one end of a rope and swam toward her. We
had just stretched out and grabbed one another when
I ran out of rope. The captain was scarcely able to
haul us back to the ship. Now I demand that everybody who goes swimming tie himself with a rope.
In addition we have to watch constantly for sharks.
They are always about, but in the daytime they keep
their distance.

5 J u l y.

I was again tormented by insomnia last night. And
I heard from time to time how somebody was knocking
against the hull from the outside. It was only toward morning that I understood what it was. Flying
fish! In the daytime they see the ship and swim out
of its way, but at night they jump blindly out of the
water and bump into the side. Unfortunately none
of them have flown onto the deck. The sides are too
high. I told the captain about my discovery. We decided
to try something. We worked all day. The difficulty
is that the only tools we have are two knives, a
needle and thread, and Lin Chan's manicure set (the
pirates didn't get into their cabin, so all their stuff
was saved. Including the gun. Pablo-Pedro admitted that the gun and two clips had been handed to
him in Montreal by Mr. Kozulin.) What we rigged
up looked like a cross between a coffin and a canoe. The body is made of boards (the planks of the
decking were sacrificed to the cause), wrapped with
sheeting. We hung our contraption over the side.
We were left with no rope, so we are using electrical wires that we rip out of the walls. I have read
that birds at sea are a sign that land is nearby. There
are a fair number of birds about us, but there can
not be any land nearby, if the maps are to be believed. I can recognize frigate birds (broad wings
and a red stripe on the male's throat) and gannets
(white heads) but don't know the others. It would
be interesting to know where they spend the night.

They can't continue to sail about in the sky, can they? Or do they come down to rest on the water? Toward evening we saw another ship. It passed us two miles to the east. We jumped and waved our shirts for a half hour, but the sun was setting right behind us then. They could scarcely have noticed us, even if they had been looking for us. Now I recall how even I, when we were sailing the Babylonia on Lake Erie, never stopped when we saw motor-boats or sailboats still in the water. The people might have stopped for any number of reasons! You could scarcely begin sailing up to each of them and checking. We are no more prepared to encounter the victim of trouble than we are a visitor from another planet. We are also done in by the invention of the radio. A ship which sends no radio signals might as well not exist, so far as other ships are concerned. But hey, here we are! You can see us with a naked eye!

6 J u l y.

Hurray! Hurray! Hurray! A couple dozen flying fish have fallen into our coffin-canoe-trough over night. And our line made of electrical wire has caught a two-foot shark. The flesh isn't very tasty, but the liver is extremely useful. We were able to squeeze a good deal of juice from it. We are getting used to the taste. I am making everyone eat the fish heads as well, especially the eyes. They have vitamin C, to prevent scurvy. We have no way of knowing how long we are to drift about the ocean. We have to be prepared for the worst. We only have one small pot with a lid to cook with (it also was in Lin Chan's cabin). We make a fire of wood splinters under it, but soon we will run out of them. The Babylonia has proved to have very few wooden parts. Plastic, aluminum and glass everywhere. We cannot con-tinue to tear up the decking forever. Otherwise the first storm will swamp us and send us to the bot-tom. Little by little we are trying to train ourselves to eat fish raw. If you cut it into chunks and salt it, it is almost like sushi in a Japanese restaurant. Incidentally, for all the salt in the ocean salt here is also not so easy to get. We dunk the sheets in sea water and hang them up to dry. Then we shake the sheets over a clean table. That way we get a sprinkling, enough to use for a meal. The next day we have to do it all over again.

7 J u l y.

The ninth day adrift. We fished a big fishing net cork float out of the water. The captain made a fire from oily rags and threw the cork in there for a minute. After that we all crawled about the deck for an hour, writing SOS in big letters with the burnt cork. If a plane were to fly over low he might see the letters. Then we realized that we should have put the letters on the sides, not the deck. It was too late, the cork was used up. And we have no other paint. SOS! SOS! SOS!

"How you can shout, sweetheart," Jill repeated, admiring and charmed. "How you can shout!"

Then she sat in front of the mirror, pensively toying with her bare breast as if it were an orange, bouncing it on her palm and tried mistrustfully to peer out from the smooth glass an explanation or reason or cause for his unbecoming shrieks. Yes, of course she had heard, had read in books and seen in movies. Love is a terribly powerful thing. Love can overcome heart and mind. It can even overcome the natural disgust one has to the body of another person. Of course she had felt love; how else could she have had two children? But her husband had never lost self-control, had never gone into such an amusing ecstasy. She was befuddled, knocked off balance, shocked, flattered.

Yes, maybe her attitude toward all things fleshy was exaggerated caution. A Protestant family, a religious upbringing. The words "fleshy delights" were said over their table with the exact same intonation as the words "food poisoning." Probably that attitude had soaked into her, had entered her subconscious. She wasn't proud of it, though. She didn't want to infect her children with it. Quite the opposite, she wanted them to be free and knowing. She kept textbooks at home, showed her children pictures. Two years ago she had taken them to a nudist colony for a month. Even though her husband really didn't want to. She had insisted, however. That had been a wonderful month. And without delights of any sort. Her two boys were still friends with two girls they had met there. After all, in Japan men and women have been bathing together since time immemorial. And they are a very healthy nation. Still, she couldn't overcome her own taboos, try as she might. To go out on the beach undressed was as hard the last day as it had been the first. And she was someone who had gone to med school for a bit!

In general she didn't speak with much enthusiasm about her past, especially her childhood. If he were to ask a direct question, she would raise her eyes from the mirror to the ceiling for a minute, as if she were examining her clips of memories against the light, like film strips, which then she would show to him, except with obvious traces of the censor's scissors and bits blotted out here and there. Her parents? They had been teachers their entire lives. Where had they lived? They were always moving from city to city. No, not just in New Jersey, but in Pennsylvania too. One year, she remembered, they had lived in Ohio. No, they were dead already. Of course she knew where they were buried, but right now she couldn't recall the name of the place. There was a distant relative who lived there, she took care of the graves. No, they hadn't died the same day. Mamma first, then dad. Everybody knows that widowers don't live long, that solitude carries them off very quickly. They were buried side by side. Is it really so important what they died of? You don't have to be afraid, I don't suffer from anything hereditary.

He fit the picture together bit by bit. Not that it was so interesting. He just liked to wrestle with her hidden censor, to win and drag something of the truth out of her. She even kept her earlier profession in the dark, and then blurted it out by chance. More precisely, she betrayed herself, when he turned up limping, with a swollen ankle.

That was in the first months, when they were still going to enormous lengths to keep Husband #5.1 from finding anything out. Husband #5.1, who always looked straight ahead, who always went straight past people asking contributions for charity, who had gone off with his black cashier, he had said terrible things to her in the moment of the break. He said that life with her had been torture. That he had put up with her only because of the children. And that he was going to do everything he could so that the judge gave the kids to him.

The lawyer assured her that this was not just an idle threat. Husband

#5. I had connections in the world of judges. If only he could prove that she was psychologically unstable, that she was taking the children away from the normal real world (remember the month with the nudists!), that she was trampling all over their tender hearts, unfurling in curiosity, then the judge who was a pal might decide in his favor.

"This is crazy!" Jill swore, hugging Anton in the half light of the plywood cabin that they had taken on the shore of a small lake. "What we're doing is absolutely crazy. Sooner or later we're going to get caught. I've got butterflies in my stomach. I have a whole gut full of terrified butterflies."

The trips to the cabin had to be carried out with the precautions of secret agents. Her car couldn't be anywhere close by, no matter what. They would agree on a time and place, phoning from one pay phone to another ("Yes, he's capable of hiring a private detective to tap my line at home!") They would come to the parking lot of some big store (a different one every time) and she would put on dark glasses, walk slowly to his car, open the door slowly, crawl inside, and lay down on the back seat, where he had left her a pillow. The whole town was filled with people who knew her; someone might see her head in the car and would tell! They had to drive for about an hour, so that sometimes she even contrived to snatch a snooze, and later he would kiss the pillow marks from her face.

The day that he pulled up lame she simply blossomed. She caught him on the path to the cabin, took away the paper bag with groceries, ordered him to lean on her. She sat him on a chair, rolled up his pants. She made him put the swollen ankle in an ice bath. Her face glowed. Wiping his feet dry, putting on a tight bandage that she had made from her spy's scarf, she several times pressed her forehead to his knee.

There was no point in hiding her weakness further. She confessed. Yes, she adored succoring the ill. It made her quiver, made her faint. She had a nursing degree. And she had worked as a nurse for almost two years. That was her real calling. There was nothing else in life that she loved like that. But soon she found a character trait, a phobia which she simply could not overcome. She began to be afraid of a patient dying because of her. That is, she could do everything right, following the doctor's order point for point, checking it against the textbook just to be sure, and the fellow would have died nonetheless. Simply because he was too old or the disease had gone too far or the wound was too deep. This didn't happen too often, but the fear stifled her. The injustice of death destabilized her, threw her face-first against the wall. And there weren't any hospitals that treated only non-life-threatening diseases, the kind that no one died from.

She tried to attack the problem head on by going to work in an old people's home. There death was a normal end, the only exit, almost a release. No one could be at fault for death, and none of those remaining among the living grieved about them. The old men, wrapped in their parchment skins, sat quietly in their armchairs, obediently opening their mouths for the spoon, regarded relatives' presents with waxy eyes. They were like the passengers of a train pulling out of the station, who had already bidden farewell to everyone, who were departing for boundless distances, clutching one-way tickets in their hands. Sometimes the administrator of the home would let neophyte musicians earn a few bucks by giving concerts for the old people, whom they gathered into the dining room. The gay sounds of the accordion would bounce off their motionless faces. Unable to bear it, Jill would leave the hall.

All of the procedures, none complex, that she had to perform for the old people seemed nonsensical to her. The pleasant surprise of recovery had been removed from the process, and without that, nursing gave her no pleasure. However, to nurse living people after she had spent an entire year alongside the dead seemed even more awful to her. And then the coming of a second child left her no time for work, and she had to quit.

Now she had only her family to satisfy her passion for nursing. If she heard a cough or a sneeze anywhere in the depths of her home, she would rush to the sound like a paratrooper on red alert, grabbing the necessary syringes and tablets and gargles as she ran. The blisters left by poison ivy filled her with such martial fervor that the person with the blisters had to submit and meekly change the dressings with various lotions that she mixed herself following various books of necromancy. If the children should happen to be constipated, they endured it to the limit without admitting to it, because they knew their mother would never limit the remedy to a simple laxative. A callous on a heel or a finger was ripe with sessions of ultraviolet radiation. Friends never asked what to get her as a gift; they knew that any sort of medical handbook would bring sincere gratitude for a week.

Anton listened to her confession charmed and sympathetic, but still didn't get the main point, of why she was afraid that her patients would die. Sick people could be incredibly sly, knowing how to slip off to the other world no matter what medical barriers you put in their way. And anyway every hospital has insurance against accidents of that sort. This was a Great Wall of China that the Miserymaker could scarcely climb over, so it was a question of caulking up the chinks. That's what had to be done, first and foremost.

Tortured by this latest divorce, in those months he was feeling his way toward his great invention. Three large and identical misfortunes—and if you weren't going to be formal about it, you could call it four—had befallen his life. And in each of these situation he had proven to be powerless before the fangs of the Miserymaker. Half the marriages in the country end in divorce, and to date no one had invented a defense against a misfortune so common! It just couldn't be that there wasn't some workable scheme to be found in all this.

"How could you avoid cheating? Cheating avoided, how could you protect yourself against fictitious divorces, divorces just to get the insurance?" He beat his brains. And on the other hand, there was Jill's husband who always looked straight ahead and who had abandoned her for another woman; was he also to be rewarded financially for his treachery? Or Wife #4, who had abandoned him so nastily and insultingly, just disappearing with a shake of her straight shoulders? She'd get something for that too? And thus, step by step, kept at a boil by hatred for dishonest traitors, he drew closer and closer to a very simple thought, simple as a slide bolt. And he slid it open!

It was so simple, the simplicity of genius!

It wouldn't be the insurance company who would pay, but the one who left, or abandoned, or betrayed.

8 J u l y.

Pablo-Pedro's shouts woke me. He was overboard. But he didn't drown. He was holding with one hand to the gangplank, and was clutching the flipper of a big turtle in the other. I leaped into the water and grabbed the turtle by the other flipper. The captain threw us a wire. We struggled for a half hour, trying to tie the turtle's flippers. Finally we got it up on deck. She had scratched and bitten us so badly that we had no regret about killing it. We made a feast. There is nothing tastier than turtle meat. It turned out that she was also carrying eggs. They stick to your teeth. They are nothing but protein. Our shrinking organisms also need fat. I made a small discovery after the feast. Under the turtle's hind flippers I found two parasitical fish. Suckers, I think they are called. The female was under the left flipper, the male under the right. It was extremely difficult to pry their suckers loose. Just think, they spend their entire lives there. They eat, travel, reproduce, and their entire world consists of the rear armpit of a turtle. In the evening we saw a ship again. We waved at it with everything we had, but without much energy. Our hopes are fading. The ship didn't stop.

9 J u l y.

The captain is always inventing things. Today he started in the morning, taking the round glass from the instruments on the dashboard. They are slightly convex. He put them together, bound the edges with insulating tape, and poured water inside. That made a large magnifying glass. He fixed it above the little sauce pot with a fish in it, made a point of sunlight on the pot cover, and an hour later the fish inside was cooked! The cooking problem is solved. True, the water is constantly leaking out of the glasses, but we can always add more. At 2:30 in the afternoon we heard an engine. An airplane was flying over, fairly high up. But suddenly Lin Chan grabbed a knife and ran to the toilet. She ran out a minute later with the mirror she had ripped from the wall. She began to point the sun's reflection back into the sky. We laughed and clapped. Maybe the airplane noticed her signal. Who knows?

How suspiciously and cautiously the couples looked at Mister Sebich when they came to him in the first days after he put his ad in the papers. Many of them already had one or two divorces under their belts, and they knew the ropes. They didn't mess around with trifles, but went right to the heart of things.

"Who pays? How are you going to know whether people are getting divorced for real or just cheating you for the insurance? What, they pay each other? The ex-husband pays the ex-wife, or vice-versa? But what makes it different from regular alimony then? The money is put up in front? What do you mean?"

He would explain patiently. You pay insurance payments, every month, or every quarter. This is your money. If you want to separate peaceably, each of them gets back 50% of the accumulated money. But if one of the spouses says that he or she doesn't want a divorce, then he or she would get the whole 100%. The longer you live together, the more it's going to cost you to abandon your life's companion.

There were other schemes possible. You could each put in a large sum when you married. Or just one of you could. The money would stay there like a deposit, quietly gathering interest. Or you could also add insurance payments to it. But the main principle would stay the same, that in case of a divorce all the money would go to the one who was being left. Also to be taken into account: if—God forbid!—one of the two were to die, all the money would revert to the other. So for the same money that got you divorce insurance you also got a sort of life insurance.

How would the insurance firm of Sebich Inc. make money? Obvious—from dividends earned by the money entrusted to them. They wouldn't invest in risky speculative deals. No, the money would be invested in reliable government paper. And a part of the dividends would be applied to the antidivorce payments. "You can find exact figures and charts of the interest and payments in this brochure."

Naturally he hoped for success, waited for it. But he was not ready for the flood of clients, the tidal wave that he got. He had to hastily open two new offices in New Jersey and another one over the river, in New York. There was no more need to waste money on ads. News of the sensational new insurance flew by word of mouth, from house to house, from double bed to double bed. The newspaper men themselves besieged him with requests for interviews. He went on television, gave autographs. Anti-divorce insurance became a fashionable wedding gift. He had no time to juggle the millions that flowed into his hands.

In the rare moments of quiet and solitude—in the elevator, a traffic jam, in the shower—he was astonished to ponder the turnings of fate. Just six months ago he was so lonely and unhappy. An aging man burdened with alimony, abandoned by a beautiful wife, getting fat, rattling around in divorce proceedings. And now? Now he had fame, fortune, and Jill, admiringly silent Jill who asked only that occasionally he would let her swab some pimple or other with antiseptic or massage his neck or put a cold pack on a twisted knee. The Miserymaker was retreating on all fronts!

Naturally this complete triumph could not continue forever. In a few months his eternal enemy recovered from the surprise and began to marshal its forces, trying to counterattack here and there. The newspapers began to write of the dramas that were taking place in families because of the anti-divorce insurance. In one family the wife wanted to buy the insurance, but the husband considered it a waste of money, as well as a sign of insulting lack of trust, and in the end he got mad and left his wife. In another family it was the opposite; the wife got insulted at the low price her husband paid for insurance. "That's what value you put on our marriage? Idiot that I am, I had thought..." The columnists' jokes got more pointed. "Today a marriage has a price on it, so that you can boast just like you would over the make of car you drive. 'Just think, he bought himself a house for four hundred thousand, a Cadillac with silver trim for fifty, and then he couldn't get together ten grand for his marriage? Cheapskate! And how's the wife going to put up with it?'"

In general though these poisonous voices drowned in the admiring shouts of success. He had read that in Ancient Rome the triumphal chariot always had to be followed by one stentorian heckler. This was considered to be a vital bitter ingredient without which the triumph didn't have the full and proper taste. His detractors played the same role. Oh, those were the days!

Sebich Inc.'s victorious conquest of both banks of the Hudson lasted almost a year. At the end of this year Anton bumped against, or felt, or experienced something which he had lightly dismissed as impossible— a surfeit of success. The eight-figured size of his annual turnover left him cold. Food had no taste. His irises forgot how to contract under tv floodlights and the pain in his eyes wouldn't let him sleep. The richer his clients were, the more petty they seemed; the older they were, the more prone to lie. Repellent, suspicious, unloving people with no gratitude to fate. His desire to defend them against the savage Miserymaker withered day by day.

The doctor wrote him out a prescription from his pad—"Month's vacation. Absolute quiet." Then he forced Anton to sign it. "You don't want to mess around with nervous exhaustion!" Anton did as he was told. The work was going smoothly in his three offices, his staff was trained, the fear of divorce was thick in the air, driving human chains of people—like the streams of sinners in paintings of the Last Judgement—to him, people who thirsted for eternal commitment no matter what it cost.

Jill was in awe. Aunt Clarence happened to have an empty cabin in the mountains, she was always asking them to use it and spare her from always feeling the money was wasted. And she was agreeable to taking the kids too. "Aunt Clarence has a heart of gold. We could leave tomorrow, if you want."

The cabin turned out to be a one-story wooden fortress besieged by pines, oaks, and birds. There was a particular abundance of woodpeckers. They complained loudly, buzzing the new arrivals as they carried bags and bundles into the cabin, trying to sneak in through the open door. Jill waved them off in fright.

"They're trying to catch the butterflies in your tummy," Anton joked.

The furniture inside looked too nice and new, out of place in the cabin. There weren't any crippled chairs with crushed bottoms or legs askew, such as usually are put out to grass in summer homes. The sheets and towels in the linen closets were blinding white, pleasing to the touch with their faultless ironing. Only the water that came out of the faucets had some hint of abandonment; it was pinkish in color and bitter to the taste. Among the supplies they have brought to the cabin, however, was a plastic bottle of Spring Water, which was sufficient to make tea, brush teeth, and make coffee in the morning.

Nevertheless the next morning Anton decided to look at the water tank. He got a flashlight out of the trunk and went up into the attic. The flapping of wings was deafening. A flock of woodpeckers dashed away from him through an open window. One particularly insistent one attempted to fly back, hung for a second in the air, and then flung what he had had in his beak, before flying off.

Anton picked up the object, which had rolled over to the wall. It was an acorn.

He went over to the water tank. The wooden top had been pierced in a dozen places. He took the cover off, rolled up his sleeves, and began to fish around on the bottom. He brought up a handful of some sort of rubbish. He went to the light and opened his hand. Acorns. Half rotten, dissolving into bits, reddish, blackish. The woodpeckers fluttered about at the window with shrieks of alarm. Did this mean that even woodpeckers had an instinctive desire to insure themselves against the future? Anton was touched.

Cleaning the tank took better than an hour. He had to pour off the standing muck, dig out the accumulated reserves of the woodpeckers with a shovel, then use a pump to wash out the tank, then fill it with clean water. He took the box of rotting acorns into the forest, where he left it under a tree. The woodpeckers paid it no attention, but continued to fly about the house, cursing him. They behaved exactly like the stars of the most famous scary movie made by the most famous scary moviemaker of all times and peoples.

"Look at them," said Anton. "If it hadn't been for me, they wouldn't have had the slightest chance of recovering their treasure. It was just accumulation for the sake of accumulation. And do they thank me? They're exactly like people, exactly like people."

"You're an insurance agent, but you still don't get it," Jill said. "You destroyed their insurance office. They didn't need the acorns right now, they just needed to know that they were there."

12 J u l y.

A squall. A storm. Three days now. The ship shudders. Out of fish. Out of turtle. There is water. From the sky. Weak. Have to bail. We're swamped. No bucket. Just the engine cover. And the turtle shell. If this is it...Olga, I was happy. Three years with you. The mystery remains though. The Big Coach... I so love His exercises... But what for...

14 J u l y.

The storm ended. We lived. However we have almost nothing left. Everything was washed overboard or broken up or smashed. We freeze at night. The hull leaks all over and we have nothing to plug it with. We have to bail round the clock. The only good thing is that all the tossing turned up a case of cat food from somewhere. Probably stuck somewhere deep in the hold, and the pirates missed it. It's the Kitty's Breakfast sort. I read the contents label closely and found nothing that is harmful for people. I was the first to try it. It tastes like low-salt chopped liver mixed with clay. It's edible. Only Pablo-Pedro couldn't keep it down. He held his nose and dashed for the railing. Oh well, he'll get used to it. On the other hand the boat orphan ate it with pleasure. We have to be careful though. Two cans a day will last us for five days, and what then?

15 J u l y.

Vitamin deficiency and salt water are making us break out in sores that won't heal. It hurts too much to lie down or sit. The cold at night is torturous. We released Lin Chan from bailing and she spent the whole day sewing us warm vests. She gutted all the soft couches in the crew's quarters and put all the vinyl between two pieces of cloth, which makes a fairly warm pelt, to cover the front and back. Our arms and legs still freeze, though. All the fish have disappeared. Maybe because of the cold? Are we drifting to the Arctic Ocean? Just the unreachable birds circle over our heads. It is the first time in my life that I am thinking of firearms without disgust.

16 J u l y.

We are running out of cat food. They gave us a few extra days to live. To eat them though you have to drink constantly. We are quickly running out of the water that we were able to collect during the storm. We have to catch some fish. But what with? Even Pablo-Pedro couldn't cut a strip off himself now. His first wound still hasn't healed. Our skins are covered in cracks and sores. He proposed cutting one finger off the boat orphan, but Lin Chan got the pistol and made him stop. It doesn't matter anyway, since there seem to be no fish. Or ships. We are in some sort of dead zone. As ever, we are drifting east.

17 J u l y.

We are all breaking out in some strange shudders. We will suddenly begin to lick our own shoulders or hands or knees. Or else we will dig our nails into the deck. Or slap at shadows. Or scratch back and sides against corners. And today I saw the captain drop to all fours and begin to stalk a gannet that had perched on the Babylonia's prow. I am afraid that this is all something to do with Kitty's Breakfast. Pablo-Pedro tried to shoot the gannet, but he missed. We only have one bullet left.

That first day in the mountains Anton and Jill decided to give the woodpeckers time to settle down. They closed all the windows and went for a walk. In the dense forest some shrub clung to them with its thorns, not cruelly, but insistently, like a beggar who doesn't want money, but that you should listen to him. Little green triangles of some plant's wandering seeds clung to their clothes.

They came out on the banks of a stream. Every stone was wearing a gurgling lace collar. Anton had brought a rod with him, that he had found in the shed. They waded into the stream, heading upstream. The water pushed against their rubber boots, pushing their feet backwards with every step. The hook hidden in the gay bit of fluff danced along the waves somewhere far behind them. The little green triangles pulled off in the water like sleepy fare beaters who had forgotten their station stops. The branches hung right down to their faces, showing their first yellow leaves.

Jill exclaimed in surprise and dropped the fishing pole. The rod dove once, twice, and swam away, but quickly stuck on some rocks. Anton chased it down, picked it out of the water and began to reel in line. The fish was solidly hooked. It leapt about thirty feet away. It was huge. The rod bent in a U. Anton made for the shore, Jill shrieking somewhere behind him. The taut line jerked left and right like a beam from a lighthouse. At the last moment his inexperienced hands jerked the line so hard that the battle-swollen trout leapt from the water, described a glittering arc, and disappeared into the pines along the bank.

"Let's let him go, please let's let him go," Jill begged, jumping through the pines.

"What are you talking about?" Anton waved her away. "You can't throw trout like these back, didn't you know that? Once you've touched them, they're going to die anyway."

Carefully he dug into the bushes, put the flopping fish onto the grass, and fell on his knees alongside, covering the fish with his hands while he took the hook out. Now out of the stream, the fish didn't seem nearly so big and strong. Probably under a pound. And still Anton's heart hammered.

It seemed they had broken the law. Fishing in the lakes and streams there required the purchase of a license. And trout apparently had to be paid for separately, special stamps had to be purchased. They were criminals twice over, runaways from their families, from lawyers, now running amok in the forest. He wasn't afraid though. The world about them was so beautifully unpopulated, absolutely full of unpeopled magic life. Creeks bubbled, birds flitted, seeds ripened and dispersed, caterpillars turned into butterflies, grubs into dragonflies. Pines tossed, the grass rustled, and mountains floated by against a backdrop of shining clouds.

The watershed of "now" was shot through with thousands of trembling rays which stretched from yesterday into tomorrow, which filled the moment with a pulsating, reverberating radiance. What nonsense it was to carry on about our solitude inside this radiant point! Wasn't it obvious that the entire world trembled within that moment along with us, and the woodpeckers who had stored away acorns in a water tank they couldn't get into were precisely as brave and selfless battling their own Miserymaker as was he with his, the cowboy standing in front of the mirror of the Past, shooting into the thicket of the Future. Each of the million deaths which occurred each minute round the globe, contemptuously indifferent to justice, rang not with silence, but with an alarming, disturbing note, resounding in time with the dying flops of the forbidden fish which he had stuffed into the pocket of his jacket.

He got to his feet and went toward Jill. For the first time he could not feel the greed berry of love in his throat; for the first time it was not necessary to him. They were alone. They were accomplices in every-thing, everything. The laws of men, the prejudices of men, the ills of men, the costly fears of men, the heat of the cities, the crush of the airports, the silence of the hospitals, the clatter of the railroad cars, the gnawing "musts" of all species and shades, all this seemed harmlessly distant, in slumber glades, insignificant beyond many mountains.

He took another step, went around her from behind, took her arm. He stuck his neck, deer-like, ahead, and put his chin on her shoulder. He pressed his cheek to her messed-up hair and spoke slowly, precisely, "I want... I propose... I very much ask you to become my wife..."

She froze for an eternity, staring straight ahead of herself at a branch, bobbing in the water. Then she sighed deeply and replied, enunciating just as precisely, "I know... I will be... I very much want to be your wife.. But I have to ask... It's not a condition, but... I have to have two things..."

"Anything..."

"No, wait a minute. The first is easy, but still... Don't get mad... Can I find out... Will you tell me precisely which number I am in the line?"

"Fifth. You will be my fifth and—swear to God—last wife."

"The second condition is harder."

"I'm up to it."

"You can't ever, ever... I know that this is awfully difficult for a man, almost impossible even... but if you want us to be together..."

She raised her hand and clutched a fistful of pine needles tightly.

"...you can't ever demand... or look like you want... or make it seem like you need me... *to be or even look like I'm happy.* Because that's the one thing that I absolutely don't know how to do."

18 J u l y.

We are out of cat food, out of drinking water. Yet the hold is constantly filling with water. We bail with our last ounce of strength. Pablo-Pedro has fainted. He was the thinnest of us, and his energy reserves were exhausted first. I took him to the cabin. He began to babble in Spanish. He was smiling, though. Then he came to. He grabbed me by the beard I haven't been able to shave. Then he said in English, with some kind of bitter satisfaction, "See, now do you see that we're absolutely equal to laughter and to death?"

19 J u l y.

Lin Chan has also fainted. She was bailing with the pot. Now we bail in twos. The captain and I. I bail with the turtle shell, hand it up to him. The captain carries it to the side and throws it over. Then we trade places. We sleep about three hours in the night. While we do the water in the hold rises. We can't hold out very long. Our Intensive Training is coming to an end. Pablo-Pedro is right. We are all the same before the Big Coach. Our entire overgrown, puny, hungry, ragged earthly team. But what's the goal? What was His goal? What was the competition to which we were to be sent? And who were we to play against?

20 J u l y.

The Babylonia is beginning to toss. Apparently

another storm is moving in. We can't keep up bailing. The water is already up to our knees. Olga, my love, if only that day when we first... But still, how good... I thank fate for one thing, that I have not had to survive the death of anyone I love...

Article

by a Correspondent of *Insight* Magazine
Broadcast in Place of the Regular Saturday Program
on Mrs. Darcey's Radio Station

I first had to fly from New York to Lisbon, and from there to a little island about two hundred miles to the northwest.

The island has to be described separately. At one time the newspapers wrote a bit about it, but just as a curiosity. Now, however, this curiosity is being turned into what amounts to a military base.

The island arose not long ago. You won't find it on maps more than three years old. Apparently there was an explosion of an underwater volcano which threw up to the surface of the ocean a pile of stones about as big as the back of a whale. At high tide this little bit of dry land all but disappeared. It was first noticed by an English seiner which was sailing nearby. The instincts of his colonial ancestors immediately awoke in the captain, and he hurriedly raised the Union Jack in the middle of the sterile lump. This noble and natural act immediately made him a target for Fleet Street. "At last we shall have a colony which won't be demanding independence!" they wrote. "The Royal Navy sets up a volleyball court in the middle of the ocean!" "How many aircraft carriers must we build in order to defend this new possession of the British crown?"

Soon though the jokes were silenced. London also turned up some clever heads, as well as some deep purses quick to rise at the scent of quick profits. Toward this crumb of an island streamed convoys of heavily laden ships. Enormous barges towed pressed garbage from London, Plymouth, Liverpool. Behind them came other barges full of sand. A layer of garbage, a layer of sand, another layer of garbage, another of sand, and the island grew before one's very eyes. Inside a year they were raising the first houses on it, as well as a bar, a lighthouse, a harbor, customs offices and an airstrip. Two years later there was a decent-sized port, a police post, a church, and a hospital. Shipping for the sand and building materials was partly paid for by payments for accepting the trash from big cities. The major income though for the Trashfromhome Company came from fishing concerns. This was because the appearance of new British territory in the middle of the ocean gave English fishermen thousands of extra square miles where they had the primary right to fish.

Such is the history of the new-born clump of earth on which our twenty-seat Douglas landed after an hour in the air. All twenty seats were occupied by correspondents from various countries, all anxious to get a glimpse of the famous Babylonia, which had been towed here two days previously by an English rocket launcher. Still, I was the only one whom Mr. Kozulin—owner of the Pirgoroy firm and my old friend, with whom I spoke by phone before leaving New York—asked be given permission to visit the rescued travellers in the hospital.

Thus it was I came to sit alongside the bed of a very thin bearded man, a melancholy look in his red and irritated eyes. This is Mr. Sebich, captain of the Babylonia. Sun, salt, and vitamin deficiency have left bleeding sores on his face. He is forbidden to shave for now. He is also forbidden solid food, given only juices and bouillon. I feel myself a child next to him. He has been there, on the other side. He knows something which we, the living, are not given to know.

There are newspaper clippings on the table next to his bed. He has already read everything which the papers have written about the Babylonia's disappearance at sea. They spoke of the way radio contact was lost, and of the international efforts to search for the boat. Yet the area was too large and so far from land that search planes couldn't reach them. Then a shark was caught which had a tin of Kitty's Breakfast in its gut, after which the search was essentially called off. Everyone decided that the boat had sunk.

I had no wish to torment the captain with my questions. The doctors only permitted me a half hour. The reader will already have an idea of what the crew has had to go through from the excerpts of the ship's log to which this article is appended. So I simply asked the captain to speak of the final day, when they were attacked by the British cruiser.

"We were lucky that day," the captain said. "The Babylonia was already listing so low in the water that some flying fish had made it onto the deck during the night. Ronald and I gathered them up, pressed them for their juice. We gave the others drinks, lying in their cabin, and then ate ourselves. Lin Chan was even able to come up top. We sat her down on the stern, put a rod in her hand, baited the hook. Then we went down in the hold.

We knew that the Babylonia wouldn't keep afloat for more than two or three days. We had to do something. We decided to disconnect the empty fuel tank and use it as a float. We might attach some sort of life raft to it.

Naturally we didn't have the strength to drag the tank upstairs. The idea was to tear apart the deck over it, and then the water would lift it when the Babylonia began to go under. We tried not to think about what would happen after that.

Luckily the nuts weren't as tight as those on the engine cover and we were able to undo them without using our teeth. We were working on the last one below decks when we heard Lin Chan shouting. She had caught a decent fish, but didn't have the strength to pull it out of the water. We went up top to help her, and then there was a terrible blow.

It was as though the deck had been knocked from beneath our feet. We fell on top of one another. My first thought was that the ship had struck some sea monster, or perhaps a submarine. Because there was something plainly metallic about the sound of the blow. I crawled to the edge of the deck, bent over the railing. And then I noticed the rocket. It was still smoking, about five feet of it sticking out of the ship. The rest was inside. The hole was above the water line. Apparently the rocket had struck the engine head on. To this minute I still don't understand how it was we weren't blown to smithereens."

I agreed with Mr. Sebich that that was simply unbelievable. Later that same evening, however, I was able to learn from a reliable source (hush-hush! we are speaking here of top-secret things!) that the rocket was a test version of the very latest model, which has no warhead, but has a special speed dampener. A few seconds before meeting its target a braking motor cuts in, reducing the hellish machine's speed to that of a trolley bus. The testers had to get the rocket back in one piece in order to get the information from the machinery, which is what saved the Babylonia.

"Pretty soon two jet fighters flew over us," Mr. Sebich went on. "They circled, buzzed us, and left. About a half hour later we saw a ship, the destroyer. It came straight at us. We couldn't believe how lucky we were. So many ships had gone by without paying us any attention!

"But the destroyer came towards us. Soon it was a few hundred yards off. A lifeboat was put out. We waved. We didn't have the strength to jump. Lin Chan cried. Ronald says that I had tears in my eyes too. It's quite possible. Yet I think they dried quite quickly as soon as I heard what the officer on the motorboat was saying.

"'You are in illegal possession of property belonging to Her Majesty's Navy. We demand its immediate return!'

"Can you imagine it? I almost fell overboard.

"'We are in possession? You almost sent us to the bottom with your damned rocket!'

"'What is the port of registry for your vessel? How did you enter a military training zone? All countries were warned that this sector would be closed to ship traffic for four days.'

"'We are sailors who have suffered misfortune. We have had no contact with the world for more than four weeks.'

"'I must warn you that the object in your possession is extremely top secret. If I saw anyone in your party attempting to draw it or photograph it, the consequences could be most serious for you.'

"'I repeat, we have had trouble. We have no water, no food, no fuel. There are sick people on board. We need help immediately.'"

Eventually Mr. Sebich was able to convince the lieutenant of the seriousness of the situation. The lieutenant said that he had to contact the commander of the ship. However according to the conditions of the exercises they had to preserve complete radio silence. For that reason he would have to go back and report in person.

And so, while the launch was returning to the destroyer, Mr. Sebich did something for which he may be proud to the end of his days. This was one of those acts which later you tell you grandsons around the fireplace. To have kept his head about him in that sort of situation! I am in awe of this man. Because he ordered his mate to bring him all the electrical wire they could find. They hurriedly took them below and very tightly tied the head of the rocket to the motor. Fortunately the rocket had a number of convenient flanges to which wire could be attached.

How right they were to have done this, and how well they had sized up the psychology of people who are involved in top secret military exercises!

For when the lieutenant came back he was distraught to announce that they were unable to interrupt their crucial mission to save the Babylonia. They equally could not take them aboard their ship, because the ship was stuffed with secrets which no one was allowed to see. True, they had brought a launch full of food, medicine, and provisions, as well as cans of fuel. They also threw a hose into the hold and in a few minutes had pumped out all the water that had accumulated there. That however was all that they could do to help. They would radio to shore about the Babylonia just as soon as they were allowed to break radio silence.

They attached a cable to the rockets tail. They pulled. The rocket was solidly stuck. The Babylonia moved slowly toward the launch. Mr. Sebich quickly opened the boxes they had been given. He didn't touch the packets of cookies, the tins of orange juice. What self-restraint! He was looking for a wrench, pliers, a chain. And he found them. The British repair kit proved to have a full set of tools, nuts, and bolts. The captain and mate once again went into the hold and fastened down the head of the rocket as tightly as they possibly could.

"Then they passed over a tow line onto the cruiser," Mr. Sebich went on, "and pulled as hard as they could. But we had tied that rocket down like our lives depended on it, and it was stuck like glue. Then the lieutenant shouted that he would have to send his sailors across the Babylonia in order to free the secret object. He never even used the word 'rocket'. I said that I forbid anyone to come on board. I said that it would lead to conflict between the US and Great Britain if anyone did. I said that since they didn't want to help us, we would defend our territory, weapons in hand. I showed them our pistol (and they didn't know that we were out of cartridges).

"The lieutenant told me to stop playing the fool. The launch came closer. And of course they would have fished their rocket free and then abandoned us in the middle of the ocean, had it not been for Lin Chan."

Five thousand years of Chinese civilization mean something, after all. What did she do? She went to the railing and showed the lieutenant a chocolate bar wrapper from chocolate in the relief packages. "This is paper," she said. "There's a picture on it. I drew it. The whole rocket, top to bottom. All the dimensions are there. Where the lights and lenses are. How high it flies above sea level. I could make good money by selling it to either Moscow or Peking. Now watch what I'm doing. This is a plastic bag. I am rolling the paper into a little tube. I put the tube in the packet, and..." What a girl! She put the packet in her mouth, opened a tin of orange juice, and drank it all down. "Now, she said, you can abandon us in the middle of the ocean. We'll see who pays the most for the secrets in my tummy."

I begged Mr. Sebich, begged the doctors to arrange even a short visit with this remarkable woman. But she won't leave the child they have dubbed "sea orphan" for even a minute. After her stratagem, of course, the English had no choice but to tow the Babylonia to the nearest port. The closest proved to be Trash Island. It was only here that Lin Chan was taken to the hospital and the secret package was removed. Was there anything on the paper? I don't know. A question on the matter has been raised in the English parliament.

The main thing though is that the heroic quartet was saved, that all of them will recover, while the Babylonia is being hastily repaired in the dry dock at Trash Island. Can it really be that they have decided to go on with their sea journey after all that they had to survive? Who knows. In any event it is clear to all that the team which Mr. Kozulin has assembled has justified even the most audacious of his expectations.

11. TRASH ISLAND

THE SEA BREEZE
ruffled the fringe on the deck chairs, gliding gently over the thin crust
on the healing sores. Wet towels ballooned on the bars of the balcony
rail. The smoothly groomed waves rolled onto the empty beach below.
There were no tourists on the island, no old people and no children. In
fact, there was nobody with time on his hands. When the four rescued
sailors went out in the morning to swim, sometimes they felt as though
they were back in the midst of the indifferent water, forgotten forever,
abandoned to the fish and birds like some sort of soft-shelled mollusk
or dry-land jellyfish. Slugs.

But then they would go back and dance a bit in the hot shower that
spurted from the hospital wall, washing off salt and sand, gulping down
the tight spray. And the first gulp of morning coffee would crawl close
past the heart, and the wondrous mixture of honey and milk would
stroke the tongue, and the piece of toasted white bread seemed like a
temptation which the god of civilization would use each morning
without fail to hook them, and then release them generously to the white
holding tank of their hospital room.

They relished the inactivity. They read newspapers, amazed that
sometimes there were stories not about them. They waited for Admiral
Kozulin to fly in.

Anton healed more slowly than the others. His muscles behaved like
Hindus who for ages had been taught to believe in the power of quiet
resistance. "Why? For what reason did you feel it necessary to reach for
that book?" his right hand would say. "What could you find to read in

209

it that's new to you? It couldn't be anything superior to just lying here and relishing the softness of the clean sheets, could it? And why is it I who must always do these things? The left hand is a lot closer, after all. After I lifted that turtle shell full of water a million times or so, don't I deserve some rest?"

It was particularly difficult to cope with the muscles in his face. These seemed to have stiffened permanently. He could find no arguments which would wipe the smile of mindless bliss from his lips. Ronald hinted that perhaps he would need special medical attention, but neither the staff of the little hospital or of Trash Island itself had a single psychiatrist.

He constantly sensed a pleasant chill in his chest, an unknown emptiness. Distantly this recalled happy moments from his school years, when the bell had already rung, but the teacher had not yet appeared. Was the teacher late? Or perhaps the teacher was ill? Would the lesson be canceled? And what should he do with this sudden gift of freedom?

Apparently this newly empty place had once been filled by the golden cockerel of fairy tales, who for four solid weeks had roused him continuously to do battle with the many faces of death, from the waves, from the wind, from the east, from the west, from above, from below. And now this cockerel, this wing-waving imperious instructor, had either fallen into a profound sleep or had simply disappeared forever. Still, the pleasant chilliness which was left in that empty spot also concealed the terror of unwanted quiet. He wanted his instructions from the golden instructor or from something that had taken his place, that would send him out each morning as before. For he had almost forgotten why they had been at sea, where they were going and for how long.

His thoughts might wander only in the past; the future was kept away now by an impenetrable dike. On the other side of the dike everything was fluid, alarming, marked by the secret trails of the Miserymaker. He had no wish to go that way. In the past he could slither endlessly through the familiar inlets, rivers, lakes, and ponds. Time and again he found himself returning to the safe harbor called Wife #5. How rapturous she would be to see him now. How she would have rushed to his side to nurse him, to care for him and save him. How cruel could fate be, to give her two husbands and four children, all of them with iron health. True, the children of the first marriage could not be called entirely healthy, but their illness was of a sort which could give her no pleasure in the curing.

Say what you will, it was still dishonest of Wife #5 not even to try to warn Anton. They came back from their week-long honeymoon, unpacked their suitcases, wandered about the house a bit (which Husband #5.1 had not been able to take away from her!), raised the blinds, bumping into each other on the stairs and in the halls, kissing as they passed, then going onward with the chores. Aunt Clarence was to return the children the next day.

Something in Wife #5's preparations struck Anton as odd. Why did all the doors and drawers of the breakfront have to be locked? The lamps all be screwed down? The rug nailed to the floor? With his own eyes and ears Anton had heard the chubby weatherman on the TV forecast that there were no storms or tornados to be found in their region. Was this an earthquake she was getting ready for?

"I know what I'm doing," Wife #5 said sadly and mysteriously. "Trust me."

He understand everything within five minutes. Between the taxi that brought them and the mother who came out on the porch with extended arms there could not have been more than thirty feet of smooth lawn, but even so the children didn't make it across.

Seven-year old Son #5.02 (Anton had decided to denote his stepsons and stepdaughters with an initial zero) jumped from the right door of the taxi and began to move his legs in a blur, without waiting for his tennis shoes to hit hard ground. He fell, of course. This gave nine-year old Son #5.01 time to leap out of the left door (forcing the bread truck going past to steer into the bushes on the other side of the road), run around the taxi, do a bongo-drum on the trunk, and make for the finish line unopposed. But who could have the sporting discipline to run past his brother on the ground without shoving his face back into the grass? All the younger brother needed was that second; he grabbed his older brother's ankle and bit him.

They both tumbled to the grass.

Their mother ran over to separate them.

However the two of them suddenly took off on hands and knees after the cat on the neighbor's lawn. Sensing trouble, the cat began to yowl. The brothers dashed at her still on all fours, barking crazily. The cat became as light as a ballerina and flew into the near-by magnolia, her claws scarcely touching the tree's bark. It was only there, under someone else's tree, with all the barking and yowling, that Wife #5 was able to grab her sons, kiss them, and lead them into the house, past the stunned Anton.

"It's called attention deficit disorder or hyperactivity," she explained two hours later, when the exhausted children had collapsed in sleep among the things scattered about the floor. One was using a wind-up toy car for a pillow, the other, two gilded slabs of the Encyclopedia Britannica. "It's quite common now. One out of ten children in the country has it. The broken cups and broken noses, that's nothing. The main problem is that it's hard for them to concentrate on anything for very long. They have trouble in school. They are always making noise in class, interfering with the others. Last year the principal of the school said that he wouldn't let them come to school anymore if I didn't start giving them Ritalin. I think that's too strong a medicine though, it makes the kids appear to have been carved out of wood. One lady I know told me that Ritalin just about drove her seven-year old to suicide. Yes, it's true, he ate almost an entire box of salt with a spoon. He could have made his own insides into jerky. In the hospital they had to flush his stomach for a whole hour."

Hyperactivity had to be treated with diet, not with medicine. That's what Wife #5 thought. All these artificial ingredients in food, these new compounds and dyes and fragrances and moisteners and acidifiers, that was what was driving the kids mad, turning them into little animals. Every time that Son #5.01 broke a flower pot with his head, immediately after the bandaging and binding he was subjected to a detailed interrogation: what did you have for breakfast? What did they give you for lunch at school? You didn't go in the refrigerator without permission did you? You had better tell us, so that we'll know what not to buy. Pickles, chocolate, hot dogs, sweetened pineapple—there was always a culprit, which was immediately put on the blacklist of suspected or condemned foods, to be barred entrance to their house.

Anton awaited the birth of Daughter #5.3 with alarm. They knew already—O miracle of medical prophecy!—that it would be a girl, and consulted in advance about ways to defend her from her uncontrollable brothers. Her crib would be bolted to the floor, of course, but should they also add a locked grid on top, so that the girl couldn't be removed to play any games without permission? Two years before the younger child had asked his mother as she was watering the flowers why she was doing it. "So they grow up really big," she answered, and two days later they found him watering the television, his bicycle, and his toy soldiers. Wouldn't his mania for watering return when he saw his itty-bitty sister? And what would become of their most recent passion, for coloring and painting? They were not just using the paints and chalks which had been bought for them, but were also using their mother's make-up. Where was the guarantee that one fine day they wouldn't get hold of the baby and paint her cheeks, lips, lashes?

To their parents' astonishment, all these worries proved to be groundless. While with their sister the boys became blessedly quiet. To forbid them to hold her became a punishment which they feared more than any other. They reminded their mother when it was time to feed her, demanded they be told what had been said after each trip to the pediatrician, fought about whose turn it was to push the carriage, change the diapers, weigh her, give her a bath. The fights stopped only with the arrival of Daughter #5.4. Each now had a sister, and the house was thick with the balm of mutual understanding, assistance, patience, of some kind of inexhaustible blessing which only families in advertisements could enjoy, after they had purchased the correct refrigerator.

What a happy year that was! And what a successful year too!

The lawyer Simpson had disappeared into silence, having either sucked his fill or having found other victims to torment. Wife #4 had left for Europe and wasn't besieging him any more. People still streamed into his three offices to insure against divorce, policies which no one else could offer them. The unwinking Miserymaker had apparently been driven back deep into his debris, frightened by the avalanche of Anton's good fortune, disheartened forever. And Anton would drive along the flowerbed-lined streets of the little towns, each flowing unnoticed into the other, passing the flattering glass windows chock full of cakes and watches and swimming suits and faraway islands (just a plane flight away!) and wine glasses and valuables and rugs, past the sturdy one-story brick banks (built no doubt by the third of the Little Pigs) where his money was growing, flowing, clanking and clanging, past the sweet old ladies in their gray curls and orange vests, who were helping school children across the streets, past the aromatic restaurants with food of all peoples and places, listening to the sound of a Schubert sonata on his car radio, interrupted by stories of faraway fires, floods, and wars. He drove and thought how if the seekers of the Promised Lands of all times were to have wandered here today, to the banks of the great Hudson river, they would no doubt have frozen in awe, understanding that there was no need to go further, for they had found what they sought.

He was a little bit saddened that Wife #5, who spent her days fighting through the snagging "musts" (the number of which had multiplied several times with the arrival of the new children) was not able wholly to share his mood of joyous exultation. True, she had warned him, even before the wedding, and as he had promised, he honestly tried to pay no attention to her ever-melancholy preoccupation, her unexpected tricks (what had set off that two-week blindness business, for example?), but in the depths of his soul he hoped that he would eventually win and she would tell him, "Yes, today, right now, maybe just for a minute, but it's happened—I am absolutely and uncaringly happy." For the time being it was enough that she lived only for him, the house, the children, that she was so obedient to his advice, so full of respect for his victories, so dependent upon him in everything, and that she was unafraid of that dependency.

No, he had not forgotten about the lurking Miserymaker, but he had let his guard down a little. He had failed to realize that the monster would also grow wiser with the years, that his attacks would become more subtle and his moves more calculated. A checkbook accidentally left at home—who could have imagined anything bad or dangerous in so inconsequential an act? And of course Anton had to come home at an unusual time, in the middle of the workday. And Wife #5 convinced him to stay for lunch and went off to fix it. And after he found the checkbook on the night table he sat on the bed and ran through the bills he had to pay right away. And when the telephone rang he couldn't immediately tear himself away from his calculations. And as he reached for the telephone a bit of his brain even knew that there was no need, that Wife #5 had already picked it up in the kitchen. But he didn't stop and so was in time to hear a man's voice say three words: "Just one night." The voice though was so full of earnest prayer that he understood everything in a flash.

He suddenly recalled scores of little confusions, insignificant misunderstandings, flimsy explanations, which settled onto these three words and glowed like a bit of highlighted text on a computer screen. The sudden absences and the constant melancholy and the unsigned postcards that were tossed into the fireplace and the mysterious Aunt Clarence, whom he had only seen once, in a restaurant, and who for some reason never invited her niece and the niece's husband to visit her, and who even though she was poor had a castle in the mountains.

Wife #5 met him in the kitchen with a worried look—had he heard?—and now he even understood that look, and her distraction, and the bacon burning on the frying pan. He waited and was not surprised when she announced that Saturday she was going to have to go visit

Aunt Clarence, who was sick, but that she would be back the same day, for sure.

The three words which the Miserymaker had selected for him were as precise as the combination for the lock of a safe, the heavy door of which swung open to reveal crumpled in the darkness that simple truth which so many millions of other husbands had discovered but which each time came as an incredible surprise—she had someone else.

Kozulin appeared at the door of the hospital room laden with presents like Santa Claus. Ronald got a scuba outfit. Lin Chan got a gold alarm clock. Pablo-Pedro, a portable radio. Anton, a camera with a mini-computer that did all the settings for the idiot snapper. Someone sent from the restaurant brought a bottle of champagne, a basket of fruits, and a plate of shrimps. Kozulin went up to each honoree and silently embraced them. He moved his chiselled profile up and down, showing them that he was absolutely speechless. The bubbles rushed to the surface of the glasses like the souls of drowning people making for salvation.

"For courage," Kozulin raised his glass. "For endurance, faithfulness, carrying on. For success. For your faithfulness one to the other. For you, my friends."

"And for Kitty's Breakfast," Ronald added.

Kozulin listened to their stories with tears in his eyes. He wanted to know all the details. He banged himself on the head with his fist when he learned that the Babylonia had had no spare radio (as if the pirates wouldn't have carried that off too). He laughed when he heard the story of how Lin Chan had tried to get the attention of the jet liner by bouncing the sun off a mirror. Then he said, "My friends! You have gone through hell. You were on the border between life and death. You deserve a rest. However, I can't drop my plans. There are circumstances which forbid me from putting my plans off. So I have to find out, do you have the strength and desire to continue your trip? Yesterday the Babylonia was put into dry dock in Lisbon, and repairs have already begun. Suppliers are falling all over themselves to offer us new instruments, motors, sails, lifeboats, all kinds of devices. And all with either huge discounts or even free, just for the right to mention in their ads that their product is on board the famous Babylonia. As the Russian saying has it, "Bad luck is good luck's best friend." They've promised me they'll finish the repairs in a week. Your bodies should heal by then too. But what about your souls?"

Kozulin took the binoculars from the table and began to focus on each of them in turn.

"I am prepared to double your pay for the rest of the voyage. I am ready to hear and possibly to grant any desires. I will not be at all angry if you tell me you've had enough. If you do though, then I've got to get a new crew. And I'm not at all sure that I'll be able to find so faithful and proven a crew. I'd be very glad if you'd agree to go on. Okay, so who should we start with? Ronald, how about you?"

Ronald picked at a callous on his finger, rubbed at a suspicious spot on his arm. He threw his head back on the chaise longue, smiled at the ceiling. He froze, as if listening to the bubbling music of the juices of life in his own body, and then began to count on his fingers, "Two, three, four...I will still need four days, and then I'll be fine. You can count on me. I mean, Golda is still a prisoner, right? So there's nothing to say. I might only add that during the weeks we were on her I fell in love with the Babylonia for good. But I'm afraid that maybe you'll forget your promise to double my pay."

Kozulin went over to him, took his hand in both of his and shook it with feeling. "Thank you. I won't forget this, I won't. Starting today. I'll phone the bookkeeper myself. Who's next? Lin Chan? What do you say?"

"I'll do whatever Pablo-Pedro does. I have to stay with him. To the end of the period. Then I will get my citizenship. And my freedom. But there's the sea orphan too. I can't leave him. He's unique. He recognizes me and laughs. What should he be called? Could I adopt him? Let him be called Babylonian, okay?"

"He's a charming lad. We'll look out for him. We'll put him in the best care until you come back, and we'll get all the papers ready. So that means it depends on Pablo-Pedro. Our radioman, our shooter. Our seagoing William Tell. What do you say, you unfettered runaway?"

Pablo-Pedro tossed a handful of shrimp into his mouth, poured himself more champagne. He was aglow with importance, like an emissary from some tiny little country of which no one has ever heard, which suddenly proves to hold all the aces in some huge game of diplomacy. "The giants of the world have tormented us for a long time, taking no notice of us, and now it's our turn." Apparently he thought that in the world of high politics people had to discuss things exclusively with hints, silences, fragments of weighty propositions, as unfounded as possible.

"Why not go to sea, as long as there's a written guaranty? A properly notarized document. One side will promise to sail to the end if the other side promises not to interfere any more and not to put them in anymore dangerous situations. Not to send any more ships full of pirates, and to give more than just two clips of ammunition."

Astonished, Kozulin sat on the edge of the bed and wiped his brow. "You think that I set up that encounter between the Babylonia and the Flying Vietnamese?"

"Nobody said anything like that and nobody is accusing you of anything of the sort. Because all kinds of things happen, and one thing can happen after another one and you can get this great big long chain of coincidences. If two ships meet on the huge ocean, that's one coincidence. And if for some reason this encounter takes place when I am asleep and watch is being stood by a very large and very rotten intellectual, that's two coincidences. And if the pirate ship knows for some reason the sort of trick to use for catching the Babylonia's crew, that's three. And if they know where everything we have is hidden, that's four. And if they only robbed us but didn't kill us, that's five. And if they took away everything except a case of cat food, that's six. So when there's that many coincidences, all together they lead us to various sorts of suspicious conclusions."

"But if I did all that, what for?"

Pablo-Pedro slowly picked up a newspaper from the table, passed it to Ronald, pointing to a paragraph circled in red ink.

"The plight of the heroic Babylonia," Ronald began to read, "had a chance but very important scientific result. The most important difficulty facing dietologists is that for ethical reasons they are not able to test on living people. Here though, by the hand of fate, it has been experimentally demonstrated that the nutrients in the box of Pirgoroy's cat food was enough to keep four people alive for a week. The Kroger food chain has announced that recently their sales of Kitty's Breakfast have tripled."

"Aha," Kozulin said. "Then there's nothing to hide. Qui bono—who benefits? But just tell me, dear Pablo-Pedro, who then benefitted from the sinking of the Titanic? Thousands of the relatives of the people who died received enormous insurance payments. Might not it have been they who in the still of the night pushed the enormous iceberg in the path of the unlucky liner? You can't doubt that the Titanic sank in the Atlantic en route from England to America? You have seen the two halves of the ship on television, lying on the bottom of the ocean, you've seen the plates and lamps and boxes and briefcases that those untactful French have brought up, those despoilers of sea graves?"

"Of course I saw it," Pablo-Pedro said. "I have always been interested in this story. But a ship on the bottom of the sea doesn't tell us anything. That it sank is indisputable. But who saw the iceberg at night, and when? The passengers were dancing in the salon, the captain was drinking and eating. They felt a sharp blow, and that was all. The iceberg was never found or produced in court as material evidence, and it isn't lying on the bottom next to the ship. But I say you should go on with the experiment. And not just on people like you and I, but on dead objects. Take a tin box and a bunch of ice chunks. Hit the box with ice for a couple of months. Hit it, throw them, fling them as hard as you can. And you will never be able to make a hole in the box, because iron is harder than ice. You'll dent it a bit, that's all. But you'll never make a hole."

The emissary from a tiny country looked at his audience triumphantly and then lay back on his pillow.

"I give up!" Kozulin said, stunned. "You win. I am powerless in the face of such logic. Maybe there never was an iceberg. Maybe the Titanic was sunk by a bomb put there by anarchists. Or by the relatives of the passengers. I'll sign the contract. That I will never ever conduct any experiments which will threaten the lives of the crew members of the Babylonia. Even if this were to double the income of Pirgoroy. Or which would interfere with fulfilling their mission. And so...?"

"I've always wanted to go to the Upside-down Country. If you believe the rumors, they have worked out several interesting means to achieve equality, some that we haven't even heard about. But I demand that I be given five times as many bullets. And I'll need some other things for defense, some toys. I'll make a list."

"Great!" Kozulin said. "Almost the entire crew is back on board. That leaves just the captain. Anthony, what do you say? Hey, Anthony, you haven't gone to sleep, have you? You hear me?"

He didn't hear. He once again was sailing through his ancient and far-away seas. He was driving on the road that lead from their house to the yellow sunset. Cars kept passing him on the left and the right. He couldn't speed up though because he had to stay with Wife #5's car. She didn't know that he was following her. The week before the older children had tied a lilac-colored streamer to the antenna of her car. They were pretending to be explorers from another planet, who had planted the lilac flag on earth. Now the triangle of cloth flapped over the roofs of the passing cars and lead him onward.

He felt almost no bitterness. Burning curiosity, yes. We know so little of those close to us. Had there ever been anyone in his life to whom he might have told absolutely everything? No, there had been so such person. He had hidden a great deal even from Wife #3, who had no fear of any sort of truth. So why could Wife #5 not have her sad secrets? After all, she had lived thirty years in this world before meeting him. What would have made him imagine that because of him she would cut off everything, that there was no vine winding from her heart back into the debris of her past? And why had he been so certain that she was incapable of secretiveness? After all, she had escaped the surveillance of Husband #5.1 cleverly enough, lying on the back seat of Anton's car and heading for distant motels, then coming back home exactly when she had said she would, like an experienced Cinderella, and so no one had ever found out about them.

The car from the stars and its lilac flag left the highway, circled around some crowded streets, and pulled up at a newly-built high-rise hotel. Wife #5 got out, gave the key to the doorman, nodded, and went into the door he held open for her. A thousand glittering windows, and behind each of them someone waited for her. Then the light behind one would go out. If he were to watch very carefully...

Anton thought about how it was still not too late. He could turn around and drive off. Go home. The children would be happy. Or he could go to the movies. He had even wanted to see a movie, about journalists in the capital. The reviews had intrigued him. The heroes were a husband and wife. She suspected him of an affair and began to dig through his papers. She finds some receipts, because her doofus of a husband has paid for his motels with a credit card. Anton had also paid with a credit card when his affair with Wife #4 began, but he always threw out the receipt slips. So it wasn't that that Wife #3 caught him with, but the photographs. He had kept some Polaroid pictures taken on the beach in San Francisco. Pretty smart of him too. He couldn't make himself throw out those shoulders flush with sunburnt flakes of skin, those eyes wide with demanding expectation. And anyway he could always have told Susan that this was simply the photo of an important client's wife. But he hadn't noticed what she had written on the other side. "To Odd-Man-Out, with admiration and gratitude." Your Honor, the accused has nothing to say in his own defense.

He parked the car in the next street over and sat there for a half hour. Then he went back to the hotel on foot. The smiling desk clerk said that no, he couldn't find a Mrs. Sebich in the guest register (as if she would have given her real name). Perhaps he could check for her name on the guest list for a reception? Oh yes, today was a big affair. The whole eastern wing of the hotel had been rented to celebrate the sixtieth birthday of a famous singer, whom he named, whose fame had recently risen again, after falling. No, the guest list for the reception also had no Mrs. Sebich. Perhaps Mr. Sebich would care to wait? The bar is over there, beyond the palms and the azaleas.

Anton went strolling through the halls. The entrance to the east wing was crowded with the curious and fans. From time to time couples in tuxes and ball gowns passed along the corridor formed by policemen, their faces made up to project imperturbable greeting. Anton stood on tiptoes and tried to peek into the hall. The chunk of the forbidden world he could see was brassily lit and ringing with noise. The merely mortal were permitted to enter only if they had the good fortune to bear the white jacket of a waiter.

Then music sounded in the hall. The police moved their gauntlet to the bottom of the staircase. The graying singer began to descend the marble stairs towards the upraised faces, flowers, applause, and flash-bulbs. His companion hid her face behind his shoulder. Anton recalled how he had bought this singer's first records as gifts for Wife #1, when she gave birth to Golda. This man had had one song that the entire campus was singing then. "You have so many highways and byways ahead that you will forget me, like you forget the roads you race through at night, but sometime you will remember my look, when it hits you like on-coming head lights, and you'll let go of the wheel, let go of the wheel..."

The smiling singer went past quite close and then stopped for a moment, to autograph the book stuck out between the police uniforms. His companion was left undisguised, where she froze, looking about in confusion, drumming her fingers on the brooch she wore on her breast. She wore an ankle-length lilac dress with a deep décolleté, and Anton realized that he had never seen that dress on Wife #5, but he had seen the brooch once and had been surprised that she would have such an old and expensive thing, but then she had said that it was a gift from Aunt Clarence, a gift from Aunt Clarence.

"Captain Sebich! Ten-HUT! Ford HARCH!" Kozulin suddenly barked. "HUT-HUT-HUT! Double time! Knees up. Arms—out! Now run! Now squat, one-two, one-two..."

Anton obeyed with joyous alacrity. He panted, his face shining. Worried, Ronald came over to him, but Kozulin waved him away.

"Leave him. I know what I'm doing. This used to happen when I was in the Navy. A man would lose his will. From exhaustion. You have to hook him up to somebody else's. It's like hooking up to a respirator. Or an artificial kidney. Or plugging something in. One-two, one-two. Up! Rest! Hands behind the head, fingers together! Bend forward, begin! Right hand to left foot, left to right! Don't bend the knees! Don't stop! The rest of you can go. We'll meet at lunch. One-two, one-two..."

Anton gasped, licked at his sweat, laughed. The place for the golden cockerel of orders was no longer empty. How good it was to submit to an invader, how nice to submit to orders. His idle-happy muscles abandoned their Hindu nonsense and leapt to obey the orders of the new sahib.

"One-two-three-four! One-two-three-four!"

Then he stood at attention before the admiral and received his orders. His brain soaked them up automatically, not daring to doubt or inquire or object. "Yes sir, fly to London. Yes sir, go to the Soviet Embassy. Yes sir, meet Comrade Mr. Glukharev. Yes sir, get visas for everybody."

Then some sort of trouble began. His memory refused to record what it didn't understand, and there were squeaks of protest.

What did lawyer Simpson have to do with this? Why was Wife #4 in London? Why did he have to follow her and at the same time hide from Simpson?

"Simpson is coming in to take you to Europe. That's what my people tell me. Now you've got something to take away. Just the book rights to the story of the Babylonia should be worth about a hundred thousand. The only defense you have is to prove that Wife #4 has a new companion. They've built a little nest in London, in a certain hotel. And Simpson is going to be watching for you at Calais."

"In Calais?"

"That's what I said at a press conference. That once the Babylonia is repaired it will make its first stop at the French port of La Manche. In fact she'll pick you up at Dover. You have to be really careful with Simpson. He has incredible connections. Besides which, the entire brotherhood of lawyers hates you. The man who invented insurance against divorces must be crushed at all costs. You understand now how important it is to get good photos of your fourth wife in the arms of her new friend? It wasn't chance that I chose a camera for your gift..."

A camera that somebody held up over the heads of the crowd for a moment blocked out Wife #5 for Anton. When the camera was put down again and the glare from the flash had left his eyes, Anton saw that Wife #5 had doubled. More precisely, two women were now standing on either side of the singer, holding his arm. The second woman was older. This was Aunt Clarence. The women resembled each other somehow. The greater similarity though was between Wife #5 and the singer. When they stood side by side like that everyone could see how endlessly inventive genes are able to sculpt our faces, how easily uniqueness is built into the traits with which we are born. Then the sixty-year old victor of life, the conqueror of millions of hearts, plus his two nearest and dearest at his side, went solemnly into the hall, where, supported by wife and daughter, he was greeted by applause.

Anton slipped back into the crowd, left the hotel. The murk of night was like a wall, held at bay by a line of streetlamps. He went to his car. He drove very cautiously, because he felt a collapse of that part of his memory that had contained the traffic laws. Other places too. His brain was filled with the question "Why?" Why had she had to hide this? For all these years? Such secretiveness, such deceit. Was she ashamed of him, ashamed to show up in that inaccessible world with Anton? The cars honked angrily as they passed him. It was only when he pulled into his garage that he understood that he had been driving with his lights off.

"Why, why, why?" he repeated, rocking a glass of straight bourbon in front of his eyes. "What did you get from it? You're ashamed of me? You didn't really think...no, I won't be mad, but I have to know..."

Wife #5 sat in front of him in a chair, hands on her cheeks, still in the same lilac gown, which refused to turn back into a housecoat even when the clock struck twelve. She tried to explain. Of course, she was wrong. She had been meaning to tell him for a long time, but she couldn't work herself up to it. It was the nightmare of her life. Ever since she was little. Since she was twelve she had been oppressed by her father's fame. She had suddenly understood that all the smiles, the gifts, the kind words— none of these were for her. She was only a reflection.

She had been angry at first. She had begun to insult people. She suspected everybody of insincerity, of wanting to get into her graces only to get something from the fame. Then she got depressed. Torpid.

Vacations in Hawaii, skiing in Switzerland, the underwater worlds of the Caribbean islands—nothing pleased her. The sable coat she was given was too heavy. The BMW she got for finishing her junior year made her burst into tears. Where could she go in such a car? How could she park it at school alongside the modest Vegas and Hondas of her classmates?

They took her to a psychiatrist, who interrogated her in detail and made his diagnosis: affluenza. Right, that's the name of this new disease that is extremely common among rich heirs. The young people who have it are depressed, hang around, can't learn, can't find themselves. One of the worst aspects of this disease is that nobody around the victim ever has any sympathy. Try to tell somebody what a burden your millions are, and they'll only laugh, and offer to trade places. People with affluenza can't tell their friends about it. They meet with each other in small groups, but even there they don't use their real names. They exchange their sad stories under the eye of a psychiatrist. This helps, though not for long. Real poverty would cure it? But how to achieve poverty? Go broke? But the money isn't yours, so you can't give it to the poor, or donate clean needles for addicts, or give to save the whales.

She understood that she had to do something. The emptiness was killing her, the loneliness, the pointlessness. Before starting college she went to municipal court and requested that her name be changed. Her parents were in despair. Why was she rejecting them? Was she ashamed? What had they done to her? Hadn't they turned themselves inside out to give her everything that would make her happy? But they submitted. They even agreed to pay for her education anonymously, through a subsidiary trust. She chose an inexpensive college in a little town two hundred miles away, where no one would know who she was.

Oh, what a terrific thing it was, to be invited to the movies for the first time! By a classmate who thought that he was better off than she because his car was two years newer than her wreck. And to find a job! That's right, she was able to get herself a job as a clerk during the evening at the medical library, because she knew German and a little Latin. The money was nothing, of course, but it was hers! And she had decided firmly not to take a cent more than the tuition from her parents, who promised not to put their address on their letters when they wrote.

It was literally as though she had been born again. However, it turned out that she was literally unable to do anything. She burnt the toast black in the toaster, washed a beloved jacket that was dry-clean only and so spent the entire winter walking around with sleeves that were too short, not even to her wrists. She didn't know that the gas tank always has to be closed tightly, and when she lost the gas cap she drove around like that until rain got in the gas and froze overnight, so that she had to run all the way across town to make her classes. It was then that she fell into slavery to the countless "musts" from which she had yet to escape.

But what of such trivialities! For the first time in her life she had friends. Real friends. Who liked HER. Smiled at HER. And asked her to come along with them. Not because she was so-and-so's daughter, but because she was just Jill, Jill from the medical department, just like everybody else and her own self, liking some, not liking others, helping some, asking help from others, kissing some in the back seat of the car, and just sitting with others until three in the morning discussing deep things. Her friends weren't even afraid to quarrel with her. It was so strangely painful and pleasant that a person would even dare to cease talking to her, and then would later ask pardon and change his mood, and her heart would wobble with joy.

She had to be on her guard. Her happy world was very fragile. She might shatter it with a single incautious word. And of course she let things slip. In the heat of some sort of stupid fight about a famous film star and his wives, which wife was when, she blurted out that right now he was married to this one, the little freckled one, which she obviously knew because she had had dinner with them both last month. What do you mean, you had dinner with them? Your very own self? Oh, it's no big deal, he's a distant cousin of my grandfather, he loves him a lot, so he came to visit, it was a really big deal, blah-blah-blah. Another time she talked about how this same grandfather had come to visit them, he loved to drop in without warning so he could catch her parents doing something wrong, like inviting foreigners to visit, because foreigners are the main distraction to a proper life, but his transmission broke a mile from their house, and so he had walked in the improper rain, which shouldn't have been falling at that time of year, and when he showed up he was in such terrible condition that the doorman didn't recognize him and didn't want to let him in and... Hey? What doorman? Oh, that's...that's a nickname. For my brother Bill, that's what we call him because he's always the first to run to the door when it rings.... Oh, she'd never said that she had a brother named Bill?

She would get tangled up in her own hurried lies, and all that saved her was that her friends were too young to remember other people's lives, didn't know how to juxtapose things and catch her out, but still this pretending oppressed her, always oppressed her, which was why she was always sad, even though everything was a hundred times better than it had been when she was a child, so at times it seemed to her that she was right to be proud that she had known enough to break free and save herself, that of all of the group suffering from affluenza that had met at the psychiatrist's, only one other boy had been able to break free, and that by becoming a penguin specialist in Antarctica, and if Anton could only understand everything she had had to go through, he could probably forgive her, maybe not right away, but eventually...

He was touched. He couldn't be angry with her. The lilac gown from space slid from her shoulders, crumbled about her ankles. The brooch from Mama-Aunt Clarence was everywhere, slithering about and getting in the way of his kisses. She had had to go through so much. Odd-man-out had always had a weakness for melancholy women, guilty women, and that night he simply outdid himself.

But then...

Day by day, unnoted and unstoppable, the poison of his discovery flowed to the very farthest corners of his kingdom of I-Can. What of all your scrabbling up the ladder of success, if your wife has always been standing and will always be standing a hundred rungs above you? What does an invitation to a reception for the mayor of the little town mean, if your wife can glitter at a gathering of stars, where you will be invited only if she begs them? What is your five-bedroom house in a prestigious neighborhood if your wife grew up in a mansion with a doorman? How can you be proud of your three offices and your income of almost two hundred thousand if your wife will inherit millions?

No, he could feel no pride in the fact that she truly loved only him, and that she rejected and despised her luxurious glittering world. And her assurances that until she met him she had not even known what love was did nothing to warm his heart. She told him that she had married her first husband in the same way that people jump into the first elevator that comes, without noticing that it doesn't stop on the floors you need. She had been so afraid that he would find her out and that she would no longer be able to believe in his love... Had the first husband found out? No, Wife #5 assured him. Her mother had come to their wedding alone, as Aunt Clarence. And she never took the children to their grandparents more than twice a year. But when the boys got older she forbid her famous father to play with them or even show up when they were there. Because they might recognize him later on the tv or a record jacket.

But Anton didn't believe this. He thought that Husband #5.1 had also discovered the truth accidentally at some point. Perhaps the father in his clouds of fame had also begged his daughter to come to his fiftieth birthday party. And Husband #5.1 had overheard and followed her too. When had he begun the fling with the black teller from the bank? Yes, the dates would be just about right, ten years ago. Probably Husband #5.1 found out but was too crushed even to talk to his wife about it. That's probably when he had developed that straight-ahead look, that was meant to say "I have no time for other people's problems."

Oh, how Anton understood him now. And how he understood the man's choice, to go far beneath him to a simple teller from an oppressed minority. How sharply he felt the similarity of their fates, and he wasn't ashamed of it, when he went through the glass door of the barber shop beneath the rotating cylinder with the colors of the French flag, and Peggy would clack her scissors in greeting over the head of her customer. Yes, Peggy—he wanted to remember her by name, without the number six she should have had—and he looked at her every two seconds from behind his magazine while he waited his turn, and he thanked fate for the fact that men cannot be forbidden to get a shave every day, and that no local guardian of morals would be able to stew up some long-legged rumor from this.

Two days later Anton left Trash Island to fly to Lisbon, and from there to London, laden with lenses, pounds sterling, rubles, instructions, seen off by his whole crew, and by the admiral, who was everywhere and knew everything.

Radio Broadcast Prepared While Flying Over Europe
(The Parisian Terrorist)

As was later made plain, that day a large new pimple had come up right under Julien's eye, and the fate of the municipal judge was sealed. But there was still the twenty-five hundred francs, which had to be used with maximum profit. Because Julien was poor, and knew the value of money.

He set off for a certain cafe on Rue Guy Lusak, where the out-of-work actors, unsuccessful agents, wedding photographers, and industrial film directors always gathered. The cameraman that Julien picked couldn't make out what the young man wanted of him. Film his typical day? How he gets up, eats breakfast, goes out? And what next? Make a half-hour documentary, sell it to a TV station, and then give half the money to Julien? But who would buy a documentary about a young man whom nobody knew? "If they don't buy it, then I'll lose my money," Julien explained. "But you won't be out anything. Twenty-five hundred francs for a day's work isn't so bad, is it? I'll pay you half tomorrow morning when we start filming, and I'll leave the other half with a notary for you. You won't refuse to go to the notary with me, and have our contract legalized there?"

The cameraman was overdue on his rent and phone bill, so he couldn't vacillate. He agreed to everything the vain idiot said. He was a little surprised at the poverty of the room in which Julien lived. He thought that Julien might better have bought himself a lamp shade and new sheets instead of wasting money on this idiotic enterprise. But he kept quiet. He obediently filmed the young man's morning, in the bath, at the stove, over coffee at the table. At the newspaper stand on the street. In the bookstore. A close-up on the volume of Sartre that Julien leafed through. In the subway, on a bench at the Tuiléries, surrounded by pigeons.

The young man had an obvious weakness for fountains. He was photographed against the Tritons and Nereids holding up the fountains on Place de la Concorde, and then asked to be taken to Place St. Michel, where he posed next to the spray by the bronze dragon and then they went on foot to the Observatoire, where the young man was immortalized again against the glittering water spouting from dolphins and turtles.

227

Later the cameraman spoke of how he had never worked with so agreeable a client. No criticism, caprices, remarks. The only request of a directorial nature which he permitted himself was that the cameraman go to high-speed filming when he gave the sign, unbuttoning the right pocket on his shirt. The right moment did not arrive for some time, so that the cameraman almost forgot, so that Julien had not only to unbutton his pocket, but also yell to the cameraman. It was dusk and they were strolling through the pleasant little streets around Boulevard Lefèbvre, both of them tired from the day, but even so the cameraman heard the quiet call and did as he was told, putting the camera to high speed, so that all of Julien's movements showed up on film in unnatural slowness—the slow bend of the knee readying the body to jump, the slow change to running, the hair waving as if under water, the fingers leaving the unbuttoned pocket of the shirt, disappearing into the waistband, reappearing, clutching an eight-shot Spanish Astra, and at just that moment the frame shows a car pulling up to the big doors of a two-story home, and the municipal judge slowly getting out of it, to move slowly toward the slow explosions and slow puffs of smoke from the barrel of the Astra, and then falling slowly face-down to the sidewalk. Julien slowly throws the pistol away and lets the chauffeur who runs over slowly push him face-first into the fence.

The cameraman was clever enough not to wait for the police, so that the moment of the arrest wasn't filmed. However what was already on the film was more than enough. The sum that the television studio paid for the half-hour film is being kept secret, but there are rumors that it is more than the amount Life magazine paid Abram Zapruder for his twenty-second film of the assassination of President Kennedy.

The French newspapers wrote a great deal about this story. No one could understand Julien's motives. During interrogation he answered contradictorily. He said that he had wanted to register his protest against oppression and injustice. Against the unjust structure of social oppression. No, he wasn't a member of any group. Why of all the municipal judges had he chosen this one? There was nothing personal, he had just seen him once on TV and remembered the name. No, he had not gotten money or orders from anybody. His patience had just run out. When it ran out for thousands of other people, we might expect some real changes.

Psychiatric examination pronounced him normal.

Thus reporters were left with the freedom to interpret this bloody act as they thought best. Some of them averred that Julien's soul had not been able to bear the unjust treatment of alien workers. Others that he was tormented by the sight of the homeless of Paris. Others said that he dreamed of independence for France's last colonies, Corsica and Caledonia.

There were those who took up psychological explanations. Usually the person who takes to terror has a nightmare ever present in his soul, they said. The peaceful life about him seems criminally indifferent to the suffering of all mankind or some part of it. For which he avenges himself on it. He flings the nightmare of his soul into the life around him. That is the source of Belfast, Beiruts, Sri-Lankas, Punjabs. Religious, political, and nationalist slogans are simply camouflage. The only injustice is that such a person suffers every minute of his life, while other people only suffer from time to time.

Political skeptics refuted the psychologists, as did gray analysts and fanners of ever-smoldering enmity. Well, they wrote archly, isn't it odd that in a world divided into two camps all the people who have nightmares in their souls all come from just one camp? How is it that peaceful citizens of one camp die from the bombs and bullets of terrorists, while those of the other never do?

Wholly explainable, others replied. Because the terrorist is able to work effectively only where he is permitted to move freely from place to place, to buy weapons freely, to send and exchange foreign money freely, freely to get the equipment he needs, the means of transport and the false documents.

"But thousands of diplomats, journalists, and all kinds of delegations from the other camp come and go in these same free countries," the skeptics shot back. "How is it that they are never in any danger, while everybody else is wiser to stay inside if they can't come with a bodyguard? It's the same kind of miracle as if the rain were suddenly to be choosy, only falling on the fields of the unjust, but never on the fields of the just."

There were also those who explained the whole thing with human quirks. Every country has people who drink too much, or go whoring, or gamble at cards, or bum around, or climb mountains, or paint pictures. Or who kill. That's the way they were born. And in every country these people find ways to satisfy their desires. Where it is acceptable to kill for the faith, they become holy martyrs; where it is acceptable to kill because of exploitation, they go on the "Shining Path" with the Red Brigades; where you can kill for national independence, they put bombs in airplanes; and where you can kill for money they become gangsters. If you can't find a use for such people, then they have no other outlet than to seize power in the country and give themselves a monopoly on killing. That is what has happened in many countries, as we can see from examples in recent history. So it is better not to drive such maniacs to despair, but give them an application for their strengths and their tastes, in limited and controlled dimensions.

Such is the plethora of opinion about this important question on the European continent, dear radio audience. And we, as ever, would be very pleased to hear your thoughts and reactions. If someone of you feels within himself the dangerous passion described above, then he may write anonymously. His opinion will be particularly interesting to us all.

12. LONDON

"**M**R. SEBICH!? SO soon? You should have warned us! How awful! I had dreamed of meeting you in Heathrow, getting my picture taken next to you, so I could be on the front pages of the papers. When am I going to get a chance like that again? Ah, you did it on purpose, to avoid the fuss? Incognito, so to say? Of course, of course..."

It had been ages and ages since comrade Mr. Glukharev had been able to greet so valued a guest to their embassy. Yes, he would get everything done quicker than quick. Yes, entrance visas would be ready in three or four days. A week, maybe. Oh, yes, he had read about Mr. Sebich, and read his very progressive radio broadcasts, given them round to colleagues. How precisely he had fixed American's sins through the lips of the angry Canadian! Yes, Mr. Kozulin had been kind enough to send the broadcast ahead. But the rest of the members of the Babylonia's crew would have to be checked out. They might be concealing reactionary deeds in their pasts. No, that wouldn't interfere with their trip. But the local authorities in Leningrad would have to know how to behave with the visitors. And meanwhile Mr. Sebich could have a wonderful rest in London. After all that he had suffered out on the ocean, he still looked like a survivor of the Leningrad blockade. Ah, personal business? Well, even more so then. Not far from here there is a very progressive little hotel... But first he would like to introduce him to the woman who would be taking care of his documents. In case she should have questions. She ought to have your telephone number. She is a very progressive girl. She was transferred to us just two months ago from Intourist in Leningrad.

He excused himself, picked up the phone, and switched to Russian.

"Melada, come round for a minute. I'll introduce you to this dogbutt. Well, catbutt too. He's plopped down on us early. What could I do about it? The bosses said to carry him like a baby, roll out the red carpet for him. So, listen, go down to Klava in the buffet, grab a bottle and something to eat. No, not the salt pork, it was pretty reactionary even yesterday. Get some salmon and a little caviar. And some headcheese too. And better make the bottle cognac. Ask for some Georgian Gremi. If Klava isn't hung over, she'll give it to you."

Glukharev turned back to his guest with redoubled enthusiasm. He hoped that Mr. Sebich would get along with Melada. She was a fine person. She knew London like the back of her hand, even though she hadn't been there very long. She had studied books on it. No, she was a hundred percent Russian. Her name was like that because her family had quarreled about what to name her—Melania, Melodia, Mlada or Lada. And they had compromised on this hybrid. But he still suspected that her father, who was a very progressive and ideological man, had agreed to this combination of letters because it was M then E then L.

"You see?" Mr. Glukharev pointed to the three portraits of Marx, Engels, and Lenin above his head. "And the end of her name can be translated as yes. You call your children after your saints, we after ours. Everything is good, we are all people, we are all for a victorious peace, isn't that right?"

The girl backed in, trying to protect the tray from the swinging door. She was tall, a little bit pop-eyed, and held herself very erect, so that she resembled a teacher without her pointer (lost? left in class? swallowed, maybe?). Her light-colored hair was wound into tight curls that hugged her head like a cap, making you expect sparks, the crackle of short-circuiting. She had a blue rhombus on the lapel of her jacket. The absence of the statutory for-acquaintance smile put him on his guard, giving him the idea that the examination might be more difficult than he had thought.

"Oh, Mr. Sebich, Mr. Sebich, we have read all about it... It was so horrible... To have nothing to drink but the juice of fish... I couldn't have... And the baby that you saved... The articles didn't say what became of him. He survived?"

The English words occasionally paused for a split second on her lips like parachutists with second thoughts.

"The child is fine. He's gaining weight faster than any of us."

"If you want, I can help you buy him some baby food."

"Unfortunately, we are unable to take him with us. Each of the crew members has too many duties during the voyage. There will be no time to spend on the child."

Comrade Mr. Glukharev poured cognac into faceted glasses.

"To our meeting! To new friends! And to your miraculous rescue! And may the only rockets to cross the oceans be those searching for shipwreck victims!"

Melada put down her glass in order to applaud the toast. Then she suddenly began to slap herself lightly in despair.

"I forgot! I forgot! I wanted to get pistachios and I forgot. What am I going to do with me?"

"We are having a reception in the Embassy the day after tomorrow," said Glukharev. "For the visiting Soviet ships. Would you like to attend? I'll put you on the guest list just in case. Melada, get our guest an invitation. Perhaps I'll be able to introduce him to the ambassador. They are bringing the hors d'oeuvres on the flagship, so it will be something special."

Melada, red with cognac and her self-punishment, called Anton a taxi and accompanied him out to the street.

"I think I could also find a crib for you. There's a very cheap department store in Dulwich that has good things. We'll be sure to get one without wheels, so that it doesn't roll around on the ship."

Anton looked at her serious face, at the halo of radio antennae about her head, and thought that the art of not hearing what you don't wish to hear was one he should pick up as fast as possible over the few days which still stood between him and a journey to the Upside-down Country.

Across London Bridge and along the right bank, so as to admire the towers of the castle above which invisibly fluttered scores of the brightest and prettiest, but alas also severed, heads. Past the monument placed on the site of the bakery which was renowned for causing London's worst fire ever (Oh, unlucky baker, oh sacrifice of the London crowd on the altar of its own laziness and indifference!). Left on Cannon Street, aimed at the cupola of the famous church, beneath which reposed both of Napoleon's conquerors—on land and on water—at the cupola which had beckoned to the thundering flocks of bombers a half century before. A turn into the prospect bearing the name of the champion queen, surpassing all others in the expanse of her realm, the number of her subjects, the length of her reign, who when she died had thirty grandchildren and forty great grandchildren (ah, what he wouldn't give for that!). Further along the embankment toward Waterloo Bridge, which spanned the tears of millions of movie-goers. Then through the tiny streets to the Strand, slipping out right in front of the funeral-colored taxis, almost having to use his hands to turn his head first right, then left, instead of the other way as he was accustomed. Across Trafalgar Square, past the early tourists, past the punks with purple protuberances on their shaved heads, kicking up a cloud of pigeons, uncounted, but one for each sailor's soul lost in the great battle which had decided the language in which the schoolchildren of Africa and Asia would be taught, English or French. And along the park fence, the park still empty, dewy, with a lake in the center still belonging to the ducks and swans until noon, when the last of Big Ben's chimes would shower the lawns with crowds of Westminster clerks. Then toward the Hilton looming above the rooftops, from the upper windows of which, it was rumored, one could sometimes see the royal family walking in the shade of the trees behind Buckingham Palace. He had no need though of princes or princesses, nor of their guards in bearskin shakos. It was not at them he aimed his camera, focussed his lens.

Anton followed this route every morning from the right bank to the Hilton where Miss Abigail von Karlston resided, the name now used by Wife #4. Every morning, his long-range camera on his chest, he tried with difficulty to convince himself that the painful stabbing sensation he felt beneath his heart was simply a sign of photo-hunter's nervousness, nothing more. That he felt nothing more than contempt and anger for the woman who had cursed his passion for reproduction, and then set on him the dragon named Simpson. And that now he was living and acting following someone else's golden rule, that he had no need to think and choose, that he was blessed in submitting to the order of the admiral who had sent him, his will be done. And the reason he was walking, not driving in a rented car, had no connection with a desire to prolong the trip through early-morning London with an adolescent pain in his chest. He walked because it was more convenient to leave the car at the hotel all night. Otherwise you'd never find a good parking place to do your hunting from, someplace where you could see the front door.

But then he got his car in position and hid inside, pointing the camera lens. From then on he had nothing else to do save wait. And listen to the whistling of his soul leaking in and out, through the hole stabbed under his heart. And recollect, of course.

Recollect how in the first month of their life together Wife #4—with tender argument, with joshing, and sometimes with direct attacks, such as the iron that was "accidentally" left on which destroyed all of his former clothing. Sometimes she said that she was just jealous of the past, that she wanted him to wear everything new, so that nothing had been touched by other women. She chose a dozen shirts for him herself, herself bought him three pairs of Finnish slippers, five French ties, a plaid Scottish cap, cufflinks with amethysts, an Italian comb rumored to have been rescued from the ashes of Pompeii, a coin purse made from the skin of a recently extinct animal. He had to change his reliable old Oldsmobile for the fashionable Saab of that year. The Saab was the only thing they could drive to the boutique where she sought out the imported clothes with the three crowns on the inner pocket for him ("It's nothing to laugh about, you know. The sales people are very observant and if you pull up in some old rustbucket they're going to have contempt for you and just offer the cheap stuff.")

Every trip with Wife #4 around New York was like a trip through some museum of animated figures guided by someone who offered almost no explanations, but just muttered distractedly to herself in fragments of speech. "So, eh? Well, well... Whatever possessed you with that brooch, sweety pie? Oh, poor thing, what ever made you think of that as a purse? What's this then? Ah, that's a bit better, that's acceptable already, congratulations. So what if it's Dior? There's nothing too elegant to ruin, you know... Oh! Come look at this! No, no, not that one, the one over there, in blue... I'll die of laughter! What, you don't get it? You're so blind! She dug a thirty-year old dress out of a trunk so as to catch the shoulder pad business on the rebound! But that trick won't work, not even if you hold your breath till you burst, it won't..."

The way an airplane pilot can remember the scores of buttons and knobs which must be checked before take-off, Wife #4 would check her husband over before going to visit, or an exhibit, or the theater, or out to eat. Hair? On head, combed. On cheeks, shaved. In nose, clipped. Tie? Color appropriate, tie tack gold with malachite. Shirt? Tucked in. Pullover? Jacket? Handkerchief in pocket? Pants? Socks? Shoes? Polished, tied, heels not down, soles springy, out on the runway. Start engines...

Their life suddenly was flooded with a crush of new acquaintances. At every party Wife #4 surreptitiously examined fitting candidates, maneuvered subtly toward them, and then at a certain moment was at hand with her wine glass, a little lost, her shoulders charmingly shrugged, and the candidate would immediately surrender, coming toward her, to talk about a new film or last night's storm (a fallen branch—what a pity—broke the glass table in the garden!), and so swallow the hook. A week later would follow an invitation to dinner— them to us, us to them—a trip to the opera together, a trip to the country, photos going into some restaurant, an intimate trip to some favorite store. This swelling of tender friendship might last a few weeks, and sometimes even months, and then would suddenly break, like an old movie-reel. "Who? Them? I was never friendly with them! Whatever gave you that idea?" But the telephone was already ringing, and the new friends, who often as not had been found at a party at the recently rejecteds' were already coming to visit, had already flown into the fire.

At first Anton had thought that this string of temporary friendships had no system, that Wife #4 simply swept from one person to another, that it was just not in her powers to get wholly attached to any one in particular. But then he began to notice that no, these dashings to and from were not so elemental. For each new acquaintance on some vital scale—success, erudition, wealth, talent, influence, or elegance—was an inch or two higher than the predecessor.

Was it self-interest which moved her? That too was unlikely. After all she had no career, wasn't even working anywhere any more. She was more like some passionate mountain climber who was always in search of new places to grip on the face of the cliff, but every handhold must be just a bit higher than the last, if only a few centimeters, because otherwise the mystery of ascent would be broken, and with it the meaning of life, when it would be better simply to let go, and let the abyss of life swallow you.

And somewhere up above was the summit. Somewhere people were indescribably successful, world-famous, so rich nothing mattered, elegant beyond belief, amusing to the point of savagery, talented to the point of simplicity. They did not even condescend to appear in the social pages of the magazines, to glitter on the television for the pleasure of the millions. No, this was like a higher clan, an order whose members recognized each other by secret signs only they knew, like rings or jokes and catchwords or glances and hints. And it was for them, in her dreams and desires, that Wife #4 would sit hours before her mirror. If she read the day before about the French Prime Minister, she would dream of how she would look to the French Prime Minister and what he would think about when he saw her. If the tv should flash a picture of a Mexican toreador, then the role of the watcher—who looked from above but not with condescension—would be taken by the Mexican bullfighter. And if the tv showed some brave pilot who had landed his passenger jet on its belly without the wheels, she would dream of the pilot taking her into his arms right at the bottom of the inflatable slide. It was for them she dressed, for them she studied French, for them that she went to the beauty parlor, twisted herself into knots with gymnastics, read the latest books. For an incredibly fortuitous encounter with one of these she had to keep her candle ever lit and inviting. What a horror it would be if the happy moment were to find her not in the proper form, wearing the wrong stockings, her hair not done, the latest movie not seen, stressing the word "Suprématisme" on the wrong syllable, not bronzed from the sun of the Caribbean!

In the depths of his soul Anton could sense that he too was just a temporary link for her, a foothold, a leg-up out of the abyss of the tourist office. So he tried to turn himself into a human cliff, to move with her and obediently offer a convenient handhold at just the place where her hand reached, to be a strong tree root overhead, a place where the rope she threw could catch.

Although Wife #4 regarded the idea of fairness as a personal enemy, she still did not hate those who remained—whom she left—behind. She had no anger for those who refused to strive for success, because these most often were weak people who did not wish to torture themselves with dreams of the impossible. Crooked doors in the house, furniture that did not match, cheap cars, clothes from the supermarket, all these only prompted a distasteful pity. And those who were for the time being still ahead and above her she regarded without jealousy, with a certain honest, sporting admiration. However she boiled with real anger for the renegades who denied the cliff. The hypocrites who announced that they had no interest in the eternal upward climb. That life had other meaning, other goals. That human attachments weren't formed up and down, that these were more important than any cliff. Oh, she was prepared to burn such heretics on a bonfire of contempt, to send them to a zone of perpetual rejection. Anton was afraid that sooner or later he was going to give himself away and the tribunal of the high mountain inquisition would condemn him without pity. He feared this coming auto-da-fe.

He most suffered from the swift current of their friendships, the unoccasioned breaks with people. When he had to pick up the phone and tell some lie, to explain to new friends whom Wife #4 had already crossed off the list why they couldn't come to the house for dinner next Saturday—and no, not next Saturday, either, for then they would be going out of town for two weeks, and yes, "Yes, of course we'll call when we get back"—he would shiver with self-contempt.

The new friends took their retirement with quiet confusion, disappearing obediently. Only Martha Kellers forced him to meet her in a restaurant for lunch and explain everything fully. This instructor in economics enumerated all of her opinions of him and Wife #4 with mathematical honesty, that they were a) soulless social climbers; b) exploiters of human trust; c) opportunists who would stoop to anything; d) egoists who had never heard of such things as tact, sympathy, or respect for the feelings of others; e) dangerous polluters of friendship who should be branded with a scarlet letter on both cheeks. She herself had sensed this outcome at the very beginning of their friendship and so wasn't surprised, but her husband Paul was very upset by this break-up. He kept saying that there was some sort of misunderstanding, that they had probably deeply offended the Sebichs somehow, because otherwise their behavior could not be explained. He had forced Martha to come to this unpleasant lunch. So, perhaps she could tell her husband that they had not offended anyone, and the Kellers weren't guilty of any ignoble acts? That they had been chucked aside simply because they were no longer necessary, wasn't that it? So here's her share of the lunch, for the vegetable soup, cheese blintzes, plus coffee and tip. No, she didn't feel like shaking hands, for some reason. Have a nice day.

For many weeks after this Anton was still mentally composing speeches of justification addressed to Martha Kellers. He wanted to explain or prove to her—to the world, to himself—what Wife #4 had to have and how she could be forgiven more than the normal person. As we forgive a poet or an artist his arrogance, his betrayals, his inconstancy—since there is no cult of the beautiful self with them, but simply a cult of the beautiful, and they don't always know where to draw the line. An artist begins to grow a little bored with someone who has already seen all his paintings, seen all his aspects, and expressed his full admiration. Feverishly he begins to seek out other people, other audiences for his art. So it was with inconstant Abigail, his unappeasable Wife #4.

No, it wasn't true that she enjoyed charming everyone she met and then abandoning them. It was just that like a real artist she struggled to meet higher demands. Probably the people she was able to captivate were no longer of interest to her. She had the constant suspicion that somewhere there must be people of more refined tastes, and she would have to charm them. These unseen, impending, and awaited audiences played an enormous role in her life. Yes, it was for the awaited, the not-yet-met, who had not yet seen her, that she lived. Dreaming of this yet-to-come, she was unable to see the living people around her, and so could hurt and offend them.

And what of the Kellers? Don't they too chuck scores of worthy people over the back fence of their life simply because they are bored with them? Would they really have asked over an ordinary insurance man like Mr. Sebich if he had turned up in front of them alone, without his charming wife? And what was it like for their abandoned friends to realize that all their honesty, goodness, hard work, and sympathy would never open the door into the nervous, refined home of the Kellers for them, while the doors were flung wide for this idle charmer? So who were they to complain now, to fling accusations after the woman who had flashed before their eyes and then floated on farther, following the eternal unknown call?

Yes, Martha, you are a woman, you should understand her. There lives within her the premonition of the primary encounter, with an Olympian, with the bearer of fate. This premonition builds up in her like the charge in an electric ray, crackling in her look, every hair on her head springs up on its suddenly stiff stem, every leucocyte and erythrocyte doubles its pace in the dash through the tunnels of blood. And if she should suddenly decide that this he is you, that the encounter has come, then the whole charge of accumulated premonitory awe, this unspent admiration, would burn you deep and long, as I felt on my own person, when I first met her, when I was walking among the computers in the far-off tourist office and stumbled over her electric glance, which was filled with a commitment to me that I had not earned. And your Paul stumbled in just that same way, as did scores of others, and as will they too. Burnt, burning, and to be burned, then left as ashes behind.

Yes, you can drink her in, like a movie or a poem or a symphony, but no one can control her forever. Control that line of her thigh, gently filling the line of the dress. Nor the quick shoulder, which turns on lights, gets sun-burnt, gets kissed. Nor the cosmetic film of her face, framed in gold by her hair, a tight close-up of which fills your whole screen. Nor the music of her neck, nor the landscape of her chest. Could someone really expect to have as his property the staccato of stockings, which below, out of the frame, are searching for footholds, or the crescendo of silent caressing of nylon on nylon, or the choirs of smiles which fleet so in conversation and rhyme so splendidly with the flight of her lashes. Which emit rays to stimulate growth in the berry of love. Which can penetrate even from a distance, or through contact lenses, or the mirror of a camera, giving stir to a forgotten ache.

No, no one may, ever. Not you, gray-haired and important, who walks by her side now in a suit made in Paris from a design by Picasso, wearing a tie painted by Matisse, and your arm on her shoulder, registering on the film with every click of the shutter. You'll be left back too, never to overtake her in your chic Swedish-suspended Jaguar. Only oil-sheiks and caliphs know how to snare this beauty, or at least think they know, how to hide her away forever in their harems. Could she survive that? Unlikely, unlikely. As for the rest of us, we are all playing with fire, letting this cinema-poem fly freely among us, tormenting us.

After his morning photo safaris at the Hilton Anton had nothing to keep himself busy. He had already asked the doorman for the name of the gray-haired playboy—Mr. Stockbridge. Satellite telecommunications, ten million or so. Anton's lawyer would sigh with relief. Especially if Anton should be able to catch their briefly snatched kiss on film. Until then he had to find something to fill the time until the newly-repaired Babylonia arrived. So he decided to go to the reception at the embassy.

Comrade Mr. Glukharev was fussing about the entrance, sorting out the arriving guests. He was happy to see Mr. Sebich again. He shook his hand with one of his, clutching his elbow with the other.

"You want to play queues? Oh, it's like a lottery we have, but with some color of home. There'll be prizes. You get a number on your wrist. Men get odd, women get even. It takes a pair to win, so you have to find your neighbor in line. You want to play?"

"Why..."

"Let me get you a number. It's a lot of fun. Don't worry, it washes right off with normal soap. So now you're number 113. Go look for number 114. Now I'll introduce you to two German beauties. They are a little bit wild, but they are very progressive girls. They recently got out of prison. I wouldn't mind flirting a bit with them myself, but I'm working. Ingrid, Gudrun, come here. Look who's come to visit! Mr. Sebich himself, captain of the famous Babylonia!"

The beauties surfaced from the crowd, fastened themselves to him, began to chatter.

"How are you? You probably are still having nightmares about fish, aren't you? We were on a hunger strike in prison, so we can understand you. But we always had water at least. Just don't go to Germany. There's an incredible anti-cat madness there now. People are smothering cats, and cutting them and shooting them. The newspapers have been writing about it. Why? Ask us something easier. The racial laws turned out to be a mistake, but somebody has to be responsible for all our problems. They catch cats by the hundred and sell them for experiments. You'll sell no Pirgoroy products there."

"And things aren't much better in America. I saw on the television how in one town in Texas it has been forbidden to take cats outside that aren't on a leash. They passed a special law about it. Because people who didn't have cats complained that the cats were running all over their lawns. If only you could see those pitiful things now, being dragged along on their leashes. They dig all their feet in, howl, scratch at the asphalt. It's horrible!"

"Why were you in prison?"

"We broke the windows in a stamp shop. More like blew it up a little. As a protest. Our group has uncovered a world conspiracy of philatelists. And collectors in general. After all, collecting is the epitome of the most horrible of man's passions—greed in its purest form. Accumulation for the sake of accumulation, collection addiction. Philatelism is the secret ruler of the world."

"What about numismatics?"

"Them too, but philately is the heart of the conspiracy. It's no accident that philately was born at the same time as imperialism, in the middle of the last century. What were the colonies for, anyway? To allow them to put out those deceptively pretty stamps and confuse people. Have you ever seen stamps from Borneo, the Ivory Coast, Curaçao, Guinea? This entire gaudy deception has always had only one purpose, to tighten the impulse to greed a few turns tighter. Or purposely to issue twenty stamps with like the incorrect number of teeth on the edge, and then ten years later sell them for a million each as incredible rarities. Our leader has very convincingly unmasked all this in his book *The Cancer of Philately*. If you'd like, we'll send you a copy."

Anton said of course. After he got back from his trip to the Upsidedown Land. Until then he just wouldn't have the time. The Babylonia, repaired, was already sailing to England, and would be in La Manche in a day or two. By then he would get his Soviet visas and join his crew.

The dance of diplomacy was circling them, drawing in tighter and tighter. Progressive mixed with reactionary. Anton felt that he was getting drunk on more than one cup of punch, but not more than five. Were they putting vodka into all the drinks? They say that in olden times their merchants used to drink champagne out of teapots in the morning. And that the tsar forced his guests to drain a Great Eagle Cup that was the size of a bucket. Whoever survived had the chance to wake up a minister the next day.

The naval officers and the diplomats, heated by hidden vodka, were dashing about, roaring with laughter, to find their place in line. "You weren't standing here!" "What do you mean I wasn't standing here?!" "Look at the number! Look at my number!" "That's no 8, that's how they write a 3!" "Hey, I'm calling the police!"

Number 114 turned out to be Melada. A coincidence?

"Having a good time? It's fun today, isn't it?"

The line crushed them together. All of his powers of touch hastened from the ends of his fingers to the skin of his back. It seemed to him that he could have described all of her straps and garters and such in great detail. The line moved forward in little surges. One in ten couples got prizes, while the rest went away empty-handed. During the jolts he would lose her, and then search greedily for her with his entire back.

They won a plush bear, his paws open wide to embrace the entire world. They picked their way clear of the crush and went to the emptier end of the hall, where the bar was, holding their prize by the ear. Laughing, they tried to decide what they were to do with one toy for the two of them. Cut it half, as wise Solomon had counseled? What, she'd never heard of King Solomon? He was probably the most famous singer in the West. Sometime he'd play his records for her.

He noticed that she had let her hair pull free from its wiry curls, let them fall to her shoulders. And it seemed that her dress had not been bought in the certain cheap store in Dulwich that she had promised to show him. And her shoes, as far as he could recall, might even have occasioned a condescending but approving nod from Wife #4.

"I'm so happy that I got transferred to London. You meet so many odd people here. And the work is a lot more interesting than in Leningrad. But it's sad that my former girlfriends don't write or phone. Probably they think I got this job by scheming or that my father helped me. He's fairly high up. But I swear, he didn't know anything about it. My transfer was just as big a surprise for him as it was for me."

Her serious face swam before him, reproducing in the chandeliers along the ceiling. His powers of touch returned to where they ought to have been, and his fingers itched with rude curiosity, aching to return to the straps, clasps, and flaps which now were forbidden them. Although even if he were to let them do what they wished, no one would have noticed. Because the very drunk brotherhood of diplomats was spending its last ounces of sobriety on the attempt not to blurt out government secrets, or at least to get some secrets in return.

Anton remembered how they put him in a taxi, how they clamped his prize bear under his arm, who also had found no one who wished to embrace him, and how Glukharev said to the laughing Melada, "He's our kind of fellow, all right! Progressive to the bone! If only there were more like him, then we wouldn't have to waste so much on rockets. We could get by with nothing but Stolichnaya."

Wife #4 believed herself to be a great driver. When she was in college she had even competed in track races. The most useless part of the automobile, in her view, was the speedometer. What was the point in knowing how fast you're going, if there were all those other cars around? Just pass them, and that's that. She always felt something unbearably insulting in the fact that there was a car in front of her. The insult could be washed away, if not with blood, then with speed. She'd pass on the left or on the right, drive on the shoulder, weave through the moving stream of traffic cutting across three, even four lanes, to the accompaniment of honking, the screech of brakes, and curses, unheard behind glass. Being stuck in traffic was the same for her as being stuck in jail. She would phone Anton from the car, asking about alternate routes, even if they were two or three times longer, just so she wouldn't have to be tortured by this solitary confinement.

She protected herself against the police with radar detectors and with a sixth sense, which worked as well for her as any electronics. The situation only became dangerous when the fates of the highway brought her up against another driver as maniacal as she. Especially when he drove a truck.

Was it Cleveland they were going to then? Yes, yes, because for some reason they suddenly had to go to a concert with the German director. And what were five hundred miles if your wife was suddenly aflame with love for Wagner? Or his conductor. She had read something about him or seen his picture in the paper and made out some of the traits of the one for whom she waited eternally. (I must see him, he must see me!) Suddenly she was ready to go, they had to drop everything and race to the concert through unpeopled, undriven Pennsylvania. With all of its red maples. Past the deer licking salt from the concrete drains at the edge of the road. Past the overhanging cliffs which had torn themselves from the bowels of the earth but were ready to obey the call and sink back. (Ah, no, that was being kept in reserve by the Miserymaker for a different wife!) They raced along, until they were jammed by the rear doors of a truck. Decorated with bolts and locks like the gates of a fortress.

The truck was in the left lane. Wife #4 waited patiently for him to let her pass. There are after all some rules which even she didn't wish to violate. Having waited a decent interval, she turned on her right blinker. Anyone could see that she didn't like to be forced to overtake on the right. But there was nothing to be done, you couldn't be expected to miss the Wagner concert because of some tortoise of a truck.

Their Saab had gotten almost to the middle of a white wall of the truck, painted with some bottle with something foaming, when the truck suddenly began to move to the right. Wife #4 scarcely had time to slow down and let the roaring fortress go ahead.

"What is he? Nuts? Or blind?"

Now the truck was in the right lane. The Saab began to pass on the left. Once again when they were halfway past the foamy green bottle began to move down on them, threatening to toss them from the road onto the tops of the maples, flashing past so far below.

There was no doubt remaining. They were being challenged to a duel. Which could have had fatal consequences. For no reason, either, except the boredom of the road! And then it began!

Wife #4 bit her lip, squinted her eyes. In her hands the Saab turned into an attacking jet fighter. Which now would hang back, hiding behind the curves, now would dash up, racing at the enemy. Pass on the left, on the right? The truck began to drive zigzag, taking not just both lanes, but the shoulder as well. The painted bottle just about scraped against the cliffs. Oh, if only the Swedes had thought to make their cars just a few inches shorter! Then they might have ducked under the wheels of this bully of the highway. The fortress-like locked gates always managed to get in front of them at the last minute, and so repulse them. When the road was going downhill the truck got going so fast that the Saab's motor began to howl like an animal, trying to keep up. On the upgrades, though, the panting bottle-hauler would deceptively yield a patch of asphalt, but only to entice the enemy to move up to be struck by both flanks.

Anton sat neither dead nor alive. He had said goodbye to life, but remained silent. He glanced at his inflamed duelist, her streaming golden hair, her narrowed eyes, and thought that the Miserymaker had never leapt up before him before in so attractive a form. He thought that if they were to crash now, badly but not fatally, it would give him a certain perverse pleasure. As if he would prove something to her with a crash. As if there would be some important and necessary change in their relations. As if she might realize at last the pointlessness of her eternal competitions, her eternal scrabbling upwards.

But they had lived. At the next attempt to pass the Saab couldn't hold the shoulder, slipped into a small drainage ditch, leapt up, turned over in the air, and, slowing down, smashed its taillights against the cliff. Anton crawled out slowly, glanced at the red lacy kaleidoscope that had scattered across the grass. He carefully plucked the shaking fingers of Wife #4 from the steering wheel, pulled her from the car. He put her in the passenger seat, buckled her in.

Oh, if only she might have seen herself then, her tear-filled eyes, her lips puffy with the insult, pursed with the sound of the last, not-quite-uttered cursing! She might have discovered new colors for her ever-renewed self-portrait, perhaps would have understood and valued that astonishing beauty which defeat gives to a woman. But no, she only studied the light through the mountain tops, gave a farewell glance to the green bottle which was disappearing victoriously by the red cliff of a valley somewhere far far ahead. She could admit an enemy's victory and accept it honestly. But to learn to get pleasure from that? Oh, take your perverted tastes and go to... I don't want to hear about it!

Anton waited. He was sure that everything would change with the birth of a baby. The baby would be a bridge between them, uniting the two shores of an ever-widening gulf. Everything would be different when they would both be getting up at night to answer a baby's cry. And they would buy toys and count the new teeth and take home movies of the first steps and go all three of them to Disneyland. And what a boundless world would open before her in children's clothing shops! After all, she still hadn't tried her hand at that octave, genre, key. After all, there must be uncounted possibilities in the artistic search for new color combinations (the mother's dress and the child's romper), new rhythms (the mother's pace and the speed of the carriage), new linguistic and sound effects.

She listened to his speeches with clear interest, nodding, asking questions even with a certain respect (he was after all the father of eight children at the time), flipped through the pediatric guidebooks and catalogues of children's clothes that he brought her. But every month she unfailingly caused him a double disappointment. No, everything was fine with her. Yes, she went to the doctor, did all the necessary tests. Maybe it was inherited. She had also been a late child. You just have to be patient.

How important the if-only, if-only, if-only, if-only of our lives! If only she had not taken a bath early that Saturday! If only he had not been in the cool quiet of his office paying the house bills. If only there had not been among them his wife's latest parking ticket. If only he had had the number of her driver's license written down (as he had long ago decided he should), then he would not have had to dig in her bags and purses in search of the number that had to be copied from the license onto the receipt for the parking ticket. Then he would never have stumbled on that flat little box with the pills. Which he knew so well, because Wife #3 had refused to part with them after the birth of the second set of twins. The box was more than half empty.

It was fortunate that the bathroom door was locked, so that drumming on it with his fists, knees, and shoulders gave him time to burn off at least some of his rage; otherwise he probably would have crippled her. When the screws in the lock finally tore loose, along with big chunks of wood, and he charged into the damp fragrance of the room, Wife #4 was huddled in the corner, covered with a towel, scrabbling her heels against the wet bottom of the tub, trying to move even farther away from his rage-distorted face, from the white bones of his fingers, from the crushed box that his fist was sticking under her very nose.

"You...you...scum! You bitch! All these months! The entire year! Lies, lies, lies! Knowing how much this meant to me... Look me straight in the face and LIE! 'Oh, no, we'll paint the nursery green... I'd rather have a daughter...'"

She tried to hide behind the damp plastic curtain. She begged that he listen to her. Yes, she had been afraid. She had felt that she wasn't ready to be a mother. Neither morally nor physically. But she had been afraid to confess that to him. He had wanted it so much, had tried so hard. She had been afraid to ask him to put it off. He had to understand her. She needed time. She still had not found herself, didn't know what she should do with herself in this life. It would be irresponsible to the child.

He had to give her some time.

Anton's father had loved to repeat that family squabbles always end justly, because the winner is always the one who feels more strongly about something. The problem was that Anton did not want to win. Because a conquered wife would become helpless and therefore he would not want to take revenge on her. And after that ill-starred day he wanted only one thing, revenge. He wanted to revel in his vengeance. He got pleasure from destroying everything that she had so carefully built up in the year of their married life. He would deliberately put on some stupid spotted necktie the size of a napkin, or show up for dinner with her new friends in pink shorts, then bellow with laughter, burp, swear. He arranged surprises for her, like suddenly emptying all the money from their joint account, so as to have the pleasure of listening to her stammer explanations when the store owners called, promising to immediately return the dress she had bought, or to pay for it with a credit card. Then he would immediately phone the bank and cancel her credit cards too. If she tried for nocturnal reconciliations, he would pretend to submit, but then permit odd-man-out such a debauch of egoism that it became not peace with honor but some sort of Treaty of Versailles, or the rape of Potsdam.

"She woke up the beast in me," he would tell his chance fellow drinkers in the bar, surprised and proud. "She turned me into an asshole."

With pleasure he remembered and recounted all that Martha Kellers had said about her. He invented new terms of abuse, which he ascribed to other former friends and acquaintances. "That woman thinks that the main significance of a person in life is to ride fast and smell to high heaven." Yes, they meant you. Or another: "She lets everybody think that she's burning to share love, but what she wants is that everybody share her love of herself." Or another: "Oh, let her cut ahead in line, and then she can find out for herself that nobody has left her a ticket at will-call."

She accepted her punishment with melancholy submission. Or so it seemed to him. She didn't complain, didn't protest, didn't ask for mercy. He was certain that if he demanded that in his presence she throw the cursed pills into the toilet, she would have done it. First, though, he wanted to revel in her debasement.

The evening when he came home well after midnight and she wasn't home he wasn't alarmed, but simply began to ponder the new scenes that he would throw when she turned up, the taunting phrases and mocking accusations that he would shower on her. Even toward morning, when he discovered that almost all of her clothes had disappeared, he still thought that this was simply a tactical thrust by his enemy, like the ancient Roman's retreat to the sacred hills. But he was not going to give in, he was not! How pleasant to imagine her sitting somewhere in some motel, watching the phone, waiting for him to come looking for her. Ha-ha, got the wrong fella there, sweetie! You won't catch us beasts and assholes by appealing to our sympathy, you know! Spend a couple of days on your lonesome and you'll come crawling back, like it or not.

Except she didn't come crawling. Not the second day, and not the third. On the fifth day he got a letter from Simpson and Co., Attorneys At Law. Wife #4 had filed for divorce. On the grounds that her husband had abused her physically and psychologically. Oh, that letter had everything! Forcing her to have children when it was risky for her health. Public humiliations, mocking her in front of friends (with the names of witnesses who were prepared to testify in court). Description of the sexual perversions that he had forced her to partake in (listing all her favorite games, but with a suffering bent). And if Mr. Sebich would not care to have all of these embarrassing facts made public in court, he might wish to confer politely about proper financial compensation for the psychological traumas, which would require lengthy psychiatric therapy; for destroying her career (it appeared that when he tore her away from the keys of her computer and made her the slave to his every whim Wife #4 had been on the threshold of phenomenal success in the travel business); as well as to maintain her in the lifestyle to which he had accustomed her. This would be in the neighborhood of two or three million, but that could be paid out over a fairly long period. We are not savages, after all.

What most astonished Anton was the packet included with the letter which held the physical evidence. There were tapes of his floods of abuse and curses. Copies of the bank statements showing that he had deliberately stopped supporting her. A photo of Wife #4 with a bruise on her forehead (which she had gotten during the race with the bottle truck, but just try and prove that!). There was even a photo of the broken bathroom door in the package. Even though the door had been fixed the very next day! Which meant that even then she had been able to calculate all this in cold blood, and had begun to stockpile weapons against him... And he had thought...

Oh, our blindness to those close, to those we love!

He had even been told, had had hints, had been warned. But he hadn't believed. He had thought that he knew her. Yes, she could be monstrously unjust, could be cruel. But she lacked the power of cold calculation—or so he wished to believe. In order to be cruel, she had to stoke up her own sense of being in the right. This sense of being right was fed anger, wrath, contempt. Fury. What set it off was unimportant. You could start a gas burner with anything—a match, a spark gun, a candle. The fury knob will flare up every time, and the stew pot of justification will boil in the wink of an eye.

This bubbling self-righteousness might be used to parboil a chance passerby who had gotten in the way at a crosswalk or managed to get in front of the car. Or a distant relative who had had the temerity to send an invitation to his daughter's wedding. A girl friend who had had the gall to ask to borrow money. A store clerk who had not listened properly to her question.

What fury would be justified, then, for a man who had spied on her? Who had followed her beyond thrice-thirty seas when she imagined herself abroad in safety? Who made secret photos from a hiding place in his car? What bad luck not to have a baseball bat in hand, but only an umbrella and purse. And that all she could do was bang them ineffectually against the hastily-slammed door, the hurriedly raised windowglass. Dashing from the arms of the grayhaired playboy. Shrieking curses and threats after the departing auto.

Anton was in a panic. How could he have let his guard down so far, why had he gotten out with his camera? Now she would race to phone that dragon Simpson. Who would fly in, breathing flame, and find him, release his poisonous fumes and throw him into some Dickensian prison packed wall to wall with debtors.

Anton raced to the embassy, looking for Melada. The visas? Yes, they were nearly ready. There was just the third stamp to get, the last. But today was impossible. Why? The second stamp still wasn't dry. Every stamp had to dry for three days. That was the way it was done. All right, if he was in such a hurry, she could try to do something. To dry it with a fan. But not right now. Now she had to take the sailors on a bus tour. She'd be back in about three hours, and then she'd get right on the visas. He didn't want to be alone for that time? Why not come along with them? There was still room in the bus.

She was wearing the jacket with the rhombus again, her hair done in antenna curls. The sailors, weary from their long voyage, could not take their eyes from her. A youthful lieutenant with a bouquet was constantly jumping up in excitement to put questions of an arithmetical nature. "The height of Nelson's column? What's that in meters? The load capacity of Tower Bridge? And in tons? The maximum width of the Thames?"

They drove around a London of which Anton knew nothing. That is, the streets, bridges, palaces, and monuments which went past were the same, but they all were wrapped in other memories, populated by ghosts he didn't know. This is where our leader and his wife lived in year such-and-such. And if you can imagine such a thing, the lady from whom they rented the apartment began to put tactless questions about why she didn't wear a wedding ring. They had to threaten her with a libel suit to make her stop. It was in this mailbox—yes, yes, that same red box—that he probably dropped his parcels with his articles for the émigré newspapers. That's where the founder lived, over there. Just think, they were separated only by about twenty years. If only they had met, what they might have been able to say to one another. Instead of that meeting, however, there was another one. With the person who subsequently was to betray the leader and his cause. For which he was expelled from our country. And later was axed in Mexico without benefit of sentence. Even his name has been expunged from our books and encyclopedias.

The English driver bent over his microphone and surreptitiously asked Miss Intourist to stop running up and down the aisle. Traffic here was quite heavy and the traffic laws said that everyone in the bus had to be sitting in a seat. Melada reluctantly took the guide's place, but ten minutes later she jumped up again, ran to the rear door, and pointed her finger at some balcony on the fifth floor. Thirty crewcut heads obediently turned to follow her, like sunflowers. The lieutenant snapped a photo.

"On the right you will see the library of the British Museum. They have ten million volumes here. If the bookshelves were laid in a row they would stretch for two hundred miles. It was here that the founder worked, and then twenty years later, the leader himself. Perhaps he held some of the books in his hands that still bore marks made by the founder, though we may never know."

"Ma'am, I must insist that you sit back down," the driver said icily. "I don't want to be responsible if something happens to you."

Now they were driving through regions where not even the most curious of tourists would ever wander. Here too though they had found sacred buildings for them, worthy of their pilgrimage. Here, more than a century before, had lived a great Russian thinker, an exile. Who had been visited by a great—and equally exiled—rebel. They had talked and dreamed of our radiant future. We recall them thankfully, naming the streets of our cities after them, our factories and schools. And just think, now we see the building where they met. Perhaps they strolled this very sidewalk. Or perhaps went for a cup of coffee in that coffee shop right over there. Yes, beyond those very doors.

Now she was running up and down the aisle again. The bus began to speed up after a curve. Anton saw the bicyclist who dashed out in front of the wheels and instinctively grabbed his seat. The good British brakes worked instantaneously. The thirty crewcut heads almost flew out of their blue-and-white collars. The bicyclist was unharmed. But poor Miss Intourist flew down the aisle as if the bus wanted to shoot her at the man who had gotten in their way. She whacked her back against the metal railing. From the sound of the blow Anton knew that it was she whom the Miserymaker had attacked this time. And on whom he had scored the decisive winning goal.

The lieutenant raced to pick her up, to sit her down, to calm her. She was gasping for air, unable to make a sound. The driver raised his index finger at those in the front row and kept repeating, "I warned her, didn't I? You all heard, how many times did I warn her?"

Upset, Anton went up the aisle.

"Do you know where the nearest hospital is?"

Melada was recovering. She tried to sit up.

"No hospitals, what are you talking about? The tour will continue. Just because of some little bruise..."

The bus moved. She took the microphone, began to speak through clenched teeth, but at the first bump she blacked out.

"To the hospital!" Anton ordered.

"To the cemetery!" Melada groaned, coming to. "Go to Highgate Cemetery. The tour must be completed."

The driver raised his eyes to the ceiling, shook his head, but submitted. Anton sat next to Melada. She quivered, swallowing back tears at every jolt.

"I think you have a broken rib," Anton said. "Probably more than one."

The bus stopped at the cemetery gates. Guiltily averting their eyes the sailors filed slowly out.

"I can't get up," she said, as if relaying some interesting bit of news that would cheer everyone up. "No, it's true, I really can't get up."

"I'll phone for an ambulance."

"No."

"Miss, in these sorts of cases the English doctors are free," the driver said. "They don't have any use for your rubles."

"Mr. Sebich, perhaps you could..." she didn't look at the driver. "It's quite easy to find... the bust of the founder can be seen from some ways away... Any one of the groundsmen can show you the way."

Anton nodded silently and got out of the bus. He waved, and the sailors fell to and followed, in step. The sparrows and pigeons ran in front of them like children greeting a parade. There was a soft grassy carpet between the road and the crosses. Forest anemone, celandine, plantain, wild garlic... The travelling vegetarian pet food salesman was pleased to have an opportunity to test his knowledge of this new sphere.

At the monument to the founder the lieutenant stuck his camera in Anton's hands and gesticulated how to take a picture. Anton photographed him laying his flowers at the base of the monument, then photographed the whole tour squadron. The sailors removed their caps.

"This moment of our lives..." the lieutenant said. "Until the day we die... Our children and grandchildren... Forever... Just touching this granite... The memory of the heart... But we are running out of time..."

On the way back Melada found strength enough to raise the microphone to her pain-white lips. "Somewhere in this area... The very first congress... Passions were raised... The delegates continued to argue out on the street... Little boys began to laugh, hearing the Russian... The hooligans threw spitballs... The next day police were sent to guard the congress... It's a good thing that they did not speak Russian and so did not know what the delegates were saying..."

She asked the driver to let her out a block before the embassy. Anton helped her get down, then followed her. The lieutenant leaned out of the window and shook her hand so hard that she screamed. The black streaks of tears stretched to the corners of her mouth.

"To the port," she ordered the driver. "Take them back to the port."

Walking with tiny steps and held up by Anton she made it to the door of a cafe, went inside, then sat carefully at a table.

"Could you call comrade Glukharev? Tell him what happened and ask him to come here? I don't want them to see me like this in the embassy."

Glukharev came, upset and clicking his tongue.

"What is this, old girl? How come you didn't take more care? No, sit,

sit. I broke my rib when I was young too. Kolka Vikulov hooked me into the boards, so I remember what it's like. Ah, you forces of reaction! Oh well, it's nothing, we'll just put you on the ship, and while you're sailing to Leningrad the thing will heal just fine."

"No! Please, no! Tolya, sweet sweet Tolya, please think up something else! I don't want to go back to Leningrad!"

"Well, old girl, think what you're asking here, eh? You know the rules..."

"They'd never send me back here. I'll be closed out of everything, it'll be the end..."

"Why do you say that? There've been cases..."

"When? Name me one! Did Galya Chervonnaya get sent back? Did Ira Kosheleva?"

"Why are you comparing yourself to them? Ira wanted to saddle her Frenchie with a baby, such a scatterbrain she was. But you've done this without any attempt to deceive, it's an honest industrial accident..."

"Even so..."

She took a napkin from the plastic box on the table, pressed it to her damp eyes. They were talking Russian, and Anton pretended that he didn't understand. The wheels in his head though were whirring away, calculating, measuring, marking out the contours of a dimly emerging scheme.

"Pardon me for intruding... but I'd like to know... what exactly is going on? I mean, normally a broken rib mends quite easily... It doesn't leave a person a cripple."

They looked at him. They nodded at one another. They had apparently decided that it was possible. They began to explain. That workers were not usually left in the embassy when they were ill. Nor were they put into the local hospitals. That was a big expense. They were sent home to heal, but their jobs couldn't be left empty. A replacement would be hastily sent. There was no shortage of volunteers for that! And so it generally worked out that the replacement got to stay permanently. Until he or she got sick. And the duffer who got sick in the first place was found work at home, after he healed. And then was never sent abroad again. Because he was considered unreliable. In the health sense. And Melada was afraid that that would happen to her. Of course it was upsetting. And she hadn't even been here two months yet. And everyone in the embassy loved her. But what were you going to do? No, there was nothing in the rules or laws about it, but there was something stronger than laws and rules. It was called business as usual. And this was business as usual.

Anton's calculating cogs continued to whirl. He could sense that the emerging machination hid within it some sort of danger. It was too complex, he couldn't figure it out to the very end, it had too many murky branches, which was where the Miserymaker especially loved to lurk. However, its main lines were so appealing, so elegant. And of course he wouldn't be able to get by without some help in the Upside-down Country. And this girl's eyes were so dark with misery, so lost in the depths of her well of tears. And was it not fate itself which had sent from on high this broken rib? And under the continuing racket of calculation, which was still far from complete, he heard himself already speaking, already moving out his main pieces.

"I'm not sure I have a right to interfere... But if it would help Miss Melada... Tomorrow morning the Babylonia will be in Dover... And we're setting right off on the voyage... But sooner or later we'll be needing a translator... Why couldn't the embassy give us our translator right now? There's an empty cabin on the Babylonia. Miss Melada would be comfortable there, could rest. She could give the crew Russian lessons and not even have to get out of bed. The trip will take about five days, so that the vital first part of the healing... If this wouldn't violate his majesty's business as usual, of course..."

They looked at each other, then at Anton. Then at each other again.

"That's a smart son of a bitch for you," Glukharev said thoughtfully. "That's the way they know how to do things. Why do they get brains like that? So what are you sitting there saying nothing for, idiot? Go kiss your progressive little beast, kiss him like a sump pump! I'll tell the boss that I've sent you along to keep an eye on things. That traces of reaction have been noted in these foreign Babylonians, that we have to keep an eye on them. And you can be sent on business. Nothing but business! Clever, very clever! Oh, I love it when things work out smoothly like this! So are you going to kiss him or what?"

She smiled through her tears. She obediently put her arm around Anton's neck and tried to pull his head to hers. However this movement proved to be beyond her threshold of pain, so that the kiss did not reach the cheek of the savior hero, but turned instead into a long involuntary moan.

And now it was the morning of the next day. The embassy car was approaching Dover. Anton had in his pocket four visas, all the necessary stamps on them well dried. Melada, well packed in pillows, was lying on the rear seat. The day before Anton had taken her to a doctor. He had insisted on it, and paid too. Now Melada had black and white photos of her broken ribs in her suitcase. The sixth and seventh rib. On the right. In her purse she had painkillers. Which at first should be taken regularly, but not abused. The intimate translucence of the X-rays suddenly caught odd-man-out's attention. He was an incurable, insatiable old crank. In truth he should have had his own visa.

The Babylonia was at the wharf, prettier than it had been. Freshly painted, a new flag with a dog shed, a glittering anchor chain. All around, thank God, not a correspondent to be seen. After all, they were waiting in Calais, on the other side of the Manche. The crew, now healthy, in white uniforms, were standing on the deck, waving their caps in greeting.

Needles of alarm were painfully piercing Anton's chest. The Miserymaker was somewhere about, he could sense it. What if that police helicopter flying past swooped down and the dragon Simpson stepped out? Or out of the black taxi coming around that corner?

The crew studied Melada with curiosity as she slowly ascended the gangplank. Yes, this is our new crew member, our Russian translator. She'll be sailing with us. Unfortunately, she had a bit of bad luck, she fell yesterday. Pretty hard, really. Ronald, she can't give you her right hand, can't you see that? Lin Chan, take her in the empty cabin and help her lie down. We'll be casting off right away. No, you can see England on the way back. It's nothing special, you can take my word for it. Just the usual bits of old empire. No, we'll take on supplies in Oslo. Or Helsinki. That's it, all hands to their posts.

Got away with it, apparently. The police helicopter flew on, the shore was almost deserted. Two girls who could have come from a resort got out of the taxi, dressed in gay hats and shorts, their bags stuffed with what seemed to be reading, knitting, and food for a thousand and one days on the beach. The girls moved along the wharf; when they saw the Babylonia they waved their arms.

"Mr. Sebich, Mr. Sebich! Good-bye, *auf weidersehn*, bon voyage!"

It was the progressive girls, Gudrun and Ingrid! Anton sighed with relief, waved at them.

"Where's Melada? Mr. Glukharev told us that she was on business, that she was sailing with you. Can we say goodbye to her too?"

"Just for a moment. We're leaving in ten minutes. She's in the cabin below."

Gudrun and Ingrid came up on board, lugging their bags. The beauty of the Babylonia, arisen from the ashes, astonished them. They stroked the gleaming brass of the lanterns, sniffed the fresh varnish on the railings, bent over the edge of the gangplank, snatched Pablo-Pedro's cap and took turns trying it on one another.

"What a ship! What perfect lines! Couldn't we please come with you?"

Anton smiled at the two naughty things in an avuncular way.

"Another time, maybe. When we're not in such a hurry, then you can come with us for sure."

"But the thing is, you're headed our way this time. And we'll pay for our trip, naturally. We have to get to Finland."

"Why not go by plane? I think it would be fifty times faster."

"It's so romantic to go by sea. Anyway, we don't want to fool with the passport people. You know how it is, this English bureaucracy has gotten simply impossible. The bureaucrats just pick over every last detail."

"I'd like to help you, honest I would. If the Babylonia were mine, you'd be honored guests here on board. But this is a job here, it's work. We're following the orders of the admiral that sent us. And he has categorically forbidden us to take passengers."

"What a pity. Oh well... But couldn't we at least give you a wrist-watch-calculator? There's this Swiss company that asked us to pass out their new model to all the celebrities we meet. Advertising. And we haven't met anybody more famous than you. There are different sizes and different covers. Here, I think this watch would look great on the mighty hand of the navigator. Can I try it on you?"

Ronald politely held out his wrist, then admired the gift.

"You like it?"

"It's a little heavy. But it's nice. And such a strong strap. Like handcuffs. How do you undo it?"

"Oh, there's a little trick to that, we'll tell you in a moment. Here's another model. Imitation gold. The kind young sailors like to show off with. You wouldn't say no?"

Pablo-Pedro studied the watch they held out, then suddenly covered his head with his hands and ran off. He ran to the stern, jumped over the railing. Then, saying not a word, not looking about, not removing his white pants or jacket, he leapt into the water.

"He knows, he knows!" the progressive German girls laughed.

They bowed to one another, bowed to the astonished Babylonians, like circus magicians after a successful trick. Ingrid dug a black box with an antenna out of her bag. Gudrun theatrically flung the watches far out into the water. Just as the watches disappeared under the water, Ingrid pulled a little switch. A small foamy white cone burst to the surface, followed by the muffled sound of an explosion. The two beach beauties once again bowed to one another and then to their audience, who had forgotten to clap.

While the fuss was dying down and Ronald was numbly studying the ticking fetter on his wrist and the oily wet and ashamed Pablo-Pedro climbed back on board, Anton found within himself the strength to overcome his confusion and meet this latest victory of his age-old enemy with a bit of dignity. He even felt a certain satisfaction—at least it meant that his warning rooster was working properly, and had been sounding the alarm since morning. The Miserymaker, as if mocking the stupidity of the loser, held up a newspaper for him, sticking out of the girls' bag.

"Explosion in a stamp store on Charing Cross Road," the headline screamed, "Two wounded. Losses of 50,000 pounds. Police are looking for two illegal immigrant girls..."

The fugitive beauties hastened to comfort the upset Ronald.

"There's nothing to be upset about... The timer is set for eight this evening. But at eight we can set it twelve hours ahead. That's what we'll do every morning and evening. The main thing is not to try to take the watch off yourself, understand? The trigger, you understand? Unless you know the code you can't do it. And we're the only ones who know the code. In Helsinki we'll take off the watch and we can all part friends. You shouldn't be mad at us. We had no choice. This wet little sailor that's looking at us so crossly... He'd very much like to toss us overboard or turn us in to the police... But then there'd be nobody to set the watch ahead this evening. So you keep a sharp eye out that nothing bad happens to us."

From behind the stern of a passenger ship a shore patrol cutter flew out, made for them.

"Hey! Babylonia! We were told that you have a man overboard!"

"He's rescued already, he's back on board."

Ingrid was waving her brightly-colored hat and laughing. Gudrun went over to her.

"Everything is in order, constable, nobody was hurt."

"But what about that wet little rooster there?"

"We'll give him a bath to wash the oil off him."

"But isn't it about time that the management of Dover harbor did something about cleaning up the water?"

"We're casting off in ten minutes. Isn't that right, captain?"

Anton looked at his crestfallen crew, at the gay beauties, at the police in their plump life preservers, at the ticking alarm on Ronald's wrist. He sighed, nodded. To accept defeat with dignity, to walk under everyone's eyes to the table and sign the act of capitulation with a firm hand—what else was there to do? He saluted and went to the helm.

The Babylonia's new diesel obediently filled the ship with an impatient tremble.

(Existing and existence, or the names of anxiety)

*Once I had to spend nearly twenty four hours on a bus going from
Chicago to New York. The next seat was taken by a woman, no longer
young, who taught philosophy in one of the New York universities. We got
to talking. She tried to explain to me the difference between existing and
existence.*

*"Existing and existence are both present in every second of our lives,"
she said, "but they are separated from one another by an invisible barrier.
We wake up in the morning, put the coffee pot on the gas, think for a
moment over the jars—decaf or caf?—go past the window, notice that the
temperature is five degrees lower this morning, think 'better take a
sweater,' we're late, we go out on the porch and the door squeaks—damn,
better oil it, except that the oil has disappeared someplace again—and
then we get distracted and remember that we never took the letters out of
the box yesterday, and so get the mail now and there's the phone bill, and
thirty dollars higher than last month. How come? We sigh.*

"That's existing.

*"And at the same time, but in a different dimension, the hand eternally
clutches the coffee pot, the door eternally squeaks, we are eternally going
out onto the porch, the eternally green and rustling oak is always bending
over our heads, we are always getting the letters from the box, blinding
white in the sun, and forgetting the amount of the telephone bill we
suddenly sigh with happiness at our participation—through the squeak,
the cool breeze sneaking under our raincoat, the smell of the new-cut
grass, the warmth of the key in our hand—in existence.*

*"When first you discover these two faces of life for yourself you feel an
unusual joy. How good it is to know how to abandon dreary existing
whenever you wish! How good to know how to encounter the eternal so
easily! The escape from existing into existence will become your favorite*

game. It will seem to you that existence might save you from any daily wears and cares. Ah, how sweet not to hurry anywhere, because in existence there is nowhere you may arrive too late, for there are neither beginnings nor ends there. How good to forget about one's mistakes and oversights and losses, because in existence they don't mean anything, since you are powerless to change anything there. How good it is to forgive all the insults and rebukes made in our address, since it is clear that we obviously are guilty of nothing, since we already are somewhere where nothing can be improved or made worse.

You float in bliss. You try to open the eyes of those near and dear to you, to summon them. With pleasure you reread familiar books, study paintings you have seen before, discovering the valuable gloss of existence in them which you had not seen before through the film of existing. For real poets and artists are great adepts of this, and the whole of their secret is that they are able unerringly to search out and convey that drop of existence in the dewdrop in the grass blade, to fix the eternal in the fleeting moment.

What a new and magical life, you think. What a gift of fate this awakening is, this discovery of a new world. For there are those unfortunates who until the day they die never discover the treasures which have been given them, who to the end of their days will imagine that there is nothing in this life save the fleeting moment of existing.

If fate is kind to you, you will preserve this joyous and grateful sense for some time, and so pass on to the next world with a light heart— unafraid, will simply drop your head onto the pillow or the chair back, or onto your arms as they lay on the table, and so flow wholly into existence.

However, there are few, very few, whom fate has chosen. Much more often this play of existence does not come without cost. Like a young and naive heir who has just moved into the ancestral home, you begin to notice elements of the supernatural, to hear the voices of evil spirits. Gradually— or sometimes suddenly, as suddenly as an avalanche, or when the ground opens up beneath your feet—clouds, waves, tornadoes of uncertain anxiety will fly over you, wash over you, twist down upon you. You will suddenly begin to realize that if existence has no time, then your own death is always at hand, right here, every second, inseparable, nearer than an arm's length away. And death's arm, not yours. That all of your cleverness, including the most elegant imaginings, including the very fine distinction between existing and existence, will remain forever feeble nonsense in a world where nothing may ever be changed. And that all of your efforts to become better or prettier or kinder, to earn approval or love or acceptance or forgiveness, all of this is laughable flapdoodle, since in existence each of us is eternally alone, initially justified, endlessly condemned, needed by no one, needing no one, faceless, alone, unloved, rejected, and damned.

Eternal collapse, eternal nonsense, eternal condemnation—these are the names of the three main anxieties which creep upon us from out of existence.

This three-headed anxiety spreads through the soul like a cancer, intruding everywhere like a metastasizing horror, sowing pustulant sores of doubt. Many people have been through this, and many have tried to describe what they have endured. From Abraham to Kierkegaard, from the Ecclesiastes poet to Tolstoy, from Job to Dostoevsky, from Luther to Nietzsche and Kafka, from Pascal to Camus, there have been written the most detailed guidebooks conceivable to all nine circles of hell, maps of torment, flow charts of pain, flung roses, gone with the winds of despair.

However, the billions of simple and weak souls have no need to refer to these colorful atlases. After all, for them there is always an easy path of salvation back from existence, into existing. A quick slam of the door that puts a long cordon of years-yet-to-be-lived between themselves and death, hours and days filled with unfounded hopes, saving surprises, chores to be done. And they throw all the snakes of doubt over a high fence of science and knowledge, then raise that fence high, to the clouds, to the sky, by degrees making it into a closed cupola. And they press together with other souls into tight clans, tribes, bands, parties, and churches, to find salvation from rejection and solitude in their density, and so gain guaranteed immunity for plea-bargaining away their participation in existence.

And woe now to them who would try to coax us back, into the freezing light and horror of existence. We would regard such a person as a criminal, someone who would bomb our dikes, an arsonist with his Moscow penny candle, like a poisoner of wells, a warlock bearing Colorado beetle-bacteria of bubonic plague. Hey, all you unacknowledged artists with your hacked-off ears, you philosophers of the concentration camps, you heretics on the bonfire, you prophets under the flying stones! Enough whining, enough complaints about injustice, enough trying to convince us that you want only good for us. Opening our eyes and our souls to existence— this you call good? You are rabblerousers and gadflies, you want to make us share your horror and despair, when even you, you with your double lives, you haven't the strength to bear it yourselves?! You also have to dump it on feeble us, of little strength? Quick, bring here the torch, the stones, the bullet, the arrows, the barbed wire!"

At this point my companion lost control of herself and her story became disjointed, thick with outbursts of deeply personal suffering, accusations, self-justifications, and self-accusations. However, I remembered her reflections on the double nature of existing and existence, and long before *Real Trouble* I tried to learn how to extract the best from both these worlds, to leap now here, now there, the way people jump from ice chunk to ice chunk when crossing a dangerous inlet.

And you, dear radio audience? Have you had occasion to feel this profound difference between the two aspects of our life? And if you have, won't you share with us the ways you have found to pass most easily from one realm to another, and—reliably, solidly, hermetically—slam shut the door between them?

13. THE BALTIC

"CAPTAIN, YOU can't do that," Pablo-Pedro said, "you can't put me on the morning watch. Graveyard is the only one. Otherwise I'll cut loose and scatter them all over the waves. Full throttle, onto a battering ram, or a rock. So that they go flying head first. The seagulls will come flocking in, peck them to pieces, and what's left will be clean and bright. I lose control very easily, and then there's no going back."

He was staring at the two untroubled beauties who were stretched out in the deck chairs in Babylonia's prow. They wore identical little covers on theirs noses, identical rosy glasses, identically turned their palms to the sun, so that they were as alike as two dolls, trustingly fragile, defenselessly friendly. Anton had noted that the Babylonia was being steered in a circle. He put his hand on the arm of the dreamy helmsman, gave the rudder a shove.

"No panic, Pablo," he said. "No nerviness. There's three days to Helsinki yet. We'll let them off there, they'll take Ronald's watch off, and the voyage will continue nice and peaceful."

"I don't believe it. We never get nice and peaceful. We can tell the police too easily. It's nothing to lie and offer up a bouquet of words. It's hard for witnesses to stay alive. Harder than it is for dynamiters. Why should they leave us as witnesses? They'll do something at the last minute. And then nobody will ever hear anything about us, what depth we're at, and what latitude."

"What do you know about the watch? Is the charge big?"

"Blow your arm off up to the elbow. And make a hole in your head

263

at the same time. Of course you can amputate the hand at the wrist, take the watch off. But Ronald won't agree to that. He values his skin too much. And anyway, where would we find a surgeon? I mean one brave enough to agree to work alongside a bomb?"

"Who might know the code for the fuse? If we could get the inventor on the radio and find out the combination, then we could disarm..."

"You won't get it on the radio, and you won't get it in a letter. Each alarm has its own code, like a car key. They're the only ones who could tell you. Because they are the ones who put it in. I've been telling you that for two days already."

"You know perfectly well that I'll never agree, and that's why you keep telling me."

"I understand. You've been brought up to fear words. You're afraid that the newspapers will print that Captain Sebich is a sea-going executioner. Who tortured two beautiful young girls. He'll be shamed in black and white for the rest of his life. Much better to have a big headline: NAVIGATOR MAIMED BUT PRINCIPLES INTACT."

"Listen, I'm curious. Are you teasing me, or is this serious? How do you suggest we do this? Put them on the electric burner and slowly turn the juice up? Crush their fingers with the anchor chain? Take turns lashing them with the signal flags?"

"No need to set up a sea-going inquisition, no need to invent a thing. There are proven tortures which leave no scars, and which won't show up on any x-rays, so that no one can prove a thing. You know them well, because you suffered them yourself not long ago. As they did to you you should do to them. Tie their legs and put them headfirst overboard. Give them a glimpse of the watery world. For a minute, then for two minutes, then for three. Pretty quick they'll be telling you the code and be falling all over themselves to disarm the bomb. We can find out whatever we want. Secret signs, passwords, the names of their lovers, the number of abortions they've had."

One of the beauties raised her head (she couldn't have heard, could she?), cast a rosy-hued glance about the far seas, shivered, and stretched out more languorously in the deck chair.

Thoughtful Ronald came up on the deck. He went over to the tanning sirens, held out his left wrist, turned away. They were saying something to him, stroking his arm, pulling at him. Ingrid did her trick with the watch, then tried to get their sad hostage to speak again. He listened with the silent submission of a student who has utterly lost faith in the words of his mentors, but who is forced to endure them and submit. Then, as silently as he had come, he left.

The sirens turned on their radio and began to sing along with a Swedish song, nodding their heads in time. Their unconcern was insulting, genuine, and infectious. Yes, life might even be savored when you were sailing with a man on Death Row. You just had to work on having the right attitude. You had to be patient and understanding. Pablo-Pedro's naked hatred was fruitless and unjust. And the fact that Anton kept asking him about what to do over and over again was no more than a rote action, like someone feeling a growing boil, to see whether it was inflamed yet.

"I've read that now they bring a whole team of specially trained psychologists to negotiate with terrorists. But these two you couldn't even call terrorists. They aren't making any demands. They keep apologizing for the inconvenience. Just take them to where they want to go and that's that, they don't ask for anything more."

"From here I could cut them down with one burst."

"And when the twelve hours is up? You going to reset the watch yourself? No, I'll try to talk them out of it again at lunch. I'll give them my solemn promise to take them to Helsinki and not to tell the police, may the philatelists of Finland forgive me."

"I'd sure like to ask our admiral how it was that these girlies knew the Babylonia would be in Dover just that day, at just that time. He'd say it was coincidence again, of course. And how many more of these coincidences has he put together for us?"

"You on about that again?"

The conversation kept going around in fruitless circles, stuck on a merry-go-round. Anton waved his hand and left. After a moment's thought, he went to the passenger compartment. It was the only place left on all of the Babylonia where he might rest from the ticking nightmare, in Melada's cabin. Nothing had been said to her. They had simply taken the two progressive passengers on board, because the girls didn't have the money for an airplane.

The passengers would run round to her cabin to smoke and chat. Anton would sit by her bed for hours. Melada asked him about life in America, told him about herself. She was happy to see him drop in. She would push up a bit from her pillow, check her hair with her left hand, smoothing it down, straightening the collar of her gown. She wanted to know everything. She was an A student, putting to the professor the hardest questions she could, trying to corner him.

That day she asked him to speak of his childhood. His teachers, his parents, his schoolchums. In your country what grade are children in before they are told that people are mortal? When do they begin to study stamens and pistils? That's so important in the growing up years. No, she didn't believe that all children secretly dream of winning mama away from papa for themselves, or papa away from mama. She hoped that the theories of the Viennese doctor would eventually go out of fashion. But the egoism of a child was generally quite strong, and very difficult to overcome.

She for example still remembers the day when she first—for the first time!—gave the neighbor girl her plastic bathtub doll. And not because she was tired of the doll. She was sad to part with it. And she didn't even like the neighbor girl. It was simply that that was the day when she believed what they had been teaching her since her milk teeth, that it is always good to give. And bad to take. She had very very much wished to be good. What of him? Did he recall the most important day of his childhood? What was it?

Of course he remembered. It was the day on the beach when he had met Robin, a little girl. He was six. They buried each other in the sand and he kept trying to touch her long curly hair. And then Robin's mother had peeled off her shorts and ordered her to run into the water and wash all the sand off. When it turned out that Robin was a boy. But one with long hair and a thin little neck and the girlish habit of puckering his lips. It was only later that Anton had understood that. At that moment he froze, petrified with horrible disillusionment, because it had turned out that underneath their pants girls and boys were identical. From somewhere or other he had somehow guessed (or hoped?) that they had to be different. And now—this blow.

No, she couldn't understand his misery. If it had been his trousers that had been removed and the entire beach had seen and had laughed at him... Yes, she would have remembered that sort of shame for a long time. But her parents would never have done such a thing with her. Even as a punishment. If she did something forbidden, they called her "nasty girl" and that was enough. To be "nasty" or "bad," to make her parents angry, seemed to her the most terrifying thing in childhood. Her father had many different ways of being angry—at his children, at his wife, at his underlings, at the dog, at the shopgirls, at coworkers, at fate, at the country's enemies... But never at his bosses, somehow. And incidentally that had just hopped out of her mouth... In Russian she never could have said something like that about her father.

"My father never got angry with me," Anton said. "Or at least I don't recall being afraid of him. The only thing I was ever afraid of was losing him in a crowd. He loved to be in crowds, in a big crush. If there was a crowd at a fire or a car wreck, he had to be there and he'd leap right in, push up against the people, asking everybody, giving advice. I would lose him and then cry in fear. And every Sunday, baseball or football. For vacations it was always some sort of very crowded resort. Where somebody was always stepping on you on the beach or spilling popcorn on you or asking you for the time or borrowing the suntan lotion or talking about the weather."

He hadn't liked it when people began to be more prosperous and everybody moved out to his own house, his own vacation place, or his own television. The movies got emptier, the resorts became strings of empty high-rise hotels all along the beach. Even the baseball games started to be played in half-empty stadiums. "And when we moved from New York to Indiana, dad was really lost. He used anything he could to get away at least to Chicago, where he could ride the El and spend the evening in some crowded bar."

"Poor, poor fellow," Melada said, her lips bent in genuine sympathy. "How he must have wanted to lose himself, drown it out."

"Drown out what?" Anton didn't understand.

"You said yourself that he was an ad man."

"Yeah. So?"

"It's such horrible, demeaning work. I would have died of shame. To spend all day every day trying to convince people to buy things they don't need."

"Why things they don't need?"

"Because if they need them, then they'd buy them without having to be convinced."

"I'm told that in your country it's written on the walls that 'All labor is honorable.'"

"Of course. Because we don't have ad men. Just gypsies who try to get you to let them read your palms or read your cards. But there's no reforming them."

"So all the professions are equal?"

"Alas, no. Doctors, or let's say musicians or pilots are more respected than cleaning women or bus conductors. Even if you are a bad doctor or pilot, people are going to respect you. That's even more true because it's so hard to know who is good and who isn't. At least until they fail to cure you or smash you into the ground. There are even people who try to deceive, who invent different professions for themselves in order to make new acquaintances like them. No one would ever admit for example that he is a salesclerk."

"So it's a shame to be a clerk?"

"I don't think so. It's perfectly possible in my country to be a good or honest clerk. It's not London. I was just stunned the first few days there. The exact same item in one store can be one price and a completely different price in the store next door. How is that possible? I didn't make a fuss about it. When you are a guest, you don't criticize your hosts. But still... I can't make any sense of it. I mean, they are forcing the buyers into eternal torment. Everyone in spite of himself is always going to be wondering, and what if I could buy this exact same thing three blocks over for less? You can't take any pleasure in anything you buy. And I'm told that it's like that everywhere in the west."

"What about when the same store changes its prices? Drops them, let's say. Yesterday the price was four pounds, now it's three. On sale. Is this a good thing?"

"Of course it's not good. It means that yesterday they deceived me, trying to sell something too dear. Every object has to have one set price, everywhere and for always. And as for advertisements, that's like taking someone by the elbow and trying to talk them into something, and so insistently, too, with music and half-naked girlies, that's nothing but, but... Oh, my lord, excuse me! I didn't mean your father."

Anton looked out the porthole. The clouds were three-storied, the lowest ones moving west, the middle ones north. The topmost layer was motionless. Melada in fact had the talent of transforming everything into some sort of awkward direction, to threaten the peaceful flow of minutes and words. Like that time in the bus, jumping up insistently, running up and down the aisle, then breaking her own ribs.

He tried to bring the conversation back to the innocent meadows of youth. He began to speak of his mother. His mother had not shared her husband's love of crowds. It was she, after all, who had made them move to quiet Indiana. People oppressed his mother with their unpredictability. It was always impossible to know in advance what they would be thinking about you. If you were to dress up would they then think you were showing off? But if you wore modest clothing, then wouldn't they take that as a sign of ill respect? Always before going to visit someone she would force the children to try on first this, then that, muttering to herself, "No, Uncle Robert won't like this, he doesn't like anything too loud... But Mrs. Gorsky is very strict about shoes... She holds that you should only wear English-made boots and shoes... I was going to buy you some last week too, but they didn't have your sizes... What am I going to do?"

Little Anton rebelled. Why should he worry only whether he was going to please Uncle Robert and Mrs. Gorsky? They hadn't tried to please him, had they? He deliberately put his socks on inside out, slouched, laughed louder than he felt like, ate with his fingers, drank his soup with a straw. His father, who didn't wish to upset his wife with direct protests, was secretly pleased at his son's antics and giggled, covering himself with the newspaper. His mother had put her hands to her head and silently left for the bedroom.

At first this was called migraine. Migraines could flare up even without any obvious aggravation. It was as though the curious, judgmental, condemnatory looks of the neighbors which were constantly cast in her direction met somewhere behind the wall of her tender brow, just as the searchlights pick out the silver dot of the airplane, threatening to blow it up, destroy it, send it crashing to the ground. Then came illness. Real illness. It had no name. The doctors could not define it, or cure it. There would be flash attacks of fever and vomiting, following which his mother could not get out of bed for a couple of days. No medicines helped, nor any trips to special spas. The attacks came again and again, and after each his mother was prostrated, powerless, dreamy, and satisfied.

Later Anton thought that even as a child he had understood his mother's illness better than any of the doctors. He had noted that it was only during and just after these attacks that his mother's face lost her expression of tense fear. He saw that it brought his mother an enormous relief to be sick and so guilty of nothing. Who could expect anything of a feeble woman who is pressed flat to the sheets by some mysterious illness?

Anton feared these clearing spells on the sick woman's face. He fooled around even more, acting up, making fun of the grownups, dressing up in their clothes, using dirty words. But he had no wish to upset his mother. He wanted to show by example how there was no need to fear condemnation, judgmental looks, or people talking behind your back.

His mother had no wish to understand him. She was upset. And so hid even deeper in her disease. The attacks came more frequently. It began to give her great pleasure to make plans for her funeral. She made her husband long lists of what he would have to buy, whom he had to invite, what the service should be like. Should she be cremated or buried? A plain coffin or a fancy lined one? And what should she wear? When she finally died, quiet and cozy, her ten-year-old son's strongest feeling was indignation, because it seemed to him that his mother had run away from him, had abandoned him, deliberately letting herself die solely to avoid having Mrs. Gorsky criticize the shoes she bought.

Anton finally interrupted his stream of reminiscence because his audience began to behave very oddly. She squinched up her face and pulled the sheet over her head, moaning softly and shaking her head side to side.

"Another attack? Should I give you another pill? I've got an American painkiller in my cabin, you want me to bring it?"

"No, no need. I'm fine. But your story... what a horrible childhood. Can it really be that your mother didn't love you at all?"

"Where did you get that idea? She worshipped me. I was her whole life."

"But then how... I don't understand."

"What?"

"The way you talk about her so unsympathetically. She could be someone you don't even know..."

"But everything I said is absolutely true."

"I'd be terrified to think that my children would ever talk about me like that."

"What do you want? That they do nothing but sing choruses of what a golden mother we have, how unworthy we are of her?"

"Isn't the love of the children for the parents something that we have a right to count on?"

"Do you think all children always love their parents?"

"Of course not. But they have to. If they don't, that's terrible."

He looked at her. She was peeking over the sheet she had pulled over her face like a timid child peeking over her fence—the grownups had gone off warning her not to let any strangers in, but how was she to know whether this was a stranger or a friend?

"I don't know how it sounds in Russian, but in English the words 'have to' and 'love' really don't go together."

His voice was filled with anger. And he didn't regret it; you have to draw the line somewhere. He got up, put on his jacket, and dryly saluted. Then he left.

20 A u g u s t.

We are sailing along the shores of Denmark. The
sea is calm. When I'm not on watch I am reading
books about the Vikings. I study the drawings of
their ships. They had ideal form. Just 75 feet long,
18 across. Held an average of 30 warriors. Oars
and a sail. No superstructure of any sort. Could
they really have stayed under open skies the whole
time they were at sea? They made it to Gibraltar,
raided for booty in the Mediterranean. Their hulls
drew so little water that they could go up even shallow
rivers. No one could be safe from them anywhere.
But why? What forced them from these pleasant
green shores, these rich pastures, these fish-filled
waters? It is a mystery. And why were they so incredibly cruel? And why did they always win? Ten
against a hundred, a hundred against a thousand?
Our girl guests are also unpredictable and cruel.
They tan for hours, chattering to each other and to
us, trying to be of service. Suddenly yesterday they
asked permission and made us all a very tasty German dinner. Schnitzel in mushroom sauce and steamed
cod. For some reason then they got gloomy and started
attacking everything and making fun. Ingrid today
right in front of everyone took out her box that has
the radio detonator and began to play catch with it,
with Gudrun. Naturally I shuddered at every toss.
And they just laughed. Could it be that their watch
is not a bomb at all, but just a toy? But do I have the
guts to find out?

21 A u g u s t.

We passed through the straits separating Denmark
from Sweden. Now we are in the Baltic Sea. I watch
the albatrosses. They skim down, right down, sketching
with their wing feathers on the water, as if they are
testing how warm it is, then suddenly they zoom up
and shoot themselves straight down at some underwater target, like an arrow. For some reason we are
convinced that birds only think about food. That

271

they never do anything but hunt, looking for food. The more I watch them though the more it seems to me that they are simply enjoying themselves, admiring the way they fly. And that final slash, like a sword into the water, might actually be for nothing, just showing off in front of each other. Or it could just be that I am becoming sentimental. When death is lurking about so close at hand, everything seems tinted with a melancholy wash of farewell.

The history books say that the Vikings believed in life after death. That the Valkyrie took warriors who had died valiantly in battle to the halls of Valhalla, where the war god Odin adopted them. Could that have been why they fought so fearlessly? But the Christians too believed in the immortality of the soul, in the rewards of the next world. So why did those little bands of Vikings always conquer the Christian cities and monasteries, sacking and plundering them? The rich kingdoms preferred to pay tribute rather than put together real armies, build strong navies, and fight them off once and for all.

I have read that by the beginning of the 12th century almost all the thrones of Europe had been seized by Norman kings, counts, and princes. That's the land over there, a peaceful blue on the horizon, that a thousand years ago was some sort of breeding ground for producing savage kings. What was the nutritional microclimate for that? Could the northern lights be what develops unconquerability? But then why is this the most peaceful of nations, which hasn't been in a war for 200 years or better? Maybe they are just waiting for their time, when there will once again be a need for bold kings? It is a mystery. My wrist is beginning to hurt under the watch. Skin irritation? Nervous eczema? Odd that they should choose me. Was it chance? Or did they sense a weakness?

22 A u g u s t.
The last few days Pablo-Pedro has been spending

a lot of time with our passengers. He asks them questions, listens respectfully to their answers. From the snatches I overhear it seems that they are explaining the world-wide conspiracy of philatelists to him. He keeps nodding, and sometimes takes notes in his pad. Lin Chan just sighs when she looks at them and makes circles against her forehead.

How easy it is for man to grow accustomed to living alongside death. A time bomb on my wrist already doesn't seem so horrible to me. The danger is even giving life a new flavor, a new piquancy. But I am always wanting to reflect and think about how I would redo my past acts and affairs.

We are heading north along the coast of Sweden. This is where the Vikings came back with their booty. The scientists have found enormous stashes of coins in archeological digs, from the Franks, the Angles, the Byzantine, the Arabs. It is as though the Vikings had no idea what to do with the coins and so kept them the same way sportsmeñ keep their prizes and trophies.

Some historians think their voyages began when they were running out of land at home. I have trouble believing this. They conquered huge tracts of land but never took up plowing or herding. Either they became the rulers of the obedient peoples or returned to take up their eternal internecine battles.

Their legends tell of the kingdom of the other world, which is ruled by the repulsive goddess Hel, who resembles a decaying corpse. She has dominion over those poor souls who did not die in battle, but from old age or disease or accidents. Naturally nobody wanted to wind up in the paws of this goddess after death.

Still, how humiliating it is to go to the cabin of our passengers in the mornings and watch the clock—7:30, 7:35, 7:40—and still they don't come out, so I knock and listen to their sleepy and grumpy voices, remind them that it is time to reset the watch...

"Part-kom, prof-kom, ob-kom, rai-kom, dom-kom..." Anton diligently repeated after Melada these vital words from the Upside-down Land. Such words weren't in the old books that grandfather Yaroslav had taught him from, and it was not difficult for him to play the part of an obedient first-year student, who had only just mastered the alphabet of a foreign tongue. But once he couldn't help himself and almost gave himself away, going on to mutter, "How-come, wel-come, they-come, here-it-comes..."

"Stop, stop," Melada laughed. "That's not it at all. Where did you get such words?"

"Probably from the book you gave me to read from."

She began very patiently to explain the difference between these "koms," short for committees, and his other "comes." Then they began to speak of untranslatable words. She told him how there was no way to say "privacy" in Russian. No doubt because there was no such idea, or feeling, or thing. Why should a people have a word in their language for something which they did not possess, of which they knew nothing, and which they did not value? On the other hand, there was no word in English for the Russian "sokrovennost." The translations which the dictionary offered—secrecy, the innermost—were completely wrong. What did the word mean in fact? The thing held most dearly and secretly, to be preserved deep in the soul. The thing which might be revealed only to the very very closest of friends. Or to the person you love. Not to a confessor and even more so, not to a psychoanalyst. A "sokrovennost" in general was hard to express in conversation. "You want to learn the word? Here, I'll write it out in Latin letters for you. Yes, it is almost like the Russian word for 'treasure.' In Russian dictionaries you'll find it next to the word 'skryt,' or conceal. In English dictionaries 'treasure' is right next to 'treason.' Odd, isn't it?"

She looked at her watch. "The lesson time is over. Do you have to go? No? You can stay by the sickbed a bit yet? Then maybe you'll want to turn into a teacher, so I can turn into a student? There are English words that I don't understand at all. Like 'pass' for example. I always thought that it just meant moving the ball from one player to another in sports. Or that it's a term in cards. Not long ago I discovered that this word has a new meaning. Something to do with the relations between a man and a woman. Is that right?"

He smiled, settled himself more comfortably on the chair. She had no idea of the important subject she was opening up. The answer to her dangerous question could turn into an entire lecture. And as luck would have it she had stumbled onto a professor, a Ph.D. of passes. Yes, the pass exists in thousands of shapes and shades. No, the word cannot be translated with words such as "courting" or "flirting" or "teasing." The pass is a test run in anticipation of courting and flirting. In recent years though the pass had developed and spread so in America that many people tried to get by entirely without courting. They would make a pass, and then it was straight to "Your place or mine?" People were always in a hurry about everything.

Yes, a pass could be made with a word or an intonation or a look or a touch. There are some with particular skills, who can make a pass with the headlights on their car. And there are corresponding experts who are able to make out such passes and send one in return. To hold open the elevator doors or ask the time or sing a snatch from a song in the latest film or brush hair from the brow or light a cigarette or toss a chunk of ice into a glass or do up a button or show a picture of their dog or share a banana—any of these innocent acts could be made into a pass. After that it was up to the addressee of the pass, whether to respond in kind or not.

Oh yes, he could recall some brilliant passes which he had happened to witness. Once his friend had chanced on a charming jogger when he was out running one morning. He had quickly gotten off the sidewalk and run to his car, followed her in it a couple of blocks until he got ahead of her, then ran toward her again, then got back in the car and did it all again. And again. The fourth time she laughed, at which point he turned around and ran alongside her.

One young lady he knew who was working in a travel agency could not, try as she might, catch the attention of her boss, who was a preoccupied bachelor who was always humming popular songs to himself, but with no intention of making them into a pass. Once he was dictating some sort of business letter to her while he stared at the screen of her computer, and this woman, as if she were unaware of it, took up the refrain of the song he had been singing a half hour before, and typed it: "I know I'll never love this way again..." That was the first time that he really took any notice of her, and then after that they lived together long and happily, until the owner of an insurance company who chanced to be passing through made her a pass she couldn't refuse—he offered his apartment on the shores of the Hudson, complete with his hand and heart.

Or once a cousin of his at a big party just went up to some woman who caught his eye and said, "Excuse me, for God's sake, but couldn't you help me, perhaps? An old girlfriend of mine is here and is following me. She knows that I'm very shy and I'm afraid that she'll start flirting with me in front of all these people. Look, look, there she is, another crude pass! Couldn't I just pretend that I've come with you? Otherwise she's going to follow me all night." The real genius of this was that the woman he was pointing to was his wife.

The main virtue in a pass is its apparent guilelessness. A pass can always be disowned. You can say, I didn't have anything of the sort in mind. A wink for example isn't really a pass. That's a straight proposition, even a sign that you are assuming certain obligations. In principle you could be sued if you don't carry through with your significant winking. Or you could be cited for lewd behavior. Probably the art of the pass has grown so precisely because the devices of old-fashioned courting have become so dangerous.

"Of course, it's easier to explain using examples. So let's say for example that I wanted to make a pass at you. In tight quarters like this cabin, what are the possible variants? I could puff up your pillow and 'by chance' touch your cheek—like this. And when I see that you jump away and 'by chance' wipe off where I touched, then I understand that my pass has been rejected. Or I might begin asking you about your tastes in things. Do you like tall men?"

"Yes."

"And I'm short. So that means my pass fails to score again. So now I might try some sort of intimate confession. For instance, that under-wear made of artificial fibers makes my skin break out. Without specifying exactly where. And if you don't immediately shudder or aren't completely indifferent to my skin problems, then I could try another pass and ask how your husband feels about synthetics."

"I'm not married."

"That's just what the guy making the pass hopes you'll say. But you know, if you had wanted to decline my pass, then you'd say something like, 'Listen, I'm not asking you anything about your wife's under-wear.'"

"What kind of underwear does your wife wear?"

"Ah-ha. A capable student. I'm not married. I was widowed two years ago. An unlucky incident. I'll tell you about it sometime, about how it happened. But now I don't want to talk about sad things. Let's go back to the theory of passes. In general knowing how to decipher passes properly and respond to them correctly is also a great art.

Especially for women. Especially if there are a lot of people around when the pass is made, or she's at work. Let's say that she works in a barber shop, and she catches a customer making moon-eyes at her. Somebody who comes in every day for a shave. And tries to sit in her chair. Naturally the barbering profession gives a lot of opportunity to respond to a pass. Perhaps while you're shaving the customer's lip you can take his nose by the tip and give it a tug, wiggle it side to side without anyone noticing. Or a thigh against his hand where it rested on the arm of the barber chair. Or tucking the napkin into his collar stick the fingers a little deeper down than was strictly necessary. Or do all of them, keep sending these passes and thinking up others, without even waiting for any answer, with no submission to any codes of modesty, pushing and pulling both him and yourself in some rapid dance or going downhill in a sled, pressing together closer and closer, against the speed, the wind, the fear."

That summer the wind knocked down several old trees in the town, and their heavy branches often broke wires. The blowdryers in the barbershop fell silent, the hood dryers cooled off, the clippers ceased buzzing, and he and Peggy would leave as if by chance, as if they were just headed in the same direction. She was never bored with him. She did not believe him when he said that probably even signs of tenderness and affection could be boring, that they have to be varied and doled out sparingly, that they should be spaced with answering gestures, so that they held their worth. But no, she only was interested in doing it her way, in a flood, gesture after gesture, smile after touch, touch after gift, arm over shoulder after wave goodbye, wave hello after telephone call in the middle of the night, and then start all over again, exactly the same, and don't you worry, brother, I won't get bored.

Even when passes had long become unnecessary, when he would go to her in the evenings with a bunch of flowers, she would ask him to leave the flowers in the hall outside and bring in the flowers one by one over the course of the evening, and she would find each one of them a delight. One she would stand before her in a little vase while they had dinner. The next one would go in her hair, while they danced. The third she would rub against her cheek while they watched television. This game of gift-giving would help them fill the time until the girlfriend that Peggy shared the apartment with would finally leave. No, the girlfriend knew all about their affair and had no objection to it, and her room was on the other side of the corridor. But still she might hear the loud singing which would bother her studying for tests. Peggy knew she had a weakness for singing at the very last moment, which embarrassed her a bit, and she had warned him in advance, so that he wouldn't be startled if she were to stop groaning and begin to sing at the top of her lungs instead. She didn't have an especially good ear, but she knew dozens of opera arias and had no hesitation about skipping from Tatyana Larina's "Why did you come to us?" to unfaithful Delilah's "Not so swift the arrow," then to end with Carmen's cry of abandonment, "Not even wings may snare her!" When she forgot the words she could put in her own words, or fake it, but there was one fan of her musical talents (without a musical gift himself, but impulsive in the extreme, and most responsive) who always leapt up when she sang, even if it happened to be in the car as they drove, which interfered with Anton's driving.

She believed in signs, but only in good ones. When she left the house in the morning she would guess what she would see first, a cat or a squirrel. A cat meant that she would have good luck, while a squirrel meant she would have an unexpected pleasant surprise.

If there were more women than men at the bus stop, that meant she would meet an old girlfriend, and if more men than women, then she would meet a handsome stranger. If she saw a jogger coming towards her, that meant money, while a bicyclist meant a gift.

Everybody loved her, admired her. Or so she thought. The landlady left her umbrella open in the hallway not because she had simply forgotten it, but because she wanted to shield her beloved tenant from the rain. The policeman waved their bus through the intersection out of turn because he had noticed her face in the window. The customers lined up at her barbershop not because of the cheap prices but because they liked her. In the stores the clerks gave her a special hello, not the way they usually said it. And in church the Madonna knew her by name and watched for her, and every time Peggy prayed to Her she always began with her full name, as though she were making a telephone call to a very busy office.

Of course there were occasional people who were coarse with her, who didn't greet her or were even cruel. But they only made her laugh heartily. Eccentrics of some sort, evidently—madmen from some other planet, walking jokes.

"Just imagine," she told him, laughing, "the teller in the bank refused to cash my check today. My own personal check! And the way he talked to me, like somebody was choking him! 'You know our rules! I have to see some ID!' It was so funny!"

Another time, at a big cookout at the Kellers, who had forgiven Anton and now invited him round occasionally with Wife #6, Peggy laughed on the way back as she recalled how she had suddenly broken into the conversation ("By the way, what was the film you were discussing? Maybe we should go see it too?") to announce in a loud voice that a new store had opened in the next street over, which had made everyone fall quiet and stare at her. It had been so funny, this little bit of news from real life that you could forget right away if you wanted—but what could it hurt to remember, you might want to know it someday—so funny that a little thing like that would make people so crazy, that it was all she could do not to laugh when she looked at their confused faces.

No, she never embarrassed Anton. It seemed to him that on some other level which he could not yet attain she was wiser than the Kellers and their guests and the *auteurs* of the arty films and the authors of all the books she had never read, and never would. He wanted to learn from her, to discover the secret of her sunny acceptance of each day, each minute, each person.

They had a church wedding. And then he went several times with her to Sunday services. He listened each time how Peggy reminded the Madonna of her maiden name and her married name, not trusting Her memory, because She had so much to worry about. Then Peggy would request happiness, health, and peace for herself, her husband, and her future child.

He hoped that by marrying a Catholic he had at last broken the ill-starred chain of his divorces. No matter that he was so much older than she; all of his insurance was changed to her name, so that she would be well provided for if he should die. It never even crossed his mind that she might die before him.

Sometimes he thought that she had died so suddenly precisely because the Madonna or fate or the Fates of old had been unable to answer her prayers but had not been able to refuse her either, and that the jugglers in the sky had just run out of the strength necessary to keep her balanced on the thinnest edge of unshakable bliss.

"Mr. Sebich?" Melada called.

He stopped in her door.

"Might I... Could I say something? About your story? That story about your wife, tell me honestly... Could I maybe think that that wasn't just a pass?"

He studied her face. This wasn't irony, was it? She wasn't capable of that, was she? She looked upset. But then she smiled. A little nervously. He shook his finger at her.

> 23 A u g u s t.
>
> Today our passengers asked the captain to stop the Babylonia. Following their orders Pablo-Pedro let down the skiff, rowed out a hundred yards and put the small thermos the girls had given him into a life ring. Then he rowed back. They handed him the radio control box. He flipped the switch and the thermos exploded like a grenade. Then he went back out to the place where the explosion had been and gathered up the dead fish. All three of them were very gay, getting ready to make bouillabaisse, that fish soup from Marseilles. We didn't feel like laughing though.
>
> We can't see the shore anymore. We are heading east. This was how the Vikings sailed on their way to conquer Rus, old Russia. Actually, it was they who were the "Rus," since that's what the old chronicles of Byzantium call them. It was they too who subdued the tribes of Finns, Slavs, Ests, and Chuds who lived along the banks of the Volkhov river, the Dnepr, the Volga, and the other rivers. The Slavs called their conquerors Varangians. The Varangians reached the Black Sea quite quickly, and began to threaten Constantinople. One of their commanders even nailed his shield to the city gates so that people would remember him and be afraid.
>
> When I see how mercilessly people compete, how passionately they strive to outdo one another, how they fight each other, I feel so alone and rejected. "Are you blind?" I mutter. But perhaps this is only my own envy. Perhaps I am the one blinded by fate.
>
> 24 A u g u s t.
> Today our passengers decided to take photographs.

And they demanded that we take part. They snapped
us in pairs and in groups, in our uniforms and in
swimming suits, hugging and holding hands, laughing
forcedly and smiling acidly. Then they collected
all the Polaroid snaps and hid them somewhere in
their bags. In general they are always trying to give
the impression that nothing in particular is going
on, that we are all friends off on a jolly little jaunt.
They get bent out of shape if we aren't friendly
with them. They insist that we all eat together, that
we have dances and watch TV together. Pablo-Pedro
is the first to respond to their suggestions. He does
whatever they ask. Even if the captain asks him to
do one thing—such as, for example, bring white
wine, and they want red—he listens to them. Maybe
he is just suffering from Stockholm Syndrome? The
desire to please those upon whom your life depends?
After all, I have something like that, and I smile at
the girls every time they reset the hands on my watch,
even though I don't want to. I read that Odin, the
Vikings' main god, once offered himself as a sacrifice. He hung himself from the Tree of Knowledge and hung there nine days, so as to learn higher
wisdom. When the Vikings wanted to offer Odin
human sacrifices—which was fairly often—they hung
captives or slaves on trees. In the evenings when I
am meditating in front of my own picture I sometimes start to wonder whether I am being offered as
a sacrifice or am being hung by the thin thread of
the fuse in the watch in order to gain new knowledge that I never asked to get. What am I going to
learn at the end of the ninth day? Tomorrow morning we sight Finland.

The flat Baltic sun, which had spent so much of itself on Karelian
huckleberries, Neva pines, Estonian cows, and Pskov daisies still
warmed the skin pleasantly. Melada pressed a dew-covered glass of
Pepsi to her cheek. Today was the first time that she came up on the deck
by herself. She was in bliss. From time to time she stretched out a bare
foot from the deck chair to run it along the smooth warm decking. Anton

hated to disturb her tranquillity, but a sudden confused guess was burning a hole in his tongue. He had to share his idea with someone. He plunked down in the chair next to her and asked whether she felt up to discussing something heavy and unpleasant.

"The death of your wife, you mean?"

"Yes," Anton said hopefully.

"I haven't been able to get it out of my head. Such a horrible way to die. But maybe it's only for us that such things are terrible? For those close to the person, those of us left behind? A mutilated body, the blood... I don't know... If we were able to choose... I'd want to go like that too, instantaneously. I mean death probably came before she felt any pain."

"Something like that happens once in a decade, in two decades. Chances are one-in-a-billion. But it was like she anticipated it. Every time we passed that place on the highway she would make a joke about the sign, 'Watch For Falling Rock.' 'What do they mean, watch for falling rock? What are we supposed to do, get out and push the car, keep one eye up on the cliff? Or look for another road? Open an umbrella maybe?' The police told me that there were no tire marks on the road. That means that she didn't even have time to hit the brakes. Bang, and that was it."

"See? I know it's not much consolation, but..."

"Later I read the statistics. About fifty thousand people die every year in auto accidents. About a thousand in air crashes. Flood and tornado get about the same, same as collapsing buildings, explosions, fires, poisoning, drowning, and suicide. However, in every one of these deaths there is somebody you can say is guilty—indirectly, at least. A drunk driver, failed brakes, a mistake by the air traffic controller. You can see a tornado or a flood coming, or someone warns you, and you can get to shelter. There are smoke detectors for fire, and sprinklers and fire extinguishers. Even if a bridge collapses and your car goes into the river the construction firm is at fault, because of an oversight or an error. But when a rock falls out of the sky, there is nobody at fault. And that is what is so horrible. There aren't even any statistics about it."

"When my younger brother was in the army he was in a car wreck. He won't say much about it, because it's a military secret, but I think it wasn't really a car wreck, but a tank wreck. He lost four fingers on his right hand."

"I turned into some sort of mannequin. My friends said that I just couldn't shake the grief. It wasn't grief though, but rather some sort of fainting spell that wouldn't end. It was as if consciousness were hiding inside it, like a snail pulled back in its shell. Misery like a hermit crab. All the time I walked and talked and worked, or at least I thought I was. When my clerks said I hadn't done what I had promised to do, that I hadn't signed the papers that had to be signed or hadn't paid overdue bills, I would get angry and yell at them. It would have been a lot better if I had taken up the bottle or gone into a psychiatric hospital for a couple of months. I had a well-trained staff, and somehow or other they would have held things together until I got well. Instead though I showed up at the office every day, picked up the mound of letters my secretary had slit open for me, told her no calls, and locked myself in my study, where I would look at them and understand not a single word. Sometimes when I surfaced I would notice that I had been sitting with a blank piece of paper cranked into my typewriter for four hours or better. But then consciousness would retract again, go back into its shell, and I would spend the rest of the day sitting over the same blank page.

"Business got worse and worse. My assistants began to quit. My clients began to sue for losses I had caused. Still I spent day after day in a stupor, angrily chasing away everyone who tried to help me, yelling 'Quit reading me lessons! I know what I'm doing!' I went bust inside of a year."

"There was nobody close who could have brought you out of this lethargy? Who would have known what to say, who could have shaken you out of it or forced his way in and taken over your business or chased off your terrible Miserymaker?"

"Forced his way in? No, that's not done in America. Every person has to cope with his problems on his own. Little or big. Sometimes it seems to me that every American begins his morning with the exact same prayer, 'O all-powerful and all-knowing God, I pray, please don't let me get involved today and forever in anyone else's troubles or problems...' You mention the Miserymaker, though... Something strange happened... I've never told anyone about this. See, when I got the word about my wife's death... I know it sounds terrible, but the Miserymaker wasn't close. Or more exactly he was, but he wasn't himself, as if he were upset and confused. You understand what I'm trying to say? Maybe that was the worst part of all. He could have been trying to apologize. He wanted to prove to me that he hadn't done it, or it wasn't his fault... Maybe that's what I was banging my head against all those hours and days that I was sitting locked in my office. I had encountered an unsolvable puzzle. If the Miserymaker had been made to do something he hadn't wanted to, then who on earth was it who had made him do it?"

In his excitement Anton put his feet on the deck, turned to face Melada. She looked expectantly at him, as if she knew the answer but couldn't break the rules by giving him a hint.

"Yes, I'm convinced now that it wasn't so much the loss of my wife that put me in a coma for an entire year, but terror of a One Who Sends The Miserymaker. It was precisely as though I had been deprived of the age-old enemy whom I knew and with whom I could cope, in place of which I was suddenly face-to-face with the Unknown. The whole familiar set-up of life collapsed around me. You know when I finally understood that? After our talk yesterday. Yes, I'm out of the fit now, I'm alive again. But not like I used to be. Because I think about it almost every day. Who, who in the name of all that's holy, who is it that forces the Miserymaker to come?"

Melada studied the hazy Baltic horizon in silence, pushing the sharp little cocktail straw around with her tongue. If people had been capable of inventing negative numbers, then why had no one invented negative gestures? Her minus-smile alarmed Anton, upset him.

"Of course, I don't have an answer to that question," she finally said. "But I think... or more exactly, I am completely convinced... That out of this whole story... Your unhappiness and your meditations are going to let you make... that you will write a very interesting radio program..."

Once again he couldn't make out whether she was being ironic or serious.

> 25 A u g u s t.
> Eight o'clock in the evening. The Babylonia is a mile off Finland. Everything is over. Pablo-Pedro has betrayed us, gone over to the terrorists. He has a pistol. They have fastened a thermos to the fuel tank. They assure us that this is simply a precaution so that we can't turn off the motor and radio the police. That in two hours they will be safe with their friends on shore and that they will turn the bomb off by radio. The bomb in my watch too. Then the watchband will open by itself and fall off. I don't believe them. I think that they are capable of anything. At Dachau they told the people that there were no gas chambers, they were being taken to a

shower. They played music. Isn't that why they had us take the photos with them? So that if they were arrested they could prove that we were all friends. They came on the cruise with us, and then went ashore, and that's all they know. What caused the explosion and when it happened, they couldn't say. I should have sacrificed myself right at the very first in order to save the others. But I was afraid. Olga, you know that I have no fear of pain, but even the thought of human flesh being ripped to bits...

"Everybody kneel along the gunwales!" Ingrid clapped her hands like a nursery school teacher. "Hands on the railing!"

"What's going on?" Melada asked, upset. "Is this some new game? I don't want to kneel, why should I? It hurts me a lot to bend..."

"You have to, you have to, you have to," Ingrid sang as she clapped handcuffs onto the outstretched wrists of the Babylonians.

"Do as they say," Anton said.

Gudrun was already over the side in the skiff, stowing the bags and supplies. The strugglers against world philately had also taken the ship's radio. Their frozen doll-like smiles didn't leave their faces for a second.

On her knees Lin Chan looked at Pablo-Pedro and said thoughtfully, "I had a feeling this would happen. When we met. Just think! I put out five thousand. The worst bargain of my life. But still I'd like to know. You haven't forgotten your pills?"

Pablo-Pedro silently slapped himself on the shirt pocket.

"There's enough for a couple of days. They're probably called something else in Finland. Show the box to a druggist. He'll understand."

"What a stupid childish game," Melada muttered, "How in the world could you ever agree to it?"

Far far overhead a plane decorated with twin lights followed the stars toward Europe. A rosy path stretched over the waves toward the electric glow above Helsinki. Ingrid walked once last time along the row of prisoners handcuffed to the rails.

"You shouldn't be upset. Everything will be tip-top okay. But the most important thing to us is our own safety. After all we have the whole world after us, because the philatelists have deceived them. The main thing is to try to suppress your hostile feelings these next two hours."

Pablo-Pedro started down into the boat. Ingrid followed him. Pablo-Pedro stopped, handed her a bunch of cloth napkins with dog's heads embroidered in the corners.

"Probably better to blindfold them. So that they don't see which direction we row off in."

"Good idea."

"And I'll start the engine."

Lin Chan tried to turn away, but Ingrid got a neat head lock on her and put the blindfold on. Ronald offered his sad and resigned face without opposition, his eyes closed.

"This is idiotic, you're going to find out that this is just idiotic," Melada said.

"Miss Melada doesn't know anything," Anton said. "She has never collected stamps. Moreover, Mr. Glukharev will be very upset when he finds out how you've treated her. This is going to shut the doors of all the Soviet embassies everywhere for you. So why don't you take her with you and leave her on the shore someplace? It's already a tradition with you to release hostages who need medical attention."

The motor fired down below. Two boiling white plumes stretched behind the boat as it pulled away.

Ingrid was suddenly angry. "What do you mean 'you'? What are you hinting at, Captain Sebich? Are you comparing us with ordinary terrorists? And that after everything we've told you about our movement? After all the wonderful hours we've spent together on this trip? What a tiny little soul someone would have to have to..."

She was suddenly silent, and threw aside the napkins as she dashed to the railing.

The skiff was bobbing about some forty meters off. The Babylonia's lights twinkled and sparkled on its rubber sides. The noise of the engine died away, replaced by a thin plaintive inhuman shriek from inside the little boat.

"Hey, what's going on over there?" Ingrid shouted.

"*Er verdreht meine Ohren!*" Gudrun's sobbing voice wafted over to them.

"*Was macht er?*"

"*Er verdreht meine Ohren!* He's pulling on my ear! OW! OUCH! NO OW OW OW!"

"*Er wagt es nicht!* (Of all the nerve!)"

"*Aber doch, aber doch!*"

"Aber es kann doch nicht so schmerzen."

"Er Fut es mit Zangen!"

"What do you mean with pliers?! Torturer! Scoundrel! Stop it, stop it this instant! Stop it or I'll..."

A new shriek flew to heaven like a needle and began to dash about there, as if it had been assigned the task of threading up all the spilled and beady stars.

Ingrid ran along the deck, now blocking her ears with her hands, now biting her fingers, now clutching at the railing and staring into the moan-filled black.

"I'll blow the ship up! You hear me! I don't care about myself! I'll blow the whole of the Pirgoroy band to high heaven!"

"Do it!" Pablo-Pedro's voice drifted over. "I'd like that. Then I could start in on her nose. Have to straighten her nose a little. Anybody would tell you that. I mean to start with there's that little German spud on the end. If I was to just give it a little squeeze..."

A new series of shrieks, like the nasal honks of dolphins, rose up over the lapping black waves.

Ingrid fell to her knees alongside Anton. "Enough! I beg you, enough! What do you want? I'll do anything, you swine, you traitor, you scum... What are you trying to do?!"

The shrieks were replaced by a stifled sobbing.

"Go below!" Pablo-Pedro ordered. "Go down below and bring out the thermos. And no tricks!"

Ingrid jumped up, disappeared into the engine room and reappeared a minute later, carrying the red and ready bomb in her hands.

"Open the top! Captain, she isn't playing tricks there is she? She's playing honest?"

"I see dials of some sort!" Anton shouted back.

"That's it. Okay, throw it overboard."

The fiendish little container filled with a TNT cocktail bubbled its way to the bottom of the Gulf of Finland.

The motor roared again. The boat emerged from the murk, began to draw nearer. Now they could see Pablo-Pedro's silhouette, holding the rudder with one hand and a tight little bundle of doll-hair in the other. His victim lay on her back in the rubber bottom of the boat, her knees twitching feebly.

"Undo the handcuffs! No, start with the captain. Okay... Now everybody get away from Ronald. Ronald, hold out the hand with the watch. And you, bitch, you stand with your back to him...and put his hand between your legs, like you're riding him. That's the best way to make sure nothing goes wrong. Okay, now undo his watchband. It's off? Throw it over board. Let the Baltic herring live on Swiss time for a while. As for you, you jump too!"

"What?"

"You heard what I said!"

"But I have to change into my swim suit."

"You're fine as you are."

"I don't swim very well."

"Good time to learn then. You going to keep me waiting much longer?"

Pablo-Pedro let go of the wheel, grabbed the pliers, and a new shriek cut through the deep night air.

"I'm coming, I'm coming! Gudrun, don't...here...I'm..."

She climbed over the railing and hung indecisively over the mysterious and innocently smooth water. Anton, too weak to interfere, hugged the astonished Melada, stroking her trembling spine. Ronald was at the lantern, studying his now-returned hand with thankful puzzlement.

"Wait!" Lin Chan said. "You can't do it that way. It's inhuman, somehow."

She went over to Ingrid, looked in her tortured and weepy face, which had suddenly came back to life a little, then, with a little leap, gave her a resounding slap on the cheek. Ingrid fell into the water with a shriek.

Pablo-Pedro laughed, gave his victim a final squeeze, then grabbed her under the knees and chucked her overboard with a splash.

The two heads bobbed at the edge of a lighted ring, complaining in English, threatening in German, cursing in Russian. Machine-like, robot-like, obeying only the sacred laws of the sea, Ronald went to the railing, took down the life ring, and threw it toward the girls. They quickly splashed over to it, grabbed the rope, then turned and swam away from the pitiless, ungrateful, and unpredictable slaves of world philately. Two pairs of plastic heels foamed in the water and quickly disappeared into the night.

The Babylonia was celebrating.

The two red lights hung one above the other on the mast told all passing ships that the crew was unable to continue their voyage that evening, that they had to recover after all they had suffered.

Pablo-Pedro sat at the head of the table, accepting the toasts and praise with condescension, hiding his grin behind a glass of wine.

"Let's drink to cruelty!" Ronald bellowed, a bit drunk. "And cynicism, hypocrisy, and the law of the jungle! To everything that we no longer have the guts to do! Tomorrow we will be sober and will once again spurn this man here. We will call him a torturer, a double-crosser, a sly dog. We will run our hands over our arms, our legs, our necks—which he saved—and say that we have nothing in common with him. That we condemn his inhuman methods of self-defense absolutely. But today, under cover of night? Long life and health to you, you sea pirate! May you live a hundred years, you Bluebeard with pliers!"

The glasses were once again raised in the direction of the hero. What was left in the fridge? A canned ham, a jar of pickles, pear juice, smoked oysters? Put it all on the table! Leave nothing! If we feast, then feast we shall! Tomorrow in Helsinki we will buy a mountain of chow, a sea of swill! And then we shall set off into the unknown debris of the Upside-down Land. But today...

"Still, I think that we ought to warn the Finnish authorities," Melada kept repeating, smiling, propped up in pillows. "Those psychotic little girls could be extremely dangerous. I'd at least like to phone our embassy. It's only right that..."

"Down with what's right!" Ronald shouted. "Down with justice! I know what's going to happen! The Finnish police will find two sopping wet little urchins on the shore, and ask what happened to them. And they'll get a horror story in reply. They'll see the swollen ear. And then tomorrow morning they will arrest our savior as soon as we dock. He'll be sent to prison for disfigurement and for attempted murder by drowning. And we'll all be sent to jail as accessories after the fact. And Melada will have to be a witness at the trial."

"I was blindfolded. I didn't see anything."

Lin Chan flung her husband's arm around her neck, nuzzled him. "Stinker, you were playing with our lives. And you went off to a nice safe distance. But that was clever and proper. You figured it out perfectly. She couldn't blow us up and leave you alive. That's psychology. All you stinkers understand each other very well."

Suddenly she broke free, then whispered something in Melada's ear. Melada nodded, then gave her the key to her cabin. Both women then began giggling and making faces. Lin Chan ran off and then came back a few minutes later, solemnly carrying in arms outstretched before her an ordinary notebook. She put it on the edge of the table, then studied the faces turned expectantly toward her. Then she flipped back the cardboard cover.

The flock of brightly colored little squares trembled, fastened firmly to the pages by a strip of adhesive. Their serrated edges slipped one atop the other. The Kremlin, a Chinese dragon, an American president, the Queen of England, a white magnolia...

The Babylonians greeted this evidence of their participation in the world conspiracy of philatelists with great roars. The wine flowed free again, knives and forks clanked, glasses glittered, the radio tinkled with guitars and balalaikas.

And it seemed that just for an instant, as Captain Anthony Sebich looked over the joyous faces of his crew, did his glance strike, even stumble on, catch an answering pair of light, damp, and foreign eyes. But that instant was enough. Their rays shot him through, penetrated deep into his chest. He felt the forgotten pain of the swelling, inflaming berry. Felt how it hurts.

PART THREE

THE RESCUE

Radio Broadcast Begun in the Gulf of Finland and Finished in the Mouth of the Neva

(The Melancholy Diplomat)

The American cultural attaché to the embassy in Moscow was given a three-day leave to Helsinki to treat his eyes and get new glasses (Either there was no good oculist nearer to Moscow than the Finnish capital, or else our diplomats are afraid that the Russians have figured out how to implant bugs even in the bows of eyeglasses.) He was passing the time between two appointments to the doctor and so came to the port to meet us and give us some advice, which of course was a nice thing for him to have done. And while my crew was engaged in buying and stowing supplies, he told me a lot of interesting things about the country we were heading for.

"This is the third year that I've lived there," he said, "so I've already gotten used to putting up with a lot of the peculiarities of local life. Yet I remember how during my first days there I was simply stunned and traumatized by one characteristic that is absolutely strange for us, the way everybody hates everybody else, to the point of rage. Rage literally splashes you in the face every step you take. And that's not because you're a foreigner. People's hatred for each other saturates the air in the cities, oozes out of the overcrowded trolleybuses and three-block-long lines, it's stamped on the faces of the salesgirls, waiters, cabbies, the porters. Sometimes it seems that the main job of each is to show you that you haven't the slightest right to ask anything of them, or even to be there. You pay them money of course, but they take the money from you with the air of a tremendous, condescending favor. Always, no matter what the situation, you are nothing but a pitiful petitioner. Sometimes you're even going to think that the customers of your firm Pirgoroy, the cats and dogs, will be looking at you and thinking just one thing, 'Boy, wouldn't I like to take a bite out of you!'

"But sooner or later, and sometimes really soon, you'll run into a particular breed of people who don't have 'Abandon hope all who enter here' stamped on their foreheads. You'll run into them for sure, because one of their characteristics is that they aren't afraid of relations with

293

foreigners. It's highly possible that pretty soon they'll invite you to be their guests. Not in a restaurant or cafe, because there that same sea of anger at high tide will be splashing on the shores of hate. So it will be at their homes. You'll visit, and immediately at the door you'll be enveloped by an air of sincere warmth, almost love. You'll feel it almost physically, like a puff of warm air. It's like wandering around Chicago for an hour in January when it's sleeting and blowing, and then coming back to a hot bath in your hotel.

"All around you are welcoming faces, full of interest and anticipating little miracles. Soon after the short ceremony of greetings and introductions is over these people may forget about you, but not out of indifference, simply because they will cease regarding you as an outsider. You will feel that you have already been included into the discussion, accepted into this little underground sect of mutual participation and admiration. Guests come and go in the crowded little room, or even in the kitchen; somebody brings a can of tinned fish, somebody a bottle of grain alcohol that he stole at work, somebody else a homemade rice pie, if there was rice in the stores, or a cabbage, if one of their relatives had been sent to the country to harvest cabbage. Sometimes children will come in after a nap, climb onto the lap of the hosts or the guests, and with silent seriousness, finger in mouth, will watch how others perform the new religious act called Conversation.

"There is no more precise a term for this heretical sect than to call them 'word-worshippers.'

"Russian conversation is like Russian ballet. It can flow about in various corners and in the center simultaneously, with the rooms as stages. The soloist does his turn, but the corps de ballet lives its life on the edges. You can listen to the main story, being told by the latest guest, or you can be distracted by a quiet conversation in a corner, or you can begin to chat about something with the girl at your side, answering her sympathetic questions, slithering on the thin line between flirting and courting. The line there is still stretched awfully high, and doesn't come down for making an everyday pass. Then in the sudden silence, in the turned faces, you sense that the soloist raconteur is just about to do some brilliant pirouette, you shut up just in time, and in fact, the leap and turn in words come, there is an explosion of laughter, glasses are raised, and then later, the soloist changes.

"Yes, our parties too are similar to ballet, but there is a subtle and important difference in how completely people throw themselves into this. I can't explain it, you'll just have to see it for yourself.

"What do the word-worshippers talk about? The rings of Saturn and the

language of dolphins, military revolution in Latin America and the battle of Thermopylae, the causes of cancer and semiprecious stones from the Ural, ways to pickle mushrooms and the dispute between Martin Luther and Erasmus of Rotterdam, about last year's trip to Kamchatka and the police search yesterday at a mutual friend's house, about the difference between an impressionist and a pointillist, about the similarities of good and evil, the stupidity of the government and the indifference of the governed, about the kids' grades in school and global overpopulation, about the competition for places in the university and telling the future from the stars.

"The major theme, though, and the one they love most is their new Holy Writ, literature. It can be difficult for a foreigner to understand and value this aspect of the cult of conversation, because as a rule he doesn't know the sacred texts to the necessary degree. He may understand that just now a quote from St. Dostoevsky was crossed with a quote from St. Lermontov, and that then another conversant was able to cross out an entire chapter of St. Chekhov with a few lines from St. Pushkin. You won't always understand who is being talked about either, because the practice is to refer to the main saints by their names and patronymics, instead of their family names, so it's Lev Nikolaevich and Anna Andreevna and Mikhail Afanasievich, instead of Tolstoy or Akhmatova or Bulgakov. In some cases, though, this can be taken as overly familiar and out of place. There's a lot of subtlety to this. And besides the main holy texts there are miles and miles of secondary figures, and libraries and libraries of commentaries and commentaries on the commentaries, all of which are brought into conversations to be fed on like an endless verbal plankton.

"In fact these and millions of similar vigils around the teapot and the vodka bottle every evening are debates which will define the next, new names in the literary pantheon. Every candidate is examined and discussed with the same pickiness that we use to examine candidates for the Supreme Court. But then Supreme Court judges are only chosen for life, so if you don't like someone, you can quietly and patiently wait for him to die. Yet the Russian literary figure is moved into the pantheon for time immemorial, and everything that he writes or wrote will influence future leaders for centuries. That's why discussion of the candidacies can go on for decades, with an ebb and flow of passion that seem disproportionate and incomprehensible to us.

"Tourists might get the idea that the country is settled by nothing but word-worshippers. In fact there aren't very many of them, it's just that they aren't afraid to have guests from abroad. And when you live here a

long time, you begin to see the other social levels. You meet the bureau-crats, from all levels; their major activity is to hide their privileges and riches. They literally know that their wellbeing is concocted from some-thing unclean. They never will say `this is mine;' instead they use a special word which you won't find in a single dictionary: `spets', for special. Special clinic, special airplane, special dacha, special distributor, special train, special resort. The word-worshippers don't envy them, and in fact make fun of them. In general it's the done thing to have contempt for the bureaucrats, and to condemn them. But in fact, if you want to live long, what you have to look out for is the word-worshippers.

"How can I explain that to you?"

When you go back out on the street after your first communion in the mystery of conversation, your soul will be overflowing with excitement. What do you care now if the entire city is flooded to the rooftops with despair and anger! After all, you have just been in an atmosphere of such warmth and heart-felt admiration, you were accepted into a tight circle of friends just for what you are, not for what you can do or have done, friends who know how to take joy from one another, to bring beauty to one another's lives, to exist on so full and self-giving a level of human intercourse, such as you have never had the opportunity to experience before. Even the sullenness of the faces flowing before your eyes is less depressing. You begin to think, or fantasize, that each of these people about you has his own domestic shrine of goodness and gentility some-where, with his own circle of dear ones, within the bosom of which this mask of 'Who do I bite now?' slips away, and the dumbstruck lips regain their ability to part in a smile.

"Then you begin to go to the homes of the word-worshippers regularly. You are passed from circle to circle. People are always happy to see you, they always have time for you. You understand their language better and better, bit by bit you become aware of the sub-texts of irony, the hidden quotes, the gentle parodying, the poetic teasing. You begin to take some part in their affairs, to help as you can—bringing in a book from abroad, or a medicine, taking out a letter. It's always easy to please them; they need so little from life, from fate, from us. Your heart is stolen, it melts, you are filled with grateful love for these people.

"But have a care, and don't succumb.

"This climate isn't for us, our skins aren't made for that sort of constant heat. Quite soon you will begin to feel sharp pangs. At first in little things. One of your new friends doesn't call when he promised he would. Someone doesn't invite you to a party where there is roast wood grouse, brought by *a visiting poacher-friend. And at a party that you were invited to every-body there forgot about you too easily, giving all their attention, and with a great deal more awe, to some visitor who has brought with him a new tape of songs by the latest unsung genius.*

"This jealous pang will hit you more and more often, and it won't go away. It will build up, layer after layer. In vain you try to convince yourself that nobody is avoiding you, that that's how they are with each other. That the woman with whom you shared the most precious of feelings for two whole hours, alone out in the hall, still remembers you a month later and just isn't coming over now because for some reason in this new crowd it's awkward for her. And the familiar husband and wife who always give you a lift to the embassy didn't forget to do so today simply because you already got the medical handbook they wanted for them, but because today they had to return home immediately. And anyway, what makes you think that a trusting friendly conversation obligates your partner in conversation to pick you out of the ringing, tightly packed crowd some-how the next time you meet?

"It's impossible to understand whether we are incorrigible property-owners who are unable to leave the soul of another as available to all, like a village commons, instead always trying to turn it into our own little garden, with a sign that says `No Trespassing'? Or are they careless seducers, knocking us off base with their souls that are open to all sides, without even a word in their language for that sacred fencing off of the soul, like 'privacy?' Or is the cause of the whole thing that deep-freeze of unending crackling hatred which flows through the streets of their cities, and to escape which you too easily run to the gatherings of the word-worshippers, as to a warm—a scalding hot!—sauna?

"What I mean is, what I want to tell you is, don't be afraid of their poverty, their denunciations, their crowding, their crushing, their surveil-lance. Don't worry about roof tiles falling on you from their buildings, don't worry about open manhole covers underfoot, don't worry about passages and dark entryways. With a little luck and some practice you can keep out of the way of their crazy trucks, can cross the shaky wooden bridges above the sea of mud, eat the soup in a restaurant car and not die. Fear rather the friendship of the word-worshippers. They will inflame you, melt you, break your heart. And we have no defenses against that friend-ship either."

In farewell the melancholy diplomat gave me a book by a famous French traveller, who had visited these places a century and a half before. The diplomat assured me that the book hadn't lost its significance even today.

"You'll be interested to read it and compare," he said. Following his advice, I am sitting now in the bow of the Babylonia as we enter the mouth of the Neva, flipping through the book, and am astonished to find everything where it was then. I am convinced that there is no need for me to describe the famous city for you, dear radio audience, because I can simply read you bits from the notes that were made a century and half ago.

The hazy outline of the land, which may be perceived far off between the sky and the sea, becomes as you advance a little more unequal at some points than at others: these scarcely perceptible irregularities are found on nearer approach to be the gigantic architectural monuments... We first begin to recognize the Greek steeples and gilded cupolas of convents; then some modern public buildings—the front of the Exchange, and the white colonnades of the colleges, museums, barracks, and palaces which border the quays of granite, become discernible. On entering the city you pass some sphinxes, also of granite. Soon the stranger is struck with the form and multitude of turrets and metallic spires which rise in every direction: this at least is national architecture. Petersburg is flanked with numbers of large convents, surmounted by steeples; pious edifices, which serve as a rampart to the profane city...

Spires, gilded and tapering like electric conductors; porticos, the bases of which almost disappear under the water; squares, ornamented with columns which seem lost in the immense space that surrounds them; antique statues, the character and attire of which so ill accord with the aspect of the country, the tint of the sky, the costume and manners of the inhabitants as to suggest the idea of their being captive heroes in a hostile land...

And here—isn't it incredible!—is a description of those same jealous feelings that my melancholy American diplomat described for me. During his voyage the French traveller, author of these notes, made the acquaintance of several Russians, who to judge by appearances seem to have been the forebears of today's word-worshippers. They charmed him utterly, and he was painfully put out that they all but forgot about him when the voyage ended.

Beware of grace in woman, and poetry in man—weapons the more dangerous because the least dreaded!

...We were still all together but we were no longer united. That circle, animated but the previous evening, by a secret harmony which rarely exists in society, now lacked its vital principle.

Few things had ever appeared to me more melancholy than this sudden change... They were returning into real life, while I was left alone to wander from place to place...I felt myself abandoned...I was no longer an object of concern to them. The people of the North have changeable hearts; their affections, like the faint rays of their sun, are always dying...Where would have been the use of adieus? I was as dead to them...Not one cordial word, not one look, not one thought was bestowed upon me. It was the white curtain of the magic lantern, after the shadows have passed...I had expected this denouement, but I had not expected the pain which it caused me...

So, dear radio audience, if something similar happens to be my fate in the Upside-down land, then I can't even complain to you about it, because you will all remember this broadcast and tell me, "You were warned twice, it's your own fault."

14. LENINGRAD

THE WET ASPHALT glistened, steaming. The croup on the bronze horse burned in a glistening point. The cupola of the cathedral glistened. Tiny little tourists walked along way up there, behind the rails, and looked down at the tiny little cars and trolley buses below.

"Our mayor liked you a great deal," said Melada. "I can't recall him ever seeing one of his guests as far as the stairs before. I think that he will do everything you ask."

"Still, the decisive meeting is tomorrow. Everything depends on what they say at the canning factory. You're sure that they got our models?"

"I phoned first thing in the morning. The crate was received entire and in good condition. They promised to look it over before the meeting tomorrow."

"Great, terrific. Who's that on the horse?"

"One of our tsars."

"What? You left monuments to the tsars? After the revolution in America all the bronze kings were melted down into cannon."

"On the other side of the cathedral there's another one, the most famous. The founder of this city. He broke open a window, so that the Russians could go out into Europe. Instead Europe crawled through the window into Russia, and built itself this city on the Neva. Would you like to look at it?"

"Happily. You're not tired though, are you? How are your ribs?"

"If we go slowly they don't hurt at all. I love to show people around

Leningrad, but sometimes I get too carried away and begin to boast. I talk as if I took part myself in all the great events. As if I was one of the ones standing up to grapeshot here on this square, that cold December day so many many years ago."

"I've read about that. It was a military uprising, right? An unsuccessful putsch that they put down the same day. What did they want?"

"Probably to be spared the shame of petty insults. That's what one of our poets said anyway. The textbooks put it differently, of course: that they wanted to overthrow the tsar and liberate the people, but the people didn't support them. People stood around the square and just watched. Toward evening the tsar had cannon brought up and fired on the rebels."

"The same tsar who's on horseback in front of the mayor's office?"

"Yes."

"And where are the monuments to the rebels?"

"There aren't any. However, streets, squares, and alleys are named after them."

"But why did they wait until evening? Why didn't they seize the palace, the ships and bridges?"

"They had no leader. The officer whom they had chosen as their commander didn't show up at the square. Besides, I think they were trying to behave as if it were a duel. They were all duelists and tried to do everything by the rules of a duelling. Tsarism had offended them, so they called tsarism out. And then they waited for their opponent either to apologize or else send his seconds to make arrangements. To agree about the type of weapon, the distance they would stand apart. Instead though their opponent brought up cannon and fired on them without any rules at all. The survivors were arrested. During the investigation they behaved badly, betraying one another. No doubt because investigations weren't mentioned in the duelist's rule book. Then they were sent off to work in the mines, as prisoners. And five of them were hung in that fortress there, across the river."

"The fortress looks old. It must have withstood a number of attacks?"

"Not a one. Haven't you ever noticed, that if a fortress is well built, then no one dares to attack it? Think of the Tower of London. It also became a prison and a place for executions. It was the palaces that got stormed. This one, for example. That was already a hundred years after the duelists' uprising. Of course a palace is hard to defend. The windows are close to the ground, and there are doors and gates

301

everywhere. If the defenders had thought to get themselves across to the fortress in time, then maybe they would have beaten back the attack. Apparently though they preferred to perish in a palace rather than survive in a prison fortress. They loved the comfort too much."

"I like that gallery, above the canal."

"Oh, this is a remarkable spot. This is supposed to be the exact spot where the heroine of a famous opera drowned herself. When I used to do tours, my Russian tourists, as soon as they saw the bridge, would immediately start to sing, 'Night and day, I torment myself with thoughts only of him. Where, oh where is the joy which once was?' Your late wife didn't sing that aria?"

"I don't think so...What's that column with the angel?"

"It's a triumphal column, the highest in the world. For the victory over Napoleon, which had to be marked by something extraordinary. They brought a chunk of granite weighing thousands of tons from a Finnish quarry on a special boat. At that time, remember, there was none of our technology. Instead of getting a crane to lift it, they called in two thousand soldiers. Isn't it strange, that in Paris there's a column to honor Napoleon, and in all the other capitals there are columns praising those who defeated him. I once tried to find out whether there are any peoples anywhere who have monuments to a great defeat. Nobody could think of one."

"What about the Wailing Wall, in Jerusalem?"

"That's right, I'll have to think about that one. You see those granite atlantes there? I never told this to my tourists, of course, but I can confess to you, that when I was in school, my girl friend and I used to arrange to meet our dates here, and if the boys didn't show up, then we would begin to fantasize that we were in love with the atlantes. We'd stroke their stone heels and throw snowballs at their bare backs and laugh like crazy. She loved that one, the last on the right. Grisha, she called him. During the winter Grisha had a snow collar frozen to him. My Ignaty is in the middle. And when the boy did show up, I use to apologize to Ignaty and tell him not to get upset. I'd tell him that this boy wasn't serious, a passing thing. And that's how it always turned out, in fact. Now I don't even remember the names of the boys, but Ignaty I remember. Bye-bye Ignaty! All the same, let's avoid him and cross over. He always was unpredictably jealous."

"All these Europeans that crawled in the tsar's window opening," Anton said, "look how they wanted to copy the towns of their youth. The cathedral is like Rome's, the palace is like Versailles, the bridges and canals are like Venice's. What a miserable profession architecture is! A painter can always find a fresh canvas, and a poet can find a sheaf of paper. But architects have to have a clean, unbuilt city, and there's never enough of those to go around. They must have been awfully happy when they were brought here."

"Since you mentioned poets, over there across the canal is the museum where our greatest poet lived. How I feared him in school! You open some volume, read about twenty lines, any you come on, and you could die. Then ten minutes later, there's my hand, reaching out by itself to open the book again. Like dope. 'Pointless present, gift of chance, for what am I sent life?' I couldn't understand the teachers, how they could give us such agonizing books. But they always acted as if there was nothing dangerous in the books. Someday I'll read you a few poems. They do say that this sweet poison disappears in translation, so that you might be getting something like non-alcoholic wine, or no-nicotine cigarettes."

They came out into a paved square that was filled with trams, not moving. People sat in the trams being as quiet and obedient as if it were a library. One of the windows had the white cheek of a sleeping woman pressed against the glass.

"This is my house of shame," Melada pointed. "This is where they give driving tests. The examiner and I came out of the gate and I asked which way to turn, right or left. He said, why ask stupid questions? Come back in a month when you've learned the rules. Because of the trams I had forgotten that this is a square, not a street. And you can only go right in a square. Every time I think of that, I blush."

"What's that line for?"

"For whatever they're going to sell."

"You're joking, right?"

"Not at all. The store is still closed for lunch. See? They aren't letting any one in. The people are waiting. Maybe they'll sell sunflower oil or sugar or soap or cheese or maybe even sausage."

"But what if the store doesn't have what they need?"

"They'll buy what there is. For their relatives or their neighbors or their friends."

"But what if it's too expensive?"

"I told you once already, our prices never change."

"You mean they'll accept a hunk of soap as if it were an unexpected surprise, like something they won in a lottery?"

"More or less. Where you live the force of human desire is measured in the number of dollars that a person is prepared to spend. Here it's the number of hours that he is prepared to stand in line. But you too have to spend many hours to begin with, in order to earn your dollars. So isn't it simpler to spend the hours directly in the line, and save yourself the strain?"

"We are now sinking into the depths of political economy, and we shouldn't. What's that church? I've never seen one like that in Europe. It's like a multi-colored ice cream wedding cake with towers."

"It's called Saviour on the Blood. Built where the tsar who freed the serfs was killed. It's always hard to explain to foreign tourists why the bridge that goes over to the church is named after the person who killed the tsar, and all the other streets leading to this spot are named after other conspirators. And the street where the beautiful palace with the atlantes is isn't named for the person who built it, but for the man who blew it up."

"Oh, that's foreigners," Anton said. "Poor slobs, we always measure everything against ourselves. We try to imagine what we'd think about on streets and bridges like the one in Dallas. You come out of the house in the morning, get in your car, head for work. Down Oswald Boulevard, then onto the Charles Manson Highway. Ten minutes later you turn off onto Chapman Avenue, that takes you to Sirhan Sirhan Plaza, that's just a hop, skip, and jump from your office on John Wilkes Booth Street. When you think about something like that, you get upset."

"It was even hard for me to get used to that contradiction until one particularly smart guide told me to explain it as a peculiarity of the Russian character and its literature. It seems we are fascinated by the amorous merger of the killer with his victim. Aleko and Zemfira, Arbenin and Nina, Rogozhin and Nastasia Fillipovna, Lieutenant Romashev and another man's wife Shurochka, Lieutenant Yarovoy and his own wife Liuba... Do these names mean anything to you? Usually when you spell them all out there's at least one that makes people nod that they understand... Then the confusion disappears. But I've walked enough for today, I think. Let's sit a bit in front of the Philharmonia."

He took her over to a bench. She studied the bench, looked around, and then took him over to another, exactly like the first.

"Let's go, come on, this is an unlucky bench, I remember it... Graduation night, and the white nights, and we walked around until dawn, but the boy turned out to be oh so stupid...That's where we sat, he and I... God, what kind of city is this, that no matter where you go, there are memories?!"

A wall of maples closed off half the sky. A ray of sun, sent through the main layers of the leaves, fell on two women pushing carriages before them, whispering to one another of the most recent injustices committed against them. A lame old drunk tried to herd a flock of pigeons on the grass with his cane, beckoned them with a finger, offered them tobacco shreds.

"Melada," Anton asked, "can I ask you for help? I'm afraid that I won't be able to do what I need to do alone."

"Is that right? It would be a great relief to me. I'm tired of feeling I owe something."

"I have to meet a certain man. He lives out of town somewhere. About an hour away, but I was asked not to use the telephone. I'm supposed to try hard to make the visit as quiet as possible. So that no one knows about it."

She leaned forward, putting her chin onto her two palms. She said nothing. She shook her head cautiously.

Anton looked at her from the side. He already knew these sudden lapses into weighty silence, which had occurred several times during their working conversations on the Babylonia. Lips pressed together, eyes glassy, she was pulling in like a snail. She had plainly ceased to see what was around her, but was seeing only whatever was going on inside her. Which was a raging rebellion. Dark feelings of a sort which have no right to exist had broken out of their cell, overthrowing the usual order, and were now making for the outer perimeter. Her skin puckered on her brow and tender skull, shaking as if from internal blows and kicks. There was no point in negotiating with the rebels. Every effort had to be made to prevent them from reaching the muscles of the arms and legs, taking over the body, breaking out in the shape of an angry cry. The suppression took time. Two minutes. Five. It hurt to watch her.

At last she straightened, sighed, permitted blood back to her again-open lips. Then she looked at him, her face exhausted from the struggle.

"So there we are, open for business. Now I understand why you took me onto the Babylonia. All our long talks, that whole game of sincerity... And in fact all you needed was a reliable agent here. For some kind of dirty business..."

"Passing gifts and greetings from one old man to another, that's the full extent of my dirty business."

"But don't you understand that I've got to put the mere request into my report today?"

"Report?"

"Every Intourist guide has to write a report about his or her foreigners every day, and turn it in to the boss. That's the rule. No one warned you about it?"

Now it was Anton's turn to fall into a stunned silence. But he wasn't able, nor did he want to contain his anger.

"You? So calmly...it's all true then! The walls do have eyes and ears...every evening, about every foreigner! Where do they keep all those reports? It's no wonder that you don't have any paper and that there's no place for people to live...and what you were writing while we were on board, that was for the boss too?"

"No, that I was writing for me. Out of habit. Like a diary. And I didn't show it to anyone. As soon as we crossed the border, though... You have to understand, it's my duty, it's part of my job..."

Anton ran ahead of her along the path, pointed at her, grabbed his head. The stunned mamas, their children forgotten, studied the wild foreign hooligan. The pensioner raised his cane, but then decided not to interfere until something valuable was destroyed or bodily harm was caused.

"Okay, do your duty, write it all down, everything! Tell them that the representative of the Pirgoroy firm tried to get you involved in some low-down operation, recruited you for a spy network. Maybe a narcotics ring...And they'll give you a reward. Let them give you a brace of stuffed teddy bears or something...No, no, don't get up, I can see my hotel from here. I'll make it myself...what an idiot I am, what a fool!"

And then, already leaving, "Hey! Don't forget to tell them about my criminal meeting with Grisha and Ignaty. How do you know I didn't recruit them for my network too?"

The office of the director of the canning factory was as round and as bare as an emptied glass. The people around the table were patiently and skeptically hearing out the man giving the report. Even Anton's unfamiliar eye could note that each of the people there had access to some secret warehouse, where their services were rewarded with spets-gifts unavailable to the rest of the populace. Their cheeks glistened smoothly, shaved by spets-shavers, creamed with spets-cream. The women sported fur collars, made of spets-beaver.

On the wall was a huge multicolored atlas of a beef carcass, resembling a map of the United States, cut up into states. The Florida of the front legs was bathed by the red, blue, and green waves of ascending diagrams. The voice of Melada the translator rang softly, a distorted echo. All day she had been silent, distant, and sad.

Anton studied the director, who was plainly differentiated from the other bureaucrats of canning. His gray full head of hair bunched over his knobby brow, flowed over his ears. His brows were black and fierce. When he spoke, his tongue writhed noticeably and grossly in his mouth, like a prisoner in a too-small dungeon. His reddish little fists would pop way out of the sleeves of his brown spets-sportcoat.

"So all right," he suddenly interrupted the speaker in the middle of a word, "good job and sit down, we get the picture. Like they say, don't feel obligated to empty your head. Otherwise we're going to be here until evening, and there's still two very important things we have to do. One is the tasting, the other's the guest from abroad. That's him over there, flapping his ears. And don't bother to translate that bit, beautiful. But I guess you know what you can translate and what you can't. The tasting today is going to be blind, ministry's orders. The new canned product is called Student's Dinner, but we haven't been told what factory makes it. So that everything is on the up and up. Otherwise, we know what you're all like, praising your friends to the skies, and covering your enemies with mud. Like they say, your friend will build you a tower, your enemy will make your coffin."

Two waitresses in lace caps began to distribute blue plates to the people in the room. On each was an open tin with no label, a glass of mineral water, a little silver spoon, and a piece of bread. Anton and Melada didn't get plates.

The tasting began in a reverential silence. The owner of a spets-necktie threw his glistening face towards the ceiling, rolled back his eyes, and concentrated on the symphony of his taste buds. The owner of a gold spets-pen kept a big unchewed lump in his cheek, pushing it back and forth with his tongue, jotting down impressions on a piece of paper. A thin old man with a translucent, icon-like beard attacked the can as if no one had offered him any breakfast today, and he had his doubts that there would be dinner. The director dug out precise little hemispheres with his spoon, chucked them in his mouth, and smacked his lips as if this were ice cream.

Then he got up and went around the table, collecting the pieces of paper.

"Let's see...'a successful combination of lightness and nourishment'...'the outstanding taste qualities of the beef jelly on the edges should be particularly noted'...'adding liver was an excellent idea'...'good saltiness but shouldn't maybe some pepper be added, to make it last better?'...In other words, what are we saying? What's the verdict? Is it good? If you were a student, would you eat it for supper? How about for breakfast and lunch, too? The mill needs water and the man needs food? Everything's useful that gives you a faceful?"

The people nodded agreement. The director went over to a tall window, his back to the round room, looking over his shoulders occasionally, with a teasing glance. Then he went back to his place. He shook his white head of director's hair, raised his little fist with the crushed papers, and then sang an instructive recitative.

"I deceived you, my dear comrades, I tricked you like children, my priceless colleagues. There's no beef in these cans, no liver or sows' ears or lamb's tails. And it wasn't the ministry that sent them to us. They were brought in by our dear guest from abroad, Anton...what was his father's name? Harvey? So that would make him Anton Gavrilovich, I guess. He brought them for us to try, and to inquire whether we wouldn't wish to buy their entire production line that turns out these tasty little cans. And what I see is that we do want to, very much. Because these tins that we unanimously liked and admired, they aren't made with meat or fat or chicken or duck or fish or crayfish, all of which are in such incredibly short supply in this country, but they are made from twenty different sorts of meadow grasses, which, thank God, we still have enough of. We applaud the remarkable accomplishments of the far-away imperialists, dear comrades, showing due respect for their beastly mastery in exploiting man and nature."

Anton had to stand and bow all about for several minutes, shaking hands, replying to the gold-toothed smiles flying from all sides.

"I don't think we should be bothered by the fact," the director continued, "that over there, in their decaying world, these tasty tins are not sold for students or soldiers or lumbermen, but for dogs and cats. That's right, Galaktion Semenovich, and don't go getting pale and grabbing your stomach. Klavdia Parfenovna, if you're not feeling well, you can go out in the hall, to your right. Such sensitive types all of a sudden. You should remember the meat that your grandfathers ate in their warships and cruisers. Didn't bother them, did it? They just whacked the harder at the class enemy. What's the important thing here, after all? The important thing is that we are on the threshold of a scientific revolution, a revolution that the rotting imperialists made with their own hands but which they won't be able to make use of, because they don't know the progressive theory. Now, if he's lucky, man feeds on mutton and beef, pork and goat, forgetting at times that all this meat and fat is nothing more than grass, processed by mammals. To take away meat production as an unnecessary intermediate step in the process of man's assimilation of the nourishing qualities of grass, that's what our goal should be!"

He looked over his cowed workers like a conductor waiting for the final chords to die away in the upper reaches of the hall.

"I've already spoken to my comrades in the ministry and got their full support. We are going to build a new factory for this foreign production line. The only question is where. Naturally we have to site it so that we won't have to haul grass for a hundred kilometers. So that the hayers can drive into the place directly from the field and unload at one end, and out the other end will tumble tinned vegetarian dinners for students and construction workers and sailors and farmers. Here of course we need the advice of our dear rotting guest, Anton Gavrilovich, so tell us the truth, what's the name of the grass that you enemies of mankind use to whip up this tasty little item? And do we have this grass? And if we do, where? After all, like the good old peasant saying has it, 'I could even feed a wolf, if he'd only eat grass.'"

Anton stood up. He could feel that he was excited. He lay out before himself the pages with instructions from Admiral Kozulin. "The thing is," he said, "the names of the grasses are an incredible jumble. Our botanists and yours haven't applied themselves seriously to problems of translation. There's no certainty that the dictionaries actually correspond. In addition, it may be that two kinds of grass are really very similar, that one of them, the Russian one, could easily take the place of the American one, but the dictionaries and handbooks would all say no, that kind of grass doesn't grow in Russia, and that would be that. So we at Pirgoroy think that we should begin with a small expedition to a Russian meadow. I would need a week or two to investigate the presence of the necessary grasses and choose the optimum place to build the factory. This expedition wouldn't cost much because I will leave my crew on board the Babylonia. I would need only a car, local maps, and letters of introduction to the authorities. I already have a translator, as you see. According to the information we have in America, the best meadows for the grass we need should be in the region of Pskov."

The participants of the meeting made noises of approval and relief. They had gotten a simple foreigner, inexperienced. He hadn't known to take advantage of their new director's mistake, for having so obviously and incautiously waxed enthusiastic about the vegetarian production line. After all a real capitalist would have immediately taken them by the throat, demanding an advance in hard currency, plus free passes to all the ballets, plus the return of some northern islands or other, or else the liberation of some crazies or some shiftless Jews, stewing in their Hebrew sauce. All this silly hick wants to make him happy is a trip around Pskov (not even the Crimea, for crying out loud!). We can help you here, rolling along with the visiting Paganelli. The bandits of Pskov will fix him up a merry life, so he'll find out how to fix the proper people up with cat food. Melada, blushing, omitted the sharpest phrases and strongest words.

The lace-hatted waitresses brought in champagne. The foaming flow of bubbles raced to wash clean the hard-worked taste buds. Anton toasted each of the approaching well-wishers three times, for a bon voyage. With one ear he listened to the director gossiping to Melada under the map of the dissected United States of Beef.

"Your name is familiar somehow, beautiful...you're not Pashka Sukhumin's daughter, are you? Maybe he's Pavel Kasianovich to other people, but for me he's going to be Pashka until they put us in the box! He and I started out together, we did! Fertilized Karelia, did the reclamation too. We started the Chinese silk-spinning on the Kola peninsula, but then they separated us. I got sent to Novgorod to be the director of the opera (because I've got a voice. Such a voice! Lemeshev heard me sing!) and he got sent into education. I always use to tell him at the Party brush-up courses, don't bust a gut to be one of the best, no good will come of it. I got chucked out of the opera to come here not so long ago. To strengthen it. And where's he now? No, come on?! Chief assistant!? For all of Pskov? Ho-ho! He's done all right! So you take your cat-eater there and you can visit your family too, see how great it works out!? So, give papa a kiss from me. Tell him that if he wants any canned goods, just call, don't be shy. Right now we're making stuff out of something other than grass. I could dig up some crab for an old friend, and some caviar and sturgeon too."

The director led them along the hall to the main stairs, shook hands, then struggled with himself for a few moments. Anton understood what had to happen, but didn't have time to get out of the way. The director quickly bent forward and rubbed his forehead, brows, and hair against Anton's shoulder.

The Intourist car was moving along a wide prospect. Precisely cropped globes of pollarded trees stretched along the sidewalk like balloons threatening to float off with the road.

"Are you happy now?" Melada asked, looking out the window.

"I'd say everything turned out perfectly. They really can get the okays I need?"

"Without a doubt. You've become an important specialist now, with that fateful prefix 'spets.' It will take them about two days to get it, so we can leave the day after tomorrow."

"Fantastic. By the way, today is the first time I heard your last name. What does it mean?"

"Sukhumin means from the city of Sukhumi. On the Black Sea coast. Thousands of years ago another foreigner adventurer came there by sea, from Greece. He also hid his real intentions at first."

"At least it isn't a golden fleece I'm interested in, or a bronze or tin one either."

"It would be nice to believe that."

Once again she looked out the window at the leafy balloons bearing past.

"I've thought about what you asked yesterday...after all, when you come right down to it, I don't have to know the name of the man you want to visit. You have the address on a piece of paper with you? Bend it over, so that I can't see the name. And cover up the house number with your finger, just the city and street. Yes, I know where that is. It's about forty minutes by suburban train, on the shores of the Gulf of Finland, a resort town. Does this man speak English? All right, so you don't need a translator. I can write in my report that you wanted to swim a bit and suntan, so I took you to the beach. You want to get a Finnish autumn suntan, don't you? That wouldn't be lying to anybody, would it?"

Anton tried to take her hand, but she pulled her hands away.

"Melada, believe me, I understand that I'm making you break all your sacred rules... You feel obligated to me. In any other situation I would refuse, I'd tell you to just forget it and don't worry about it, but in this case what I have to do is too important, and I can't allow myself grand gestures. The thing is, the person whom I have to visit..."

She clamped her hands over her ears and turned toward him, face angry.

"Don't you understand? I don't want to know anything about it. Nothing! I'll meet you in the hotel lobby at four."

The pine dachas stretched through the pine forest behind even ranks of pine fences. Squirrels, woodpeckers, and sparrows had flung open their travelling bazaar among the housetops and treetops, making no distinctions between them, acknowledging no boundaries. It seemed strange that the television antennas weren't sprouting green branches with pine cones, and that the pine trunks, rosy in the evening light, weren't glittering with windows.

When he got to number 35, Anton looked back. Melada had disappeared, an honest woman. "You know a lot, you get old fast," his grandfather Yaroslav use to tell him when he was young. Melada didn't want to know what she didn't need to know, wanted to stay young. She had said that she would wait for him on the beach. He promised to hurry, not drag out his conspiracy.

A tall, erect old man came slowly toward him from the house, walking on the slippery pine needles. A black Newfoundland followed, his confused muzzle raised as if to say that he could easily take care of this uninvited visitor alone. The chiselled family profile on the elder Kozulin was touched at all its peaks by a bluish gray, on the little beard, the mustache, the brows.

Anton took the photo which had crossed the ocean out of his wallet and silently extended it to the old man over the fence of pine spears. The old man took a close look at the picture of his brother, surrounded by his grandchildren; he was standing behind a massive chair, gesturing invitingly toward the empty seat. The old man turned it over, read the short message on the other side. Then he crossed himself three times, raised his face to the silent branches and muttered a prayer of thanks. The Newfoundland put his nose under the gate latch and opened the gate.

After he had taken his guest into the house, the first thing the elder Kozulin did was to get a dewy decanter from the refrigerator and set it carefully on the table. He got out a hunk of cheese, a jar of pickles. The pine walls of the room were scarcely visible in the spaces between the gilded frames of the pictures. Suitcases in the style of the later Cézanne, trunks imitating Degas, Van Gogh valises, *nécessaires aux itinérants*, cubist packages...

"Well, all right then, let's have a look at what's bothering you," the host said, unexpectedly loudly. "Take off your shirt."

Anton obediently fingered his top button, but the elder Kozulin stopped him with a gesture. Then he pointed at the telephone, his ear, then struck himself on the shoulder with two fingers. Then he took a prescription pad and wrote "When?"

"About ten days," Anton wrote in reply. "I have to find my daughter first. Will you have time to get ready?"

"All I have to do is take the pictures out of their frames, pack them, and I'm ready."

"Lie down here," he said, "that's right...no, relax the stomach...here? This is where you say it stings? Higher? How about on this side?"

As he was saying this, the host was carefully filling the glasses, then made a gesture of invitation and drank himself. Anton followed his example, but then screamed, muffled it, coughed hoarsely.

"It's nothing, it's nothing, it'll pass...I won't do it again," Kozulin said, "You have to watch your kidneys, dear fellow, don't abuse strong drink."

He took Anton's hand, led him across the veranda to a rear door. There he saw laid out a miniature alley of thick elderberry bushes.

"This is my 'path of frankness,' the only place that I can speak cleanly with people. Let's just stand for a minute, my heart is twinging badly. Your coming like that...I believed that it would happen sooner or later, that my brother would think of something, that the Lord wouldn't let me die among foreigners, aliens... But I did have my moments of despair...My faith grew weak, and I doubted that I would live to see the day...

"Why do I say foreigners? No, dear fellow, there are no Russians in this world, no Frenchman or Americans or Finns or Jews or Hindus. There are just two eternal tribes, the Varangians and the Chuds, and they live among all sorts of peoples. They need each other, and as long as they keep to their proper places, the Varangians on top and the Chuds underneath, everything is fine, but the Chuds get tired of being on the bottom, and the Varangians get tired of everything going along smoothly, and so the Varangians start to fight with other Varangians. That gets the Chuds worked up, when they see the Varangians fighting Varangians, and that's when the whole structure falls apart, and blood is spilled, the Varangian blood getting mixed up with Chud blood, so that you can't tell which is whose...

"No, no, don't you go refuting my theory. My theory has helped me survive the last fifty years, it gave me a tidy picture of the world, and if you're going to prove to me now that I was wrong, I'm not going to have time to think up a new theory. Varangian blood is just a little thicker than Chud blood, but you can't tell that by eye. You have to have experience...but how could I not know? How many times have I seen the blood get mixed right on these very hands? You can't even get your scalpel out of some Varangian's belly and already they're laying out some Chud's ripped throat. Ah, what a war that was, the Finnish Varangians fighting the Russian Chuds... One man against a hundred...in these very pines...you see, there's still some anti-tank traps sticking up over there? But the Chuds kept coming on and coming on, in their tanks and planes, with cannon and automatics, wave after wave...and there was nobody to help, because the English and French Varangians at that time were just barely coping with their German Chuds...

"Chuds always use numbers. They know how to get together in hordes and herds, attacking like a plague of locusts...but the worst of it is when they are able to get even a couple hundred Varangians to fight for them...For some reason they are usually able to do that, and then there's no saving yourself from them. You line them up and there's no end to them...the only thing you can call them is empty eyes. They broke into our hospital and rounded everybody up. When they were marching us off to their rear, I said to their officer, 'Why are you taking these two? They're yours, after all, and I operated on them yesterday. They won't make it, see how the blood is oozing out of the bandages again? And look, they've got stars on their shirts...' But the officer says, 'The ones who are really ours don't let themselves get captured. If they got captured they aren't ours anymore, I'd shoot them like dogs, and you too, you white Finnish dogskin whore...'

"But I'm wandering, excuse me. Since my wife died I don't have anyone to talk with. She was a little Chud girl, from the Crimea. She could listen better than anyone I've ever known. Varangian women don't have that charm, because they can't forget themselves, dissolve...they always have to contest with you, at least to come out even. It's a big temptation, when they make a god of you...and the others too, all the Chuds that I've treated. They look at me as if I'm the one who will decide their fate. Even their most powerful khans. It can get downright funny sometimes. I don't start operations without praying first, and they would ask—they're atheists, remember!—to say the words after me. Even though their own idols and cult figures could have punished them terribly for that...

"So what do you say, we're going to sail on a yacht? Will there be enough room there for my pictures? A Varangian can't part with his booty, his treasure...Ah, this is a yacht without a sail, a diesel-powered ship? But how am I going to get onto it? They've got everything controlled, and the border is locked up, they know how to do that sort of thing. All right, all right, I'll trust you, let everything go according to your plan. If we get out of here, I'll give you one of my paintings...who knows, maybe you'll be able to make some money on it pretty soon....

"Yes, the last lonely Varangian, a valued rarity among Chud people...That's what I felt like all these years...Were they right to chase out and destroy all of my fellow tribesmen, all the local and foreign Varangians, seventy years ago? What right or not right does history know? Were we in the right to hold sway here for a thousand years before that? Yes, we built the largest empire in the world, but did we ever ask the Chuds whether they needed this empire, and whether all those marble palaces didn't press down maybe a little bit hard on their shoulders? And were the European Varangians right to start up their internecine struggle—and with no reason!—at the beginning of the century? That's the thing that drove the Chuds to the mindlessness of all our revolutions.

"Still, in one way at least this defeat was to our benefit, because it spared us from having to feel guilty about the Chuds. When you live among them, on the bottom, and you get a good long look at how they are capable of carrying on with each other, without us around, how they crush and trample and burn and cripple each other, when you experience all of that yourself, then your blood is literally cleansed of any of the rot of guilt...

"When I was young of course I took everything on faith, so from my parents I got the plague of Russian Varangians, an eternal sense of guilt...But after the war, being in captivity, starving, all the searches, the contemptuous treatment, that cured me. There's no better cure for guilt than to live among the Chuds, with the rights of Chuds. Then instead of guilt you get contempt. If your entire soul becomes filled with contempt, you can live on that. Not for long, though, because pretty soon you understand that this is an illness too, just like a feeling of guilt. Especially if you have a wife and relatives and patients and neighbors, and they are all Chuds. They can have a lot of good in them, and propriety too, and emotions, and charm, and industry. There's just one thing they don't have—maturity. Chuds are eternal adolescents. But then that's why you won't find that terrible Varangian pride among them, that terrible self-assuredness. After all, even that sense of guilt that the Varangians have grows out of their rabid feeling of self-assurance...I mean, good heavens, for them to imagine that it's they, pitiful little people, who are the main purveyors of suffering and joy in this world, and not the Lord!

"Yes, I know, you have to hurry. Just a second, just a second, you can go in a minute...Show me one more time how to work this box...this is the receiver, that's the transmitter...this is the antenna. All right, I'll keep it with me all the time, even in the hospital. Sometimes they still call me in to consult...but mostly I take patients at home. Yes, I'll pack up the pictures in several bundles...about thirty kilos each, no more. I'll start today, just as soon as my hands quit shaking...

"What do you think? Will I find a place over there that's like this place? Where the pines are exactly that tall, and there are squirrels and boulders and a gray sea with sand along the edges? It would be awfully silly to get homesick in my ninth decade, but who knows... I've read some poems by the Russian Varangians that they exiled, and some of the lines just bury themselves deep in your memory...'But if by the road there's a bush, just one, especially a rowan...' Except for me it would have to be an elderberry...

"Here, I'll let you out the back gate...This street will also take you to the beach...So, you think that in Maine I'll find pines and these kinds of boulders and even elderberry bushes? Is that far from where my brother lives? Two days' drive? You know, it's not beyond the realm that after a month together we'd be on each other's nerves. Varangians are so hard to get along with...What? How do you tell a Varangian from a Chud? That's simple, by their prayers. No matter what god they are praying to, Jupiter, Odin, Christ, Perun, Mohammed, Yahweh, Buddha, the Chud always has the same kind of prayer: 'O Great and Powerful One, hear me and do my desire.' The Varangian's prayer is always: 'O Great and Powerful One, let me hear you and do your will. Not as I desire, O Father, but as You do...'"

The evening breeze was plucking the first yellow leaves from the birches. Melada walked from the beach to the station at Anton's side, saying nothing, shivering, hands clasping bare elbows. Once again the shades of feelings condemned to life imprisonment, unjustly and without rights, beating on the bars of their cells, ran across her face. Once again all her strength was deployed to put down the insurrection.

Anton too was silent.

The long shadows of legs lay across the high platform. The heads and trunks of the patient passengers lay cut off by the rails, stretching all the way to the water tower in the distance.

The suburban train arrived.

"I'm going stay at the end and have a smoke, is that all right with you?" Melada asked.

Anton nodded thoughtfully and went into the car. He sat next to a window, with his back to the front of the train. The woman opposite him, in a felt cap with felt flowers pinned to it, looked at him and asked pleasantly what parts he hailed from. Anton answered honestly that he hailed from distant parts, American parts.

"No kidding!" the woman clapped. "My daughter moved over there not too long ago. With her husband, the bum. She got herself such an unlucky husband that he couldn't find what he wanted in life anywhere. He was an engineer, got a good wage. But then he got into a funk, started moping around. I want to go into real science, he says. So all right, so be a scientist, what are you going to do? Four years my daughter works overtime, while he's cooking up his dissertation. Finally he finishes it, turns it in, defends it in front of everybody, and hotsy-totsy, he's a scientist. In a research institute, making a measly one seventy a month. He's studying metal corrosion, so he comes home all covered in rust. And the table was always ready for him, he got respect and admiration. So what didn't he have? What did he need your America for? Say, is it true what they say, that there's a lot of lying there? When there are only five buildings on the whole street the first will be number 12 and the last will have like 90 or something on it?"

"It's the God's honest truth," Anton said. "The last place I lived was number 65, the house to the left was 59 and on the right there was a little garden, but at the end, on the corner, there was a bank, number 79."

"So there you go, see! How do you poor folks ever find each other, with addresses like that? It's no wonder that my daughter doesn't get all the letters I send. They live in the town of Brooklyn there, and at first they were incredibly poor. Their apartment had cockroaches and rats, and the little black kids teased their children, called them 'commie, commie' in school, and my son-in-law couldn't find work anywhere, I guess because your rust is totally different from ours, or else nobody wants to study it, but just slap grease on it instead, since you've got so much oil. And then his pals thought up this one. Hey, they say, listen bud, go work as a poor man in a big firm called Welfare. He did what they said, now my daughter writes that things are fine, they're living high, with a car and an apartment...but I get insomnia wondering, probably she's just lying and lying and lying, to make her momma feel better? I mean, what kind of job is that, working as a poor man in this

Welfare firm? Something crooked, I'll bet, or else everybody would want to become one. So look, you tell me honestly now, is there such a job in America or not?"

"Well, there are plenty of poor people, and they get by somehow, make ends meet...there are a lot of different ways and means..."

"She writes me that let's say they went and got an education loan that is only given to the poorest of the poor, and then they used that money to buy a car, so that my son-in-law could start taking poor old ladies to this doctor called Ed. Medic Ed. The government pays this Ed for everything, even for bringing the poor patients to him. Except they aren't sick, any of them, my son-in-law just takes the healthy ones where they have to go. And that's what started the money coming in. More and more of it. My son-in-law talked my daughter into getting divorced from him, for show, so that she could be an absolutely down and out single mother, the sort that gets a free apartment. So they got the apartment, but stayed in their old one, so that they can rent out the new one for such good money that here even a butcher doesn't make that. Can I believe any of this?"

"You know," Anton said, "I'm very interested in what you're saying. All eyes and ears. There's a lot that's new to me in what you're saying, but it all seems pretty likely. I'll try to keep it in mind, in case I lose the job I'm on now. It could come in pretty handy for me."

"So all right, listen to some more then..."

Then the woman suddenly shook her felt flowers and sent an angry glare over Anton's head.

"What do you want, beautiful? Hanging around here like that? There's lots of empty seats, go find yourself one somewhere and enjoy the ride without all the looking around."

Anton turned around.

Melada was standing over them, still clasping her bare elbows and shivering, though whether from chill or disgust wasn't clear. Her brow was furrowed and her eyes were narrowed. Her cheeks bulged and emptied, as if it were no longer the prisoner-feelings dashing against them, but winged sparrows of words, which if released would later be regretted ever and again.

So having said nothing she turned and ran away.

Anton dashed after her.

They ran from car to car, followed by doors slamming, drafts, the din of the wheels. Passengers, alarmed, raised their heads from their magazines and books, then, misinterpreting the reason for the running, touched the cardboard rectangles of their tickets in their pockets.

One of the doors at the end of a car was wedged shut.

He caught her, tugging on the iron handle, and grabbed her shoulder.

"What is this? What did I do wrong this time? I shouldn't be talking to that lady? I shouldn't have admitted that I'm an American? But what's so bad about that? Thousands of us come here...You think she's going to turn me in? And you'll get fired?"

She didn't turn toward him, but didn't tear herself away either. She pressed her forehead against the glass of the door. She was muttering in Russian. Several times he heard the word "lie." Finally he was able to turn her towards him.

"What lie?"

"What lie? What lie?"

"Yes, that's what I said, what lie?"

"That...that...you..."

"I what?"

"You speak Russian fluently!"

Surprised, he felt himself blushing. The long conversation with the elder Kozulin had apparently melted his caution, drawn him into Russian life, making him cross the linguistic border as well when he did.

He began to assure her that he didn't, that his unconscious had just somehow served up the ancient lessons he had once gotten from his Russian grandfather, and besides her working with him on the Babylonia had helped him a great deal. That was the only reason that he had been able to stumble through the story of this chance travelling companion. But there's no way you could call that knowing the language. Nor could there be any discussion of not needing the services of a translator. He needed her, for the whole of the journey to the provinces.

A look of melancholy submission to fate wandered across her face. Then she had a new thought, and began to push him away, covering herself with elbows, hands, tossing her head and slapping herself on the cheeks.

"That means you understood everything! Everything that we said about you in the embassy, at the mayor's, at the factory? All those stupid quips and the insults...Oh, how embarrassing, how shameful! How could you treat me like this? What did I do? It's like...like...tapping a telephone or watching through a peephole or spying, like opening someone else's letters..."

"Like writing reports every day?" he helped her.

She fell silent, in confusion. She removed his hands from her shoulders and went back into the car.

They were silent the rest of the trip.

The train stopped.

They went out onto the platform, passed the little locomotive, now in a glass cell, that had brought Lenin into the city and came out onto the square. Across the river the forests of antennas glistened on the roof of the palace of the secret police. The bronze leader whom the legendary steam locomotive had once brought in from Finland was standing on the turret of the armored car, pointing a bronze hand at the antennae.

A taxi took them along the embankment, the humped bridges giving a sweet sense of cosmic weightlessness in the pit of the stomach. She suddenly covered his hand with hers. Her tense, frozen face appeared, disappeared in the light of the street-lights they passed. Anton could feel how the suddenly enlivened berry-size balloon in his chest had a sudden burst of growth, the sprout pricking him as it pushed right and left, as if searching for some promised chink or crack, for a taut chord.

"Turn onto Palace Square," Melada told the driver. "Stop here. We'll walk the rest of the way."

Anton didn't immediately recognize the street in the evening lights, but then he saw the little bridge over the opera-setting canal, the granite giants, bent beneath the weight of the balcony. Melada beckoned him to follow her. The gently sloping carriageway was paved by black granite squares, concealed beneath its arches the rattle of ancient carriages. Melada sat down on Ignaty's enormous granite foot, setting Anton before her. With a tap of a finger sharp as a pointer in his chest, she stunned him with the difficult, impossible question, the one that should not be part of the examination.

"Who are you?"

He looked at the starry blackboard above her head and was silent. The sharp painful shoot in his chest was crawling slowly upward, towards his throat.

"Who are you who are you who are you? Why are you here? Why have you come to visit us? What are you looking for? Why should you make me violate my native order of things? I had everything set up so well, everything fit together just so...fear couldn't get through, and shame couldn't, and doubt. I was solid and firm on my own little island...and now my island is floating away from under my feet. Why did you have to turn toward London? You should have kept on going straight for the Neva, like the Varangians from the opera *Sadko*, you could have sold your kittie cat meatballs just fine without me, and not any worse either..."

He made her get up. Stumbling just a bit, and choosing his Russian carefully, he said, "I can't tell you all my *sokrovennost* right now... But I must make you aware of one thing...that if I don't kiss you right now, I could well die."

She thought about it, like a teacher who had been given an unusual answer, an evasive one, not worth more than a C. But then with a sanitary efficiency she positioned her face for him and froze. Already clasping her to himself, he tried to recall what it was he was supposed to do with her lips—after all, how long had it been since he'd had to do this? The sprout in his chest gathered strength and suddenly shot upwards, as though it had suddenly been wafted with a long-needed breath of oxygen, as if it had finally discovered where the sought-after cord was stretched.

Granite Ignaty patiently held his stone canopy above them.

Radio Broadcast Taped in the Evropeiskaya Hotel
the Night Before Departure for the Meadows of Pskov

(Boss Diver)

We spent almost half a day buying up supplies in the hard currency store for our trip to provincial Russia. The list of foods and things that my translator had drawn up was so long that we might have been preparing for the Antarctic. Yet I felt I had no right to object. I kept still even when along with a case of vodka she also bought a whole box of flashlights. Who knows, maybe the nights are really so black there that the street lights are too feeble to chase away the murk?

After shopping I went to the port to say goodbye to the crew of the Babylonia, to make sure everything was in good order, and to leave my final orders. When I was there Pablo-Pedro introduced me to his new friend, the boss of the underwater repair crew. In the course of his life this unusual man had changed his profession a number of times, working in many places, including Cuba. He had learned to speak a little Spanish there, and so could talk with Pablo-Pedro.

At first I couldn't understand what it was about this man which so enraptured Pablo-Pedro. His life was absolute ordinary, save perhaps for the fact that success dogged him the way failure dogs other people. In his childhood he was thin and sickly, but also did so poorly in school that he was always left back in the second grade. Thus he quickly became the oldest and the strongest in the class, and so was spared those torments which the world over fall to the fate of runts.

Then he was drafted, sent into the navy. It soon became clear that no teachers and no punishments could ever force him to learn to swim. So they began to use him to train lifeguards. They would throw him into the water, and he would sink so readily that any of the lifeguards could work out all sorts of devices for raising him, draining the water from his lungs, and giving him artificial respiration. He was an excellent drowner, faking nothing, and so was given badges. After each session he was given an extra bottle of milk and a day off, which he would spend on the beaches of the Black Sea. He had only the most blissful of memories about his spell in the

322

navy.

When he came back to non-military life our drowning diver got a blue-collar job in a textile factory. In this country the workers of such factories are exclusively female, so that even a short and skinny blue-collar worker can be surrounded by eternal attention and affection. At first his pay wasn't much, but then the union sector head took him on as an assistant and he got a big raise. This head would get very tired from being cursed as stupid and disorganized by the bosses above him, and needed an assistant who was even stupider and more disorganized than he was, so as to have someone to feel superior to, and blame things on. The volunteer drowning victim was a real find for him. His inability to remember even the least of the rules for collecting union dues was impenetrable and awesome. This boss came to love him so much that just before he retired he transferred him to the job of chief safety inspector.

When Pablo-Pedro asked it this new friend was happy to give me a full explanation of what his new post required of him. He had to walk around the factory floor every day making sure that the girls at the looms were wearing scarves on their heads and were keeping the belts of their smocks tucked in. If it seemed to him that a belt was too loose, then as part of his professional obligation he would sneak up behind the girl, grab her by the waist, and tug the belt tight. Sometimes the main office sent down new posters warning people not to stand under heavy weights, grab wires with their bare hands, or drink vodka on the job. These posters had to be put up where everybody could see them. When this happened he would get into conflicts with the head of the fire department, who (the smoke-eating son-of-a-bitch!) was also always looking for walls on which to put his posters. Naturally there weren't so many bare walls left for either of them after the fellow from the Party office had glued up his posters with slogans and pictures of the Party leaders. This war of posters demanded considerable stamina and invention. The rest of the work day, though, he could sit quietly in his office and answer all other requests, proposals, ideas, and plans with a confident "No, that won't do, it hasn't been ordered, it isn't needed." It was only if somebody from one of the big offices upstairs were to call and give the go-ahead that he could say "yes." But that didn't happen at all often.

It was as a safety engineer that this man had been sent to where a port was being built in Cuba. There had of course been other people trying to get posted to this attractive spot, people with real engineering diplomas, but each of them proved to have some sort of spot on their histories. However, this man had no relatives overseas, had no ancestors from the exploiting classes, had never been in a part of the country occupied by foreign enemies (which was a pretty serious offense there), knew no foreign languages, had never read a single book, had no friends, and never wrote letters. He was as clean and transparent as a soap bubble, which was why he was the one chosen to be sent abroad, where he got double pay, and then was able when he got back to set himself up in the prestigious post of supervisor of the harbor divers.

I confess I soon grew bored listening to tales of these enviable and undeserved successes. This mite of a man sat at the little table in our state room, sucking down our whiskey and smiling beatifically. From time to time one of his underlings would poke his head through the door to ask a question of some sort. Whereupon he would grow scarlet and roar, "Can't you see I'm busy!?" Then he would go back to his glassful of overseas bibulation.

I asked Pablo-Pedro what he found so attractive about this man. He tried to explain. The radical movement to which Pablo-Pedro belonged, "The Leveling Way," had long ago been riven by arguments over whether it was possible in practical terms to achieve absolute equality of people. They weren't arguing about inequality of class or property or race; those problems had long ago been solved in theory, leaving only the necessity to translate theory into deed. The Levellers were attentively following the progress of plastic surgery and organ transplants, because these seemed to the Levellers to hold great potential for making tall equal to short, beautiful equal to ugly, healthy equal to handicapped, and so forth. But what of inequality of native ability? That was their stumbling block, the source of endless argument. How might the intelligent be made equal to the stupid, the energetic to the inert, the talented with the untalented? It was a real puzzle.

So it was that the fate of this underwater repairman who never went into the water and who didn't know how to repair anything seemed to Pablo-Pedro a shining example of how the problem might be solved in the Upside-down Land and nowhere else. There would be no need to hobble the energetic, make it impossible for bright ones to get an education, take the brushes, paper, paints, and pens away from the talented. No, it would be enough simply to give all the administrative posts to the lazy, the stupid, and the talentless. It would be necessary to compensate their feeling of inferiority by giving them power, high wages, second homes, and freedom from responsibility. After all, talented and energetic people are always saying that what they really like about working is the work itself. So let them keep on enjoying their simple pleasures. As for the poor people *whom fate had deprived of all talent, these should be given material riches, since spiritual ones were inaccessible to such as they. Let the poor in spirit have not only the Kingdom of Heaven, but the one on earth as well.*

I said that introducing that principle would quickly lead to the collapse of the state. The harvest would rot in the fields, the rivers would silt up, sick people would die, ships would sink, the roads would crumble, and the airplanes would crash. All of which were occurring in the Upside-down Land with incredible frequency. To which Pablo-Pedro replied that that was precisely what most impressed him, to see the sorts of material sacrifice that this country was prepared to make in order to observe the higher principle of equality among people. Pablo-Pedro is going to use his time here to study their experience in this sphere as fully as he might. However, for his part he would also like to introduce into their customs and habits something progressive and useful. Which is why he has promised to teach the diver and his helpers how to play communist poker.

You will have guessed, dear listeners, that I took Pablo-Pedro's sermonizing with a certain degree of skepticism. On the other hand though, I recall the director of the food-tinning factory, his tangled career, which took in both cultivation of silkworms and administration of the regional opera company, and indeed begin to wonder whether the selection and advancement of administrators in this country might not indeed be subject to some sort of eccentric principles which we do not fully understand.

I shall be informing you of all new observations in this most interesting of spheres, you may be very sure.

15. PSKOV

IT WAS A SHADY, wooded land which flew past the windows of the Fiat-like Zhiguli car. Little wooden houses surrounded by little wooden fences, covered by wooden lathing, decorated with wooden gingerbread. Stacks of logs and boards, wooden well booms, wooden posts, wooden signs, wooden barriers. Woodpiles, in the shape of towers, walls, staircases, ruins. Wooden carts, wooden harness bows, wooden traces. Wooden wheels rattled over wooden bridges. Birches, oaks, firs, pines—these were just another stage in the life cycle of wood. The fruit within the skin, the beetle in grub form. Little wooden boats stood motionless on the surface of the lakes, and in each was a little figure with a long wooden pole, which made man move faster than fish. Logs cleaned of branches and bark glistened at the sites where huts were planned, silver from the weather where the huts were no longer new, black with rot where huts had collapsed, the green sprouts of logs still to be pushing through here and there. New boards were decorated with designs of many branches. It sometimes even seemed that the glass in the house windows was made of the finest transparent slices of wood.

"When I was little," Melada recounted, "just the word 'forest' could make my mouth water. Blackberries, raspberries, wild strawberries, huckleberries, cloud-berries, those were our candy and ice cream. Going into the forest for us was like going to a candy store. It was only about two hundred meters from our village to the woods. Once when I was six I took my four-year old brother and we went off to pick. The thickets were so high already that no one noticed us as we went along the road into the clearing. And then we got into it. From one blackberry bush to the next, step by step, running from here to there... And then there were raspberry bushes. When we knew that we just couldn't fit anything more in we decided to go back, but didn't know how. There was no path, no clearing, no field to be seen. Just pines and oaks all around. My brother began to cry. Instead of being tasty and pretty, now it was quiet and scary. The bird sailing overhead must be a vulture, wanting to sink his claws into us. That leaf wiggling under the branch over there, that must be a snake hiding. That bumblebee nosing about in that flower, any minute he'll start buzzing angrily and fly up and sting one of us in the eye..."

Anton looked at her from the side. She was steering confidently, easily passing the ponderous dump trucks, the dawdling cement mixers, the buses groaning beneath their passengers, illegally crammed into the aisles. Her hair was tied back with a brightly colored scarf which he had bought for her the day before in the hard currency store. He had had to talk her into accepting it. She kept waving him away, saying, "Whatever are you thinking of? We can't accept presents from tourists!" Later she took it. Snatched it with a desperate fever, as if to say, "If breaking rules, then let's break them!" The vise grip of Omnipresent Order slipped a millimeter. Anton was proud of himself.

"They found us when it was already growing dark. Greatgrandmother Pelageia whipped me with a willow switch, but kept saying, 'You were a good girl not to abandon your brother, such a good girl, but take that, take that! So you'll remember that you never should abandon little ones in trouble...' But what I felt in those dark and deserted woods made a much stronger impression on me. The forest seemed like something alive, getting ready to swallow me. As if we were the berries. And that gave me a very sharp and curious sense of how I might taste sweet to something else..."

A ring of famous tourist towers and columns danced around the scarf—Eiffel, Pisa, the Tower of London, the Vendôme. However this was the last glimmer of the exotic upon Melada—with each passing day, each passing hour, with every turn of the wheels she was more at home. She was changing before his eyes, becoming more confident, commanding, calm. It was her nest, her hexagon in the beehive. She knew what to expect of people and of things. Her eye was accustomed to picking out in the rear view mirror the militia vehicle that was creeping up behind, her foot accustomed to slipping from accelerator to brake. Her ear was accustomed to picking from all the radio nonsense the vital information about the weather. Her fingers could dig blind in her purse for the money to pay for gas. Her lips parted in a smile of the correct width—and not a millimeter wider!—in response to the flung kisses and broad gestures of invitation from the soldiers in a truck they passed.

Her forest, her road, her horizon, her clouds, her soldiers, her memories. Anton felt himself cheated, lost, dependent. How quickly their roles had changed! Could it really have been that at the point of intersection, in the shade of some granite giant idol, that they had kissed passionately? Or had he dreamed it? In any event she behaved as though nothing at all had happened. As though there had been no secret trip to the summer settlement on the shores of the Gulf of Finland, no secret conversations in Russian, no secret kissing.

"Stop!" Anton suddenly shouted. "Stop the car! I have to..."

"What's wrong? You feel sick?"

The Russified Fiat winked a right turn, pulled onto the verge. Anton jumped out onto the edge, hurdled the drainage ditch. He walked quickly over a plowed field stuck over with stalks of potato plants. The roar of the highway diminished behind him, softer with every step. In the distance a combine crept soundlessly over the yellow stubble.

The women working at the edge of the field noticed the stranger getting nearer, stood up, straightening themselves. Even Anton's inexperienced eye could make out—from their bright jackets? fashionable eyeglasses? tight pants?—that these were city girls, sent to save the harvest. One of them was still on her knees, her back to him, trying with her hands deep in the cold mud of a furrow to dig out the last clump of potatoes. Anton was already on top of her when she turned around, glanced at him in astonishment, shading her eyes with her hand. Blonde eyelashes, light colored eyes, greedy white teeth... No, not like Golda at all... The angle of the shoulders?

"You from Moscow, my beauties?" he tried as hard as he could to disguise his accent, to imitate the loose manner of the boss of the divers.

"No, from Leningrad. From the Red Triangle factory. And what would you be, a journalist?"

"Something like that. I'm on the radio. You wouldn't know whether there are teams from Moscow anywhere around here, would you? I need the International Institute."

"We don't know, we haven't heard of them. But what have they got that we haven't? You can tell your Estonians about us too. Describe our heroic triumphs, our deeds of labor and so on. Because it's always

Moscow, Moscow, Moscow...”

Giggling, the women began to gather round. Anton stepped back. “Next time, maybe, for sure... I’ll make you all world-famous...”

Melada greeted his return with a puzzled, alarmed look. She looked as though that difficult question “just who are you?” was ready to burst from her—kissed or unkissed?—lips. But she kept silent.

“We mustn’t be late. My father doesn’t like it when people are late for meals. In honor of your visit he’s ordered that they slaughter and prepare a spets-suckling pig.”

The stone two-story building was hidden from prying eyes by a high fence. It was only after driving through the tall solid gates that a visitor had the opportunity to admire the tall windows, old-fashioned plaster garlanding, the slender half-columns in the façade, all of which elevated the building to the status of a small palace. A teen-age palace.

Two women dashed from the doors to hug Melada. Anton tried to guess which of them was the secretary Gulia and which was the housekeeper Katia, and got it wrong. The secretary turned out to be the dumpy older woman whose hair dye was five weeks overdue. Katia the housekeeper (meaning she was cook, launderer, and gardener, Melada explained) boasted a sportswoman’s waist and strong calves which probably could have sent their owner jumping a full head above the top of a volleyball net. Melada’s mother had died about five years earlier from vascular, cardiac, nervous, and hormonal insufficiencies—or so it said in the autopsy.

The master of the house, Pavel Kasianovich Sukhumin, was waiting for his daughter and guest in his office. The main feature of the man was a universal thin angularity, of nose, elbow, ears, knees, opinions. Also notable was the contrast between his frozen posture and the unusually gusty energy of his speech. It was as though Pavel Kasianovich’s tongue had been strictly ordered that no matter what it cost it had to protect the calm of his hands and feet. Both hands as if instantly exhausted from their short exertions (one to shake Anton’s, the other to clap his daughter on the shoulder—”A business trip? So soon? Important visitor? Good for you!”) returned hastily to his stomach, across which they locked fingers. The tongue did everything for them, ordering who should sit in which chair, invited the guest to come closer so as to see the fountain in the garden, ordered the secretary to telephone the person in charge of flowers and then hold the receiver up while he gave the order to bring in fresh dahlias for the table.

"So, Anton Gavrilovich, you have been so kind as to visit us because of our grass? Important business, a good thing. But does that mean you have none of your own left in America? Ah, for comparison and study, so to say? To exploit local resources for purposes of a fruitful cooperative venture? Hey, Gulia my girl, pour us a little of that Czech beer for a chaser, will you? All right, now blow off the foam for me and my guest, show a little respect, all right? But why have you come so late then? All around here the hay has already been cut, it's in the haystacks and barns now. There's just a little widow grass left here and there. Problems on your journey here held you up? It happens, it happens... Well, you can still go to my native village. Kon-Kolodets, they call it, Horsewell. The only people left there are too lazy or old to leave, so they never get the hay cut in time. In some places the grass is up to the old women's waist, and I won't tell you what that is on the men... And our old house is still there, a big strong building that my grandfather built. So go live there. My little Melada will take you there, show you everything, introduce you to the old men, translate all their old stories for you My grandmother Pelageia is still alive, she was the one who knew the most about the grasses there...If you go tomorrow, you'll be in time for a wedding. Melada, you'll never guess who's getting married! Anisim and Agrippina, that's who! So what if they are both almost sixty! You young people think that when you're sixty life is over, that you can dump all of us onto the garbage heap. But no, don't hold your breath for it, we'll let you go down that path ahead of us! She's waited thirty years for him, never married. To be sure, there was never a parade of village swains strolling around squeezing their concertinas in front of her. There was almost nobody left to marry in the village. But just as soon as he was widowed he waited the forty days mourning and then started courting her. Miracles, eh? Except that her sister almost killed him. She's lived with Agrippina all these years and now she'll be living alone. She's incredibly jealous. Say, did you know that that Vitka of yours, Polusvetov, he still hasn't married either? People say he's waiting for you. I'm not sure I know why he's yours. Did you shoot at him? You shot at him. So it's like buck shot, stuck in the heart..."

Katya the sporty cook peeked in the door and announced that dinner was served. Melada took her father by the arm, the secretary Gulia took the foreign guest, and then proceeded down the stairs of the little palace to the dining room. A floral tablecloth was draped to the floor, carrying a glittering parade of salad bowls, glasses, decanters, plates, serving boats.

"All of this is ours, old man, everything is fresh from the garden. The vodka is store-bought of course, but that's a sacred business for the government. And you'll understand of course that it's not an ordinary sort of store, not just anybody gets in. And what did you think, that we spilled our blood for nothing, freed you ungrateful wretches? Well, let that pass... We'll drink to our meeting and to getting acquainted and to peace between the hemispheres. You can have one of them, we'll take the other, all right? Your health!"

Once at the table Pavel Kasianovich was finally forced to unknit his fingers and permit them to grasp fork, knife, and glass. Here too though the three women were frequently forced to rise to his endless commands of "pour," "pass," "put," "push," "wipe." It seemed, incidentally, that they did so without the least irritation, accepting the commands as pleasant signs of attention.

"So, old man, you didn't get the chance to fight, eh? Me, I did my spell, the whole four years. Eh, I remember how when we got to Austria...the little houses there are so clean, so perfect, every cobble-stone in the street is washed, the glass glistens, there are flowers in all the squares... And you know, this incredible spite wells up in your soul... That's why we really took the battle to them, to the death. The pressure was terrible, we pushed on and on. To the Manche! To Paris! Marshall Zhukov even put the question to Stalin, said, 'It's the Atlantic Ocean for us, or death.' But Stalin, even though he was a great man, he had his weakness. He was a one for keeping to agreements. 'I can't, comrade Marshall, I gave Roosevelt my word.' So we stopped at the Elbe. But if the order had come down, none of your Shermans or Eisenhowers could have held us back. How many tanks and cannons did you have then? You don't remember? I've forgotten too. Gulia, go phone the head of the institute, ask him to come over. Tell him there's an urgent question. While we're waiting, old man, I've got another question to put to you. About our people. The great and unconquered, but first, let's drink."

Tender bits of the spets-suckling pig were laid out on the plates, framed by a border of green pickles. Pavel Kasianovich parked his sharp elbow on the tabletop, let household and guest click glasses with him, then found the rim of the glass with his sharp lips and sucked the vodka up in a single gulp, with a savage whistle.

"So naturally, old thing, you're thinking that the Russian people are poor, that the stores are empty and the roads are a mess, that the land is endless, but that the entire way from Leningrad to Pskov there isn't a single place where a traveller could get a bite to eat. However, we have one priceless treasure, one fortune which you foreigners don't understand and don't value, but which we wouldn't exchange for anything else in the world. This treasure is GUILTLESSNESS. Our people can get by without bread and milk, without clothes and a roof over the head, without wood for the stove and tobacco for the pipe, but they can't do without this main treasure. Our people are very scrupulous, and simply can't live in guilt. You can tell that from our whole history. When we had the tsar people lived all kinds of ways, some thick, some thin, but the people always had their guiltlessness. If something bad happened, the ministers and the police blamed it on troublemakers, and the troublemakers blamed it on the police and the ministers, while that well-practiced giant among men Lev Tolstoy also got a shot in about the priests. However nobody dared raise an eyebrow at the people. A bit later there appeared a couple of scribblers and squabblers who began to kick the people in the shins a bit. You do this wrong, and you do that wrong, and you put the wrong end of the plow in the dirt, and you've got the cow by the wrong teat, and it's the wrong stallion that you're letting in with the wrong mare. That's when the people got confused, depressed, doubtful. They got so depressed that they had a revolution. But when everything fell apart and went to the devil, when the tsar's power fell apart, who did the people follow? They followed the party who returned their guiltlessness to them. Who said, my golden fellow, that you are a thief? What you stole was stolen already, and it wasn't that you set fire to a house with children and old people inside, it was a nest of enemies of humankind, and you took your axes to evil men, exploiters, to prevent them from drinking the blood of workers and peasants...

"And why do you think the people came to love the least guilty leader of all times and peoples, why did they weep so at his funeral? In the beginning after all he had no great power and didn't even speak Russian properly. However he never left the people alone in their greatest need, he always found them enemies and apostates who were guilty for all our troubles. At first the cause was class enemies who needed more beating, then it was the kulaks and kulak sympathizers, then it was the *basmachi* and the hirelings of capitalism, then spies and wreckers, then rootless cosmopolitans. Even so, though, we failed to protect him, we let the killers in white coats get their hands on him...

"The scribblers have been set free again, their leashes let slip for criticizing and revision. But here, just read some of them...they don't dare to attack the people. It's just bad governors and secretaries who distort the party line and volunteeristic presidents. They write about the collapse of the economy and millions of innocent dead. Millions is of course a distortion, there could have been fewer. But again they are missing the most important mitigating moment, that they almost always shot people who weren't guilty. So every person, even when he was being taken into the basement for liquidation, could preserve his major happiness right up to the very last minute, his consciousness of not being at fault. Judge for yourself—it would have been impossible to kill no one, because otherwise the people would have ceased to respect authority. And you couldn't kill the guilty—that would have been cruelty of the worst order, fanaticism of some sort. So here too..."

The dining room door opened to admit a plumpish man who looked to have hastily tossed on the variously colored parts of his good clothing, taking whatever was at hand.

"Do you call for me, Pavel Kasianovich?"

"I did, old bean...You...I...let me think a minute, what was it I wanted you for?"

"Pavel Kasianovich, you wanted to ask him how many cannons and tanks we had at the end of the war and how many the Americans had," Katya the volleyballer-cook reminded him in a ringing voice.

The secretary Gulia turned her heavy lids toward Katya, stroked the gray roots of her hair, but remained silent.

"Yes, that's it. So tell us, old bean, how many men at arms we had in May '45 and how much of what kind of war material. And then let's have a comparison with the Americans who seized the other half of Europe."

"How can I...have some mercy, Pavel Kasianovich...to know figures like that... I'm not a Jew, you know."

"You don't remember? And you call yourself head of an institute? You've muddled me up here, and in front of a visitor from abroad."

"If you'd said something earlier, I could have phoned the proper people, sent somebody to look in the reference books, to copy something out of the encyclopedias..."

"So go phone, go look, go copy! If that were only all it took with you types, that you send someone... Gulya, pour him one for the road. Let's drink to our world-leading scholarship! For our scholars, never ever at fault! Who maybe don't know so much about the past, but have the future in the palms of their hands!"

The head of the institute respectfully poured the glass of vodka into himself, closed his eyes, as if wishing to following the drink with his mind's eye into the secret places of his organism, waiting until it had safely arrived in the proper centers of quiet exultation, only after which did he sigh a spirits-thickened breath. Then he bolted from the room.

"I learned that from our platoon commander in the army," Pavel Kasianovich said, looking at the door. "Never leave your men without something to do. Sometimes we might be sitting around after training, waiting for the trucks. We'd wait an hour, two hours... 'Up!' the platoon commander would shout. 'Shovels! Fill in trenches!' 'Comrade commander!' someone would shout. 'But we've got to come back here tomorrow for training. We aren't really going to dig these same trenches again are we?' 'You talk too much! That's an order, soldier!' So that's what we did. In the morning we'd dig trenches, and in the afternoon we'd fill them in again. But we always had something to do. There simply was no time for stupid mischief-makers to get up to tricks, and no weedy little ideas could take root in anybody's head."

Pavel Kasianovich drifted dreamily in recollection. Then he went off on something else.

"That crack in passing about the Jewish nation now. The people here say a lot of stupid things about that nation. That Jews don't like to fight wars and that all they want to do is commerce and getting on, that they always crawl themselves into someplace warm and ready. It's all lies. I fought side by side with Sanka Zalmanovich, and there wasn't a better grenade tosser in the whole platoon! He could chuck a lemon grenade down the barrel of a tank as it drove by. And they never get higher than engineer or first violin or cameraman now. You won't find any Jews anywhere in our top echelons. Not among the generals, not among the first secretaries, not even among the second secretaries. Georgians are a lot more nimble in that regard. How many years did just two of them run the entire country, and even now we've got one who's a minister. But our people don't hate the Georgians and they do the Jews. Why?"

Pavel Kasianovich froze with a pickled mushroom speared on his fork, anticipating the pleasure of sharing a beloved idea.

"It's all because our people can feel, really feel deep down in their gut, that the Jews don't place any value on not being at fault, that they don't understand it, and aren't even willing to give a kopek for it. From childhood this is so developed in Jews that they don't even have to spank their children, but just use guilt feelings. We whale away at ours, for nothing, mind, from the time they're little, beating the fear of God and the fear of socialism into them so that we can have some order and some respect. But the Jews, sly ones that they are, want everything to be soft, gentle. They have no wish to share the burdens of living together with the rest of the peoples in hateful companionship. When I was a boy, if father happened to whip me for stealing a kopek, then the sense of guilt would pass immediately, because a swollen bottom is the best fulcrum of guiltlessness. Jews never have that. People say that they don't even beat their wives. What more can you say? And their Bible makes it clear that their prophets not only let the rulers have it, but raised their voices against the people as a whole. 'You are sunk in sin,' they'd say, 'and God shall never forgive you for these sins!' It's a terrible thing to say, but sometimes you'd almost think that this people even puts guilt above guiltlessness. And that, as you yourself obviously understand, can only speak to their complete, national lack of sensitivity."

Pavel Kasianovich looked over the quiet serious audience, stopped and looked directly at Anton, and then suddenly began to speak with even more force and explosiveness.

"Our treasure is guiltlessness. That's true. But do you know what our wealth is? What do we have more of than any other nation? Of which we have the right to be proud? Unbounded suffering. That's what we have in surplus, no one can ever outdo us. Out there you go into raptures over every little renegade who spends forty days in the wilderness living on dry rations and grasshoppers, or who gets stigmata on his hands and feet, over psychotics who cross the oceans without taking along fresh water and over all sorts of religious fanatics who force the authorities to burn them at the stake. You honor those among you who walk on coals barefoot or who dive deeper than everybody else or sleep in one sack with snakes or climb up a frozen waterfall to the top. So why don't you stand in awe of the people which has outdone all other peoples in the pain they have brought upon themselves? Why do you say that these sufferings might have been lessened or foreseen, that they were senseless and led to nothing? You lie, you damned wolves in the night! It's you who lead us on in our stations of the cross, and then you study our sufferings and jump out of the way in time! Like you did the last time, luring us on with the incredible dream of universal satiation, universal equality, the end to all wars and struggles. And then you let us go first so you could see what came of it. And it scared you. All right, all right, so you sneaked one by us again. But at least we were climbing toward something high, something impossible. So don't you dare tell us, you and your radio liberties, don't dare tell us that this was all for nothing! Because we have gotten well into it, have gotten ourselves well and truly lost, but just as soon as we get back onto a solid road again, we're going to hit you upside your western heads with our guiltlessness..."

From somewhere behind the tubs of tangerine trees came the gentle ringing of the Kremlin carillon. Volleyball Katya dashed over, grabbed a red telephone and carried it to the host. He had jumped hastily up, wiped his hands and lips with a napkin, then took the receiver.

"Yes, Emelian Stepanovich... Of course, yes... Whatever you wish, Emelian Stepanovich, how could you imagine... When? In an hour? I'll be there in an hour... It will be my pleasure... I can't thank you enough... I'll bring them both right over... You're a wit, Emelian Stepanovich!...Come on, when have I never refused to drink? And the rest of it too, of course... I'm like a Young Pioneer, Always Ready!"

Pavel Kasianovich carefully replaced the receiver and shook his head mournfully. "The big boss himself invites us. Too bad, it didn't work out so well then. He's going to entertain us, and what can I do about it? I couldn't fit another crumb in... What an insult it's going to be to the boss... Gulia, tell Styopka to get the jeep ready, not the Chaika. We'll go the long way round, through Malye Tsapelki. The road is such a mess there that maybe I'll get car sick and clean my stomach out. And you'll just have to grin and bear it. He's ordered that both of you be brought over. He's found an old Indian film, starring Raj Kapoor, and he loves having people in the room to cry with him when he watches. What do you mean, you couldn't possibly, what does it mean that you can't? Take an onion with you, squirt it in each other's eyes. You're going to cry tears like a cloudburst for me! You don't play tricks when it's the boss."

Pavel Kasianovich's self-important deliberateness blew away like so many clouds, replaced by a schoolboy's haste. He dashed about the dining room, giving orders, holding the jackets and morning coats he was brought up against himself in the mirror, putting first one, then another shoe under the boot brush that was flashing in Katya's hands. Melada sat at the table in silence, frozen over a plate holding a plum with a bite out of it. Her father gave her a pop in the back of the head, told her to smarten up and entertain the guest, and not to wait for his return. These special movie showings with the boss didn't have a set schedule.

Going out the door he bumped into the self-satisfied, panting institute director.

"I found everything, Pavel Kasianovich, everything is clear, we had fifteen million men at arms, and all together the allies had eighteen million. As for cannon, tanks, airplanes, and ships..."

Pavel Kasianovich simply growled, "Go to hell, you devil of guns and ships, you goddamned warmonger," pushed the man out of the way, and went out to the jeep which had pulled up. The ladies were quickly settled in the back seat, and the master sat next to the driver. For a few moments more the institute head stood in the yard and shouted, offended, at the disappearing rear lights of the jeep, "American tanks...English... Soviet... long-range cannon, short-range, and mortars... rocket-launchers... Fighter planes and bombers... and destroyers..."

Anton woke up alert, refreshed, with a sense that something good was about to happen, tasting a bit too of the local nut candies that had been given with the tea, the name of which he couldn't recall, because it was pushed out of his head by the similar name of the three-panelled mirror on the wall in the room he had been assigned. He looked at the phosphorescent hands of his pilot's watch. Seven in the evening. Time. Time to act on his own. No more need for translator or driver. Enough hanging on to the shoulders of the woman, enough putting her at risk, kicking away from beneath her feet the archipelago of the life she had arranged for herself.

He dressed quietly, stuck a flask of Canadian whiskey in his coat pocket for supplies. The carpet runner on the darkened stairs absorbed the sound of his footsteps. The walls of the oldfashioned house knew how to swallow an echo, making no response even to the rattle of the door latch. He went around the fountain in the little courtyard, opened the garden gate. Then he went outside.

The rose-bottomed clouds gathered in the dark corners of heaven for their nightly activities. The infrequent passersby glanced at, then followed with stares, the passage of the unleashed foreigner, as though debating whether it was time to tell the authorities about this laxness or to leave this necessary work to others.

Just guessing, Anton turned right, and ended up on the shore. On the other side of the river there stretched a long fortress-like wall. An old-fashioned tower with arrow-slots, a white bell tower, a tall church, five gilded onions in the evening sky... As they had driven into the city Melada had not been able to restrain herself and so had dumped an entire pile of gussied-up tourist tales into his lap. A thousand years of history, the bloom of culture, frescoes in the churches, trade with the entire world... During three centuries of the Middle Ages these walls had repelled Germans, Tartars, Lithuanians, Poles... And then, tired, they had opened the gates to Moscow voluntarily and without a fight. Apparently mysterious Moscow had known something even back then, had known how to entice, to scrape together land beneath its feet, to insinuate itself into other cities, to drawn-in peoples. Perhaps with the very "guiltlessness" that drunken Sukhumin had explained over dinner? Wasn't that the sweet narcotic that Moscow was using to draw in the naive suckers from the world over, even to this day? And then just you try to call them back from the seven lands beyond the seas, to bring them back into a world where every person is at fault for himself, for all time.

The setting sun set a brief blaze in the windows of the cathedral and then disappeared behind the clouds. A tour ship gathered up the last flock of tourists from the dock, then hammered off into the lake, rocking the little fishing boats near the shore. The round-eyed towers with helmet-like roofs peered into the distance for ancient enemies, from beyond the forest, beyond the river, beyond the lake. Anton shrank from this gaze and turned back into the maze of city streets.

He didn't understand terribly well what it was he was looking for. However if somebody besides these evening-time old ladies with their sacks lived here, if there were people a bit younger, wouldn't they have to gather someplace, to stroll, to drink, to get acquainted, to fight, to dance? Maybe they had some sort of Main Street, a promenade, a Corso, a Broadway? Maybe a favorite tavern or a movie theater where the city kids would gather, and the young people from the surrounding villages as well?

He found squat white churches on every street. The window openings in their walls were as long as tunnels. It was as if the builders had been ordered to spare no stone or mortar, but to think only of how to make this temple of God so that it would withstand any flood, tornado, earthquake, so that the little gilded cross would stand above the point of the onion dome. The ages of the churches were indicated on tablets next to the doors—three, four, even six centuries. Near one of the churches two men in rags were sitting, eating something from a tin. Melada had already explained to him that these weren't homeless people, that there weren't any homeless people in the Upside-down Land, that these since time immemorial had been called holy fools, and that they were even treated with a certain respect.

Finally Anton saw what he had been looking for. The illuminated sign above the three-story building had lost some letters, so that it read "'s House of Culture." What might that mean? Pilot's? Truck driver's? Carpenter's? Drummer's? Dancer's? But what difference did it make, if there was a clump of well-dressed people out in front, pomaded hair glistened, and music could be heard from within?

Anton squeezed his way through the crowd of smokers, bought a ticket, and went into the dance hall just at the moment when the disc jockey dug a thirty-year old American song from his stack, and Ella Fitzgerald began urging the crowd to fall in love with each other because even jellyfish, sponges and Lithuanians "do it."

Thirty years ago this record had never failed to get a laugh at their school dances, had relaxed everyone and helped them pull the girls a little closer, closing the last and most difficult millimeters of stand-offishness. A lump of nostalgia caught in his throat, misted his eyes. Was a coincidence like this really possible? That it should be precisely that song? Or had someone sent him a secret sign, a friendly greeting? The young people of Pskov clearly did not understand the words and so danced with faces slammed solidly shut.

The curled and permed girls stood patiently along the walls, trying surreptitiously to push into the front rows. Almost every one of them clutched a plastic bag. If one of the boys from the street happened to finish his cigarette and invite one of them to dance, she would hand her bag to her girlfriend. The most hopeless of the girls stood with five or six bags.

People glanced at Anton nervously and curiously, out of the corner of their eyes; where had this foreign old fart fetched up from?

The music stopped, and immediately one of the girls pushed away her partner, her high heels drumming on the floor, ran out on to the emptying dance floor, and began to sing:

> *Vanka don't come rattle my window*
> *I'm in no hurry to open it*
> *I'll put on my bright galoshes*
> *And be there in a bit*

Another girl sang to meet her, coming up to her side and also drumming her heels on the floor:

> *Petya promised me*
> *Sweet candy*

Candy melted
But I made Petya fall in love

The first girl went in a circle, twirling and clapping time to her song.

I'll take the white kerchief
I'll chase the mists from the fields
The one on whom I'd placed my hopes
Is the one who fooled me.

The second girl followed her, wringing her hands in great misery.

In our fields like two paths
Like two paths diverging
You found yourself another beauty
And left me on my lonesome.

"Ladies' choice!" the voice at the microphone instructed, before putting on the next record.

A pleasant-faced young thing split out from her friends in the corner and set bravely off for Anton. Her friends saw her off with laughs and shouts of advice. "Even we beauties don't find everything easy" might have been how the slightly worried and anxious look on her face could have been interpreted.

Anton was flattered. It would be nice, after all, not to remain a foreigner for long. And to grow two decades younger too. Lingering effects of the drinking at dinner clouded his sight a bit. The posters on the walls of the club swirled in a red and white roundabout. His partner whirled him as she wished, and he submitted with great pleasure.

He began to ask her where she was from and what she did. She said she was local and that big money went through her hands at the savings bank, but alas, the money always belonged to others. He asked what treasures the girls were hiding in their plastic bags, and she said that most of them had raincoats and their street shoes, because the cloak room for the club was closed, but that certain of the dishonest wallflowers who had had luck with neither figure nor face, they also hid little vodka bottles there, in order to divert the more unprincipled boys away from the nice girls.

He apologized for his accent and, recalling the guess made by the potato-pickers, said that he was a radio correspondent from Estonia. He had come on assignment, but also was looking for a relative who was helping bring in the harvest somewhere about. Either they had given him the wrong name for the village or her team had been sent somewhere else. By any chance had she heard of the International team from Moscow?

No, she hadn't. And to judge by her tone, she wasn't pleased by his line of questions. "Us beauties find life hard enough, and then people start asking us about other people," her face said. However, she volunteers that their group included an amateur juggler, Kostya, who might help since he went to all the villages with an amateur theatrical group and knew all the state farms and collective farms in the area. Yes, he was present. "There's his group, and he's the one that's a head above everybody else, like the church tower in Kolomenskoe."

They made the last turn of their lady's choice tango and she, disappointed, steered him into the corner, to introduce him to the rest, and share him. The juggler Kostya had moist southern eyes that poured over his interlocutor with the balm of commitment, attention, and the readiness either to share his last ruble or to steal yours. A team from Moscow? Your niece is missing? Sure, he'd drop all that he was doing, stay up all night until he found her. His pals here, they wouldn't let him tell a lie, they knew what kind of a guy he was. Reliable. A rock. Before he began, though, he would have to make a few phone calls. Would the Estonian correspondent happen to have two kopeks? And what did his niece look like?

After five minutes of a conversation that included discussions of the Sinatra record that had just been put on, flights to Mars, and how much better basketball was than any other sport, they left the club the fastest of friends, pushed their way through the clots of smokers to the telephones. Kostya bent down and ducked into the booth, but then came right out and said they'd have to wait, the line was busy.

"Getting chilly all of sudden, isn't it?" he drawled cozily. "A drink wouldn't hurt any about now, would it? But where could a fellow get one, eh?"

Well-prepared, Anton slapped himself proudly on the pocket and then pulled out the neck of the bourbon bottle. The juggler rolled his juicy eyes to the black heavens above. He had known, had sensed, that this was an exceptional man he was meeting, but that he was *this*... a man of such spirit, such fine... No, better not drink right here. Otherwise there would be a flock of so-called friends, all kinds of people trying to hang on.

They went around the corner, into a dark alleyway. Two glasses suddenly appeared in Kostya's hands. Unable to restrain himself, he tossed them into the air, caught them behind his back, then put them under the burbling flow of bourbon. He drank and then suddenly, no pretending, sincerely, he grew melancholy. "So, Anton, answer me this, would you, honestly? How is it you Estonians have everything, and we have nothing? We live side by side, the land is the same, the rain is the same, the potatoes are the same. But you have a tie made overseas and alligator shoes and a wristwatch like the clock in the Kremlin tower, and in your pocket you've got a treat that with one swallow makes your soul billow up like a white sail in a stiff breeze. And me, I'm a daredevil master at what I do, I can juggle a Buran chain saw in working condition at high speed, and still can't get hold of a bottle of that Vana Tallinn stuff of yours, and the doorman at your Vyra hotel won't let me in for love nor money."

Anton finished his glass, gave it back to Kostya and put both hands on the knot of his tie. His fingers bumped into one another clumsily and guiltily, pulling at the wrong ends, in the wrong directions. The distrustful moist eyes watched the fingers intently. When at last the tie drawled out from beneath the shirt collar and had been hung about the neck of the daredevil juggler, the young man could only sigh in surprise, "For me?!"

As a sign that it was Anton took out the Canadian whiskey and once again filled the glasses. Kostya tossed his off in a gulp.

"So, what's this niece of yours called? Golda? Golda Kozulina? Or maybe Chichikova? We'll dig her up, don't you worry. I mean, I would... for a friend like you! You got another couple kopeks? I'll run call. You wait here, don't move!"

He came back in about five minutes to say that they hadn't been at one place and they weren't in another dormitory, but then he had found a team from Moscow in another dormitory, about a hundred people, so that his good friend had had to go check the list. Now they had to wait.

They had another glass each.

"Tell the truth, Anton, just between us, friend to friend, how much you have to lay out for the overseas threads here? I mean I'm just curious how the black market stuff stands with you guys there in Tallinn. I mean there's the ships docking there, the sailors bringing stuff back, the navigators and the captains too, they probably aren't shy about that sort of stuff either. God, what I'd give to go out just once! They say that variety shows get hired for the passenger ships, to entertain the passengers during the cruises. God, how I'd entertain them, I'd do such a stunt... I've had this idea, to juggle three live poisonous snakes..."

He went to the phone again and came back at a gallop, shaking clenched hands over his head.

"She's there! We've found your Golda! As if Kostya wouldn't find her, eh? So let's kill the bottle and then off we go. About ten kilometers down the Kiev road. God, it's nice to help a buddy..."

He wouldn't let Anton throw out the empty bottle ("I'm going to put Three Sevens port in her and take a sniff of her on holidays!"). He led Anton to a light pole chained to which was a motorcycle with a sidecar. Undoing the lock, taking off the chain, he explained to Anton that the discipline for this International brigade was army-like. Doors locked at eight and that was that. However, it was a friend of his who was on duty there right now, and he had agreed to get Golda and bring her out on the street for a little.

The cold night wind raced toward them.

Hiding his face behind the plexiglass, Anton thought that this was all happening too fast. That he had not had time to get his necessary words together. What arguments might he use to convince Golda to leave with him? And did she have to leave? Maybe this army-like discipline, heavy physical labor by day and the enforced closeness of a dormitory at night, maybe that was the last and most important of lessons, which no American university could provide? But then if fate had allowed him to find her so quickly, perhaps fate would also supply him the necessary words? Might it not be smarter to trust to fate in everything, and now just drink in the speed, the liquor-buzz, the cold-cleansed wind, the melting puddle of pride in his chest. He had travelled, driven, lied, and schemed, and he had found her. He had found her!

The motorcycle turned into a village. The headlight ran over log walls, garden fences, telephone poles. The two-story building in front them bulked massive and still in the night clouds. A single light bulb was lit over the porch.

"This used to be a school," Kostya whispered. "But now the villages are shrinking and there's not enough kids. The villagers all are running to the cities, and the city people get sent to the villages. Life's a mess, it is!"

A squat little man came out of the building, approaching them soundlessly. By the light of the distant porch light they could make out a soldier's shirt, without epaulets, the stripes of a sailor's shirt visible at the throat, a dour face divided by suntan into two parts, a white upper and a leathery lower.

"Here, Anton, this is Rodya, the watchman I was telling you about. Rodya, Anton. He looks gloomy, but he's the greatest of guys, in actual fact..."

It seemed to Anton that the juggler's voice was nervous. Could it really be that their violations of All-Mighty Order right now were so serious? Rodya the guard silently took his friend by the elbow, led him to one side. Anton overheard snatches of their quiet conversation. Most of the words he didn't know. What on earth were "bashli", "shmotki", "shkary", "klevo", "fart"? Still, they managed somehow or other to come to an agreement. Coming back, Kostya nodded, stroking the air with his open palm.

"You go behind the school with him, wait a little there, and he'll bring her out for you, okey-okey? Then you can thank him however it seems right to you. I'll be here, keeping an eye out. If anybody comes, I'll whistle."

Rodya opened the sun-blackened (whose sun? Afghanistan's? Angola's? Yemen's?) bottom half of his face into a smile. Anton followed him.

"The sheets are on your head!" Kostya shouted softly after them.

A small terrace crept up to the school from behind. Rodya went up the stairs first, lighting the way with a pocket flashlight. He took a broom from a corner and began to sweep up fallen leaves, dust, bird droppings. Embarrassed, Anton said that there was no need for such a fuss, that he and Golda could happily stand and talk here as it was, not swept up.

Rodya didn't reply. He finished cleaning, shone the light around the wide circle he had swept. With his fingers he picked up something that had stuck to the boards. Then he signalled that Anton should step into the center of the circle.

Smiling condescendingly, Anton did so.

They stood across from each other for a moment. The flashlight was shining into Anton's eyes. He was amused that he was being studied like a new recruit before a big inspection. He wanted to say that he didn't have so much time and couldn't kind sweet Rodya perhaps hurry up a bit.

But he didn't have time though to say anything.

The smoked-ham of an Afghan vet's fist leapt from the blinding circle to hit him in the temple, and with the last of his departing consciousness he heard the sound of his own body falling onto the specially cleaned planks.

There was no air. It had all turned into a stick wet cold that gnawed its way into the skin of hands, feet, face, back. His arms could still move. Anton stretched them up and, gasping, began to wipe the rustling cold from his mouth and eyes. He searched for a weak spot, plunged his numbed fingers into it, then pulled with all his strength.

There was a crack.

The old sack gave way and let in a few mouthfuls of air, mixed with rain.

Consciousness returned, but brought with it pain.

The pain had two kingdoms, one in the left half of his head, the other in his left knee. A tunnel ran between the two kingdoms, through which clots of pain raced back and forth, like big trucks.

Anton ripped the sacking wider. He stuck his head out. Rivulets of mud ran past his face down a steep slope. Farther out, through the rain, the light of a lantern let him make out little waves, and beyond them, the illuminated fortress wall, with the towers. It seemed to him he had seen this wall not long ago somewhere. He had looked across the river at it today. But what was today? When did it begin, when did it end? How many hours had he been lying here, in the wet gully, stuck into an old sack?

He tried to get up. The knee's kingdom of pain rebelled with a yelp. Besides, his legs were still tangled in the sacking. He stuck one hand into a hole, reached down, felt the knot, tugged. His bare feet slipped out, began to slither in the mud. He managed to flip over onto his stomach, got up on one knee and one elbow. He crawled upwards. He grabbed some sort of railing. He pulled. The pain in his freezing body became louder than the pain in his knee. He crawled over the railing and got up, shaking, but on two feet in the middle of the night-abandoned riverside road.

Naked beneath the wet sacking, covered in mud and blood, he studied the amphitheater of dark alleyways with clouded eyes, and would probably have felt no surprise if a herd of old bears had leapt out of one of them, or leopards or wolves, running towards him along the empty road, as if in the arena.

Still, he felt as though somewhere in the very depths of his chest cavity there must remain some tiny speck of warmth, enough for a heartbeat or two, so that he could make it to the next lamp. And that was how, begging, squeezing, scraping every last calorie from his muscles, he staggered, lame from intersection to intersection, either by instinct or because the short path he had walked that evening to the river had stuck in his mind, walking until he glimpsed the tall spets-fence he remembered.

The gate next to the big doors was still open.

It took the last of his strength to limp over to the sill of the house.

At first he didn't recognize the woman who opened the door when he rang. The pink folds of her dressing gown passed unnoticed into the pink folds of the pillow marks on her cheek.

Seeing the shaking, mud-covered figure wearing only a bag Melada woke completely up and giggled, but then her face wrinkled in what might have been pity, might have been disgust.

Then he collapsed.

Then he lay in hot water, naked and guiltless, while she tried to make him drink a glass of that universal remedy of theirs of which he had already had much more than enough in the last few days.

But he drank it. And in fact began to liven up. His sensations, which had run off in terror, had begun to return, and he greeted them, stroking them and counting them (he ought to have five, right?) like runaway kittens. The hot molecules of water strained to join the hot molecules of alcohol inside him, drumming on his skin from both sides, filling him with warmth. The heat brought tears to his eyes, winding his heart to a hammering fury. The pain remained, but no longer evoked hatred and fear, now seeming only a barbed blossom which of necessity had to grace the branches of returning life.

Melada brought him pajamas, turned away while he put them on, and then helped him to bed. Then she began to fuss around him with bandages and iodine and cotton and compresses. Oh, no—forget about Wife #5!—she got no pleasure from this. She raged at his bruises and cuts, as though he were simply a valuable object, entrusted to her by the state, which had had the gall to crack and break. She fixed up her broken charge the way someone would fix up a broken old clunker of a car. Just don't drive any further, that's all!

Anton yelped under her fingers as they bandaged his cut forehead, tightened the bandage around his knee, painted the scrapes on his elbow. At times it seemed to him that she was mad enough to kick him, as people do a flat tire.

"Whatever made you go out in the street? I was sure that you were asleep, I tiptoed, I was afraid to turn on the television. Who did this to you? Where? I told you that you ought to wear that jacket from the Skorokhod factory so that nobody would want to rob you. Oh, if I could get my hands on them! I'd shoot them right where they stand!"

She shrieked happily, as if she had found the answer to a difficult problem, and then ran out of the room, to return with a double-barreled shotgun.

"What's dad got in here for shells? Duck shot? Oh well, that's okay, later I'll find a slug."

She put the gun in the corner to admire the direct and pitiless justice it concealed.

"A tall juggler, you say? With bedroom eyes? A motorcycle? And the House of Culture, what was it called? No, no, that's all right, we can find it without any problem. They don't know who they're messing with! You'll get it all back, down to the last sock, the last cent, the last credit card. God, I hate criminals. Ever since I was a child... You hated your Miserymaker, and I hated the people he sent. You were saying that now you think maybe the monster is sent by someone else, right? I only know one thing for sure, though, we don't need prisons or the death penalty or your cells with open windows. We just need a special island, that we could call something like 'Island of Brave Lads Without Treasures.' And we could send them all there. Let them all live together, since they can't live among honest people. Toss down clothes and food and medicine from an airplane the way they were once dropped off for islands of lepers. And if they started something among themselves, if they started fighting over a jar of fruit cocktail, we wouldn't send in the police. Let them settle their problems their own way."

She was marching to and fro in the room, waving her arms and shouting. He grabbed the edge of her robe, stopped her and made her sit on the bed. "It was my own fault... But I'll tell your boss that you had nothing to do with it. That I slipped away. That I had to, just had to. The most important thing is that you believe me. I had no dark plans. All that I had to do was find my own daughter and talk with her a bit. That's the truth. I have an adult daughter from my first marriage. Yes, I didn't want to admit to you that I've been married more than once. My daughter is still a student. And she ran away. She got mixed up in something and ran away here, to your country. She's somewhere in this region. And I know that she needs help..."

"Her entire childhood, the whole time she was a teenager, her favorite words were 'I'll do it myself!' It was like a slogan, or a motto. Then this started to cause problems at school, fights at home. Even before that... You asked me once, when do we let our children know that all people must die? Well, that was something I just couldn't tell her. It made me feel as if this were something we grownups had done, making such a hopeless situation for them. I told her that in some earlier life she had probably been a bird...a blue-jay, most likely. It's beautiful, loud and really skittish. You can never touch one with your hand. She laughed and asked, 'And before that? Before that?' 'Before that,' I told her, 'you were probably a mussel.' That was when she learned how to slam her lips shut like clamshells. And before that she had been a horse, who had irritated the other horses on the bus by jabbing them with her sharp knees. And before that she had been a caterpillar, who also had made its bed incredibly slowly. And before that... It became her favorite game. When she was going to sleep she wouldn't ask for a story, but instead that I tell her something from one of her former lives. 'Tell me about how I used to be a raccoon and loved chicken bones more than anything, and how mommy was a cat and was scared to death of me...no, no, you're getting mixed up, I was a raccoon after I was a dragon fly, not a tomato... You shouldn't mix things like that up.' Then we would start on the future, and she would choose what she would become in her future lives, and I had to elaborate on the plots. I remember one pretty good story that I made up about a jellyfish who wanted to become an umbrella for somebody, except that it never rains under the ocean, and it couldn't become a parasol, because it was transparent. And so once..."

"But you shouldn't have, you shouldn't have, you shouldn't have!" Melada suddenly said very loudly. "Why did you mix the child up so? That's undoubtedly why she ran away from you. From all these pretty ideas and lies... And now she'll never come back to you!"

"I was just..."

"Now I understand why sometimes it's so awkward with you, why I often get upset... I feel like I'm walking on ice, everything is so slippery and slick, and any moment it'll crack under your feet. It's like a special talent you have for wrapping everything in fog. Pink fog, black fog, pink and black fog..."

"And you.. you..." Anton tried to choke back his drunken tears of offense.

"Oh my God what have I gotten myself mixed up in? First there was that murky business at those Finnish beach houses, then it turns out you know Russian... Now, after a good blow to the head, it turns out that you've got a grown daughter! And that she lives somewhere in this region. What else do you have stored away? Why not get it all out at once?"

"At least I don't hide the main things. What I feel. But you... you...Who is it keeps every feeling locked up, like a prisoner? Isn't that the main lie, to live always under a mask?"

"No, that's not a lie, that's not a lie. Yes, I keep things back, but I don't hide things."

"Ha, take a good look at Little Miss Frankness!"

"You know perfectly well what I am feeling, what I want."

"I do?"

"Don't play make-believe."

"What do I know? How do I know it?"

"It doesn't have to be in so many words..."

"So what is it then? At least give me an example."

"For example you know perfectly well that every minute of every day I only want one thing, for you to hug and kiss me again."

Anton was struck dumb. His eyebrows obeyed the splash of astonishment from his soul and shot upwards, but the left one struck against his growing goose-egg and he squeaked in pain.

"You couldn't not see that," Melada went on. "Gulia and Katia noticed it immediately and asked me about it. But I told them that there couldn't be anything between us, because you were going to go home soon and we wouldn't see each other again. So there's nothing to ask about here, or talk about."

Anton could feel how the mixture of alcohol and blood was beginning to pound harder in his temples.

"How about me? Robbed, beaten, offended, alone? Don't my desires count for anything? Or are you going to say that you can't tell what I want by looking at me?"

"Oh, I can tell, believe me I can tell. But if I can control myself then you will have to. That's what you're a man for."

Anton got up from the pillow, looked around the room wildly. His eyes fell on the double-barrelled shotgun in the corner.

"There it is! That's what we need! Please, bring your shotgun over here. No, no, don't point it at me. I don't want to touch it. Put it over here on the bed. And you lay down on the other side. That way you'll be safe. And I can finally get a look at you. And I'll tell you what's happening to me. No, no, you look up at the ceiling. Don't interfere with me. You don't have anything to worry about. It's on safety, the firing pin won't go. Is that all right? You have enough room? So, all right then...

Andrei Moscovit

You remember when you and I first embraced
no, not under Ignaty, but still back in the embassy
how in some odd way I hugged you with my back
but after all you too, even though the line was pushing us
against each other, could have turned to the side
if you had wanted but you didn't want to and I remembered them with
my spine remembered them both left and right in turn but then
jealousy began the jealousy my eyes felt for my back
and the whole time we were on the boat and I would come
to your cabin I liked it so much and it was so interesting
talking to you but even so I sometimes suspected
that I wasn't coming to you for heart-to-hearts
but instead to catch a glimpse of them to wait until you stretched
to fix your hair so that they would peek out the opening
of your shirt and I thought how much easier it would have been
for me if you had taken off your shirt and let them free
and then both of us could have conversed easily about anything under
the sun and my thoughts would have been clearer
and more profound and wouldn't have been distracted but then
I decided not to ask you to do that we were barely acquainted
but now we've known each other for a long time and we both met
death without believing in it and maybe because I am very drunk and
I have hit the very bottom and down here in the mud
there is nothing more to be ashamed of so that I can ask
this little trifle of you I've got so much to tell you but I can't think
of anything else while they are both there under that robe
I mean even one would be enough I mean since we've already agreed
that we can't be together and there are only a few days left to us
a week maybe and it would be so dreadful to waste these last
few days on squabbling conversations about little things like...

Oh, excuse me, of course I lost my train of thought
you did that so easily so naturally that now I'm getting my breath
back and I can go on let my eyes drink it all in like kids
in front of the television so we can at last talk in peace
two grownups who have much more serious problems
just now I got the thought that a nudist colony or even
whole villages of them as in France that's not just an eccentricity
but people probably who just can't talk to each other otherwise
they are always thinking about what everybody else
has under the clothes and only after they take off all their clothes
can they finally talk about important business about feelings about
children about money about health about fate
I understand them now and understand those artists who always strip

their models no matter what I mean tell me why should Liberty on the
barricades toss off the straps of her dress from her shoulder why
undress for a *Petit déjeuner sur l'herbe* for playing the lute wouldn't
it be easier for the Maja to remain prettily dressed
but I understand the artists and I envy them the hours they spend
in blessed and justified ogling but their hands
have to be full of pallets and brushes
for ordinary people to get such props in order to pass the time
examining the most perfect aspects of creation would be considered
stupid and ridiculous besides which there would be a jealous itch
in the fingertips they are jealous like the eyes used to be
of the back and it also turns out that they know how to raise a fuss to
distract the thoughts from elevated abstract themes and I see
that you aren't angry at them it appears to you that this horde
is worthy of condescension oh you are even ready to take them
in hand and calm them you are even ready to let them
into the television room...

Yes, I have to confess a new problem breathing
probably I'm coming down with pneumonia at least certainly
fever is close to lie in the rain on the cold ground for so many hours
but it's nothing the body has handled worse but one thing is bad
that my eyes can't see anything now in moments like these
these five begin to behave as if at long last they had finally achieved
their real purpose in creation as if they are not able to do
anything else don't want to won't as though just squeezing gently like
this and feeling the enveloping compliant infinity
squeezing and releasing squeezing and releasing each little pillow
in turn they evoke some music inaudible to us which they
are capable of listening to for hours and once they in fact did spend
the entire night doing just this and furthermore
the woman was a stranger a seat companion on a bus from Chicago to
New York you will condemn me of course and call me
a degenerate but I just had to do something so as to make her quit
talking about philosophy and in fact she calmed down and
as they say passed from existing into existence and I was even
kind of proud of them and their constancy and knowledge of how
to find pleasure in just one thing I have always held
that this greed wandering to the right and to the left
and up and down is a sign of savagery is a failure to take
real and deep pleasure from one thing alone true we were sitting
pushed right against each other and they crept over under a blanket so
that the other passengers couldn't see them creeping
to the only place they might have there on the left and if they had had

any choice in the matter...

No, not like that why did you do that you are provoking
this greedy horde upsetting them of course now there's no point even
in talking to them saying that the left is exactly like the right the
children won't listen to you if you tell them that the television
in the next room has the exact same programs because even so
they are going to be trying to go there only so
that they can then want to come back here apparently
just like people they prefer above all else the moment of encounter
and recognition and they are running back and forth
not because of greed but in order to make more such happy meetings
and joyously check the growth of right and left
this is a magically competition although of course there are again
some voracious elements here and yes, of course yes both hands and
eyes begin to imagine that they have become a mouth and so must
leave from time to time the sweet objects of their lust just as the
gardener from time to time leaves his strawberry bushes alone
to let the new berries ripen but at the same time he has no wish
to waste time since he must also check other mounds he recalls
that somewhere lower down he had ripening an incomparable cross of
light pumpkin and soft mandarin yes that's right the path there went
through the cleft of the tight-knotted robe tie a simple barrier and yet
not to be overcome without the assistance of the other five ah that's it
there it is that verdant valley with a crater in the middle what bliss to
be here amidst objects from dreams a field
of endless gliding for eye and finger it is like an opening into
a new register of a thousand keyboards on which one may fly up
and down striking tormenting notes and sweet painful notes
excuse me please I don't understand too noisy notes no you don't
wish to say that your fingers too hold musical passions that they have
need for my piteous harpsichord...

But then we must open the borders complete disarmament
down all walls and barriers I already knew that your hands ache
somehow for a weapon in moments of heartfelt agitation but still
please put it down on the floor and come here pay no attention
if I scream a time or two it's just the scrape on my knee but we can
get by today without my knee let's not touch it three knees
are enough for two people your knees are so beautiful but perhaps
I'll turn my back at first let my back meet you again this time
with no textile obstructions I recognize old friends left and right
and the soft valley below them and now come here now I must
introduce a certain criminal who has crossed the border

without a visa he is a bit ashamed at this and holds himself tautly
extended oh yes how he loves to be at the very center of attention but
it would be best not to spoil him today he can't be distracted
by trifles he's no child you send to the television he's nuts about you
for ages already I guess since that night in London when I took you to
the doctor's and then the two of us examined your x-ray
secret places and if he is not permitted to go where he aches to go into
the kingdom of sweet mysteries as your poet called it he will give us
no peace won't let us talk or look at each other or hug

So, he's at home the ruffian the rebel at home completely completely
at home in the center of creation and now I can at last do
what it seems you wanted all the while that I do hug and kiss you and
he won't be in our way any more so you see now
what a terrible thing secretiveness is how much we have missed
because of it during the short voyage of life we might have done this
already in Helsinki when we saved ourselves from those bandit girls
but we'd have had to have been careful so as not to jolt your broken
ribs or maybe in the Gulf of Finland when we were sailing past
Kronstadt and you already felt much better and the porthole
was showing the far-off cupola of the church or then in the
Evropeiskaya Hotel in the evening of that day when we fought
so stupidly and I felt so utterly unbearably alone just look
what a long life we have behind us already and all
that we could have done for each other when the car stopped
in Gatchin Park or coming into Luga or in the forest near Pliussa or
coming into Pskov coming into Pskov might have occurred
what can't be put right the thing that your government fears more than
anything else that is the descent of an American army
of many millions right in the center of their beloved fatherland
it's coming it's coming it can't be stopped but no one will know
no one will know no one will know if only I can stifle this cry
from my heart cry from cry from cry from

He froze, but not like an exhausted runner collapsing drained, but
rather like the victorious hurler of a javelin, a shot, a ball, a discus,
following the flying projectile with greedy eyes, guiding it right and left
to its cherished goal, harnessing the undiscovered radiopowers of our
desires, flowing along the bleached nerves until he heard the magic
rustle of the penetrated target and so began to laugh softly.

"A hit, a hit, a hit," he muttered.

"What are you saying, you saying, you saying?" she muttered.

"A hit, a fit, a win, victory," he explained.

"I don't know, don't believe, don't hear, don't understand," she repeated.

"We've started conceived begun evoked a child!"

"Girl or boy?" she asked trustingly and businesslike.

"It hasn't decided itself yet."

"Great and while it's decided what it wants to become can you have that serious talk with me as you wanted from the beginning? Can you tell me all those magical things that you couldn't say aloud while I was far away and in clothes?"

"Yes...of course...I've waited so long for this...so long...but now...I don't know what's happening to me...it's a shameful thing, of course...but I'm falling asleep...shameful sweet sleeping...but tomorrow... tomorrow... first thing for sure..."

(The Forest Near Opochka)

Yes, dear radio listeners, I have found it out. By chance, with no special effort I stumbled on it, without knowing what awaited me. Now I understand why they keep their borders locked, why they don't permit foreigners to travel freely about their country, why they regard every stranger with suspicion. This secret stretches for tens and hundreds of kilometers, and even so the spy planes and spy satellites could never see it, nor can you glimpse it from the windows of a tourist bus. I am still not sure where I will hide this tape I am making. If the customs people were to find it they surely wouldn't let me leave. It would be wiser to wait and take this story out in my head. Yet I fear that in a month this impression will fade and I won't believe myself and so won't be able to describe what I have seen.

Probably the trick is in how fast you move. Probably if our car hadn't broken down I would have driven right through the secret and never have noticed it. Because of the breakdown, however, we had to walk more than an hour to reach the village. Take any famous masterpiece of the cinema and run it at triple speed. Would you feel anything, would you appreciate it over this thirty minutes of flitting past? No, you have to see everything frame by frame, all five thousand four hundred seconds at the proper speed, and only then does the director's art open for you.

But it isn't just speed. The effect of touching is also very important. Even through the soles of the shoes. At first you feel the softness of the dust on the road. Then the path dips into a pothole, disappears under a puddle, and you have to go around, walk between the tree stumps. Immediately your feet sink into moss. The moss is dry, whitish, cool. If you sit down and look into the moss, it recalls a winter forest, waiting for little Alice. The moss stretches on endlessly. It is true that in the distance the moss begins to change color, as if there, in the reduced world of the moss, the seasons can live side by side, the green of summer side by side with the russet of autumn, and then again the white-covered branches.

You go back to the road but the sensation of double infinity, horizontal and vertical, beneath your feet and overhead, this doesn't disappear. It *simply recedes into the background, like the sound of a double bass. To the foreground come the trumpets, the pine trunks. They too are without end. The sky winks rhythmically through the gaps overhead. The celestial accompanist begins a modest melody, a bit mechanically, as if tired of always having to accompany the same film, even if it is marvelous. However the ticketless viewer who has come into this hall wholly by chance succumbs and is bewitched without fail.*

The pine grove ends, replaced by a sea of foliage. Birch and oak. Clearings, rimmed by bushes I don't know. Yellow and orange leaves, like makeup tests in preparation for the big autumn ball. ("A bit too much carmine, perhaps? No problem, that's the fashion this year.")

Further on, a stand of fir. Ranks of Christmas trees. All in glistening white finery. Looking closer you understand that this is simply dew on the spider webs. Millions of nets heavy with drops, stretched to air between the fir needles. In a half hour the dew will evaporate and the webs will again be invisible. Then will begin the great catch of flying prey. And we will again return to the illusion that this world is made for us (certainly not for spiders!).

Beyond the firs there is a big clearing. A swamp, drying up. The moss is embroidered with beads of cranberry. Amber-like cloud-berries. Orchards of overripe, scattering gonoboli. The smell of thornapple. The white powder puffs of milkweed on tall stalks.

And now again the road rises toward pines. "The woods are shafted through by sun, the rays in dusty pillars rise" is how their poet put it, famed in the West as author of a screenplay about a good-hearted doctor.

I am trying to understand whence in me this sense of penetrating novelty. As if I have never before seen such trees. Perhaps this is because the forest is so clean, that there is no dried, rotting deadfall of woody corpses? Because underfoot are moss and grass, not branches and stones? Because the tree trunks aren't bristling with barbed, untouchable dead branches like our trees in Pennsylvania or Massachusetts?

But no, I have also been in beautifully tended parks and forest reserves, and this is still different, still different...

And suddenly I understand. As I walk, every moment I am unconsciously waiting to see signs. Or fences. A stretch of wire. The brand of someone's property. But there aren't any. Mile after mile, endless, empty, like a palace or museum, a forest that belongs to no one. You are ripped from a world which is carved up into millions of "that's mine"s. You are returned to Creation in all its integrity. It's the same thing as growing used to fragments of long symphonies which have become hits, dances, theme music for ads, and then suddenly hearing the symphony in entirety. It is familiar in bits, but unfamiliar as a whole. Played by the best of orchestras, under the direction of the Composer Himself.

Oh, now I understand the Russians!

And if I were in their place I would keep this secret too, and would fight for it on the borders and I would not let us in, we greedy pie-slicers, who see creation as simply a huge chunk of real estate.

Because what would we do with such a forest! Ha!

I look about and imagine sadly: here sprouts the Three Cossacks Motel, over there Prince Myshkin's Resort, beyond them an asphalted parking lot, a gas station with its sign stretching above the tree tops. For Sale! For Sale! Phone from 10 to 12—low financing—the finest service—air-conditioned rooms—golf course—electric bug-killers—electric wolf-repellent—best possible automated systems of protection against everything that lives— we guarantee that not a single bird will fly over your head, or your money back!

How is it that none of us have thought to grid the ocean off with nylon ropes and sell it by squares? That will undoubtedly happen just as soon as we learn how to make underwater houses. Helicopters will take each of us to our own nylon square, and we will sink to the bottom to our coral yard, and we will look nervously into the portholes of our neighbors, to check that no undesirable neighbors have moved in, or that the old neighbors haven't brought in something new and unpleasant, like maybe a new watch shark, which of course will lower the value of our cozy little bottom berth.

Dear radio listeners!

It is possible that in the near future the Russians will become infected with our passion for profit and subdividing all Creation into plots for sale. Perhaps they will allow us and our dollars to come into their major treasure. Perhaps they will lay roads here, put up barriers and begin to charge for photo safaris, of whom another of their poets so wittingly joked, "Kodak ergo sum!" ("I photograph, therefore I am"). Don't submit to this! Leave the cars at the edge of the forest! Walk! Maybe you should even take off your shoes, as people do before entering an eastern temple.

For only thus may you touch the mystical secret which opens before a wanderer in a Russian forest.

The name of this secret is inseparability.

You will sense the inseparability of your eyes from the ladybird on the grass, from the glitter of the water in a standpool, from the lilac shadow of a butterfly on a stem, from the tops of the cluster-bomb cone-heavy firs.

You will feel the inseparability of your skin from the juniper breeze, the ultraviolet warmth, the roughness of the mushroom caps. Your hearing will fuse with the whining of the bumblebees, the grumbling of the rivulets, the carpenter's blows of the woodpeckers, the rustling of the dragonflies' wings. And you will want to shout aloud like Saint Francis of Assisi did, "My brother the rivulet! My sister the birch tree! We are separate in existing, but one in existence!"

And if you should have the good fortune to be in a Russian forest with the one you love, on some overgrown clearing, surrounded by grasses, for whose names I must again take not from my text-books, but from their poet and screenwriter, "heart's-ease, St. John's wort, daisy, rose-bay, thistle, ensnared-by-wizardry, all-ogle, clustering-about-the-shrubs," then you will feel such a total flowing into your beloved that you shall not forget it to the end of your days.

16. THE VILLAGE OF KON-KOLODETS, OR HORSE-WELL

"Help... help...

Help..."

The woman's voice held no alarm, no pain, no fear. It sounded like hallooing in the woods, like curious news, like "Breakfast is on the table!" The voice flew from the street over the window sill and under the little curtain, chasing the violet fly that was attacking the wall clock from various quarters.

Not moving his head on his pillow, Anton cautiously moved his hand under the blanket. Back, forward... Empty. Nobody. He was alone. Alone in the bed. Alone in the room. Alone in the house.

However, it seemed that this was a different house. The other one had been a city house, of stone, and this was logs. Yesterday they had been drinking Gordon's vodka here with the muzhiks. And Melada had been with them, and Granny Pelageia, and then some other village women came, and Agrippina the intended, who wasn't quite sixty. Bridegroom Anisim couldn't come. Because yesterday Agrippina's sister had sneaked up somehow and hit him upside the head with a log. He had been carted off to the hospital to stitch up. The wedding was going to have to be postponed. And the sister had been hauled off to the nuthouse, to cure her jealousy and teach her how to calm down.

"Help... Help..."

The voice was growing weaker, moving along the street toward the road. That was good. He could lie a bit longer, put his memory in order.

359

Every shaped piece had to have its proper place. Putting together the picture puzzle of the last two days.

River.

A tree upside down in the water.

A pine.

The roots poking into the air.

A kayak was floating in the middle. He had dreamed this in the ocean. But now it came when he was awake. They were standing on the shore, and the car had stayed somewhere on the road. The oar of the kayak was pushing away wet needles. The rower was laughing, shouting something behind him. Of course, he had seen this place, this river bend, in a dream. But Melada says that he only thought he had. No one can dream of a place he's never been. They return to the road and drive on.

They arrive at the house. It is the biggest house in the village. It has a tin roof. The log walls are covered with boards. The boards are painted yellow. The porch is violet. A straight-backed old woman in a green sarafan steps out onto the violet porch. She puts aside her staff, enfolds Melada in her embrace. She stays on the top step, Melada stays on the bottom, so that the old woman can look over Melada's shoulder at Anton. She studies his face and shrieks, though its unclear whether from joy or from fright.

"Heavens above! Heavens above!" she shouts, "so who is this here that you've brought round, Melady? Where ever did you find the like? So young and handsome!"

She leaves Melada, takes up her staff, and lively as a bug hobbles toward the guest. She takes his hands and tries to lift it to her lips. She strokes the sleeve of his sport coat, extends trembling fingers towards his face.

"Yaroslav Garoldovich, as I live and breath! Wherever have you been hiding yourself all these years! And how is it they didn't sniff you out, those cursed wolves, how is it they didn't drag you under? I can see though that they didn't do your eye any good, the cursed devils. But whatever is there for you hereabouts now? Your mill burned to the ground years ago, and your shop they turned into a selpo shop for salt and candies, except that you won't find any of the candies nowadays."

"That was the name of my grandfather, Yaroslav Garoldovich," Anton says. "And it's true, he was a merchant in your parts. So it would seem that you had the favor of knowing him?"

"The spit and image! You're the spit and image of Yaroslav

Garoldovich, my good master," the old woman began to keen. "And how would you be christened? Anthony? Anton in Russian? Ah, Anton, my little Anton, what a joy this is! Mary Mother of God, our intercessor and our succor, what She gives me to witness in the fullness of my years..."

The news of the arrival of the miller's scion flies about the village. Old and young alike gallop up to have a look. Anisim and Agrippina are forgotten, as is the jealous sister, and the wedding itself. The chickens go unfed, the pigs unwatered, the firewood unchopped, the radio unlistened to. The people jam themselves into the big Sukhumin house, asking him about nothing, interrupting one another with memories, for him.

"And what didn't his shop have! Saddles and lamps and axes and ropes and samovars and washbasins and varnish and solder and nails and soap and kerosene and tobacco and clocks and victrolas... And a crowd of people from morning till night, no place for people to leave their wagons. And Yaroslav Garoldovich knew everybody by name, knew everybody through and through, who could be trusted with a tab and who was feeble, that you couldn't lend so much as a pin."

"He was a one, he knew how to have a good time!"

"Across the road was the other store, Solomon's. A very sad Jew, quick to cry as a girl. Let's say one of the muzhiks is buying a saw from him. He bends the saw, runs a finger along it, and the saw makes a sad hum, and Solomon would start to cry. The cat would come in with a bird in its mouth and tears would start rolling down his face again. The wind would knock the blossoms off the bird cherry bushes, and Solomon would carry on for a week. And people didn't go to him so often... Everybody went to Yaroslav."

"You're lying there, you lying whelp of a forgetful pup! You were still crawling around under the kitchen table then, you wouldn't remember a thing. But I remember! Depends on what year we're talking. Bumper years, dead right, everybody went to Yaroslav's store to buy, happy as could be. But come a skinny year, fields like ribs on a stray, and you'd get down yourself, and you didn't want any joking and jollying. You look in a bad year, you'd see all the carts over at Solomon's. The muzhiks would honk around with melancholy Solomon, buying up supplies with their last kopeks, and it warmed their hearts to see that even their money wasn't making him happier, that his Jewish sad could chase their Russian sad three times around the pond and still be first one in the barn..."

"I'll give that, that's true... Bad years most people went to Solomon's. But Yaroslav wasn't exactly asleep then. He knew that on toward winter the muzhiks would start getting worried and would start looking for any work they could get. He'd borrow some money from Solomon and start scouring the countryside, looking for cheap woods. Along about Protection they'd be sitting around his shop with saws and axes, just hanging around waiting. They watch, and then of a sudden he'd ride up on a horse, wave his cap, shout, 'My woods, lads, my woods! I'll stand a pail of vodka!' Eh, there was a lot of excitement in life then, but now..."

"How about him? He was a handsome one," granny Pelagea sticks in, "I was just a slip of a thing, but he won my heart all the same. And the girls just withered up and blew away because of him, each one worse than the next! How about them, that Yaroslav Garoldovich up and falls in love with who? Solomon's daughter, that's who! And she loved him. She was a good girl, thoughtful like. She converted on account of him, church wedding, everything by the book. They could have lived forever, except the locals just couldn't forgive him that, not the villagers, not the country folk. Our daughters aren't good enough for him, they said, he had to get himself mixed up with a heathen. They started to avoid him. Somebody doesn't invite him to a nameday party, somebody won't be a godfather, a third cusses him out in front of everybody, over nothing. And then the village bad boys get wind of who the village is on the outs with, and they come running up to do their nasty tricks. Dig a rake down into the path with the teeth up, to catch a kid's bare feet. Chuck some sharp glass in the trough for the overseas boar, that he's paid good money to bring in. Set fire to a hay stack in the night. And as soon as the tsar was overthrown, there was nothing stopping the hooligans. Yaroslav Garoldovich got himself a proper wind up then, started listening to his wife carry on, 'Let's leave, she says, let's leave, I'm scared for the children!' She finally talked him into it. He sold the house and the mill and the shop, and in the middle of the war they left, through Finland and Sweden, people say, to the far corners, to get away from our cruelty and envy. And so now you're telling me they ran themselves all the way to America? You see, Anton, when we scare somebody, we do a proper job of it. And then we think about it, reminisce, and cry."

"Help... Help..."

The voice was coming back again.

Anton hastily pulled on the old coat which Melada had found in a closet of her father's house, tied up his sagging pants, jammed on the crude Russian boots. The boots slopped around on his feet but he decided that there wasn't the time to chink them with wads of newspaper, the way Melada's brother Tolik had taught him, a war cripple in time of peace. In the mirror he saw himself as a rumpled unshaven hobo with a black eye who wouldn't be out of place in line at the beer stand first thing of a morning, in keeping with what they had seen as they left Pskov... yesterday? Two days ago? Last week?

He went out on the porch, yelled to the strange woman who was wandering the streets yelling for help.

"Hey, lady, what's the problem?"

The woman looked up at him from under her shading hand.

"Well, master, God be praised we come in to the town to the store, there was a rumor that matches was brought in and tobacco too, and we're run out of sugar so we came straight over from that Chalovnitsy of ours, but wouldn't you know it, the water was riz, the horse couldn't make the ford, so my man he says 'Hell or high water, let's take the bridge,' but I says to him that's a big risk and sure enough, 'cause it wasn't a year that my nephew just about took his motorcycle off that same bridge, and nobody fixed her since then, then when the ice went out this spring it give her a good shaking besides, but he keeps saying come on, come on, so we did it, and the horse went through, and that was the last one we have, the only horse in the whole village..."

"He fell through? Was he killed?"

"Naw, he's still hanging there. He's got his front legs on the bridge, but the back ones is completely down, just above the water. Your muzhiks is already two hours working on it over there, but the five of them can't hardly handle it, so they sent me to get some more help. But where am I going to get help? All the Kon-Kolodets folk have been out clearing logs since morning, chopping dead wood, so there's none but little kids and old women like me in the houses... so don't you refuse me, you're a good man, you'll lend us a hand, won't you? You'll see, six will do in a snap what five can't budge."

Anton followed the woman down the dusty road that lead to the river. The road went through a beet field. True, half the village held that it wasn't a beet field but a cabbage field. In order to prove their case the arguers got down on all fours in the sea of weeds, burrowing into the rape, couch-grass, and bachelor's buttons, digging around in the depths with their hands and in fact did manage to find a head of cabbage about the size of a new-born's fist. However their opponents immediately dropped down beside them, dug in the neighboring invisible mound and dug up a clutch of beet tops with rat-like tails on the end. The argument faded.

"Well, wait until Vitya Polusvetov comes on his Pskovmobile to cut the weeds, then you'll see!" said the one faction.

"When Vitya Polusvetov comes to plow, then you'll see!" said the other.

Vitya Polusvetov was a legendary local tractor-driver. People said that he had his tractor fixed so it could make homebrew. That the snacks no good man would drink without grew on the roof of his tractor, mushrooms and cucumbers. That this Vitya, who once had courted Melada, had already arrived at communism a thousand years before anybody else. They said too that if he liked somebody he could dig up a garden for them in five minutes, like some sort of tractor-driving Robin Hood, but if he didn't like somebody, he'd bump into a corner of his cowbarn with the treads of his caterpillar and then just go and try to complain, being sure to bundle up your tumbled logs and bricks along with your complaints.

Vitya could be severe, but he was also quick to soften. Let's say that his sister got to cutting up with some passing kayaker. Another kind of brother might beat a girl bloody, cripple her. Vitya, good lad that he was, simply took his ax and the no-good girl out in the yard, laid her head on the chopping block and whack! cut off her braid, right up against her neck. When Anton forgot himself a bit during the third bottle and put an arm around Melada, the villagers sighed and shook their heads, whispering one to the other, "Oh, if only Vitya doesn't find out, our boy shouldn't know, it'll break his heart."

The road tumbled over a hummock, opening a view of the river. The wooden pilings of the bridge had been driven into the river bottom at an angle and now were all askew, like the legs of a drunk, all battered and dented by spring ice breaking up. On top of them were laid boards, through which water was seen. The horse was sitting in the middle in an awkward dog-like pose, stretching out its front legs. The back legs and croup had fallen into a hole between the loose boards. Hooves were bobbing about a couple of meters above the water, spasmodically seeking a fulcrum. The horse's muzzle bore a look of melancholy guilt. The cart, unharnessed, stood in the bushes on the shore.

Anton quickened his step, started to run. He saw immediately, clearly, that if the boards were to move even a bit more then the horse with all its bulk would smash down onto the rocks below. However the muzhiks gathered about would not let that happen. Probably this wasn't the first time that they had had to drag out a fallen horse, and probably they knew what to grab and where to do it. All that was required of Anton was to offer his two hands. To which, thank God, power and strength had returned, after all that bailing water in the hold of the Babylonia.

When he reached the group of muzhiks, however, Anton could feel that something was not right. The muzhiks were obviously tired and quarrelsome after pointless exertions. They were slapping the horse on the rump, stroking its muzzle, pulling on its halter. They were recalling similar incidents, boasting, arguing, getting angry, making bets. Two geniuses had yanked a couple of boards from the planking, stuck them under the horse's belly, and were getting ready to push up, as on a lever. A minute or two more and the horse's bones would have broken, pushing through the flesh. Anton barely was in time to push aside these new-found Archimedeses.

Then everybody turned on the assistant they hadn't asked for, suspicious and taunting. "Where'd you come from? What's he know about pulling horses out of holes? Those overseas places he comes from I wouldn't wonder they've forgot which end you put the collar on and what side the saddle goes on."

Anton was thinking feverishly.

"We need a crane to lift with, but where we going to get one? Forget about machinery... In Boy Scout camp they taught us how to pull out a car stuck in the mud, tie one end of a rope to the bumper and the other to a tree, and then everybody pile on the middle...but no, that won't work, we'd only cripple the poor creature. If only there was some kind of strong branch over head, we could toss a rope over the branch and lift it like a crane, except there's no branch. So why not slap together a frame out of logs? Like a scaffolding, except to save the horse, not hang him. But would the six of us be strong enough to lift it? But wait, why just six? There's also the horse... one horsepower, one big horsepower...the horse is a lot stronger than we..."

Then Anton slapped himself on the forehead and smiled.

"Tolik! You gonna help?"

Tolik Sukhumin readily took the other end of the board, and the two of them went down under the bridge. Anton leaned one end of the board against the slope of the bank, and with gestures explained to his helper what he needed. Tolik quickly offered his strong back, and Anton hopped on, riding him out into the water and holding the other end of the board. Half a meter under the planking there was a reinforcing beam between the pilings, on which Anton put the end of the board. He tested it, found it strong. Up to his waist in water, Tolik moved his rider under the thrashing legs of the horse. Anton grabbed one of the hooves and put it on the board. The horse stopped flailing and froze, as if unable to believe its good luck. Then it kicked the other hoof, almost getting Anton in the head, but it found the board, and got on it.

Its veins throbbed under its quivering skin. A moment more, and it didn't so much step as squeeze itself upward, with a groan.

Daylight burst through the now-empty hole.

The exultant shouts of the rescue squad joined the whinny of the horse and the clatter of its hooves along the planks.

Tolik went back to shore, put Anton down, and began to pump his hand heartily.

Beaming with pride, arms about each other's shoulders, they came out from under the bridge and froze in a pose, expecting congratulations, laurels, proclamations, or at least some kind of nod hello.

No one paid them the least attention. The muzhiks had already led the horse to the other shore and harnessed it to the cart again. The woman who had been passing through bowed deeply to each in turn, then made the sign of the cross. The muzhiks clapped each other on the shoulder, passing a water bottle around.

Anton couldn't accept what had just happened. He dashed over the bridge, to the harnessed cart.

"Everybody see how to pull horses out of holes now? If you want," he shouted gaily, "we could do it again."

The muzhiks looked at him with mute incomprehension. Then they glanced at one another. They were obviously embarrassed by the importunate foreigner in mufti. "What's he expect us to be?" was plainly written on their faces. "We worked long and honestly trying to get that horse out of the bridge. And with God's help the whole of us were able to surmount this hard job. And then when everything was almost over this one comes running up and wants to claim all the credit... These foreigners just don't know how to behave. No manners, they just have no manners..."

They silently arranged themselves on the flatbed wagon and set off toward the village. Even Tolik Sukhumin ran past Anton and joined his fellows.

Anton, feeling spat upon, dragged along behind, trying to get this very difficult but obviously important lesson into his vainglorious, unaccustomed, foreign head.

Granny Pelageia was fussing about the wood-greedy Russian stove, fixing dinner. The flames raged in their brick cave. Tongues of flame flicked out, licking the sides of the two cast iron pits, roared up the chimney. The room smelled of pitch and cabbage. Slowly the stove drank up warmth, which that night it would grudgingly give back to the sleeping people of the house.

"Where's our Melada then?" Anton asked. "She's awake and up?"

Granny Pelageia put down her tongs and glanced sympathetically at him.

"Melada, she's up and about real early, Anton, up and gone away and who's to say where?"

"What do you mean up and gone away? Gone where? Without saying anything—goodbye?"

"She left you a letter, put it smack in the middle of the table next to your bed. Didn't see it then, did you? I don't know what's in the letter, 'cause it's not in how we write."

Anton dashed into his room. A page with writing was leaned against a glass holding a bouquet of dried oats. How could he have missed it?

"Good morning. Excuse me, but I had to leave. I want to find your Golda, so you can talk with her and see that it wasn't we who lured her in, but she who ran away from you. Otherwise I'll never feel at peace. There's no need for you to go with me. You would only be in the way with your black eye and Estonian accent. You can live two days in the village. Or maybe three. Look for grasses. The villagers liked you. They can understand you without a translator. And you understand them. There won't be any unpleasantness. I do beg you, though, don't go deep into the woods. Especially if you are alone. Struggle against this new passion. On a foggy day it's easy to get lost. You can walk scores of kilometers and never encounter a soul. There are no rescue rockets or ships or helicopters that can find you there. If you don't value your own life, then think of my career. They won't forgive me the loss of so valuable a specialist. To be on the safe side, burn this letter. Your M."

He went back to the kitchen, upset. Mechanically he stuck the paper into the rollicking flame. Granny Pelageia sighed and said thoughtfully, "That's how they are, those cars and motorcycles. On she hops and off she goes. Didn't use to know troubles like this, we didn't, lived side-by-side with each other, just living... So where did she go off to then?"

"I don't know exactly. The letter says it was on business. She's going to be covering the whole territory for a few days."

"I'll tell you one thing, Anton, and that's that she asked me how to get to Volokhonka village, to Irina Borisovna Tikhomirova's house."

"And what does that mean?"

"What that means is that the girls only go to Borisovna's for one thing, either they want to cast a spell on somebody else's heart, or get rid of a spell on their own. There isn't a better witch in the entire region than Borisovna."

Glimmers of the cave fire flickered on the old woman's face. She lifted her hand, pointed a finger at the icon.

"They've forgotten how to ask the Lord for things, but they still go running to witches. You wouldn't know who's got her heart worked up this time, would you, Anton?"

"No, I don't. I don't even think it is. She always has her feelings under tight control. Why? Why can't she be more open?"

"That's as it is, different for everybody. There's people with good but feeble feelings, like kids. No harm in letting that type run around and play. They won't hurt themselves and won't do any harm to anyone else either. Then there's those, any feeling they get, it's like a bandit in the woods. You let those sort out without guard dogs and soldiers, they'll make such a mess. Everything around them they'll burn to the ground, smash to bits, and destroy. Like this Vitya Polusvetov that's coming over on his tractor, you heard about him?"

"I have."

"You give him a little room at first. The tongue-waggers have already been filling his ears pretty good about you and Melada. Wouldn't wonder if he wasn't mad enough to run his tractor treads over my berries a bit. Or over you."

"They say he's her old flame."

"Don't believe it. Oh, he's stuck on her, that's right enough. That first year, she was a student, came down here for the summer, for the holidays, he lost his head right then. Hereabouts though that's considered a terrible shame to a boy. Everybody teases them, cracks all kinds of sayings, like 'he fell in love like a pig in mud,' or 'tumbled into love like a mouse into the cracker tin.' And as for bringing round flowers or giving girls some kind of spangly-jangles, no sirree! Falling in love, that's girly giggles stuff. 'Gonna give my guy a wink of my eye' and 'he's not a bad sort but he's brought me to port,' all those kinds of sayings are about girls."

"Where I come from that's called male chauvinism."

"So he started courting her like they do around here, not like in the city. Making fun of her at the dances. Or waiting for her on the paths at night, giving her a good scare. Or driving the tractor back and forth in the middle of the night. She got mad one time, ran outside with the double-barrel. And shot too!"

"She hit anything?"

"The right barrel blew all the mushrooms off the hood. And then when she pointed the left barrel at the cabin, he put her right into reverse. He got scared, and kind of backed off from her. Still hasn't forgotten her, though, and still has a boil on his heart about it. Whenever she comes to visit, he won't let anyone be around her."

"I'm not going to hide from him like an ostrich."

"You don't have to. We'll explain everything to him, that there's nothing between you, that she's doing a job, that you're sleeping in a bed in the good room, and that's she's up in the hay loft. And as for that putting your arm around her when you were drinking, that's just your foreign bad manners, something she's got to put up with in a guest. One person will say it, another will back it up, and everything will pass all right..."

Suddenly she turned to the window.

"Say, look, there's Feoktist, come after you. Where'd he promise to take you, you say?"

"To his far hayfields. He says that he's got a lot of hay still not cut there."

"It's a good thing all round. Feoktist is a reliable muzhik, a correct guy, like one of the family. Even so though, Anton, don't believe everything that he's going to be telling you. Soon's he finds a new man, then he's like a drunk. Spouts out all his stories one after the other, can't stop himself. If you get tired of it, just tell him that's it, no more, no more cooking your head in Russian. He'll shut up then. Otherwise he'll talk so much you'll forget where you came from, and how to get back home."

The stems of the reeds brushed along the edges of the boat, leaning toward the sand of the shore. Instead of a flower each stem bore a stick of velvety chocolate. Underwater forests rocked, bubbles of air floated up, schools of red-eyed fish hid in the weeds winding about boulders and snags. On the overgrown September banks were the blue berries of juniper, the red of currants, the yellow of hawthorn, and then, occasionally, like some lacquered jewel of a toy, the red-black pendants of *beresklet*.

The graybeard ancient Feoktist steadily stuck his pole into the water, transferred his body weight, hung above the canoe slipping away beneath him, and then, at the very last moment touching the boat with the pole, he would push the boat's nose directly into the stream.

"Don't even look at this meadow, Anton," Feoktist said. "There's lots of grass there, that's for sure, but it isn't grass for us. See that brownish matter sticking out from the birch, like a poppy head tied to it? That's a brigade mark, that means it's a state farm meadow, everybody's property, nobody can touch it. And we're going out to the eighth bend, the brigade leader hasn't gotten out there yet."

"Isn't it kind of late to be cutting the people's meadow? The grass has gone brown, almost like the birch."

"It's late, Anton, you couldn't be righter, my boy. They've let the time go by. Back in the spring, when he put that thing on the tree, he knew that they wouldn't be able to cut it, that they'd never get the mower in here. But he put it up anyway, so that we wouldn't get it."

"But why? How come?"

"Because that's his job. To keep order, make our life miserable."

"And it's your job to work umpty-three hours a day and cut your hay umpty-three river bends away?"

"That's about it."

"I met a kid at the Shutkoplokhovs' house. A little girl. I was talking with her about fresh fruits. I asked her how many apples she had eaten this summer. One, she said. Kolkhidonov's wife had given her one apple. That's it. And in the collective farm orchard the apples drop on the ground and the worms eat them and they rot. Why?"

"Because there aren't enough workers in the collective farm to pick them."

"So why not let the girl go in and pick apples for herself, as many as she can carry in her gingham skirtfront."

"Because that would be a violation of the law for public property.

You can go to jail for that."

"So couldn't you ask me to come pick this public property, the way we bring in Mexicans in America?"

"That would be the worst violation of all, the return of exploitation—what we had when your grandpa was alive, Yaroslav Garoldovich."

"But wouldn't the collective farm be paying me?"

"They don't have anything to pay with."

"Then I'm ready to work for nothing, just for food, like a stupid volunteer in the Peace Corps."

"You can't. That would be a violation of the law of surplus value and a contradiction of a contradiction."

"Feoktist, all these laws of yours are making my head spin. I'm going to fall overboard, I think."

"Not here, though. It's real deep right here, a bad place."

As if to confirm what he said, the surface of the water burst open with a loud splash, and the glass head of some monster with a long horn rose up. The head came nearer through the sun-dappled water, grabbed the edge of the boat. The monster opened it's teeth and spit a flopping fish into the boat.

From beneath the glass mask pushed back onto a forehead appeared the laughing face of Tolya Sukhumin. He waved, put the rubber mouthpiece of the snorkel back into his mouth, put the goggles back onto his face, pushed off from the boat with his flipper feet, and once again disappeared into the depths of the underwater forest.

"Oh my lord, what a great carp he got!" Feoktist gasped in admiration. "The boy's got a talent, a real talent! Before he was in the army he used to get more of them with his hands or a trident. Stupid fish, sitting around in the weeds or under a snag, thinks nobody can see it. He sneaks up behind real quiet and snap! Dinner on the table. But when he was in the army the tank turret crushed all his fingers, so you know what he did? Taught himself how to catch 'em with his teeth. There's a pike for you, eh? Pelageia's a lucky lady. I'd give a lot for a grandson like him."

"But isn't he violating some great Law for preserving fish schools?"

"No, there's nothing forbidding that. Catch all you want, long's you use your hands or teeth. How many can you catch that way? Can even use a fishing pole, if you want. But nets, that you can't. Seines either. And you can't use dynamite to stun them either. The muzhiks break that law, though. How you going to get on without fish? Except now even with a net you don't get but a few. They built a dam downstream and all the fish can do is beat their heads against it, they sure can't get up to us."

"But why, Feoktist, why? Why build a dam without a fish ladder? Why do your little kids grow up without big apples? Why do your chickens lay eggs without shells? Why do you feed your pigs and cows with bread and then pay gold for grain from Michigan? Why do you cart all the cabbage to town in wagons and have your relatives mail it back to you in parcels? Why does each of you lug water to his own gardens in heavy buckets, instead of getting together to buy a pump like the Kolkhidonovs', so you can sit and rest when you're old?"

Feoktist grew melancholy, wiped his beard on the pole, studied the question mark of a scarlet stork on the shore. Crowds of waterskippers danced about among the blooming water lilies, safe from whatever lived in the water below either because of their speed or how they tasted. The stab of the sun penetrated his eyes even when his lids were closed.

"Anton, I think the way I do because here everything is all cockeyed to rid us of the smart muzhiks. Or to force them to hide their brains as deep down as they can. Take my dad. Between the second famine and the third, suddenly they started giving the peasants land. He was the first to take a plot. He divided it up into a farm and started raising horses, pigs, and chickens. All of us worked, little and big, sun up to sun down. And we started to make it. Then they had a mouthful of a word for us, but nice: peasant initiativists. Five years later everything was turned upside down by the political planners and the newspapers started to curse us with a word that was a lot easier to understand: kulaks. But my dad, you won't believe it but it's true, my dad was so clever that he immediately abandoned everything and moved us all here, to his brother, in Kon-Kolodets. He stuffed the whole family into a shed and announced that he was poor. Dirt poor, so there was nobody they could take from us. That was how he saved us. The rest of the initiativists were rounded up by people who already weren't so nice, with pistols, and those we never saw again."

A sun-gilded frog croaked and slipped from a lily pad just a second before the pole would have pierced him, and then floated away downstream.

"After that our family didn't let their brains show in anything, no matter what it was. Whoever tried to stick out, even just for the neighbors or in school for the teachers, my father would beat him without mercy. So we all stuck our brains so far away in our heads that I can't even remember any more where they are. And it seems like when you don't use them, they dry up. Take me for instance. I've got brains enough for three villages, and you won't find a professor who's read as many books as I have. But intelligence? Not a drop. Absolutely no clue about when to plant my potatoes. Just keep an eye out until the others do. No idea where to dig my well, so I have holes all over my yard. If I remember a good place for mushrooms I'm going to go straight there every year even if there's nothing growing there, because I can't find a new place. Even the electricity won't pay me any mind. Soon's I plug something in, I immediately blow the transformer outside, and black out the whole village. They come running, plug in a new one."

The sandy bank rose up to the sky, seeming higher than the walls of the Pskov fortress. In the overhanging roots were bird nests and burrows, and the racket of birds was continual. Blue helmets of lupine were rocking in ranks down below, right next to the water. Here and there pine stumps poked through, like enemy cannon. One of them held an ant's forepost, a mound in constant motion, hanging over the water. And who would have believed the stories its inhabitants could tell about unidentified objects floating past in the water below? No one would, ever.

"To live with somebody who's got brains is nothing but trouble," Feoktist went on. "He's always outdoing you, passing you, doing things better, and then he makes fun of you besides. The rain comes, and everybody in the village runs out to stack up their hay. Except the smart ones, they've already got it in stacks and in the barn. Suddenly comes fall and the price of peas jumps up, and then you find out the smart ones already have a whole field of nothing but peas. Suddenly the bosses decide to let the peasant sell honey, and then it turns out that the smart ones already have so many hives put together that the woods ring from the buzzing. And your wife and your relatives and all your kids are going to give you the devil about it, that's how to do things, you good-for-nothing! You ever going to learn how to farm, you miserable excuse for a man? And what can you do? Just grind your teeth and clench your fist.

"In our village, the only smart one left is Leonid Kolkhidonov. He's always got apples somehow, and his roof is tin, and he's got a motorcycle outside and a television inside, and a pump for the garden. The village doesn't like the Kolkhidonovs, keep away from them. Leonid isn't real taken with us, either. But he did come back to us, thirty years ago, after exile. Brought a young wife, also one of the exiles. His whole family died there, except him. Scurvy got his teeth, though. And how come? Because his father wasn't as smart as mine, because he didn't want to run off and be a poor man. He held out to the very end, refused to go into the collective farm. He'd lock his gate and wouldn't come out no matter how hard the brigade leader knocked. The brigade leader then was Anisim's dad, and he figured out what to do. He got up on the Kolkhidonovs' roof and knocked their chimney in with a hammer. Like it or not, that'll make you run out into the street. He talked a lot of people into joining the collective farms by doing that."

"Anisim's dad? Is he the one that looks like a duck with a blue nose? Who talked about my grandfather Yaroslav?"

"Right, that's him. Your grandpa could read him like a book, wouldn't give him so much as a box of matches on credit."

"So how come people still treat him with respect, and put him in the front row? And the Kolkhidonovs who never did any of you any harm, who didn't take two stabs at doing you in, how come nobody has anything to do with them? But for the guy who knocks the chimneys in it's all forgive and forget?"

The pole hung in the air for a moment, dripping river water into the boat. Then the slithering across the water started again, but Feoktist was still searching for the words to explain this to the uncomprehending foreigner.

"You know, Anton, it doesn't do all the time to be coming out with these whys. They say that before this cat food thing you worked in an insurance office. Way we see it, that means you fought with fate. And that's not a good thing to be doing, way we see things. Makes a fellow's brains into oatmeal, so's he starts to forget how to understand who gets what."

"All right, I get you. That means that Anisim's dad was meant to knock down chimneys and people. And Kolkhidonov's father was meant to die in exile along with his whole family, without even tobacco to sniff. And my brainy grandpa was meant to run away before the stupid came to power. And the brigade leader is meant to take away your last blade of grass. And so nobody is ever at fault in anything, right?"

"You got it! And it seems like you've got an easy job, just feeding cats. Tolik Sukhumin now, his lot was to lose all the fingers on his left hand during basic training in the 9th Armored Division for taking the city of Stockholm. Except that so far nobody knows whether the 9th Division is supposed to actually take Stockholm or is supposed to lay their bones on the bottom of the Baltic along with all their submarines."

Anton grew thoughtful. There was something unusual, something attractive about this simple-hearted trick by which Feoktist transformed all human activities, ailments, successes, and problems. His beneficent picture left no room for a Miserymaker. Or more precisely, the monster was there, but not as a cruel and dangerous opponent, but as a dispassionate herald. The monster simply informed people of who was fated for what. And to struggle against the monster wouldn't even be presumption and arrogance; it would be just dumb.

The Miserymaker slithered majestically about the world, dispensing roles and fates. "You, pine tree on the lip of the bank, you have three winters and three summers yet to stand, and then it is fated that you will fall top first into the water, where you will lay another eight years, until kayaking tourists from free Estonia come and chop you into firewood. And you, little roach leaping out of the water, you are fated for a meeting with a big perch, who for the moment is still drowsing in the depths of the third river bend. As for you, little thistle fluff, you are fated to waft over forest and vale, over the iron bridges and belching locomotives, until you land next to a fence in a monastery near the Soroti river, where you will grow into a big blossoming bush that will gladden the eye of everyone waiting in the long line to see the grave marker by the hand of man, where Tungus, Finn, and Kalmyk still argue over who Pushkin intended should stand where, when he put them in his poem."

"You shouldn't be so proud, Anton," Feoktist sighed. "Don't be snooty about us. I mean we used to have plenty of everything too, no worse than you've got there in your America."

"When was that? In the days of wine and roses, when you had tsars and emperors?"

"Why then? Before that, before the tsars. In your America then there was nothing but wild Indians, scalping each other. And we already had the Pskov Republic! Incredibly rich it was too. The churches were full of icons, the bazaar was stuffed with food, the wheat stood higher than a horse, and you couldn't stick an oar in the river for the fish. There wasn't an enemy had the guts to cross the border, and our merchants went all over the globe with our goods. And that's the real truth, which Arkady Makarovich has read from his books where it is being kept forever."

"And who's this Arkady Makarovich?"

"Our best loved summer resident, almost one of us. If you'd come a week earlier, you'd have met him. He's such a great guy, he's made of gold. You won't find the like anymore. All summer long he fixed the old peoples' roofs for free, and brought in firewood and watered their gardens. And if the weather was no good, he'd write his books or else read to us about the olden days from somebody else's. We learned all about it from him, how famous Pskov was. What's your Moscow? Spoiled by Tatars and Turks, and nothing left there but Tatar ways. I mean Moscow was under the Mongols more than once, and the Poles, and the French. Here in Pskov though, we always drove the enemy away.

"In Moscow the merchants would drive the prices up to the clouds and then wait in an empty bazaar for some overseas idiot to turn up, and then they'd flatter him and make him feel good. Meanwhile we had caravan after caravan streaming in. Because we had everything and no tricks, everything was the best, too. People always respected capital and everyone was accounted for properly, in the bazaar or in court. You knock somebody's tooth out, then pay him twelve *grivens*. Steal the beaver out of somebody's trap? Also twelve *grivens*. You just want to give somebody a pop in the snout? Then pay three *grivens* and go to it. Even killing had a price. If it was just a peasant, forty *grivens*, but for somebody from the boyar family, that was eighty. Even women couldn't be killed for free. Cough up twenty *grivens* for every one of them. That's how people kept our Pskov laws, and that's what kept us strong."

"So where did it all go? What I mean is, when and why was it fated that you should be conquered by this turkified Moscow?"

"Hey, knock it off, Anton, knock it off! You're just a lad, to be making jokes at me! Or are you wanting to start in with your stupid whys again? If so, then I'm going to tell..."

Feoktist was so upset that he lost the rhythm of his poling, let the boat slide further under him than he should have. He lost his balance and so hung over the pole that was stuck in the mud, kicking his legs above the water. The current began to turn the nose of canoe now that it had lost its steering. Anton bellied over the side, to stand in the silty bottom.

"...to tell you," the now-angry Feoktist shouted from his pole while Anton waded waist deep in water to push the pitchy boat-bottom back under his waving legs, "I'll tell you what all the old folks said, that this happened because they didn't withstand temptation! That they forgot about God's gifts! So you look out, Anton, that the same thing doesn't happen there with you! Because you can't see God behind all your Cadillacs and pineapples and bare-boobed beauties and your little glass shack under the palm trees! Repent, while there's still time!"

They got back to the village in the evening. Samples of meadow grass that they had gathered at the eighth river bend were cooling between the pages of Anton's herbarium. The outlines of the little bathhouses were inked against a yellow sky, like backdrops for a silhouette theater. The universal soldier's widow Valentina was driving home a herd of the last seven lean cattle, who were lowing in anticipation of their evening loaves of bread made from Michigan's wheat. Tolia Sukhumin was sitting on the planks of a small pier, cleaning fish with tooth marks on their backs. A squad of the Kolkhidonovs's geese swam by against a green backdrop of reeds. Above this whole peaceful picture hung—promised? beckoned?—the growing clamor of an automobile engine.

Anton jumped out of the canoe onto a dock, ran up the bank, slipping in the geese droppings. A sharp sprout in his chest, left with no stays to guide it, grew where it wanted, turning into a shapeless painful lump. And what if the magic had worked, and her heart had been cured of the nice little guy from abroad, the one who wasn't worth the earrings in her ear? The village street flew past, blinding with the light of scores of setting suns, one in each window. Towards him, down the hill, grew two more blinding globes whose rays picked their way through the corn stocks.

But no, not even in its Russian translation would the Fiat make such a dreadful noise. The whine and rattle advanced like a wall. Something huge and heavy, almost touching the wires on the poles above, was moving towards him down the village street.

Anton backed against a fence and let the roaring enormity pass him. He could see a high quivering cage, fastened to the roof of the tractor cabin with thick cucumber vines tumbling down from above. Three rotten logs were fastened to the hood, bristling thick with clusters of mushrooms. Above the roar of the engine the clucking of chickens could be heard from inside the cage. Old and young came running out to meet their beloved guest, Vitya Polusvetov.

Billowing smoke, the tractor stopped by the house of Agrippina, the bride. The tractor driver came out onto the foot rung and began plucking fresh cucumbers from the thick vines, handing them down to the outstretched children's hands. Then he yanked on a rope, the cage opened, and chickens tumbled out like paratroopers from their plane. Only then did Vitya jump down to the ground, then turn and reach up, to help his head-bandaged passenger to get down.

"Anisim! Anisim! Vitya Polusvetov brought Anisim back from the hospital!"

"Here you go, auntie Agrippina, here's your groom back," the munificent Vitya said. "Found him out on the road. I look, and it's like in the song, a wounded man wandering along, 'head in swaths, bloodied sleeves, and a bloody trail in the cold damp grass.'"

Agrippina came up smiling, shook her groom's hand.

"I ran away, my friends, my soul couldn't endure it," Anisim said. "They stick needles in you, shine x-rays through you, don't let you walk or smoke or drink. My God! Piss in a cup from morning to night, that's all they let you do? And what kind of piss you going to make with that tea and milk of theirs? The hell with them, the devils! They hid my clothes, so I took some from a stiff in the morgue there. Got to remember to give it back to him, too."

Vitya Polusvetov took in turn each of the mugs that people were holding out to him, opened the cock on the radiator and gave each person a splash to try from the motor's first batch. He then offered some of them pickles, others baked eggs, pocketing their clanking coppers.

"I've got an oven rigged up in the exhaust pipe now, lads, do some baking. If I get the notion, I can make a chicken, roast some eggs, make a mushroom pie."

"Good for you, Vitya! You and your Pskovmobile, you got to communism a thousand years before anybody else! You don't need stores or bazaars. Everything except the sunshine is yours. We're backward, we can't even find the path to socialism yet, say nothing of communism."

"All right, lads, all right, enough wasting time!" shouted the wounded groom, who had gotten tipsy from a single swallow. "Agrippina and me, we've decided to celebrate the wedding tomorrow! She's waited thirty years, so why put things off any longer? So long as the doctors don't grab me back again, and that sister of hers doesn't get me with another log, let's make some noise tomorrow, so that the whole damn district will hear!"

"Right you are!"

"True, why wait?"

"The sun is out and life's still easy, so why not play!"

"But how we gonna to get the guests in?"

"They'll hear us!"

"They'll come running in so fast we won't have time enough to set the tables for them."

"Besides, look at the guest we've got right here, come three thousands versts, over ocean and sea he's come!"

"Hey, Vitya, come meet Anton," Granny Pelageia popped up, "he's maybe from over there, but he's our stock, from Pskov. His grandpa came here to settle from over Sebich way, became our best trader and miller. Us old folks, we still remember him as a good man."

It grew still.

The crowd began to melt back, leaving a narrow dueler's path between the two visitors from different worlds. Anton took a step or two forward, hand extended. Vitya straightened his hat, tore off a couple cucumber leaves, and began to wipe the dust off the word "Pskovmobile" that was painted on the cabin door. Then, suddenly he stuck two fingers in his mouth and gave a whistle. The tractor chickens immediately stopped their plundering raid on the village and one after another began to jump back into their cage. The rooster chased the last one in with threats and nips, then jumped in himself.

Vitya shrugged his broad shoulders, straightened his cotton-padded jacket.

"Evenings getting chilly, seems like," he said.

Paying no attention to Anton's outstretched hand, he jumped lightly onto the tractor tread and opened his cabin door.

"Got to get a lot of booze made for tomorrow. Figure I'll be driving the tractor all night to do it."

Shaking, the Pskovmobile roared, belched a blue cloud and set off, making the huts tremble and the chicken tower sway. The cucumber mane was waving in the breeze and the bunches of mushrooms were shaking.

Embarrassed, the men and women gave a wide berth to Anton, who stood frozen, hand still outstretched.

The Story of Wise Feoktist, Recorded on the Banks
of Duck Lake
(The Two Atamans: Washington and
Pugachev)

The night before Anisim and Agrippina's wedding I understood why we had had to bring in a crate of flashlights. Tolya Sukhumin and Feoktist asked me to go catch crayfish for the wedding feast. After an hour of walking we came to the shore of Duck Lake. The sun had already set, but Feoktist said that we had to wait a bit yet, to let the crayfish fall completely asleep.

When it was almost completely dark we cut firewood, then drove some uprights into the ground, then hung a kettle on the crosspiece (which incidentally made clear why their forest is so clean and pretty—they are only allowed to cut deadwood for firewood, so that every summer millions of volunteer woodsmen who have neither gas nor electric ovens cut down the dead trees for free, gather up deadfall, and so, though involuntarily, turn the forests into something like a palace with columns and carpets). Only after that was done, lighting our way with the flashlights, we went into the shallow water.

The water was still warm from the day. We walked carefully, trying not to stir up the bottom silt. When the light would hit a crayfish he would try to hide, but very slowly, sleepily. Feoktist and I had nets that we would sweep them up in, but Tolya would grab them in his hand. Even so, at the end of the hunt there was not a scratch on him, while my right hand, that I had used to dig the crayfish out of the netting, was nipped all bloody.

Each of us used up several batteries to catch two buckets of crayfish and a dozen sleeping perch and baby pike. While we were boiling the crayfish in salt water and eating the fish we had caught, washed down with sweet tea, I heard a highly unusual explanation of Russian and American history which I must share with you, my dear listeners.

Feoktist swore that he was adding nothing of his own, that everything he was saying was in Arkady Makarovich's books. I don't know whether that may be believed. I wish only to stress that I had my little Sony with me and turned it on without anyone noticing, so that I have the whole story on tape, word for word.

"The Russian land and the English land started the same, Anton, at about the same time, a thousand years ago. The Varangians came to both us and you, that you called Normans or Vikings, and they began to rule everyone. People lie about us, that we voluntarily asked them to rule us. Fat chance! It was them made that story up later. As they said to the chronicler Pimen, 'Write that your land was broad and rich, but that there was no order in it. Write that you asked us yourselves to come and rule you, and if you don't, then onto the stake with you, and we'll make somebody else write it.' We know how such things are done now, we've had a good look at the ways.

"Your language and our language even have a lot of the words the same. Your 'nose' is our 'nos,' your 'salt' is our 'sol.' You have 'yes' and we have 'est,' that is, yes sir. You've got 'army' and we've got 'armiia,' you've got 'cost' and we've got 'kosht.'

"And then things started going for us the way they were going for you. In the 14th century you beat the French, and we beat the Tatars. In the 15th century we both fought more among ourselves. In the 16th century your kings cut off a lot of heads, but then our Ivan the Terrible's count will stand up fine alongside yours. In the 17th century new clans started to rule, the Stuarts for you and the Romanovs for us. And both the one and the other started to introduce a new faith, and whoever wanted to worship God the old way got prison or the rod or torture.

"Your old believers were called Puritans. They began to run off to America. Our old believers were called schismatics, and they ran off to the Don, the Yaik river (the Ural we call it now), where they became free Cossacks.

"So what are we up to now? Oh yes, the 18th century. Our Cossacks are living how they want on the far borders of the Russian empire. They plant grain, hunt, fish, keep the Bashkir and Kalmyk tribes at bay. The American Cossacks are doing the same thing on the edge of the British empire, growing grain, getting furs, tobacco, and little by little they squeeze the Indians out. And if the French or Spanish try to stick their nose in, they get one straight off. Ours too, if necessary, take a whack at the Turks or give a hand against the Swedes. They govern themselves, get together to settle problems. Yours get together in their parishes and states, ours in their stanitsas and kureniias. And it would seem like both the one and the other give the government nothing but good.

"However kings, tsars, and emperors never have completely satisfied souls, so they can't ever just walk past a free man in peace. They always have to either jump on him or chop him down. And our kings then were similar, yours and ours, both Germans. They began to squeeze the Cossacks, ours and yours, something fierce. They'd send out their own generals and judges and priests, who were happy to mock and condemn and besmirch the old faith with all kinds of unnecessary demands. And they mocked them so badly that they drove the Cossacks to open rebellion. And what's especially interesting, both of our Cossacks rebellions began in exactly the same year, in 1773.

"But right there is also our first major difference.

"Your Cossacks found themselves a good ataman by the name of General Washington (and note that in Russian it even sounds like 'good-for-your-guys'). He understood war business and respected law and believed in God and had sympathy for people. Ours got Emelian Pugachev for their ataman. He knew how to fight as well as your Washington; he'd also served in two wars against the Germans and the Turks. But as for the rest he was an uneducated Cossack, who put crosses instead of his signature on his orders. And all his generals were famous drunkards from the Yaik. That's why the American Cossacks under Washington's command beat their king and separated from him, and formed their country, the Independent American States. The Russian Cossacks lost their war and they were punished in ways visible and invisible.

"Hey, if only we'd had generals with a little more brains and an ataman with more education! Then everything could have gone differently. We would have had a blossoming Independent Ural States, and then we would have begun to spread out too, only not into the Wild West, but into the Wild East. We might have had new states start appearing, Ishim, Tobol, Enisei, Taimyr, Baikal, Lena, Sikhote-Alin, Kamchatka, Chukotka. We'd have made it to the ocean. And then our Cossacks and yours would have started mixing it up there on the Pacific. The Russian Cossacks aren't some kind of Japs, you wouldn't have got away from us so easy. You'd never have set eyes on Alaska, that's for sure, and maybe California would have been ours too, with the capital in Fort Ross.

"But that was not the fated outcome for world Russian-American history.

"We were considerably behind you then. Even so, ninety years later we had almost caught up. Because slavery for you and for us was ended in the same year, 1861. For you that started a civil war, but God spared us that. Or so us Russians thought. It turns out that He didn't spare us, but simply put

it off for fifty years. Which made it a lot worse for us, because you can cut down a lot more people with machine guns and shrapnel than you can with muskets and balls.

"*There we sat among the rubble after our civil war, shaking our heads, wiping our bloody ears, and pounding our heads against the question, where to go from here? And so we began to say that as long as we had always gone neck and neck with America, then in the future we ought to hang on to it as well and learn everything from her. See how rich and famous America has got! So we scurried to buy up tractors and build airplanes and dams and give the farms to the farmers. Our Leonid Utesov even learned how to make movies no worse than your Charlie Chaplin did, so the whole country danced to his jazz.*

"*That didn't last long, though.*

"*Because by that time, as if we had done it on purpose, all the smart ones had either been beaten down or driven off. And again to the top came an uneducated type again, this time a Georgian who never finished school, and he upset the apple cart. 'How come you set off to catch up with America from the middle of things, lads? You'll never catch America that way. You got to catch America by doing things in the proper order, by starting with what made America rich in the first place.' 'And what's that?' his henchmen and supporters ask. 'With slavery, obviously,' he answers. 'And where are we going to get so many blacks? We only brought one in once, made a general out of him, and a poet-general out of his grandson, and that's it.' 'If we got no blacks, we'll use whites,' said that main Georgian. And people obeyed him and began to chase after America with slavery, and they called this new slavery 'kolkhoz.'*

"*And the ones with no smarts and the stupid had forgotten that we already had slavery. We had just as much of it as America did, two hundred years, and nothing good came of it there for you, and nothing came of it here, for us.*

"*And since then, Anton, we have been feeling our way like blind men, can't ever figure out what road to take to catch up with you sly-eyes. First we start sowing corn everywhere, then we go chasing off into space, then we cut the girls skirts right up to where it gets interesting. Now you've got some new sort of machine over there that you call Computer, and we've got to have that too. I stick by what I say: for us nothing will come of it until we learn how to forgive the smart ones and put up with them. If we can't get back our smart ones, no Computer is going to do anything for us, even if he's seven axe handles across the forehead and seven inches in the screen. So now you tell me, in America do they put up with clever ones, do they give* them the room they need?"

So now it was my turn to talk. And by the crackle of the fire, and the bubbling of the scarlet crayfish in the boiling pot I began to explain to Feoktist how unbearable it is to live where the clever ones have taken power, who pass you by every day in their Rolls Royces and limousines, who soar above you on the hundredth floor of their closed clubs, who buy their wives snow leopard coats, send their kids to study at Harvard and Oxford, earn as much in a minute as you do in a day, then try to convince you that everything you lost or never attained is because you're lazy and stupid. Someday I'll also record my speech, dear listeners, and broadcast it to you.

17. VERMONT BRIDGE

THE WEDDING RAGED
on in the village.

For the third straight day, with no end in sight.

Every day they sang and danced by a bonfire on the shore, then pulled the collapsed out of the weeds, then the drunk took the unconscious home, and then the next day it all started again. New guests from the surrounding villages and settlements kept coming, on foot, on flatbeds, in trucks, some bringing a bucket of potatoes fried with onion, some raspberry wine, some a pail of pickles, some a jar of pickled mushrooms. And the local women never grew weary of making blintzes and cabbage soup and carrot pie.

The river water was cold—or as the locals put it, St. Ilya had long ago tossed his ice chunk in—but that wouldn't bother Tolya Sukhumin. In the morning he'd pull on a thick sweater, put on his goggles, swim around for a bit, and then come up with a fish for the soup kettle, so that people would have something hot to greet the morning after with.

When the homebrew ran out they went to look for the golden soul with the injured heart, Vitya Polusvetov. They'd find him in a hayrack somewhere, wake him, pour water on him, lead him out to his tractor and sit him down on it. And then Vitya would drive his Pskovmobile around, making new circles in the cabbage-beet field. The weeds would tumble beneath the plow, the black mirrors of the furrow would flip belly-up. The women and kids would run along behind, picking the little cabbage heads out of the weeds, little beet roots from the clods of earth.

The cabbage would be carried to the tables, cut open, salted, buttered, and cranberries added, for something more to go with the hair of the dog. The beets were chucked into the tractor's hopper, where steel jaws ground them up and dumped them into the still inside the engine, and after two or three times around the field you'd have a whole bucket of rosy-pink brew fresh from the still, drink it down and *na zdoroviia*.

And they drank, to themselves, to each other, to Anisim and Agrippina, shouting "Bitter! Bitter! Sweeten the table with a kiss!"

Teasing couplets flew over the village, each saltier than the next.

> *Out the sky come a shooting star*
> *Fell in my sweetheart's pants*
> *Everything there can blow to France*
> *As long as there's no war!*

By now Anton knew almost everyone, and everyone had had time to tell him the story of his life.

Over there was the bride's father, Onufry, a soldier forever. When he was called for the first world war he was just a boy, and look at that, they didn't let him put the gun down for decades. He went with General Brusilov against the Austrians, with General Kornilov against the Bolsheviks, with Tuchachevsky almost captured Warsaw from the Poles, then chased the bashmachi around the deserts of Central Asia and liberated the Latvians from the bourgeoisie.

By the Second World War he was already too old, so he figured they'd pass him over. But no. The Germans came to their parts, and set up a tank repair station in their village. All the muzhiks still left were rounded up to help. They put German caps on them all, called them Hiwis, meaning "willing to assist." Then when the Reds came back all of these Hiwis, old and young, were kitted out in Soviet uniforms, handed Molotov cocktails, and driven out to set fire to the same tanks that they had been fixing the day before. Onufry had a trunkful of medals and orders from various times and peoples, and he was already too old to recall which ones he could wear now and which ones it would be better not to wear around just now. To be on the safe side he pinned a single button to his chest, a little round button that said "We Want Peace!" in various languages, and he would sit quietly by himself, drunk, not worrying about a thing.

> *I feel kind of odd*
> *Someone odd felt me*
> *My dress is back to front*
> *And got a fiver in my fist.*

To the left of Onufry was his niece, Valentina, who was also the universal soldier's wife of all times and peoples.

Of late she had been stricken by misery, or maybe happiness, or maybe just some sort of a joke—which it was she didn't know herself. She had lived her whole life through without a husband, but had had three strapping robust sons, one by a Russian soldier, one by a German, and the third by a Spaniard (some of those came through these parts too). The sons had grown up smart, finished school, and had taken off for the city, where they had families of their own. But they didn't forget their mother. They sent treats and came on their vacations to help her, had her visit them. And then, can you beat it, out of the clear blue the middle one's German father suddenly turns up, Gunther Feliksovich Schlotke. Who lives in Hanover, has his own store, but wants a family and so decides to invite his Russian son to come live with him.

Such an attack, and what for?

And the son, such an idiot, better than forty years he's alive and hasn't grown a brain. He goes! It hurt me a lot when I was a kid, he says, they called me Fritz and the whole class beat me up. Now, he says, I don't want to let my chance go. I'm sick and tired of this stupid life, four in a room. I want to be with my high-culture German people. He's turned his papers in already, he's in such a rush!

> *Hey girls, hey ladies!*
> *I'm off for over there*
> *I've got a guy, name is Vanya*
> *Who's Gordon through his mother*

Then there was Volodiia Sineglazov, a fired teacher, and the village Don Quixote. The authorities tolerated his preaching for a long time, and forgave him his letters to the newspapers, and even his acid replies to official speeches. After all, where are you going to get another teacher of literature out in this bush? But then it had to happen one winter that there was a cavalcade of government Chaikas out on the Kiev road. And the frost nip in the air made the bosses from Kiev get it into their heads to have a drink and a bite to eat, which is what made them show up at the village eatery without any warning, tumbling in in all their red-faced whooping glory.

Where, wouldn't you know it, sat Volodiia. He was nibbling his sorry compote of dried fruits and thinking about the ideological immaturity of Dostoevsky, whom it was simply impossible to present to his students in any guise remotely progressive. And when he saw how the new arrivals spread out their ham and salmon on their tables and starting hoisting their glasses of vodka, a kind of ideological rapture came over him. He stood up, white as a sheet, and screeched in a squeaky voice, "I forbid this!"

The drivers and assistants nodded at him. "What's the matter, you blind? You don't see who you're talking to?"

"I see," said the seeker of truth. "And you apparently are either blind or can't read, if you don't see what is written on the wall."

At which he points to the sign that says "The possession or consumption of alcoholic beverages here is strictly forbidden."

While he was being dragged and kicked out the door, he kept shouting, "If you don't observe your own laws, then who's going to observe them? Who?"

Seems like he ruined the fun for the passers-by. Ruined it so completely that they didn't forget him, but sent an order from the capital about firing him which was signed, people say, by Dostoevsky himself. Sineglazov went down like a meteor, clattering down, and now was shivering outside with the tally clerks.

> *I'm telling you lads*
> *It's bad without no wife*
> *Get up come morning, feel your heart*
> *Beating lonesome at your zipper*

Then there were the two refugees from the city, Sasha and Masha, married a year now. Then they came back, poor devils, to live in their native parts. "Tell you, brothers, we couldn't take all the crowding and stink in the city. Being poor and cold and worked half to death, that doesn't scare us. And as for being bored in the village, we're never bored alone." Sasha's mother died about then and they moved into her house. They fixed the door, added a porch, cleaned the chimney, plastered the stove. They got work at the state farm, earn enough for bread and salt, the rest they grow in their plot, and what else could they need?

There's one problem though. Seems among the things they brought from the city were bugs. And these bugs found such a great place between the logs and the wallpaper that they flourished incredibly. What's your village bug? A soft little critter, weak enough that a few dried daisies will curl up his toes in grace. But these new bugs were so savage, the result of genetic manipulations in the battle for urban survival, that no poisons or powders would do them in. The only thing Sasha and Masha still hadn't tried was yperite with mustard gas. They battled the bugs night after night. Their eyes were red with sleeplessness, their cheeks were bitten up and their tongues were all tangled. They wanted a baby, but how could you have a baby when the bugs would eat it all up? There they sat all melancholy, leaning their heads on each others' shoulders, to try at least to get a little sleep.

> *Come down to the beach*
> *Stretch out your feet*
> *We'll build us a castle*
> *And you be the keep*

Opposite Sasha and Masha was Fedya, a young partisan. Or he was young once, ages and ages ago, during the war, more than forty years ago, when he sent the German major back to his German ancestors. Fedya still loved to recall how that had been; he could retell it a pitiless ten times in a row. How there were two German tank officers staying in their hut, a major and a lieutenant, who loved to steam in the steam-bath. And even though Fedya was just a little boy, too small for either the Soviet or German army, he still could fire up a steam-bath, and so was kept around as a go-fer. And Gunther Schlotke would stick his head out of the door and yell, "Hey, Fedka, more wasser, more wasser!"

And Fedya would grab a bucket and an ax and go down the slippery steps to the river. He'd make a new hole in the ice over the water hole, then fill the bucket. And how did he get it back up, when both his hands were full? There wasn't even a railing to grab. So he'd put the hatchet into the bucket. He went up, went into the outer room where the Germans had left their uniforms and their holsters with their pistols, and then he went into the steam room. And that's when he remembered that he had the hatchet in the bucket. He pulled it out, started to shake the water off it. And the major didn't recognize him in the dark and so suddenly sees just a Russian muzhik in a hat and ragged sheepskin waving a hatchet. He starts shouting, "Partizanen! Partizanen!" And drops dead.

The lieutenant and Fedya drag him out into the outer room and start thumping on him, but there's not a hope in hell. He's the chunky type, plus he's got a good load of schnapps, and his German heart just couldn't take a good Russian scare. The lieutenant, Gunter Feliksovich, was a good soul, he worked hard to keep Fedya out of the Gestapo's paws, proved to them that the kid had nothing to do with it. But when our boys came back to town they started asking, who were the heroes who fought the occupiers here in the rear? For a joke people pointed out Fedya, and right away the boy got a medal, they wrote him up in the papers, even made a movie about him. So for the rest of his grown-up life Fedya stayed a young hero of the partisan movement.

> *Grenadier give me a grenade*
> *I'll hide it right down here*
> *So when the war starts up*
> *At least one enemy will die*

After Fedya there was Katerina the Informer. Even when she was a mite she had been the worst tattler in the school, and she never got any better. She couldn't put down her pen, writing and writing without thanks or reward, but just from the pure passion to be what she was meant to be. She told the Chekists about former kulaks and merchants, told the Germans about former Chekists, informed the returning Chekists and NKVD men about the Germans-yet-to-be, meaning those who were still just drumming their little German heels against the insides of their mommy's tums. She told husbands about wives, wives about husbands, brigade leaders about loafers, the farm president about people who gathered wheat they shouldn't have, the inspectors about people who sold meat they shouldn't have, the prosecutor about moonshiners. So many lives she had ruined, so many fates she had shattered, and there she sits, right alongside everyone, laughing and drinking toasts. Because that's what she had been fated to do, and there's nothing that a man can do against his fate.

There is that mighty, blessed guiltlessness in action!

Spread above the tables like a cloud, this guiltlessness has space for everyone within. For the toppler of chimneys and the poster of taboos at birch trees and the new recruit who loses his fingers through no fault of his own and the young partisan who is forever lauded for something he has not done and Vitya Polusvetov who has managed to get himself to tractor-driven communism and the writer of so many denunciations, Katerina. And should the jealous sister of the bride turn up right now, having escaped from the nuthouse, a place would have been found for her as well, although it would have been well away from axes and logs. Today even the Kolkhidonovs were forgiven their cleverness, even they were in the throng, smiling cautiously, plucking the crayfish from their shells, and treating their neighbors to the pumpkin pies they had brought.

Lord, how Anton wanted them to accept him, wanted to be wrapped in that cloud! Wasn't he from the same roots? Wasn't it his Russian-Lithuanian grandfather who had made their grandfathers chuckle at his jokes? Wasn't it his Jewish-Christian grandmother who had spilled sad tears on this sad earth? And had he really done anything in his life which could not be forgiven, for which he should be deprived of membership in Guiltlessness?

"I want to propose a toast!"

As soon as he was on his feet, he understood that he should have stayed sitting. It would have been less fearsome to fall face down into the sauerkraut from a sitting position. As it was, could he stay on his feet to the end of his speech?

"I want to praise your entire village... All of Kon, all of Kolodets, all the houses, all the stoves, all the beds, all the chairs, and all the people who sit on the one and lie on the other... I want to drink to the cows and the pigs and the chickens and the geese and even the sparrows that live under the eaves... I raise my glass to all the lamps in the houses, the electric burners in the kitchens, the street lamps, and even that tiny little transformer up there on the pole in the field that can't cope with the slightest overheating and so shuts your power off every half hour... I drink to your gardens, your roads into the village and out, to all the fields, clearings, and all the royal forests... Because I have fallen in love with it all and I want to remain here forever, for the rest of my working life, to build many houses, plant many trees, and have many children!"

"Hurray!" the wedding party shouted and held up their glasses to click with Anton's. "Hey, Anton, hey, what a foreigner!"

"The words kind of slip around one by one, but put them together and they come out just fine, don't they?"

"Hey, stay here with us, live with us!"

"We'll find a house for you, and a wife, and we'll clear some land for you."

"Come on, let me give you a hug!"

"Come here, let me make the cross over you!"

"Hey, Fedya, you fool, what you grabbing my boob for?"

"You wake up, Katerina, nobody can lean on your shoulder, that's sure!"

"Lean on my boob, my boob, good people! I'll take him to his wife right away!"

"So what do you say, neighbor, shall we give Anton our little Melada?"

"Hey, Tolik, Tolik, what do you say, will you let your sister marry a foreigner?"

"You can open up a horse rescue service with him, go around the whole county and drag horses out of holes."

"I want to help everybody," Anton shouted in rhapsody. "Everybody! Because I am fated to fight and conquer the Miserymaker no matter where he appears! We'll get the bedbugs off Sasha and Masha! I know a clever new method. We'll cover their house with a plastic sheet and fill the house with hot steam, so the bugs will steam to death. We won't import expensive wheat from America, we'll bring in grass clippings that lawn mowers will give us for free, and we'll fatten up seven times seventy seven cows! We'll fix the transformer out in the field and put all those carrots and potatoes that are now rotting in little root cellars into big deep freezers! We'll build a restaurant out by the road and sell steamed clams to the people driving past! We'll put presses under all the apple trees and use the government windfall apples to make sweet juice that belongs to nobody, and our kids can drink as much of it as they want to! We'll buy a pontoon plane and every morning it can take off from Duck Lake and fly to Pskov, Leningrad, even Moscow all full of crayfish. We'll plow up..."

He shut up, like a bird flying into a hard wall of silence. He looked where everyone else was looking, behind him. There stood Vitya Polusvetov, swaying slightly, his cap decked with fall phlox, his jacket a full-dress uniform, his pants broad blue Turkish ones that it was rumored he had been given by his brother, who was a dancer in the opera "A May Night, or the Drowned Woman." Vitya flung wide his right arm and pronounced, "Oh my brothers, hold my right arm, so that I don't kill this foreign braggart with it right now!"

Fedya the partisan, Volodya Sineglazov, and Tolik Sukhumin leapt up obediently, to hang on Vitya's right arm. Then he flung wide his left and called out, "Oh brothers, hold my left, so that I don't cripple him where he stands!"

Several people leapt up to hold Vitya's left. Spread-eagled thus by drunken peacemakers, Vitya then poured out on Anton all that had accumulated in his wounded heart.

"Who in the devil are you to come strutting around, you unwhipped bourgeois pup? Who are you to turn up here unwanted and unasked? You want to steal the last of our grass to feed your cats? You decided to steal off our best girls with your nylons and your chiffons and your Adidas? We need you like a pig needs wings or a truck needs buttons. Or maybe you got to hankering for your grandad's mill and store, eh? Wanted to come back and get them back in your filthy capitalist paws, eh?"

Drunken Anton was not frightened by his shouts, was unalarmed by his accusations, and did not shrink back.

"You shut your face better, you sugar beet moonshiner! You made everything great for yourself and didn't do a damn thing for anybody else! You couldn't plow the field properly so that there'd be no weeds. You couldn't plant cabbages and beets separate. Drunk you ran over Shutkoplokhovs' barn with your tractor tread and you never remembered to fix it! You forgot how to build up and out, you just drive around in circles farting stinking blue smoke!"

"I what? You what? Hold me, boys, hold me! I forgot how to build up?! What about you? What've you built during your pussycat and insurance life? What can you build, you pencil-neck grassnibbler?!"

"I can build a bridge."

"A bridge?!"

"Yes. All alone, I can build a bridge. A completely new bridge. In three days. Like a piece of cake for me."

"I'm going to die laughing! Let go of my arms, boys, so I can double up and laugh!"

"I am assigned by fate to build a bridge that no ice can knock out. It will stand there year after year, word after word, and the whole heaving mess can rage beneath it, wave after wave!"

"You ad man! You singer of pretty songs! You damn waggling tongue!"

"Just give me that old hog barn up on that rise. And some logs. And one helper. Even an invalid, like Tolik Sukhumin. Because each of those logs is going to have two ends, so one man can't pick it up. The two of us will build a bridge out of a hog house."

"Anisim, lend him your cap, will you? You all hear that, lads? I'm going to bet with this foreigner. If he can build this pigbarn bridge of his in three days, then he can stay here with us. If he doesn't, I'll put him in a cage myself and take him to the bus station with all you honest people watching. So that he can get himself back to where he came from. So that he gets his foreigner's backside out of here. We don't need his tinned grasses. We're not some kind of goats, to be eating grass. So what do you say, foreigner? Have we got a bet?"

Anton twisted the three-flapped cap he had been handed, took the peak, and then suddenly, unexpectedly even by him, he was seized by a strength not his but as if hidden within him by his grandfather's genes, he leapt into the air, then just as he came down, struck both heels and the cap hard against the ground.

The women gasped in awe.

Released by the men, Vitya Polusvetov came over to him, stood face to face, and then suddenly whipped off his hat and stabbed it down onto the three-flapper so hard that phlox petals floated high, high into the air, fluttering above the wedding tables.

Indian Summer ended in about an hour during the second day of work. From the west, where the enemy had always come, an icy sleet had sprung up, driven by a stinging wind. Streams of rainwater began to beat through holes in the pig shed. For a moment Anton stopped swinging his axe and turned his burning face up to the stream. The drops sizzled, as on a frying pan. It may have been that this was just the sound of the rain falling on the old clapboard. All of his senses were dulled by the pain in his shoulders, elbows, blisters.

Tolik Sukhumin was fussing alongside like something mechanical, not sparing himself. He brought up clamps and nails, turned the handle of the ax-grinder, pulled the other end of the bucksaw, carried his end of the logs. Still, he couldn't aim an axe properly using nothing but his palms. All the axe work fell to Anton. He had got used to it by noon of the first day, accurately sinking the sharp blade time after time into the submissive soft wood. Pitchy chips flew from the cut like smooth children's toys; just paint them up and give them to somebody! Splinters and bark covered the pigshed floor. When the muzhiks passed by going about their business, they would glance in the window and shake their heads approvingly.

"Sunuvabitch! Take a look at that, will you? The man's a hewer! Puts her in and gives her a wiggle, just like he's been doing it all his life! And everybody says he's a foreigner..."

From time to time Anton went over to the wall, to which he had glued his plans with bread balls. The plan was stolen, a picture taken out of a tourist guide to Vermont that had turned up in his suitcase. The picture showed an old wooden barn that had one end on each side of a rushing stream. The bridge looked as light, solid, and handy as a match box. How many times as he drove about New England had Anton crossed streams on such bridges, and never once did it occur to him that the technical ideas on which it was based were not known to the rest of mankind.

Naturally, if you have good Vermont stone on the bottom of your river, and not sand, then you have no choice but to put aside thoughts of how to drive pilings under your bridge and have to start thinking instead about how to span the current in a single bound. But how was it that after someone had thought up that sort of bridge that the idea had not gone around the world, as victorious as the idea of the wheel? Could that be what would happen now? Maybe it was precisely Anton who had been fated to carry this building idea across the waters in his head, as a poplar is carried in its little puff of seed? As at some time the means for smelting bronze had been carried, for firing clay or silvering mirrors?

As he had hoped, the pigshed floor proved still to be solid, the planking well preserved. The floor and roof had reasonably reliable beams still. Only one had to be replaced. That left only the fixing of the stabilizing and strengthening Xes that could be seen in the murk inside in Anton's picture of the Vermont bridge.

"Only"—how easy to say!

For starters, every log had to be barked. Then it had to be turned into a semblance of a wooden idol, chopping and sawing slots into the ends and middles. Two of the ready beams would be laid one over the other, then bound into an X with heavy iron clamps. Then they raised the X, fitting the bottom end into the bottom beam and the upper into the top beam. They hammered it home. If everything went right, if all the tabs fit into the rabbeting the first time, it took about three hours per. There were eight Xes to get in, four per side. Which left almost no time for food or sleep.

At a certain point Anton began to feel as though he was not building a bridge, but rather fighting a cruel battle. It was as though the logs were fighting back, blow for blow, hammering the handle of the ax up against his hands. The handle of the axe-grinder would whop him painfully in the ribs, the stepladder would trip him, a clamp schemed to nail his hand to a log. At the same time the pain that built in his body was memorialized in handsome rabbets and pegs, the transformation of a hastily conceived idea into a solid and tangible bridge. The future bridge moved painfully in the depths of his exhausted muscles, like an unborn child. He was pregnant with this bridge, loving it already, proud of it, and ready to labor to his last breath for it. How he was going to drag this thing a hundred meters to the river he tried not to think.

The second night he didn't have the strength to go back to the village and so went to sleep right there in the hog house, on a pile of shavings and straw, wrapped tight in a rough sheepskin that granny Pelageia had brought round. His overworked blood continued to race around his brain, not letting the brain cells settle into the oblivion which would save them. Through this racket in his brain his consciousness made out the crackle of twigs in the stove and Tolik's voice, self-importantly explaining to the girls and women gathered about all the American marvels.

"Believe it if you want to, girls, or don't if you don't, I'm not going to bother to lie to you. What Anton Gavrilich told me, that's what I'm telling you. Their cucumbers grow as big as a boot, their watermelons are as big as a barrel, their chokecherries are as big as cherries, they ripen up on the trees and then they pick them with ladders, not on hands and knees like us."

"Saints above, can that be true?" the old women whispered to one another in awe.

"There's no clerks in their stores. The goods and food lie there in heaps, go and take what you want. They even give you a little cage for that, on wheels. But you won't get away with anything, because at the door they'll search you for sure."

"They strip you to the buff?"

"They not only don't strip you, they don't even lay a finger on you. But they can see right through you, with some kind of rays. Under your belt, in your pockets, between your legs, you can't hide anything anywhere. And if they find anything, then they'll invite you real polite into the office, then on with the cuffs and you're off to a place where Makar don't keep no cows."

"They've got God on their side!"

"That they do! In the airport, the library, the museums, at work, they always search you. You, Nikiforovna, you'd have to pay for your sunflower oil, you'd have to forget about sneaking it out of the school under your skirt. Even the money is different there with them though. I don't know whether to believe this or not myself. But what Anton Gavrilovich told me is that you can take money right out of the wall in the banks there. You just have to know some kind of secret codeword. Come driving up in your car, knock on the wall, say the magic word, and there's your bundle of green!"

"Give us something like that!"

"Sure thing! And around the next corner there's your husband, who'll take more than your money. Couple three slaps and you'll give him the secret word yourself, and then how in the devil will you ever get him out of the dry-up tank?"

"They don't slap women around there. They don't even touch them. They've got so much power there that the muzhiks got nothing left. They've even got special like bars there just for women, where hired men dance around in front of them and take their clothes off!"

"Tfu! Tfu!"

"If there's any of you want to crack a bottle for me, then next Saturday I'll come prancing out of the bathhouse in all my beauty."

"We'll show you 'crack a bottle!'"

"We'll give you beauty with stinging nettles on your backside!"

"They're richer than us in everything. And you know why? Because they don't let anything go to waste. They use everything there, even human meat. You heard about this? If some fellow gets himself killed in an accident, they chuck him up fresh on the slab, and start hacking him up. You need to change something of yours, then get in line. You need an elbow, you need an eye, you want a kidney, a heart for you, and lungs for you? How much you charging for fresh human liver today? That's a lot, but nothing's too good for my favorite grandpa!"

"Tfu, Tolik, what a blasphemer you are!"

"Not to mention a liar whose like has never been born."

"You think that's all? Well, not long ago people even started to keep umbilical cords. Fools that we are, we chuck them out, but over there, as soon as somebody has a baby, off goes the cord, the blood gets washed off, stash it in the fridge, and then off to market early the next morning. Who buys them? The doctors. They use these umbilical cords in place of ruined veins. And then the man gets up and walks around and his blood can do what it wants. And who's ever to know that from his knees to his butt the blood's running through umbilical cords?"

"Tfu, Tolik, tfu, you shameless liar!"

"Come on, girls, let's tickle him to death so that he'll quit with his nasty stories."

"Get his leg, get his leg!"

"Grab his coat."

"Stop!"

"Catch him!"

"Cut him off from the trees!"

"Tolik!"

"Tolik, come back!"

"We won't do it!"

"We'll forgive you this time!"

"Come on back, tell us more!"

They had cut and placed the last of the Xes by the middle of the third day. Now they had to pull free the big nails that held the pigshed tight to the foundation. Anton's hands shook with fatigue. Even so he ordered Tolik to drop everything and take his bicycle to go find a tractor driver who would help. It was now obvious that there was no way they could drag the heavy pigshed to the river without the aid of a tractor.

Left alone, Anton began to kick the remaining logs into place, making a short path towards the river. He laid them out even distances from one another, already dreaming of how his baby would glide along them, to perch elegantly on the two banks of the river alongside the old bridge. It would have been great if Melada had returned by then, if she could witness his triumph. But she had gone off somewhere on some business that could not be put off.

What kind of business was it that had sprung up at so inopportune a time?

He tried to remember and couldn't. There was someone that she had to go see? Or look for someone? His memory was cloudy with fatigue, like the screen of a decrepit TV that threw up all sorts of extra snow. He wanted to ask her something, about some people that the villagers mentioned often in their conversations, people he didn't know but was too shy to ask about. Like yesterday when Tolya had mentioned that mysterious Makar and his cows again. People often spoke too of some Sidor and his goat, and the hat of some Senka, and some fellow Emil's mill. She shouldn't have left him here all alone, with no one to help him. Say what you will, he was her work, and she was getting a salary precisely because she was supposed to relieve him of the little worries.

Towards sundown granny Pelageia brought hot potatoes in a pot, a clump of green onion, salt, and a half loaf of Kansas bread. She looked the refashioned pigshed over, touched the Xes suspiciously, shook her head, then said that she had never seen the like in those parts and she only hoped that nothing bad would come of all this. Then she left.

It was almost completely black when Tolik got back, bringing the sad news that Anton should have expected all along, that all the local tractor drivers had already been warned off by Vitya Polusvetov. Whoever dared to help the foreigner with his bridge was sure to come up against the Pskovmobile on a narrow path someday. In the gathering damp dark the pigshed seemed to have been poured full of heaviness, swollen immobile, cast into the earth forever.

Anton went inside and threw himself down on the grass, almost indifferent.

They'd done everything they could, right? Maybe sometime next year or next century the village would understand the good of this and talk Vitya Polusvetov out of his madness and into some mercy. Then he could hook the hogshed up to his Pskovmobile and put the bridge in place. Everyone who crossed it would be grateful, and they could even call it Polusvetov's Bridge. Everybody would forget Anton. And let them. Of course he wouldn't wait around to be shamed tomorrow. He wouldn't let himself be tossed in the chicken cage and carried off with all the chickens clucking around him. No, he'd get up quietly at daybreak and take off by himself. Somewhere out on the roads Melada would pick him up and take him to another village, surrounded by other royal forests. This Kon-Kolodets wasn't the end of the world. Old man Sukhumin assured him that blessed guiltlessness was spread evenly over the whole of the Upside-down Land.

He and Melada could marry and settle anywhere, among anyone of the hundred different peoples who live in this country. He had long been taken by the thought that there must somewhere on the planet exist, even if among the wildest of savages, a tongue in which the words of love weren't also used as curses. That's the people he'd like to seek out! It seemed to him that this linguistic peculiarity would have to be evidence of an unusual delicacy of the heart. Probably when these people learned other languages they would not understand and become upset when it came time for them to learn the swear words. "What?" they would ask, "What did you say? You meant to say 'flick your mother,' didn't you? 'Flick me in the mouth?' 'Flick me?' You didn't? You really meant what you said? But how is it that that wonderful action could become a curse, a threat? We don't understand. Or can it be that for you this is associated with painful and difficult sensations somehow?" Yes, he would have to talk to Melada about this. And then they would have to go there, to wherever on the other side of the Urals there was a tribe like that, where they would live, only among them...

Anton woke up from the jolts, and the light of a flashlight shone in his eyes.

"Up you get, Gavrilich, wake up! I can't do this myself, you know!"

The man who woke him shone the torch on himself, and Anton recognized the toothless smile of Lenya Kolkhidonov.

Still not understanding anything, Anton got up, fumbled his way into a coat, stumbled outside behind his uninvited guest.

In the dawn murk Kolkhidonov led him to his motorcycle, pointed at the sidecar, and said something in a strange language, maybe Greek?

"Block-and-tackle."

"What?" Anton didn't understand.

"Pull!" Kolkhidonov mimed what he meant, then spoke, breaking the words up into chunks as you would for a deaf man. "Pull It Up! Help Me! Then We Drag Bridge! Side Ways!"

They pulled the heavy device out of the side car, then carried it to a solid oak which grew between the pigshed and the river. They fastened it to the trunk. Then Kolkhidonov gave Anton a pair of work gloves and showed him how to unroll the steel cable from the drum. They pulled the winch cable across the wet grass, fastened it to the beam under the front door of the hog shed. Another cable stretched from the block and tackle to the motorcycle. Kolkhidonov got on the machine, turned on the engine, and then carefully, looking over his shoulder, drove away from the river.

The pulleys turned, the oak bark squeaked, the cables and ropes stretched tight.

The heavy block-and-tackle lifted from the ground and hung in the air.

One motorcycle's worth of power ran along the cables to the ancient mechanism, where it was multiplied tenfold just as faithfully as it had when the pyramids were being built, the parthenons and coliseums, multiplying tenfold their horsepowers and oxenpowers, transferring all this titanic power to the box from Vermont, trying to rip free the front beam.

There was a scraping noise, a crack, a creak.

The last shards of glass popped from the window frames.

The mighty drawing force spread along the beams and Xes like the first jolt of a locomotive spreads along the train, and just as if convinced that they were not to be separated one from the other, the elements of the building began to move as one entity.

In a single second destroying the lives of millions of woodlice, maggots, beetles, and lizards, the pigshed tore free of its old foundation and set off down the log slide which had been prepared for it.

Tolik, suddenly wide awake, leapt with a shriek from the back door. But then he understood and in awe began to gallop alongside the sliding walls.

Like a blacked-out ship leaving the harbor in time of war the pigshed floated through the floods of mist. It moved as if fastened firm to the tow rope of the motorcycle's headlight. An early-awakened flock of ducks winged up from their hidden clearing and rustling flew low over this site of alarming changes.

They had to change where the block was three times, nearer and nearer to the spot they wanted it along the shore. As soon as the rear of the creeping structure freed a scraped log, Anton and Tolik grabbed it and raced forward. The sky was already greenish white when Kolkhidonov returned the powerful device to the sidecar and then carefully drove across the old bridge to the other side of the river. There they found the right kind of forked pine, threw a line across fork, and stretched it over the river.

The front door of the pigshed hung over the water.

The shadow of Vermont fell over the sedge of Pskov.

One by one the logs began to roll out from under the bottom, falling into the shallows, and quietly floated away in the mist.

The line pulling upwards did not let the pigshed touch the water, but kept pulling it across and up.

When the first beam lay on the sand of the far side, demobbed soldier Sukhumin let out the ear-shattering "Hurray!" that he had been storing up ever since the Ninth Motorized Cavalry days, when they took Stockholm.

Stunned, still not believing his victory, Anton went in the back doors, then carefully crossed to the middle of his new-born bridge, then jumped. The boards responded with an unaccustomed hollow and solemn ring.

Kolkhidonov was winding up his cables, putting all his heavy lifting equipment back in the sidecar. He got on the motorcycle, carefully drove across the bridge from the other side. A toothless smile shone on his face.

"I wasn't even here, and I didn't give anybody a hand, right? You keep me out of this, like a fox out of the barn, got it? A bet is something sacred, but then we can't live without a bridge, am I right? Hey, that American thing of yours looks all right. All right, lads, think kindly of me..."

He turned down the side path and set off toward the forest.

Anton and Tolik took up shovels and started to level the approach from the road to the bridge.

First to come from the village was a herd of cows. The universal soldier's wife Valentina was driving them along with gentle persuasion—"Schnell! Schnell!" When she glimpsed the refigured pigshed floating out off the mist she gasped in astonishment and turned to the two record-breaking builders, who were sitting modestly to one side.

"It'll hold the cows?"

"A motorcycle went across and didn't have any complaints," Tolik said slyly.

Suspiciously the cows followed one another through the open doors, their hooves ringing on the boards.

"It's been a month or better since we've grazed on that side," Valentina explained. "I was scared of the old bridge and I couldn't ford them, the water's high already, it would carry them off. So thank you lads, you've made my cows happy, you have!"

Then the school wise-guy, Vanya Shutkoplokhov, came up on his bike. He saw the bridge and went whistling back, to spread the news. And then the rest of the village came along, young and old.

The newlyweds, Anisim and Agrippina came, shook the builders' hands, said that they had never expected such a wedding gift.

Fedya the partisan, came out on his buckboard, bringing the soldier Onufry, who now wore bravely both crosses and stars on his breast.

Katerina the informer came too, with a clean sheet of paper, which she rolled into a tube, through which she studied the bridge from up on the rise, like Napoleon.

Sasha and Masha ran up smiling, slapping the most adventurous of the bedbugs from their cheeks, and immediately cut branches to use as brooms, to sweep up the shavings and chips.

Volodya Sineglazov walked back and forth on the bridge several times, checking and checking again to see whether there wasn't something there that wasn't right.

The preschool kids kept stamping inside the bridge, running through the slanting rays of the rising sun.

And finally, to complete the triumph, the Zhiguli Fiat rolled quietly down the hill.

The car came trustingly up to the doors, as if to a garage, and stopped, to let the kids pile inside and onto the hood, and then drove through to the other side. And while the car was turning about over there, in order to drive back, clever Tolik ran to the door and stretched across it a clean white bandage from his soldier's first-aid kit.

The Fiat Zhiguli burst through the ribbon magnificently and stopped on the side of the road.

The kids all piled out.

Melada came after them, took off her gloves, and went up to Anton.

"What's going on here? Is it true? You didn't really make this beauty with your own hands, did you? You and my brother? I can't believe it... There's no end of surprises... What else do you know how to do, you overseas spets of all trades?"

They stood, fingers intertwined, looking one another in the eye. He was forcibly keeping himself in check, doing all he could to prevent the triumph hammering his chest from coming out as a wild Indian yelp. A sharp shoot of love was poking indiscriminately in all directions, like a fork in the hands of a drunk. It seemed as though all they lacked were the wedding party's cries of "Bitter! Bitter!" and they would begin kissing and hugging, right there, in front of everybody.

Instead of such cries though they heard the roar of an engine.

Like a smoldering dragon, like a blast furnace gone for a walk, like a cross between a tank and a hen coop, a volcano on caterpillar tracks, the Pskovmobile appeared on the little hill.

The children fell still, the adults stepped back, and Fedya the Partisan took his horse's bridle, to lead him into the shrubs.

A cloud covered the fleeting sunny slant, bringing a wind.

The Pskovmobile stood for a moment, as if enjoying the general fright it had caused.

Then it went down hill, toward the bridge.

Melada barely had time enough to run to the car, jump in the driver's seat and move it into the roadside burdocks.

"No!" Anton shouted, running to cut off the approaching bulk, "Not for you! You have to use the ford! That's dishonest!"

Tolik flew toward him, head down, like a real quarterback, grabbed him by the shoulder, and tossed him to one side, away from the treads that were almost upon him.

The chicken tower hit the top of the door and split in clouds of clucking white clumps.

The Pskovmobile disappeared inside the hog shed.

Smoke and dust poured from the windows.

The beams groaned, the Xes cracked, the boards twisted.

For a split of a second, when the Pskovmobile appeared on the other shore, everyone had a fleeting hope that things had passed off all right, that this incredible Vermont bridge had withstood even this unfair test.

The tractor though immediately went into reverse and once again disappeared into the tunnel made of boards.

The maddened machine began to batter at the walls from within.

The window frames, splinters, bits of the roof fell into the water.

Five, six, ten blows, and the treads beat through one of the bottom bearing beams, appearing for a second through the hole, and then began to tumble out, bringing with it the whole fire-breathing, distilling-not-sit-stilling aggregate from the future, breaking the pig hut in half, at the same time taking with it the pilings of the old bridge...

The river greeted its unexpected catch with a huge splash and a cloud of steam.

The waves were painted with floods of oily rainbows.

The cows, cut off on the far shore, lowed mournfully.

The cucumber vines, egg shells, the stunned white-bellied fish, the bunches of mushrooms on the logs, and a cap with phlox stuck in it set off on the long float to Lake Chudsky.

The driver himself crawled out of the cabin that was just above water, and swam to the far shore.

There he stood, one hand on his scalded cheek, the other on his aching heart, to look at what he had done. Tossed in an instant from his cozy tractor future into the overcast skies of today, he clearly had no idea what to do with himself on the even and unshaking earth. The bridging timbers which had been chucked into the river seemed to affirm with all their hopelessness that there would be no return to the past.

Vitya Polusvetov turned and without releasing his love-impaled heart, he wandered shaking into the depths of the forest beyond the river.

Anton stood with his head buried in Melada's shoulder, moaning as if in pain. She comforted him as if he were in first grade, promising him good marks and happy holidays and interesting meetings.

"I found her, that's the main thing. We'll go there tomorrow. You have to get washed up and changed, get a grip on yourself a bit. I found her, you hear what I'm saying? We'll go to the town of Velikie Luki."

He didn't hear her.

He was looking stupidly at Sineglazov the bookkeeper, trying to understand what the columns of figures that were written all over the notebook meant, and why they were being shoved under his nose.

"The thing of it is, Anton Gavrilovich, I've totted it all up here quickly... Maybe I've missed something, we can add that on later... fifteen cubic meters of logs wasted, and maybe forty rubles worth of tools, and then there's all the repair... I figure the loss can't be less than four thousand... I'm not counting the tractor now, the tractor will have to be figured in by itself... So are you paying in dollars or in rubles?"

"Me? On top of all this you want me to pay? You think that I'm the one who caused all this?"

"No one's caused anything." The adder-up was taken aback. "But somebody has to answer for the losses. Vitya's got nothing we can take, apart from the tractor he didn't have a thing in the world, and even the tractor wasn't his, but the government's, temporarily alienated to him..."

Anton pulled away from Melada and began to run from person to person.

"Good people, what is this? You saw everything! Why are you silent? Everything happened right in front of your eyes! I was fated to build the Vermont bridge... And I did, I built it! Feoktist, you tell them!"

Feoktist sighed, looked at the glowering sky, looked away.

"Well, you look at it yourself, Anton. Before you came to our village, we had a bridge. Wasn't much, but it was a bridge. And we had a pig barn, even if it was empty and old. And there was a tractor that made vodka and grew cucumbers. And where is all that stuff now? Where? Right over there, with the waves washing over it. So how are we going to live now?"

Anton couldn't find an answer.

He covered his face with his hands and shook his head, as if trying to wake up.

Melada took his elbow, moved the fact-finder with his list of losses out of the way, and led Anton to the car.

(The young against the old)

How numerous, how various the faces of enmity! Our scientists and thinkers try to study the sources of enmity, to analyze the reasons, to control epidemic eruptions of mass disorders. Many books have been written about religious hatred, racial hatred, inter-ethnic hatred. The hatred of poor for rich has been well studied, of nomads for land-tillers, of those without rights for those who have power, those without talent for those who have.

But have you not noticed, dear listeners, that in the past decades a new face is appearing more often and more insistently in the frames of this bloody newsreel? Have you not noticed how many young people, some- times even children, there are in the ranks of partisans, who are trying the shining path in the jungles, mountains, and deserts of your televisions? Hasn't it seemed noteworthy that those same half-childish faces have become the major part of the crowds which hang red slogans from the necks of old professors? In the crowds which rip off the iron rails and spread fatal panic among fans at a soccer match? In the crowd that puts a burning tire around the neck of some unhappy victim? That throw stones at a bus? That poke women and old people in the back with Kalashnikovs to drive them out of the cities and into the open fields, where they have been condemned to die of hunger or be smothered in blue plastic bags?

No, I am not saying that the young inevitably are responsible for blood, cruelty, and destructiveness. We have also seen them without arms, and face to face with tanks, have seen them setting fire to themselves in squares to defend the idea of liberty, climbing over the walls that divide, sticking flowers in the barrels of the guns that are pointed at them. Here too, though, there is this new, threatening, and insurmountable fact, of Them against Us. Those looking ahead against those looking back. The riches of years yet to be lived against the riches of wisdom accumulated over the years.

Again and again I rummaged through these worrisome thoughts, flipping through newspapers, magazines, and books in the library of a provincial Russian city, while waiting for a meeting of great importance to me with a certain young person, again and again coming up against the unnaturally young faces of those who caused other people death or who hastened toward their own. As if on purpose there was in the stack of books I had taken at random from the shelves one book in which the inimical feelings and moods of the young were elaborated, named, and fixed in brilliant lines by a half-forgotten local poet, as it turns out, seventy years before.

"We are beautiful in the unavoidable betrayal of our past," he wrote, "and in the unavoidable madness of the lifting of the next hammer over this earth, which is atremble already with the tramping of our feet... We opened the sealed train car pulled by the locomotive of our daring. There's nothing there but the graves of youths... How to free the winged motor from the fat treads of a goods wagon of old ages?

"The ages should separate and live apart.

"Let those who are closer to death than to birth surrender! Let them fall on their shoulder blades in the fight against time, under the push of our wildness.

"We are heading there, young men, and suddenly someone dead, someone skeletal, grabs us, stops us from molting the feathers of stupid today. Is that good?

"The state of the young will unfurl the winged sails of time!"

The poet is imbued with a tender sense of understanding for the youths of other countries, and returns constantly to the idea of uniting them into a world union to wage war between the ages.

"I can more easily understand a young Japanese, speaking in Old Japanese, than certain of my fellow countrymen as they speak modern Russian...

"The right of world unions according to age. The divorce of ages, and the right to live separately and to act alone."

The older ages, in the terminology of this poet, are called "acquirers," while the younger are "inventors." What sort of inventions does the poet envision for the joy of mankind?

"It is necessary," he writes, "to breed predatory animals to fight since the transformation of people into rabbits... To breed crocodiles in the rivers. To study the condition of mental abilities among the older ages...

"To breed in the rivers some kind of edible, invisible creatures so that every lake could be a kettle full of fish soup, even if raw...

"To introduce new forms of land ownership, acknowledging that the

amount of land to be owned and used by one person cannot be less than the surface of the globe.

"To bring apes into the family of man and accord them certain of the rights of citizenship.

"All the thoughts of the earthly globe (which are so few) are like the houses of a street, and so should be given a particular number so that people could converse and exchange thoughts just by using the thought number.

"In common warfare to use weapons of sleep (sleeping bullets).

"To erect running and travelling monuments on railroads.

"To measure the units of working rights and working duties of heart-beats. A heartbeat is the money of the future. Hunger and health are the account books, while joy and bright eyes are the signature on the receipt."

Oh, how shameful not to submit to this poetic intoxication, how shameful to feel oneself forever among the old, the acquirers. Perhaps, if we but knew how to master ourselves, if we but agreed to lay back under the mad swings of their hammer, they might forgive us? Forgive us for the fact that without even opening our mouths, but just by how we look, remind them that their fortune in life yet unlived grows less with each passing day. After all when we speak to them of our love and ask them, or even just wait silently, for even a glimmer of feeling to return, with justice they answer us, or snort silently, that love is not something to be presented like a bill for payment; that all our talk of feelings is a self-interested comedy written in order to force them to die uncomplainingly in our wars, to work obediently and pay the taxes which go for our pensions, our medicines, our vacation homes, our old men's greedy appetites, our tired amusements.

Dear listeners! If their slogans are sometimes hard to understand, why not just repeat after them: "The world is like a ray. You (the old) are a structure of space. We (the young) are a structure of time." And sooner or later you will find in their shouts, their pamphlets, their graffiti, the simple, understandable orders, a listing of what you must do if you are to earn even condescension from them:

"In our picturesque realms taken for temporary use to set up camps of inventors (have we not seen such camps through our guitar strings and the smoke of our marijuana?) where they can live as their tastes and mores please. The neighboring towns and villages are obligated to feed them, and bow down before them."

You hear? Is that so hard?

"To feed and bow down before." That's all there is to it.

18. VELIKIE LUKI

"**S**TEPMOTHER." THE thought was unexpected even for Anton when he saw Melada coming into the library reading room with Golda. "I want her to become Golda's stepmother. Good stepmother, not wicked. And I want her to give Golda half-brothers and sisters. Seven is a holy number. The seventh wife. And the last."

The entire way to Velikie Luki he had tried to get the details out of Melada, how and where she had found Golda, what had happened to her, how did she look, what shape was she in?

Melada's answers were evasive.

"She's in a study and labor camp. No, the work isn't bad. The food is all right. If you don't break the rules. If you do, they can cut your rations pretty sharply. But that's not just a punishment, it's also part of the learning process. They are being taught according to some new theory, that holds that a person who has not experienced hunger can not be a complete citizen. All contacts with the outside world are forbidden. But I was very lucky... A fellow I know from school is working as an instructor there. He said I could meet her. Not face to face, of course. I couldn't tell her you are here, and I didn't want to, either. She is obligated to tell her commander everything. And then there's no way that she'd ever get out. But I want you two to see each other. Now I'm willing... I think it would be better if she would leave, this isn't for her. That's what I think, anyway...so I thought up something we might try..."

The rain lashed through the whole area with the feverish haste of a cleaning woman late for work, who is slapping her wet rag into the various corners, trying to make up for lost time. The windshield seemed twice as thick because of the layer of water, and Melada had to bend low over the wheel in order to see ahead. Her face was preoccupied and melancholy. On-coming trucks would for a moment transform the little Russian Fiat into a submarine.

"They have to work in the fields and shops all the time, but they also have to take all these tests and competitions. For example, I saw them playing Cossacks and bandits. You know the game? It's like your cowboys and Indians. The Cossack looks for the bandit, who has hidden; when he catches him, he jumps on him like a horse and then rides him around in a circle. In this camp, though, they play it a bit differently. There's an illuminated sign that keeps changing the roles. Just at the moment that a Cossack catches a bandit, it can happen that the sign changes to say that they should switch roles. And the bandit gets up on the Cossack. I saw how this one skinny little girl collapsed during the second circle under the weight of an enormous clod of a boy. No, you can't refuse, you can't not find someone, because for that you get fined and sent to the blockhouse."

"What fanaticism!" Anton said.

"But at least that made their methods clear to me. And so I was able to think up a good task for Golda. A bit of a brain-buster. They were intrigued and so agreed to release her to me for the day, to take her to the town library. She has to help me arrange the books in the foreign division. Alphabetically, by author. English and Russian at the same time."

"Is that possible?"

"That's the tricky part. Students are supposed to do whatever work they are assigned energetically and enthusiastically, without thinking of whether or not the task can be accomplished. They have a whole series of tests and exercises for that. They call it liberation from the rational, I think. It's absolutely essential for foreigners who have decided to live in our country. Their minds are too subservient to rationality, and that has to be destroyed first of all, and replaced by blind obedience to an order. I have an agreement with the head of the library. She promised to let us in before they open."

And here they are now, walking between the library tables. Two women. And nowhere in the world are there any dearer to him than these. Large overalls flapped on a much thinner Golda, and her hair was cut like a fuzzy ball. Had he ever predicted for her that in some future life she would become a gopher? Cautiously frozen in its burrow, looking about in alarm, ready to disappear again at the slightest rustling of the grass? Exactly as she froze now, when she saw him.

"That's my father," she said softly.

"Yes," Melada said.

"How did he get here?"

"He came to see you."

"How did he find out that I'm here?"

"He looked for you. It wasn't easy, but he found you."

"Can I say hello to him?"

"Of course."

"Hi, dad."

"Hi, Golda."

"Can I hug him?"

"Yes."

The fabric of the overalls reluctantly yielded to his hands. Why had he not realized before that the words "waist" and "waste" sounded the same? And what was the Russian word for this chain of bumps that were now sliding past beneath his fingertips? Backbells? And it was true, in a minute they would ring out. It seemed to him that she was trembling a bit.

"I'd like to start work as quickly as possible," Golda said, freeing herself and turning to Melada.

"You don't want to know about your mother? Your brother? Your grandfather and grandmother?" Anton asked.

"Maybe later. During lunch break. I'll have a lunch break?"

"Of course."

"They told me that this is a very serious job. I wouldn't want to muck it up. As it is we've lost a lot of time on the road from the camp."

"All right," Melada said. "You can start with this shelf. The letters A and B won't give you any trouble. They are in the same places in both Russian and English. What are you going to do after that though? Russian B or English C? You'll have to do some thinking there."

"I can do it. But, one last question. It's pretty hot in here. May I undo the top button on my blouse?"

"Yes. And I don't think that you need special permission to do so."

"Whatever are you saying?! Of course it's necessary. The condition of your clothing is a most important paragraph in the rules."

Golda pushed a little step-stool over to the shelves, got up on it, and reached for the book jackets. Anton felt that even on the day when she had fallen off her bicycle and he had carried her to the hospital, wiping blood from her face, holding her hand while the doctor stitched her torn lip, he had not felt so staggering a pity for her.

"You see now?" Melada said quietly.

"Yes."

"You have to take her away."

"But how?"

"There are people who like to have other people decide everything for them. Or to have rules. Things are very good in the camp for that sort."

"If I ask your authorities they will think up some other excuse again?"

"There are also people who are too independent. You talked about how when she was little she was always demanding to do things 'by myself,' 'I wanna do it.' For people like that the camp is very difficult. She is trying to completely remake her self, but nothing good will come of it."

"I can threaten to tell the whole story to the newspapers. A scandal like this might be front page news."

"That isn't likely to help. And then your Golda will spend the rest of her life branded as a runaway and a failure. She'll always be under suspicion. No, this all has to be done quietly. Now you know everything about her, where she is, what she's doing. She is found, so there's no point in keeping her hidden anymore. I know the people we need, who can help. Even my boss in Intourist. If he won't help himself, he'll at least say who we have to go to up above. If you'd like, I could call him right now."

"Yes, please."

"The head librarian said I could use her telephone. You stay with your daughter. How many years is it you haven't seen each other? Three? Quite a father. A person would have to think it over real hard before she'd have a child by someone like you."

She left.

Anton went cautiously up to Golda. How does a wrinkled brow help solve the hard questions of life? Does it improve the blood supply to the brain? Or does adding the wrinkles of an old person automatically give you the wisdom of an old person? How about that habit of shaking the head a little, as if not agreeing with one's own thoughts? Who had she taken that from? Wife #1 had had that habit in her school years, he thought. But then the habit had disappeared. When she learned how to agree with everything that went on within her. And to disagree only with

Anton.

"May I help you?"

"That's against the rules."

"I might at least hold the books you are taking down. You can use me as a bookshelf."

"The difficulties have begun even earlier than I expected, with A."

"I'm not surprised."

"Obviously Henry Adams has to come after this collection of Kobo Abe. Then Andersen's fairy tales. But what happens with Isaac Asimov then? In English he has to be close to the end of the A shelf, but in Russian he should be in the middle."

"We were upset the first three days. Your mother, me, grandpa Kozulin. Until they called from the embassy."

"It doesn't get any easier further down. Look, here's Aldington, Aldridge, Jane Austen. In Russian they all start with O. And then there's Kingsley Amis; in Russian his first letter is almost at the end of the alphabet."

"For the time being put him over here. Pablo-Pedro and Lin Chan say hi."

The mole in its burrow ducked its head nervously, looked about, its nostrils flaring.

"They agreed to sail with me. We sailed over on your grandfather's yacht. On the Babylonia. You could have read about us in the papers."

She got a nub of pencil out of her overalls, quickly jotted something on a library card, handed it to him.

It said: "Don't name names."

"We aren't hiding anything from anyone. They received me very well in Leningrad. Our business proposals were accepted with awe. As you see, they even gave me a personal automobile and a translator."

Golda jotted again.

"Don't trust her!" Anton read. "She has a hidden microphone!"

In answer to his suspicious glance she nodded energetically and poked herself several times with a finger—"Here! Here!"

Anton wanted to say that she was wrong. That Melada had no microphone there and that he had had the possibility to be sure of it with both his eyes and his hands as recently as this morning, when they stopped briefly in the forest. He thought better of it though. It was better to appear to agree to everything. He turned the card over and wrote, "Do you want to go home?"

She thought. Then she wrote something lengthy in reply. He read it.

413

"I've forgotten how to think that far ahead. Just an hour or two. The longest is until the end of the day. There's no point in thinking farther ahead than that. Because the sign can always change and then all the roles change."

"There's nothing for you to fear," Anton said quietly. "I have spoken with the people from the Agency. They swore that they have nothing against you. Maybe they'll have a few questions for you, but that's all."

Golda wrote again. As she did, however, there was the heavy sound of footsteps from the hall. She hastily ripped the card into bits and stuck the bits into the pages of Aristotle. (Who would ever open these pages in Velikie Luki, and when?)

The excited head librarian ran into the room, excitedly took Anton to one side.

"Mister American, comrade citizen sir! Something happened to Melada Pavlovna by the phone. She's sick. She's all contorted and can't speak. She didn't eat anything in our railway station buffet, did she? For somebody who's not used to it that can be a bad thing."

Melada was lying on a sofa in the librarian's office. She was lying still, save that her face, eyes closed, was twitching with controlled convulsions. Her green dress was hiked up unattractively on one side, showing a garter strap. The white teeth marks on her hand were slowly turning blood-scarlet.

With a gesture she indicated that they should wait. That they shouldn't ask her about anything. Then, with difficulty, she got up, sat, leaning against the leather cushion. She put her legs down, smoothed her dress.

"Could you leave us alone?" she asked the librarian. "We have something important to discuss."

"Of course, of course, I'm going right now," the woman said, relieved. "And I'll get you some tea from downstairs. Sweet, sweet tea, and very very hot. So it almost boils in your mouth. There's no better help for your stomach than sweet tea. You can believe me, how many years have I suffered from this!"

Melada waited until she had shut the door, then patted the seat next to her. Anton sat hastily, tried to hug her. She removed his hand, put it back into his lap. She spoke with a dead voice.

"You are being expelled from the country. Twenty-four hours notice. I have to take you right back."

"Why?!"

She wanted to answer, but a small band of offenses which had been hidden away for life imprisonment suddenly broke free from their cell and strangled her throat with a fresh convulsion. It took about two minutes to round them up and put them back in their cell.

"I never forgot for a moment that we didn't have a lot of days left to us, and that the number was getting smaller and smaller. But still, so sharply, so wrenchingly... That's like telling a beggar that it's not even ten kopeks that he has in his hands, as he'd thought, but just one lousy kopek..."

"But it's undoubtedly some sort of misunderstanding! I haven't given them any cause! Probably this is just some trick by Pirgoroy's competitors, or slander of some sort. Or the lawyer Simpson has found some way to threaten me even here. We have to find out the reason right away and explain..."

"What did you say in your radio broadcasts over there? And didn't anybody explain to you that you can't use the regular mails for such things?"

"What radio broadcast?"

"The one you sent from Leningrad. Somebody's prying hands opened it, translated it, and sent it all the way up to the Leningrad bosses. My Intourist boss was called in to explain himself. He said that he's never been yelled at like that before. And he's never yelled at me like he just did either."

"But what was it I said? It was just the usual chat with listeners, travel remarks..."

"You claim there..."

"Never! Never in any of my broadcasts have I ever claimed anything! I only ask questions and share observations, share observations and ask."

"You claim, or so my boss shouted at me, that in our country the only people who can make it to top jobs are those who have no education or talent."

"I didn't say anything of the kind..."

"That you tell about some half-literate boss of divers..."

"Character sketches, the passing thoughts of a traveller..."

"And have the gall to claim that he is a very typical case, a characteristic example..."

"I described him sympathetically even, the little guy was so funny... They'll make laughing stocks of themselves, reacting to it in such an exaggerated way. We have to phone..."

"The crew of the Babylonia has already been warned and they are getting ready to cast off."

"And what a nasty thing, to open other people's mail! To listen to other people's conversations! It's worse than theft! You really would have to be a complete nonentity..."

"That's it, my love, it's over!" She suddenly took his face and turned him towards her. "There's nothing we can do. Believe me. This is the wall. Maybe you didn't want to, but...you hit them where it hurts the most. I can imagine what my father is going to say, when he hears about it..."

He was distracted for a moment by her hands, but then grew livelier, took her elbows, pulled her to himself.

"The hell with them! If I have to leave, I'll leave... It's all for the best. Let them do without my canned goods, bridges, without moonshine tractors. I'll find you in London, and there nobody can get in our way. We can be together for real there, for the first time, neither of us at work, but just each of us for the other..."

"Yes, darling, yes..."

"And what about Golda?"

"I'll take her back to the camp. It's on the way."

"But now they can't hide her. They lost and that's it! I'll take it to Congress! To the Senate! If she wants, she can come back at any moment!"

"Of course. You have to leave immediately. It's eight hours drive to Leningrad, and with the weather like this, more like ten. That's how much time we have left together. You'll probably have to take a turn at the wheel for a while."

"Of course, naturally. I'll drive so fast that we'll gain a whole hour that we can spend together on the Babylonia."

"You're always on about that, about your..."

"We'll have a television room, for big and little, children and grown-ups..."

"Why does it sometimes seem to me that the closer I get to you, the farther away I get?"

"And all the keyboards in all the keys."

"And when I'm alongside, you forget about me completely."

"I thought of you every minute of all those days when you were travelling around seeing all your warlocks and Sibyls! I can't forget you for a second, even if I wanted to!"

"You forget me just like you forgot about your own daughter."

"Me? Me, who came four thousand miles by sea to get her?"

"Probably you only know how to remember those far away and forget about those close to you."

"That's not true, it's not true, it's not true!"

"But now I am going to be the farthest away of all for you, and you're going to remember me for a long, long time. Isn't that right? You will? No, say it in words! No nodding, say it!"

He said it.

And now they were riding, the three of them, in the car. Family, strangers. Good-byes not yet said, and yet already apart. A sweet family, composed of father, daughter, berry of love, odd-man-out, mother-stepmother, and unborn brother in her mandarin belly. Strangers, who had lived without one another and who would live on. "In our fields like three paths, like three paths diverging..." Three roads leading away from the inscribed stone, and each of them was already setting out on his own.

The ground couldn't soak up the water tumbling from the heavens, and so it swelled everywhere in bubbling seas, bubbles chasing bubbles in muddy rivulets. A tiny world of warmth and dryness rolled through the flood, improbable and insistent, like a bird's nest on wheels.

Anton sat on the back seat alongside Golda. He had his arm on her shoulder. She had a pack of library cards in her hands with all the authors at least from Russian A to English F on them. She had gotten upset and alarmed when they took her off her task. Now she could continue the job in her camp.

Even now she was sorting the cards, laying them out on her knees. She was absorbed in the job. The mole had hidden in its hole again, surrounding itself with a strong wall of urgent tasks. She could wait behind this wall, sitting out all troubles. She could even avoid finding out what was happening, why the work was interrupted, why they had so hurriedly to go back, and why the air was so tense.

Anton tried to talk with her, to talk about the last few months. She answered monosyllabically: "yes"; "no"; "some"; "later." Or suddenly she'd turn her face to him, warning him with her eyes about Melada, who was in front. A in Suspicion. A+ in Distrust. She had always been an excellent student. Even when there was no need to be.

The car stopped at a rain-blackened house.

"We're there?" Anton asked.

"Not yet. This is the crossroads where we have to turn off for the camp. But I don't want them to see you there."

"You really think it matters now?"

"It'll be better for Golda if they didn't. And for me too. This is the local post office. You can wait inside for me."

Anton faced his daughter. He bent to kiss her.

She jerked away. It was as though she had only now understood what was happening. She shook her head, repeating the word "no" several times.

"There's nothing I can do, darling," Anton said. "I've been ordered to get out of here immediately. But if you decide that you've had enough, you can leave at once. Right now, even. Just write a request in this notebook, sign it, and as soon as I get back I'll give it to the Agency. The wheels will start turning, and we'll have you out of here in two shakes."

Golda shook her head again.

"You don't understand. You don't know anything about things here. These people... the sign lights up and all the roles change immediately," she muttered.

Her fingers dug into his hand so hard that his mind again recalled that old scene: her head on the paper-covered pillow, the cotton wad soaking up the blood from her chin, the doctor's needle piercing the softness of her lip, and then the transparent thread lacing up the gaping edges of the wound, tugging them together again, and brave girls are absolutely forbidden to cry, but you can hold Daddy's hand, can't you? Hard, when it hurts. So that it hurts him a bit too? So that he has to suffer at least a little bit of this too?

"Oh, daddy, daddy, daddy..."

The library cards scattered over the cramped space. She buried her face in his chest and began to sob softly.

She was saying something, but he couldn't make out the words.

The wailing changed into a thin, pulsing moan. As if the gopher now understood that the fox's toothy muzzle had penetrated the burrow, that it was right there, and that there was no longer any sense in hiding and cowering.

"Daddy, daddy, daddy!"

It was the only word that he could make out. All the others flowed together, mixed themselves up, gulping, drowning in the sound of the rain. Somewhere lower, though, on the animal or fish (prehuman) level this howl of farewell could apparently be understood, heard, deciphered. Probably this was her unborn brother moving in answer to this cry for help. Probably it was he, probably his order that made the wooden Melada's left foot put in the clutch. The right hand moved the gear shift to first. And the right foot stepped on the gas.

A hot oily mixture was thrown into the cylinders.

The smooth pistons hammered.

The spark-plugs sparked bright.

The sturdy crankshaft turned.

The wheels turned too, the rainy ocean splashed, the postoffice building went past, as did the necessary, unnecessary, despised cross-road and they dashed onward, ahead, where in a gap between the clouds...

Radio Broadcast Conceived While Passing By
the Station of Dno (or Bottom)
(Jail the fathers)

Once in my earlier life I met a man who was broken by grief. His son was in prison. The man didn't say what crime the son had committed.

"That's not important," he said. "Maybe he robbed a poor old woman. Or a rich bank. Maybe he ran over somebody and took off, didn't stay to help. Maybe he was an arsonist, for the insurance. Or an airplane hijacker. The point is that I'm the one who's guilty in all this. So I should be the one who's in jail instead of him, or at least alongside him. But our stupid criminal system doesn't accept this obvious fact. I have offered myself to the judges and the prison wardens many times, but they only want to send me to the psychiatrists."

It was impossible to argue with the man. He was absolutely convinced of his own guilt. He said that any man who has had a child takes upon himself in advance by doing so responsibility for whatever the child does in the future.

"It's not important how you raised him," he said. "If you were a strict father, punishing your son for the bad things he did, putting him in the corner, pulling his ear, spanking him with your belt, then he comes to hate your strength, your corners and your belts. His deformed and constrained will seek an outlet in breaking of rules, will try to find freedom at whatever price, even the freedom to commit crimes. If you have been a good father, if you have tried to influence him by examples of justice, honesty, and sympathy, then he will hate justice, honor, and sympathy, since for him these will again be only the walls of the cage into which you are always trying to drive him and keep him.

"Obviously there is no salvation in flight for you, since if you leave your children and go to another woman or other man, or even go off to wander on your own, you are a criminal who has broken a child's heart, and so you are obligated to take upon yourself all the sad consequences as your guilt.

"This truth flows not just from logic, but from our unconscious emotions as well. All people were children at one time, but have you ever known even

420

one child who did not blame his parents for everything? 'Did we ask to be born?' they throw back in our faces. 'You had us for your pleasure, not ours!' they shout. And what about the people who are afraid to have children? What else holds them back, do you think, if it isn't a presentiment of that heavy conscious guilt that the birth of a child bears with it? And so mankind is able to continue only because of its most irresponsible representatives, which means that we are condemned to remain from century to century on our present primitive level.

"The sins of the fathers always fall on the heads of the children, so that the fathers are always guilty and so must pay for this guilt. We can only pray that our children don't do anything monstrous before we die. But if this happens we must accept our punishment without a word of protest and go sit in the cell next door. Until our laws are changed to permit that, our jails will stay packed with nothing but innocent people, while the real culprits—their parents—will be free, showing righteous anger or false sympathy."

Naturally I argued with this man. I said that in that sort of system evil children would have enormous power over their parents, and could easily blackmail them, threaten to send them to prison at any moment (to which he replied that parents who have given birth to children of that sort deserve no better). I said too that according to that logic everybody could pass their guilt even further, on to their own parents, grandparents, and great grandparents, in fact all the way back to Adam, and so it would turn out that no one was guilty of anything. I also offered a number of other arguments, which seemed convincing to me then.

Now, though, I am in doubt. Perhaps misfortune has undercut my self-confidence. Or the birth of a tenth child has forced me finally to reflect. Today I would not know what to say to this grief-stricken man. And so I turn to you, my radio listeners, both the responsible childless and the feckless parents, asking that you give me new ideas I might use in this far from frivolous argument.

19. LANDS AND WATERS

...WHERE IN A GAP
between the night clouds glittered the spire of the Peter-Paul fortress.

"This is the Summer Garden, right?" Anton asked.

"Yes," Melada answered.

"Stop here. Please."

"But we are very late..."

"One! Just one minute! Golda, you have that empty milk bottle there? And the paper bag that the danish came in? I'll be right back."

He got out into the rain, his raincoat over his head, and went down the granite stairs to the black Neva. He rinsed the bottle a couple of times, then dunked it under the water. The bubble floated to the top with a soft pop.

He gave the full bottle to Golda, told her to hold it straight and tight. Then he dashed across the road and into the empty, rain-soaked garden, went briskly down a tree-lined alley. An old bronze man sat in a chair, surrounded by bronze foxes, wolves, cats, storks. It looked as though they were running up to seek protection from the naked nymphs, muses, goddesses, and cupids that had seized the rest of the park. The old fabulist Krylov had his nose sunk in a book, as if he had no idea why anybody had felt it necessary to plant him here in the middle of this marble shamelessness.

A lone watchwoman with a sharp-peaked slicker wandered somewhere ahead. Anton hid from her behind a monument, scraped the fallen leaves away with his foot. He bent down. His pen knife sunk easily into the dirt. A rain-soaked night crawler silently began a new existence as two worms. One half, along with a clump of dirt, set off for a long journey in the bag that had held the cheese danish.

Again the palaces flashed past, the columns and monuments. Melada braked near the granite giants. To light incense, burn a clump of fleece, drop ram's blood? But no, she just looked at her Ignaty for some moments, as if wanting advice or a nod or some kind word. Then they drove on.

They were almost silent. They had had time enough to discuss everything on the road from Velikie Luki. They had all agreed to lie, to insist that Golda had decided to run away on her own. Then there was some slight chance that Melada would not be punished quite so severely. Still, she had been ordered by her director to immediately bring the American specialist in her care back to Leningrad. Where he was to be met by a well-deserved boot in the rear. And she had fulfilled her main order. And Melada (they would say) had put Golda on the passing truck headed for camp. But Golda (they would say) had gotten out of the truck halfway there and then had come on by train into Leningrad and had gotten herself to the American consulate, where she would announce that she wanted to go home. Authoritative American opinion would be that there would be no further basis on which to detain a citizen of the United States, of which they would inform the higher-ups of the other side.

They went over the details again. What was the name of the train station where Golda had gotten on? Novosokolniki. Which train? The one from Lvov, that stops at 12:30, for five minutes. Where did she get the money for a ticket? The American canned grass and slander specialist, who had just learned that he would have no further need of rubles, had given what he had left to his fellow countryman for ice cream (they had decided not to mention that they were related). Where had the train come into? Vitebsk station in Leningrad. How had she gotten to the consulate? On the subway, to Chernyshevsky station.

They grew more lively, believed that the escape might work. Melada had even been able to force herself to sleep for an hour, letting Anton drive. She even remembered her professional obligations and entertained them with short accounts of the little towns they passed through. She even tried to explain a historical pun to them, when they went through the town of Dno, where the last Russian emperor had signed his renunciation of the throne, and thus had left the empire, so to say, *na dne*, or on the bottom. In answer to that Anton recalled that in New Mexico there is a town called Truth or Consequences, and then asked which half she'd want to live in, and they had laughed, weighing all the pros and cons of each side.

In the wet night glimmer of Leningard's streets fear and melancholy had returned to the nest on wheels. And when they stopped not far from the American consulate and they could make out through the trees not one and not two, but for some reason three militia men strolling around the entrance. When she saw them Golda began to tremble so badly that they had to abandon all hope that she might walk confidently up to them, nonchalantly ask them to call some night-duty diplomat, and nonchalantly duck inside. ("American citizen? So where's your passport? Ah, they took it away from you? So why don't you telephone the consulate tomorrow? It's urgent? What kind of urgent business is there at ten at night?")

One thing was left. One last possibility. Which Anton didn't even want to discuss while there were others still alive. Because he was going to have to ask Melada for help again. And so reveal to her another bit of the truth about himself. And so once again have to face her searching, astonished tired look.

"You think they've already put the alarm up in the camp?" Anton asked.

"Of course, they understood that something was wrong. They might have phoned the library. The local militia. But they wouldn't have been likely to call Leningrad. They'll be hoping to find us on their own. Nobody wants to admit his own mistakes. In the morning they'll phone for sure, though."

"That means all we have is tonight."

Anton got out of the car, went around to the front, got in next to Melada. He put his arm back, resting his hand on the cheek of Golda, who was jammed into the corner; he may have been reassuring her, may have been stroking her, may have been pushing her away, or may have been asking her forgiveness for what he was going to have to whisper in her presence.

Melada listened silently.

To his astonishment, she didn't get upset, wasn't frightened. She even interrupted him somewhere in the middle of his salespitch.

"I already know that you are—how is it you say it?—full of surprises. You want me to do that? That means I'll do it. That's it. I remember the name of the village and the street. Just give me the house number. And the man's first name. I don't need his last."

The whole rest of the way to the harbor she never once went back to the forbidden theme.

She stopped the car not far from the customs building.

Anton hugged his daughter.

"Don't be afraid of anything. We'll see each other again in a few hours. Everything will be all right. You're not afraid of Melada anymore? Good. There's not going to be any change of the sign, and she's not going to be declared the Evil Bastinda. And I won't turn into a Cossack with a Mauser. Do whatever she tells you to do. We'll be headed home pretty soon."

He kissed both of them and got out of the car. The rain was thinning, turning into a fog dust that wasn't strong enough even to fly all the way down to the asphalt. He got his suitcases out of the trunk and walked up to the customs shed.

Everything on the Babylonia was ready. The diesel engine throbbed quietly, warming as it idled.

"What happened out there?" Ronald asked in alarm, helping Anton get on board. "We weren't even allowed to go to the consulate. Get your things together and get out of here! In two shakes! What did we do to them?"

"I'll tell you later. You refueled? You tested the radar? The night binoculars? We'll be needing them tonight. It's very important. Test them before we cast off."

Pablo-Pedro stuck his face out of the engine room, covered with a black netting, like a mask. He glanced up, then froze, expecting an order.

"How did you get on here?" Anton asked. "Did you see anything of the town or the country? How are your new friends?"

Pablo-Pedro just waved him off and went back into his cramped diesel cave.

"What's his problem?" Anton asked Lin Chan.

"He's very let down. At first everything was great. He played cards with the Russian diving boss. And taught the others too. They were all friendly, throwing the money overboard. Dollars and rubles. They praised the new game a lot. Communist poker is good, very good! But once he happened to stay by the gunwale. And he saw a rubber hand. It was a diver that had been specially sent. Picking up the dollars from the water. Then he threw them all out and broke off the friendship. After that he didn't even go into the city."

"And how are you?"

"I very much want to go home. I can't understand anything here. I wanted to sell my pants suit and old slippers. I asked where. They said must have passport. No passport, just visa. Then legally nowhere, they said, but illegally, right here. They pointed down. Under the counter. They laughed. But I was afraid without the law. I just understood one thing. I've got to get my family to America. Fast, fast. If they aren't allowed to trade, then things will be bad. They don't know how to do anything else."

The customs officials had combed the Babylonia in the daylight as well, confiscating the bronze soccer player that Ronald had bought (A people's treasure! A work of art! Where is your special permission?) and before putting their stamps on the documents. Then the border guards came. A lieutenant and two soldiers with dogs. They went from cabin to cabin, looked in all the lockers, the showers, the cupboards, and even in the refrigerator. Anton waited until the lieutenant was alone, then called him to one side and took out a carton of cigarettes.

"I've decided to quit smoking. I wanted to throw the temptation overboard. But the rules forbid littering the harbor. Could you be so kind as to confiscate this for me?"

"It can be done," the lieutenant said. "As a favor, one nation to another. But would you maybe have some kind of bag here? One you can't see through?"

The bag was found. Into it was also put—with approving nods by the lieutenant—a handful of magazines with eye-popping beauties. It was a lucky thing that the beads, bracelets, mirrors, and other traditional gifts for savages could be so easily replaced. But no—just then the lieutenant of the border guards showed that he was not so simple by stunning Captain Sebich with an unanticipated request.

"What? What?" Anton did not believe his ears.

"You wouldn't have any recent numbers of the *Wall Street Journal*, would you?"

"I'm afraid I haven't."

"You see, of late I've gotten hooked on reading the market news. The way the prices have dropped for Eastern's shares is terribly upsetting. You wouldn't know what they're getting today, would you?"

"I'm ashamed to say I don't... But I promise I'll bring one next time. I hadn't expected to run into someone with such broad interests."

"We follow it with pleasure. Poke into things, read a few things. Maybe there is something about talking dolphins? Or the Dead Sea scrolls?"

"I'm terribly ashamed to say..."

"It's a pity, it really is..."

"I've been thinking that our engine has starting acting up while we've been here," Anton changed the subject. "But I haven't wanted to put off the departure. Who knows what kind of second thoughts your bosses will have in the morning."

"Yes, there's no way of telling that."

"We can fiddle with it as we go. If we have to, can we stop in the bay for a half hour? I'd like you to warn the radar stations, if you would."

"We can do that. If we're going to help then we'll help all the way. Except don't be long. Otherwise they'll send a cutter out to check."

The guards climbed up from the machine room. Their dog snorted and tried to rub the grease from its nose with a paw. The lieutenant stamped their passports. Lin Chan gave each of the soldiers a tin of Brunch of the Baskervilles and with gestures told them that they were for their four-footed friend, not for them.

"A happy voyage," the lieutenant saluted.

"Thanks," Anton said.

"Duty is duty," the lieutenant said, as if apologizing. Then he suddenly recalled a fitting quotation from a a classic and declaimed it with the heat of a school boy: "To serve is a pleasure! To submit a disgrace!"

And, seeing his sharp silhouette on the receding wharf, Anton suddenly recalled the warnings of the melancholy diplomat and thought how fate had nevertheless been kind to him in this country, if it had sent him his only encounter with a multifaceted word-worshipper only at the very last and very short minute, when it no longer could wound.

A green ray circled the radar screen like a watch hand set off in pursuit of time passing. Lights dimmed, the Babylonia floated slowly through the Finnish shallows. Through the eyepieces of the night glasses the pines and empty beaches along the shore stretched like a transparent, distant undiscovered land, a tiny ribbon pressed between sky and sea.

"Contact!" Ronald said. "They made contact!"

He handed Anton the box with the radio-telephone.

The elder Kozulin's voice sounded tense and excited.

"Yes, yes, everything's ready. I'm waiting how many days already for you, months, years... And both young ladies came just fine. My great-niece is charming. Obviously of Varangian blood. But why is she so suspicious of everything? She won't believe that her grandfather is my brother. She nods politely and agrees with me, but her eyes give away that she doesn't believe me. What are we to do now? Where are you? Of course we can take the pictures down to the shore. I have a special cart. All right, we'll try to keep out of the open. Varangians know how to hide when they have to, otherwise the Chuds would have destroyed them down to the last. Pull the antenna out all the way? Point it toward the sea? And periodically press on the red button? How often? Every two-three seconds? Nothing could be easier. And you'll find us? Not very likely. But no, of course, I believe you."

They had to crawl another fifteen minutes before the radio could pluck out from the damp darkness the sound of the radio beacon. The Babylonia turned to the north and began to approach the invisible shore.

"Fifteen... fourteen... thirteen..." Ronald announced aloud, not taking his eyes from the depthmeter. "That's it! We can't go any closer. The shallows by the shore are too treacherous."

The two anchor chains hammered happily as they dropped. The dinghy, inflated beforehand, was already on the deck, filling it completely, the rubber gunwales flopping off the edge of the yacht. Somewhere up above in the catacombs of the clouds the rain and wind were gathering strength for a new attack. For the moment, though, things were calm. The bottom of the dinghy slapped against the water with unexpected loudness.

"Back!" Pablo-Pedro whispered, taking Ronald's arm as Ronald tried to bring up a powerful gas engine. "I have an electric motor ready, a silent one. There it is, over under the superstructure."

While they were setting the motor and putting the heavy batteries in one by one, Anton was putting on armpit-high rubber boots, doing up the straps.

Ronald helped him crawl over the edge, then held out the peeping radio-telephone.

"It's not more than a mile to the shore. You can do it in ten minutes. You sure that two of you are enough?"

"The question is whether the dinghy will be enough. I have absolutely no idea how much baggage our passenger will be bringing."

Pablo-Pedro sat on the soft edge, took the tiller. The blades of the screw, manufactured in the western hemisphere, churned the waters of the eastern half. The rubber gunwale moved along the metal one, then separated, plunging silently into the murk. Anton sat in the prow, the antenna pointing ahead, to catch the signals coming toward them, threading them like rings on the invisible guiding thread. Pablo-Pedro could not see his hands, but he could see the rocking of the glowing face of the watch. To the left. To the right. Straight on.

After about ten minutes a line of surf showed white. Almost at the same moment the eastern sand began to scrape against the western propeller. They had to turn the engine off, raise it to the horizontal.

Anton stepped over the edge and walked to shore, pulling the dinghy on a line. Pablo-Pedro helped him with an oar. The gurgle of the surf and the noise of the pines fought with one another on the no-man's-land of silence. Overtaking both of them, however, was the ever more insistent and urgent pipping of the radio beacon, moving toward them.

A dog barked softly.

The light of a torch flickered between the tree trunks.

And immediately a dark shape ran out onto the cold beach toward Anton, arms flung wide.

He was ready to catch her, but just then Pablo-Pedro stepped forward, grabbed her, raised her into the air, spun her around, and kissed her hard. Only then did he hand her over to her father.

"It's true then daddy? It's true? We are leaving? We're going home? And the sign won't change? You are really you? And I am really me? And that's how it's going to stay forever?"

"My congratulations," Ronald's voice came over the radio-tele-phone. "My heartiest congratulations. Golda, sweetie, say something to me."

"How's your externus adominis? Mine has gotten shamefully soft."

"We'll work on it tomorrow. Right now though you don't have a minute to spare. Even for kisses. Load up and cast off immediately."

Pablo-Pedro ran toward the elder Kozulin to help him pull the cart, dragging the heavy freight toward the little vessel that lay on its rubber belly. The Newfoundland pushed from behind. Anton put Golda back on the sand, gave her a pat to "go and help" and then went quickly over to the lone figure that stood dark alongside some kind of foundation (a machine-gun emplacement? anti-landing barrier? a sacrificial altar?).

She didn't move toward him.

"What's wrong?" he asked, running up.

"I can't go any farther." Melada pointed to a broad plowed strip at her feet. "This is the border."

"If it was light," Anton said, "I would write all the way across it in the sand. Every letter big enough to stretch from the trees to the water. T and H and A and N and K and so on."

"I'm glad I could help."

"When are you going to be in London? A week? Two weeks? After all, once I'm gone there's no point in keeping you here anymore..."

"Just a second sweetheart..."

"The main thing is that I really want you to come to America to have the baby. Then our baby will be an American citizen right from the beginning."

"You were talking in the car about the name of a town..."

"It's not that I want him to become President, but still, who's to say what will be?"

"In New Mexico, I think it was."

"Truth or Consequences?"

"That's the one."

"Why are you talking about it now?"

"The truth is that I won't be forgiven Golda's escape. And especially the old man's escape."

"But how are they ever going to find out? You don't have anything to do with this!"

"And the consequences are that I'm never going to be allowed out again. Never. This is our last meeting. So hug me as tight as you can, and be still."

A stern pedagogic intonation again colored her voice. But the pupil didn't give a damn about discipline. He was disobedient. He crossed the border. Now it was his turn to give orders.

"If that's the case, then you have to sail with us. Yes you do! Right now!"

"You're crazy!"

"There's nothing to keep you here."

"My relatives, my friends, my whole life."

"You've already said good-bye to Ignaty, and you won't see your father or brother for a year no matter what."

"No matter what it's like, I have my own place here."

"I had wanted to put off this serious conversation, get on my feet first..."

"And what would I have waiting for me over there?"

"But if that's how it has to be, then it's better that I go down on my knee right here, in the wet sand..."

"Everything will be foreign to me there."

"And ask you to become my wife immediately."

"You know yourself that that is impossible."

"Melada, are you willing to take as your lawfully wedded husband this man, who has nothing for a soul save that child which is already in your belly?"

"These are more of your rosy cloud castles, your fairy stories and dreams."

"I can give you five seconds to think it over. Starting now. Five. Four..."

"Don't torture me!"

"Three. Two..."

"Come on, I can't, it's too sudden."

"One. Go!"

"No!"

"No? No? Pablo! Here, on the double!" Anton shouted, forgetting about caution.

Sweaty Pablo-Pedro emerged from the dark.

"Get your pistol!" Anton ordered. "Get it, come on! Enough pretending. I know that you always have it on you. Okay. And now kidnap that woman for me. I want her for my wife. But she doesn't believe in the power of words. Only in the power of arms. It's magical."

"This is like jumping off a cliff for me, try to understand that!"

"So jump! I'll catch you! Here are my arms! Come on!"

Not taking her eyes from the pistol in the hand of the alarmed Pablo-Pedro, as if convincing herself, as if dredging up strength and lack of responsibility—"Yes, you can see that I don't want to do this, they're making me!"—Melada stepped onto the sacred furrow of the border, but then, after letting Anton catch her up and hug her, she couldn't stop herself from saying the melancholy, joking words from an old film that they had used in the institute to study the American accent.

"You'll get me? But who's going to get you, my beloved, my dear one, my fated, newly-appeared, and self-appointed superman?"

It seemed incredible that the little rubber bathtub could hold all the refugees, the parcels of paintings, and, to top it off, the huge heavy dog. As each passenger got in the boat had to be tugged a little farther out, to deeper water. The water was up to Anton's thighs when he finally pulled himself over the round gunwale, which was barely sticking up above the side, and waved to the helmsman. Pablo-Pedro turned on the silent motor. Violating the border regime, they were at the same time violating the laws of Archimedes, Bernoulli and Toricelli as they moved slowly back along their radio lifeline toward the Babylonia.

Every wave threw a little salty puddle into the boat. Golda found something to bail with, and the others helped with their hands, then wrung their soaked clothing out over the side. They crawled ahead so slowly that it was better not to look at the watch. The half hour they had allotted for this had long ago run out.

Then a signal light shone on the Babylonia.

Then there came the fuss of transshipping, crazy hugs, stifled cries, and Lin Chan's order: "Everyone change clothes. Everything is soaked. Come here. You can be shy later. Quickly, quickly."

Then the excited Newfoundland raced up and down the stairs of his new home, barking furiously at the traces left by the border guard's German shepherd.

They weighed the anchor without a snag and headed west, trying to make up some of their lost time, already beginning to believe that their wild plan had worked.

The pursuit appeared only toward morning.

It appeared as a simple little dot on the shining screen, then began to grow, to come closer.

Anton tried to change course, but the dot followed them.

The radar detector began to squeal.

The omnipresent radar tentacles had found them, and were attaching themselves firmly to the Babylonia.

Anton went to full ahead.

A white storm surf grew on both sides of the stem and spread over the watery wastes like a frightened ostrich.

The green dot on the radar screen stayed right with them. Soon after a break in the fog showed the silhouette of an approaching ship. A border patrol cutter. Not more than a half mile off.

"You don't know how many years for kidnapping, do you?" Ronald shouted.

"In English or in Russian?"

"What's the difference?"

"In English you're always 'the defendant,' but in Russian you're 'the accused.'"

"Looks like it's time to wake the others," Ronald said wearily.

But the passengers of the Babylonia had already woken from the roar of the engine and were coming up on deck. Melada and Lin Chan stood side by side at the railing, exactly where they had been handcuffed on their knees three weeks before. They watched the closing pursuit vessel sadly and seriously. The elder Kozulin held the barking Newfoundland by the collar. Golda hid her gopher's head in Ronald's chest. Suddenly she pointed at Melada and screamed, "I know what it is, I know! She has a hidden transmitter! She's signalling them! Throw her overboard!"

Ronald covered her mouth with his iron hand.

Pablo-Pedro was the last to come up. He saw the cutter on the brightening horizon, shook his fist, and shouted, "Again!? Again when I'm sleeping?! And naturally it's all coincidence again!?"

Then he ducked behind the door leading to the hold.

The Babylonia flew into a cloud that lay upon the water. The morning light darkened. The fog did its honest best to surround the ship, to hide it from its enemies, as it had done for centuries. Oh, poor brother fog! Can't you see how you've become transparent, vulnerable, pierceable by evil burrowing electrons?

Pablo-Pedro appeared again on the deck. He was dragging a heavy box in his left hand and had some sort of heavy stick on his right shoulder.

Ronald ran towards him.

Pablo-Pedro pointed the stick at him, and Ronald jumped back.

"It's a bazooka!" Anton thought. "This madman had a bazooka hidden! He's going to get us all killed!"

He was so upset as literally to turn to stone. His hand froze, the throttle held wide open.

Pablo-Pedro now lifted the rod to the sky. The shot threw a rosy spot onto the cloud of fog that whipped past. Pablo-Pedro bent down to his box, got out a second shell, which even to Anton's civilian eyes looked odd, and fired it straight ahead, in the direction Babylonia was racing.

"Cease fire!" the radio suddenly barked, in an unexpectedly loud voice. "I order you to stop the ship immediately. Surrender! Otherwise I'll open fire!"

Pablo-Pedro continued to dash around the deck, firing into the air. As if they were being overtaken not from behind, but from above, as if he could see paratroopers of some sort through the white blanket around them, dropping down on them from helicopters.

These paratroopers must have been awfully small, because Melada suddenly began swatting them away with her hands. Then the others began to do the same. Then Anton noticed a strip of aluminum foil sticking to the window.

And only then did he get it.

He glanced at the radar screen.

A green blizzard raged there, saving them like a wall.

The shells fired into the air broke into millions of silver ribbons and then fluttered slowly back to the water like a fancy-dress rain, covering their faces, the masts, the gunwales. What brother fog could not do sister foil had, covering the Babylonia with a screen many kilometers long, hiding the ship from the electronic beams, ripping free the deadly tentacles.

The radar detector gave a final shriek, then fell silent.

Anton threw the rudder to the right so sharply that the celebrating passengers had to grab a hold. Somewhere to their rear the blinded cutter raced straight ahead, disappearing in the electronic foil blizzard. The radio's threats and orders died to a weak rasp.

The ostrich feather wake at the Babylonia's prow, now turned by the falling foil into silver wings, raced nearer and nearer to the border and neutral waters.

And once again—silence.

A pale sun winked through the cranes of Helsinki's port.

A little wave slapped an orange peel against the Babylonia's sides, then against the mooring.

Sleep. Can't sleep. The fingers continue to tingle with nerves, and the eyes. Dry mouth.

Only the elder Kozulin seemed to have been unfazed, and was wild with joy. He was chattering on about something, standing in the prow of the yacht. He was rummaging in one of the parcels of his pictures. The word "unique" flashed past quite often.

"People are paying enormous money for this right now. Just imagine some rich guy who has everything. A mansion, a yacht, private jet, a Hollywood lover, some lover in Europe, photos of him hugging the President. But everybody else in his club has the same thing. What's he to do? He's dying to get hold of something unique. No matter what he has to pay. He's going to be ready to pay whatever money you want so as to get something unique. A million, fifty million. He's terrified at the thought of remaining lost forever, just a face in the crowd of million-aires. And then he buys a Gauguin. He's saved. He's got something unique. He's the man who owns 'Bathing in the Red Stream,' now not to be confused with the millionaire who only has some 'Flight into

Egypt' from the school of Rembrandt. You have something unique to sell? A prize race horse? An Egyptian sphinx? A baseball player? A Mozart wig? You can ask any price you want, and you'll find a buyer."

Anton wanted to gather his forces, get out of his deck chair, and go over to Melada, who was standing along the rail. He was worried by the look on her face. He wanted to hug her in front of everybody, and say loudly that everything was going to be fine. That everything dangerous and alien in reality was back there, behind them, in the land of the blacksmith-brigade leaders, drowning divers, innocent betrayers, moonshining tractors. That what lay before her was unknown, but not alien. That soon she would feel the new land to be hers, familiar and comprehensible, all the houses, people, flowers, roads. The words she already knew, sung and written, scrawled on the sides of buildings and shimmering in the sky, blasting from loudspeakers and creeping across the screen. However a canvas with a picture of two suitcases rose up between him and Melada.

"Here's the present I promised you, captain."

Anton had strength enough to sit up, put his feet on the deck. He politely studied the muddy brown colors, the shiny leather of the belts painted there, praising the picture, thanking the old man.

"We'll hang it in the living room of our new house, won't we, Melada?"

She nodded suspiciously.

"Just a second," Kozulin said. "You still haven't seen everything. Please, all of you, attention."

He waved a piece of wrapping cloth like a magician would his cape. Then he did something with the frame support and, with a single gesture, took the canvas off the frame. There was a second picture underneath. A green man was walking along a snowy street carrying a yellow samovar, in the glowing middle of which was floating a ram's head. Over the bowing church flew a fish with a bouquet in its mouth. A glittering pink buckboard was carrying two embracing lovers over the sea as if it were dry land, without the need for any bridges from Vermont.

"My father didn't have any millions," Kozulin explained. "But he had uniqueness in his soul. And he knew how to recognize it, to find it and value it and to buy it when other people still considered it to be foolishness, daubings, something nobody else wanted. He put together an entire collection, traveling from one crazy eccentric to another, creeping up the rickety stairs to their attics, giving them his hard-earned rubles, marks, thalers, and then he returned home with his loot, like a real Varangian returning from a voyage overseas. His entire life went into this collection. Once our famous neighbor came to look at it. He was a great hand at painting Volga boatmen and Cossacks from the Zaporozhie, but his uniqueness was later stolen by imitators. And the collection became my life too. To hide it, and not let the Chuds get their hands on it. I painted my trunks and suitcases to disguise them with such passion that I think maybe they too have some real art in them. How could I leave without them? To leave our enemies the treasure that my father had worked so hard to accumulate? Odin would have chucked me out of his hall for that, sent me to the cave of loathsome Hel for doing that. And quite right, too."

Naturally Anton had seen pictures by this artist before. He had an odd name in Russian, like a verb. Juggle? Goggle? Haggle? And something like two years ago one of his pictures had been sold in London for some millions. And if in everyone of the old man's pictures of trunks and suitcases there was painting like this one hidden it would be hard to say which of the two Kozulin brothers would prove to be the richer.

His tired, exhausted brain tried to grasp the improbability of what had happened. A day ago he had had nothing. A failure, a flop at everything, who had blown his last chance, letting all his hopes and bridges collapse, his and those of others, fit to bring home only a clump of dirt and jug of water. And now just 24 hours later he had everything back, had been given everything—his rescued daughter, his beloved wife, and unexpected wealth.

Why? For what? Had he done something in the dark hold of his existence that merited such a reward up on the decks of existing? Or was it really as Feoktist believed, that indifferent time simply brings us in turn the goblets as they are set out, now with wormwood, now with honey, asking of us only that we drink each to the lees, gulping them down with gratitude?

And, trying to rein in his racing thoughts, before they could wander into reaches where lay the serpentine doubts and fears of existence, trying to stay on the point of the moment's joy, which pierced him to the heart, he at the same moment also noted without comprehension that the enormity of the gifts which had been showered down upon him evoked in him the same paralyzing horror at the Donor as he had felt two years before in the face of the Remover, the one who had sent the Miserymaker.

Even more, maybe.

EPILOGUE

FAREWELL

the Notebook Left Behind
by the Creator's Unasked Defender

I recently returned to my favorite resort town on the Maine coast. The house of the solitary island dweller still sticks dismally up beyond the bay. However a bartender I knew told me that the old eccentric had died the year before. The mayor's office was trying to find any relatives before putting the house up for auction.

On one of his last visits the old man had left the barman a thick notebook, asking him to send it off to a publisher after his death. The barman didn't know anything about the publishing business, though, and so didn't know how to do this. On the other hand, he couldn't bring himself to chuck the notebook in the trash. After all, this was the last relic of the old man. And then who knows? Maybe there was a best seller in it, something that was worth millions? Would I agree to look through it overnight? Because judging by how easily I put words together, he felt that I would know how and where to sell them for a good price. He would be very grateful for my advice.

Before going to bed back at the hotel I leafed through the notebook. The old man had not abandoned his topic. Now though his praise of the Creator had acquired a certain ambiguity, even what I might call a bitterly ironic tinge. It seemed as though the writer had spent a lot of time in front of the television, turning from one news program to another, then transferring his impressions of what he had seen to his notebook.

"Praise the Lord, without whose will not a single airliner would fall onto a sleeping town, would explode in a fire ball, bringing hundreds of unprepared souls up to You...

"And without Your knowledge and consent the walls of a school cafeteria would not burst before a tornado, showering down onto kids drinking their milk.

"Maybe someday we shall be lucky, and some victim of an earthquake who has been buried alive in his home will happen to have a tape recorder

in his hands. Then we shall know at last what a person says to You as he slowly dies of hunger and thirst, able to feel only the pain of his shattered legs, crushed under the rubble.

"However we mustn't always trust to chance. After all, modern banks are now equipped with automatic cameras. Shouldn't we put cameras like that on all ships, so that when the next ship is dispatched to the bottom we will be able to see the faces of those who have been fated to meet You underwater?

"Oh, how naive the relatives of those tourists who die in a bus, showered by the bullets of bandits! Don't they understand that without Your will not a single firing pin will touch a firing cap, the mercury will not flare, the powder flash, the all-powerful gases won't expand, the slug won't leave the barrel.

"And how unenlightened, how ignorant the mother who sobs beside the flaming house where her two-year old son remains, as she curses everyone about her but doesn't send a single curse aloft."

Apparently the television had then broken, and the praises to the Creator took on a slightly different cast.

"Praise be to You, oh, great genius of the advertisement. Your inde-scribable art draws us to Your main product, Your good, Your invention, the gift of life. Your millions of salesmen from age to age try—with great success—to convince us that this is not a commercial deal, that Your company is engaged in free distribution, that we insignificant creatures are given life for free. And that there is no office or bureau where we might file a complaint of false advertising. In fact, what we are always talking about is a deal. We are offered life, for which we pay with suffering. Suffering is the golden coin, coin of the realm which for some reason Your bankers take so willingly and so readily in all their branches.

It would seem that You like simple-minded customers who take the goods You offer without complaint, lightly agreeing to live life from beginning to end and always pay their bills promptly, with all Your piratical interest points. However, those who figure out the swindle and who politely refuse, meaning that they kill themselves, sometimes even before they reach twenty, arouse implacable ire in You. It is no accident that Your servants long ago began refusing to bury such people.

Like every Trader, though, You pay particular attention to Your rich customers, those whose pockets are fat with pain. Those who stroke their fat wallets in their pockets, vacillating eternally, dickering with You, trying what You offer for size and taste, counting their capital over and over again, their funds of pain, wondering whether they have enough to pay with. You serve these ones with incredible inventiveness, giving them discounts, offering better terms, like success and beauty and talent and dreams and love. You even let them leave Your shop and then come back in, breaking the pain into bits until finally the insistent customer without noticing it himself lives his life to old age. 'I'm giving back Your gift!' one of these wrote with great pride not long ago. But it was too late, the deal had already occurred."

Then the television had apparently been fixed, and the notebook began again to note bitterly ironic hosannas: for a huge mudslide, a terrific fire, a record-breaking psychopath who had managed to choke thirty women to death in a very short time, for wars, hurricanes, earthquakes, pestilence. Yet towards the end of the notebook another note began to sound more and more insistently: "DON'T LEAVE US!"

"Yes, I understand that You grow weary with us, the way a merchant gets tired of dealing with impoverished customers, or a teacher gets tired with dull students. We only understand constant repetition. Which bores You. Twenty, thirty, forty times we have to be flooded before we figure out to build our houses on pillars or dikes. Millions have to die of smallpox, plague, malaria before we finally get down to looking for a vaccine, and as many must die before we agree to take the injections. And these are all instances in which we are trying to save our own skin. How can we ever be taught anything higher, anything selfless? Anything unpredictable, original, unique, with which we might amuse You, or even amaze You?

"Even so I pray, let us have one more chance, hold us over the same grade next year, don't expel us from Your school.

"Yes, we don't understand single instances. We kill Your prophets precisely because they are the only ones in the world who are able to hear You. Nothing exists for us until it has been repeated a hundred times. The ants in their anthill out in the forest are given only one glimpse of the man who pensively digs at their structures with a stick. 'If he is rational,' the skeptics among the ants will say, 'if he belongs to another civilization, as some of our psychopaths and weirdos insist, then why doesn't he try to communicate with us? Why doesn't he try to tell us about his world, and ask us about ours?' But why should we talk with you pitiful crawlers and biters? How can anything be explained to you if you have already slammed your little world shut with the self-satisfied slogan ALL THAT IS IS RATIONAL? How can you believe anything that lies beyond the bounds of your reason?

"However, if Your patience has been boundless so far, is there not hope that it might extend a few days more, a few years, centuries, millennia? That You might send us a new messenger with a stick, who will try to let *some light into the murk of our spirits?*

"The only thing in which we show endless invention (and You have to give us credit where it's due) is in the means of killing one another. Knives and slings, spears and arrows, Greek fire and arbalest, ball and shot, machine gun and flame thrower, bomb and gas, electrons and bacilli, lasers and nuclear devices. In this regard we are certainly A+ students without peer. Oh, if we had used but one hundredth part of that same inventiveness in the attempt to understand why it is we kill each other! Astonishing things might have opened up before us.

"At the same time, however, I ask You not to listen to the cries of those who pray You to spare us the nightmare of unending war. They do not understand for what they ask. They take no account of the fact that only the horror of war saves horrible us from the horrors of absolute tyranny. If the tyrants reigning over us had no wars to fear, if they did not have to worry about being left absolutely without soldiers, then they would destroy us all to the last person for having the wrong faith or the wrong nose, the wrong mama and papa, the wrong skin color, but most of all just because, to satisfy the lust of ruling.

"We have been most successful in one other sphere as well—concealing ourselves from Your face. Scientists hide behind their knowledge, soldiers behind their victory banners, musicians behind their sweet strains, poets behind their dark lines, doctors behind those whom they restore to life, teachers behind those they save from ignorance, laborers behind the daily bread they earn by the sweat of their brows, and lovers behind one another. But please do not turn Your face away! Remember that there have been among us those who sought You alone, who harkened only to You, who spoke only with You. Not many, not often, once in a millennium, but what for You is a millennium? An instant, a minute for a change of scenery.

"Don't leave us, not for any reason! Don't let us disappear along with the pterodactyls and ichthyosauruses. We may still find a way to amuse You, to touch You, maybe even—who knows?—to move!"

The next day I told the bartender that I doubted that a publisher would want to print these notes. Even so I advised him to send the notebook to be kept in the enormous underground archive which was recently built in Utah. As far as I know, the creators of this unique archive are trying to gather and preserve information about as many people who have ever lived on Earth as they possibly can, so that no one shall be overlooked on Resurrection Day. The granite tunnels dug seven hundred feet into a cliff not far from Salt Lake City stretch endlessly with shelves of microfilms and computer disks full of accounts of the lives and relatives of billions of *people. This project seems so original to me that sooner or later I am going to have to go there myself, dear listeners, and then I will tell you about all that I see, in my next broadcast.*

20. HOLIDAY ON WATER, FIVE YEARS LATER

IN THE DUSK THE last helicopter full of photographers left the north-bound Babylonia 2 and turned back toward Detroit. In an hour the booty now hidden on the little rolls of film would come to life, turn into negatives, into prints, would be multiplied and disseminated across the whole land in millions of morning newspapers. The horde of journalists had been free to get their fill today. They had been allowed to snap pictures as the boat left Cleveland too, and when it stopped at Toledo and Windsor. Now, though, it was enough. From the first this celebration of five years since the Kozulin brothers' reunion had been intended to be an intimate family affair. Even very famous people have a right to a few days of peace and solitude. Tomorrow they would enter Lake Huron, making for a secret island on which is a small resort that the elder Kozulin had recently received in exchange for a unique early Kandinsky.

Anton could not get accustomed to his fame. Even today, when he and the father of Wife #5 stood by the handrail peacefully discussing their children and grandchildren, and what pitiful songs you heard nowadays, and then some fatso with a television camera had begun to shout from a motorboat down below, "Sir! Sir! A big smile for our viewers on Channel 7!" Anton had turned expectantly to the famous singer, only to be told that the request was to him.

"They made me from a 'Sir' into 'Bobby' a long time ago. So there's no good pretending. Wave your hand, blow him some kisses. Seven of them, if you can. So that the viewers on Channel 7 will feel that you care specially about them."

The journalists had begun to pester Mr. Sebich back when he opened his office again, reintroducing divorce insurance. However his real fame had come only after he began to air his ten-minute program on tv. In every show he managed to attack someone, and so provoke a whole wave of angry responses. He had particularly stirred something up with his story of the old doctor ("We know your tricks! Always hiding behind someone else! You trouble-making devil!") who had wanted to split the medical association into at least two competing parts.

What a storm that blew up!

He was accused of ignorance, superstition, irresponsibility, rabble-rousing and incitement to riot. Two doctors' corporations? Very interesting? And what, they'll cure in different ways? Use different methods, or different medicines? Conceal the latest medical developments from each other? And so the patients in one corporation would die and the others would get better?

Naturally there were also those who defended the daring idea. The bills that doctors write are a national disgrace, these shouted. Chop the hydra into ten pieces, not two! There's no other way to check their greed. You won't be able to hide any healing secrets from people, just as you can't conceal the secrets of automobile construction. But automobile manufacturers are forbidden to have monopolies—doctors are not! You're right a thousand times over, Mr. Sebich! Time to put an end to this.

The praise flowed in with the attacks, congratulations took turns with anonymous telephone threats. When Melada came down with a neurological pain in her elbow, he was afraid to send her to the local doctor and so forced her to go to New York, where he signed her in under a false name. His producer did everything he could to hush the scandal up, making all sorts of conciliatory announcements. He swore that the old doctor actually existed, and that he had simply gotten bitter after he had been deprived of his right to practice, for some sort of violation of medical ethics. Soon other scandals and sensations distracted the greedy viewers, but public interest in Mr. Sebich had obviously jumped up several notches, just as it does in any of us when we notice that the sign beneath the wild animal's cage says "Poisonous."

Anton laughed, poured himself more beer. The foam ran down the outside of the glass, splashing overboard and stretching in a white trail toward the five glass cylinders huddled close together that were still darkling above the horizon near Detroit. The banquet hall windows spilled music as the famous Bobby sang softly, just for family, a song from their youth: "You'll remember my look when it hits you like oncoming headlights, and you'll lose the wheel, lose the wheel." A familiar urge, to go share favorite memories with his wife, almost forced Anton to get up and go inside. He didn't though. There were too many of his wives in the room, and the hour was so late that he might make a mistake and go to the wrong one.

He was glad that Melada had agreed to take part in the holiday cruise. He had been glad to see her today, and the children too, repressed, walled off from him and the world, too intense upon one another, but at the same time calm, placid, and polite as they offered their cheeks for relatives to kiss.

How long had it been since he had seen Melada? Almost seven months? It had been good for everyone, everyone felt better. There was no going back to the past, they had tortured each other too much. He wondered whether Melada knew that he was going back to Wife #5, to Jill. Probably she could guess. There had been something alarmingly unfamiliar in her look today, something had flitted across it that morning in Cleveland, when she and the children came on board. Or had it been in Windsor? Might it be the shadow of the Miserymaker? But when exactly? He couldn't remember.

> CLOSE UP OF RINGING ALARM CLOCK. THEN CRAWL ALONG EDGE OF BLANKET, THEN UP. A WOMAN'S FEET COME TO THE FLOOR, FEEL ABOUT FOR SLIPPERS. THE WOMAN GETS UP. WE SEE HER FROM BEHIND. SHE TIES HER ROBE, FREES HER HAIR FROM THE COLLAR. GOES TO THE WINDOW, OPENS THE BLINDS. MORNING NEWSPAPERS LIE IN VARIOUS COLORED PLASTIC BAGS ON THE LAWN. THE NEIGHBOR IS HOSING OFF HIS CAR. THE WOMAN WALKS ALONG THE CORRIDOR, TOUCHES PHOTOS OF THE CHILDREN ON THE WALL. THE SLIPPERS REMAIN ON THE RUG. A BARE LEG STEPS OVER THE EDGE OF A YELLOW TUB. SOUND OF WATER.

Then, five years ago, they had decided to fly directly from Helsinki to Mexico. More exactly, Anton had decided, and Melada had agreed. He had convinced her that they would never have another chance. That life in America would ensnare them, suck them dry, never leave them a day free for peaceful contemplation of the new sky, the new grass, the new monuments, new bridges, and one another. That he had to gather himself after all that they had been through. And that she did, too.

She had liked travelling to a new country. She smiled a lot. She turned her head to look at every palm, every donkey, every sombrero. She bought a mountain of bright postcards at the gas stations. And when they stopped at the mayor's office in the border town and he had explained to her that there was nowhere in the entire western hemisphere where it was cheaper or faster to get married, and he had chanced to buy a ring at a souvenir stand at their last stop, she seemed not fully to believe him. She took it to be some sort of exotic local game, a tourist attraction, and she took her part in it, smiling obediently, readily offering her lips to be kissed, lithely skipping away from the rice that was thrown at them as they went back out to the square.

The American customs officer congratulated Mr. and Mrs. Sebich on their safe return home.

Anton was in seventh heaven. Yes, he had been hasty! Yes, he had wanted to take advantage of her shock, her disorientation. And let her rebuke him later that he had taken her by deceit, by force, that he had abducted her at gun point, that he had slapped an off-the-rack Mexican wedding veil on her befuddled head. He was terribly frightened that she would reconsider, that some of her incorrigible prisoners would manage to break out of their cells and take control of her, force her to regret what she had done, abandon him, and go back to the Upside-down World.

Their first house was on the Hudson. Bought with the money that Sotheby's had sent when he offered his gift Chagall through them ("Oh, Mr. Sebich, this is an absolute sensation of the art world. You're like some sort of Jason, came back with his Argonauts from his voyages. What are you saying? You not only brought back the golden fleece, but a wife too? I hope her name isn't Medea, is it? And does Mr. Kozulin have a lot of these surprises? You think at least thirty? May we trust that you will inform him of our firm's reputation? We would be very happy indeed to undertake to sell them for him. We might discuss the matter of a commission...")

The seven-figure sum in the check they sent must have put him in a state of euphoria for many days. Otherwise he would have thought and rethought a score of times before buying this suburban mansion with a marble swimming pool. During the process of its construction the mansion had passed from one diplomat to another, and each diplomat added new details from his national architectural traditions. The problem wasn't the price (a freshly-hatched millionaire could permit himself such expenses) but that he often misplaced Melada in all the endless bedrooms, bathrooms, and studies. While searching for her he would wander from the Arab wing into the Spanish one, crossing the Chinese hall into the French orangery, obeying a muddled inner voice which kept telling him "cold, freezing, warmer, warmer," as in the children's game.

Sometimes he had to go up to the third floor and down again several times, shouting for her, before she would answer from some hidden Gothic tower which looked to have been built by some German descendant of Bluebeard. She would answer and then fling herself at him. Whereupon things would become blazing hot.

These first days together remained in his memory precisely in the heat emanating from her. The heat poured from her cheeks, her eyes, her hands. As though a roaring wood fire was burning within her, leaving her nothing of her own, filling her with another flaming nature which belonged to him alone. Only the burning outer skin pressed against him. She so flowed into him, so hung from him, that it was difficult to imagine that she might ever be able to return to independent existence. There was no lightness within her, not a drop. But he was in bliss beneath this burning weight which was so new to him.

WINDING WET HAIR INTO TOWEL TURBAN, THE WOMAN GOES INTO THE NURSERY. SHE WAKES THE CHILDREN, KISSES THEM, SENDS THEM ALONG TO THE BATHROOM. SHE GOES TO THE KITCHEN. KETTLE ON THE STOVE, BREAD IN THE TOASTER, EGGS IN THE FRY PAN. PANCAKES, JAM, ORANGE JUICE. SALT SHAKER IN THE SHAPE OF A MATRYOSHKA DOLL. NAPKINS WITH A RED ROOSTER ON THEM. REFRIGERATOR STICKERED OVER WITH NOTES—TELEPHONE NUMBERS, RECIPES, BILLS TO BE PAID, THE CLEANING LADY'S SCHEDULE. SUDDENLY THE WOMAN BEGINS TO RIP THESE NOTES FROM UNDER THE MAGNETS AND TOSSES THEM INTO THE GARBAGE WITHOUT LOOKING AT THEM.

Anton got up from where he was sitting and walked quietly along the now-cooling deck, glass in hand, toward the banquet room. Bobby was still singing, accompanying himself on electric piano. The audience was nodding dreamily along, forgetting about the furious Now as they drifted one after another off into their individual Yesterdays, Tomorrows, and Forevers.

Anton glanced at each in turn.

The elder Kozulin sat straight-backed in his motorized wheelchair, peering into the Varangian blackness outside the windows, from time to time wiping his cheek against the hand of the nurse who kept straightening his fluffy neck brace. The tenderness and dedication of this 40-year old woman seemed genuine, and even if they were warmed up a notch or two by the Malevich she had been promised in the will, who might raise a tongue in protest?

The old man's lapel bore a white button with a dog's head. The unforgettable Newfoundland had in a few years become the most famous dog in the country. His face smiled from Pirgoroy's ads on millions of television screens.

Wife #1 had gotten even fatter over the years. She said that she detested the universal dieting madness which had gripped the country, that she had no desire to descend to the level of the crazy women who fish out their pocket calculators after every spoonful of soup in order to ask the machine's permission to swallow a couple more calories. Do you like the ambulatory skeletons in skirts that clog New York? Well, that's your problem. The ham that she had baked for the last family supper had swum in splattering, bubbling fat. Son #1.2 told Anton in secret that almost no students took Professor Kozulin's courses, which upset her terribly. But she wasn't going to give in. A few chance political revolutions in Eastern Europe could not disturb the proper course of world history. And if the capricious students no longer wished to study the correct and scientifically based course then she was not going to suck up to their limitations by abandoning her convictions.

The only thing she could not come to terms with was Golda's betrayal. When the girl got back from the Upside-down Land she flat-out refused to live with her mother. She moved into a dorm and changed majors, and friends as well. There were rumors that she had been seen in the church. When she finished the university she went to work for some government agency whose name was suspiciously vague: Bureau of International Research. Her fiancé, who had come on the cruise, had a short soldier's crewcut and the condescending look of a man who knows more about you than you do yourself. From time to time they turned to each other and kissed carefully, paying no attention to those around them.

Incorrigible unforgiving Susan, Wife #3, had refused to come, as always. She had not even permitted the older twins to come, although they asked. But Mrs. Darcey was present. She was radiant. Blissful. What an evil lie, to say that she loved to manipulate people, to jerk them around on strings. If she took someone under her wing it was solely for that person's benefit. To help, to guide, to let the person regain strength, embark on a new path. Just as she had helped, directed, and given a push to Mr. Sebich, who was now famous. And if anyone were to ask her advice—such as for example the former second wife of Mr. Sebich—she would feel in no position to refuse that person.

Caitlin bent over her in the breaks between musical numbers, saying something softly. Then she listened to the answer, nodding thoughtfully. Wife #2 now had a very full business life. A few years previously she and two girl friends had started a new magazine called Complete Safety. There were departments in it like "Travel Without Surprises" and "Consequences of Risk." Despite what the skeptics predicted the magazine quickly gathered subscribers, its popularity growing with every month. Anton let them interview him several times for the column "Survivors' Tales." He was happy that Wife #2 had finally found an activity which suited her, and he was proud of her success. In his own way he had taught her a thing or two about how to fire at the enemy who was creeping up behind by means of the mirror of the Future. They were real friends by now. They always had things to talk about, because there were still so many things in life that they loved in common: their grown children, the battle against the Miserymaker, the sweet secret of the teapot, and the unforgettable proud little thing that was Susan.

Lin Chan was rocking a sleeping boy on her lap. The Babylonian, orphan of the sea, had grown up to be a sturdy plump lad who at five years had already mastered eighth grade math. Pablo-Pedro had left them, unable to endure the arrival of the family from Hong Kong, dreary merchants all, who had immediately opened bakeries whose main product was an endless cake in the shape of the Great Wall of China (sold by the inch, centimeter or section, with a slightly higher charge for the towers). Lin Chan hadn't stayed single long though. Both clans, the Kozulins and the Sebichs, were mightily surprised when Ronald Ironhand began to call them in turn to invite them to his wedding, hinting in embarrassment that they all more or less knew the bride.

Now he sat alongside his wife, glittering in captain's braids, and from time to time with one of his iron hands he would brush the hair from the face of the sleeping Babylonian. Lin Chan always complained that in family arguments about how the child was to be raised Ronald always prevailed over her because he would ask, "Who plucked this creature from the abyss of watery oblivion to God's world above, you or me?"

Wife #5 was right against the wall in the last row, hiding behind Mama-Aunt Clarence's back. She had agreed to come on one condition only, that neither by word nor gesture would Anton give away the secret of their renewed relations. No, no, she still hadn't decided anything, and she couldn't promise him anything. She hadn't spent her entire life hiding from her father's riches and fame just to drown in the riches and fame of her husband. And the children! Think of the children! How could they live under the burden of a double fame? Famous Grandpa Bobby had already phoned Famous Papa Anthony several times, and they were conspiring at tactics by which to convince Jill that affluenza was in the end not the most dangerous of diseases, and that her children might even prove immune to it.

The younger Kozulin had aged greatly after the death of his wife. She had died a few months after the happy reunion of the brothers, as if she indeed had only been waiting for the cup of water from the Neva and the clump of earth from the Summer Garden. Had it not been her blessings which had brought down on Anton's head all the unbelievable successes of the past few years? But on the other hand, wasn't it because of them, the old Kozulin brothers, that Melada had remained a stranger in the new world? Why had they disliked her so? They even tried not to use her name, getting by with just pronouns or numbers: "her," "that one," "your seventh." Even a week ago, when Anton had called the old man to ask whether Melada might not bring a girlfriend along on the cruise ("after all, she hardly knows any of the guests, she'll feel lonely") he had heard a long pause for an answer. "Anthony, what do you want with all that?" Admiral Kozulin finally said. "Why do you have to get all of your wives together? You sure there won't be a scene? They won't spoil the cruise? If your seventh is afraid that she'll be lonely with fifty guests there, shouldn't she stay home?"

Still, he had let himself be talked into it. Anton had noticed the girlfriend in passing, when they got on in Cleveland. Now, though, Melada was sitting alone. The girlfriend had probably stayed in the cabin with the children. Melada had gotten thinner and much prettier in the past months. She had had good success with fashions. Not like Wife #4, of course, but with a noticeable difference from the others. It couldn't be that she would remain alone for long. She had only to meet a man who would value devotion above all else. And seriousness. A lack of desire to laugh or joke about trifles. And a belief in the power of rules. And the ability to control oneself. And who was at least six feet tall. And who could calmly endure long offended silences.

She had promised Anton that at the end of the cruise she would tell him her conditions for an amicable divorce.

THE WOMAN SITS IN FRONT OF A THREE-PART MIRROR DOING HER EYELASHES AND BROWS. A THREE-YEAR OLD DAUGHTER PLAYS BE-HIND HER, IMITATING HER MOTHER, TURN-ING ABOUT TO GET A PROFILE IN THE MIRROR, ADMIRING HERSELF, CROSSING HER EYES. THE MOTHER PUTS THE COSMETICS DOWN, PICKS UP A COMB. SHE BEGINS TO COMB HER DAUGHTER'S HAIR. SHE TRIES ONE RIBBON, ANOTHER. A FOUR-YEAR OLD SON CREEPS UP BEHIND HER WITH A PLASTIC WATER PISTOL. HE AIMS AT THE MIRRORED REFLECTION OF THE MOTHER AND HIS SISTER. HE FIRES. THE DROPS, REFLECTED, DRIP DOWN THE GLASS.

The first year of their life in the mansion with the pool Anton was care and attention incarnate. He did not forget for a moment how difficult it would be for Wife #7 to get used to her new life. Ten times a day she had to cope with something she did not understand, do something that she did not know how to. And she loathed having to ask anyone for help, even him.

The toaster would burn her morning waffles black. The smoke detector on the wall would pierce her ears with his wail, and she would rip it out along with the screws, then hide it under her pillow. Once the washing machine, upset at being handled clumsily, wrapped itself in a mountain of sweet-smelling foam and began to dance about inside it. After that Melada wouldn't go near the machine, washing everything by hand. The obsequious American automobile tried to help her figure out the pedals, but she couldn't get used to it and every time tromped on them so hard that she just about put her forehead through the windshield.

Plus the language. To admit that she (a professional translator!) couldn't understand spoken American, which refused to separate words and phrases with proper pauses—this was beyond her powers. She was too proud ever to ask people who telephoned to repeat, and so said "yes" to everything, "wonderful," "how kind of you." After which it would turn out that she had promised to help collect money for building a new hospital, to join the religious group Jews for Jesus, subscribe to Golf magazine, join the neighbors in celebrating their anniversary. People then got offended, cursing the strange Russian lady under their breath. Only telephone salesmen and solicitors were happy with her. They seized upon her incautious "yes," taking her at her word, and then Anton had to send apologies and penalty payments back with the radios, vacuum cleaners, rugs, and refrigerators.

Hardest of all for Mrs. Sebich #7 were situations in which she had to submit to someone's assistance, good will, or hospitality. For example, to let Anton's secretary take her to a store she didn't know. Or go for an interview in the college where a friend of Mrs. Darcey had promised to help her find a teaching job. As for spending the night in someone else's house, that was out of the question. She would only agree to go to dinner if she would be permitted to bring expensive gifts of some sort that cost two or three times more than the hosts had paid—a case of fine wine, a fancy china vase, a samovar that no one wanted or needed.

Of his old friends the warmest to Wife #7 were the Kellers. For them, who had lived together thirty years, each of Anthony Sebich's new marriages was like the newest volume of a beloved novel, which they looked forward to reading with a dreamy and slightly envious curiosity. Both the Kellers and their guests tried to restrain their usual causticity when Melada was there. It was as if they were covering her with sterile bandages to prevent any microbes of irony from entering.

Anton had thought that Melada also loved these visits. She tried in every way she might to satisfy Martha Kellers's curiosity, as well as that of their friends from the college, economists who asked about the mysteries of the upside-down economy, where the consumer was always wrong. Sometimes, if there were a particularly large number of guests, Melada would excuse herself and ask permission to go off a bit by herself, to walk a bit along the stream. Once when she had returned unnoticed to the house and rejoined the jolly crowd, Anton heard one of the Kellers' neighbors, who had come about five minutes after Melada, say softly to her friend, "Hey, look, that's the woman."

"Where?"

"There, by the bar, pouring herself the juice. Remember, I told you? How she always sobs down by the stream, hugging the larch? I guess she thinks that the bushes hide her, doesn't know that you can see the larch from my bedroom window."

After that Anton no longer insisted when Melada said that she didn't feel like visiting.

THE GARAGE DOOR FLIES UP SILENT AND A BLUE TOYOTA PULLS SLOWLY OUT ONTO THE DRIVEWAY. THE CHILDREN ARE ALREADY INSIDE, SEAT-BELTED. THE YOUNGEST IS IN A CAR SEAT IN THE BACK, THE OLDER BOY IS IN THE FRONT, ALONGSIDE THE MOTHER. SHE BRAKES, SHUTS THE ENGINE OFF, GETS OUT. SHE GOES BACK, LOOKING THROUGH THE KEYS. SHE LOCKS THE GARAGE, THEN THE FRONT DOOR. THE BLINDS IN THE HOUSE ARE DOWN. THE WOMAN UNDOES THE KEYS FROM THE KEY CHAIN, PUTS THEM IN AN ENVE-LOPE, SEALS IT. SHE GETS BACK IN THE CAR. GRASSY SPACES, BUSHES, PORCHES SWIM PAST, DROWNING IN AUTUMN DAHLIAS. ON ONE OF THE LAWNS THERE IS A PLASTER DOLPHIN SPOUTING A CRUMBLING UM-BRELLA OF WATER. THE TOYOTA STOPS AT THE POST BOX. THE WOMAN ROLLS THE WIN-DOW DOWN AND THROWS THE ENVELOPE WITH THE KEYS INTO IT.

"Always sobs down by the stream, hugging the larch..." The phrase stuck in Anton's head for a long time. "Why?" he asked himself. "What doesn't she have? Can things really be so awful for her here? A loving husband, good friends, amusements, security, health. She's got every-thing. How many years is it going to take her to get used to her new life?"

To his mind the only real grounds for upset had come the first months. For example she had taken the newspaper scandals about their escape very much to heart. "Theft of National Treasures!" "Russia Demands Return of Stolen Pictures." "Who Owns Art?" "Theft of the Century!" Melada had to meet with diplomats from the Upside-down Motherland

and officially announce that she had not been kidnapped, that she had left voluntarily, but that she had had nothing to do with removal of the paintings. No, her reasons for leaving were entirely personal in nature, the desire to marry the man she loved. No, he is not a swindler or an adventurer. He wanted to teach them how to make good canned goods and build good bridges. While he was looking for his lost daughter. He also knew nothing about the paintings. He had simply helped an old eccentric man to leave.

Nevertheless she was declared an accessory to the crime, and a request for extradition was made. Even her father, Pavel Kasianovich Sukhumin, published a renunciation of his daughter the traitor in a central Moscow newspaper, expunging her forever from his heart, as well as from the list of the guiltless.

The newspaper abuse could have been ignored by shutting herself up on the edge of her marble swimming pool in her multinational suburban mansion. But where could she hide from the specters of former wives? They turned up everywhere, reminding her of their presence with a gift inscription on a lamp, or with a photograph forgotten between the pages of a book, or with the phone calls from the children, or by the chance misspeaking of the new acquaintances.

"What difference does it make how many there were before you?" Anton exclaimed. "Is it really so important? The important thing is that now I don't need anybody other than you. I don't ask you how many men you loved before we met. My ex-wives haven't done anything bad to you, and your former admirer almost mashed me into the sand with his tractor treads back there in Kon-Kolodets."

It was important to her, though. Very important. Each time she discovered another wife in his past it hurt as much as if she were discovering an adultery. Today's, in full heat. Yet it wasn't jealousy. The bitterness of loss, rather. As if the growth of the number she was moved her farther and farther away from something without which life was no longer life for her. But from what? Trying to explain it to him, she used a Russian word that at first he did not understand.

"You've just forgotten. It's the same thing that old Kozulin was babbling about in the port in Helsinki. Uniqueness. How everybody tries to get something unique, how they'll pay any money you want to get it. I hadn't understood how important that is to me, until I began to lose it. Every time one of your old wives floats up out of the past, my uniqueness gets smaller. How much do I have left? A fifth?" (This conversation was before she had learned of Wives #3 and #4.)

As ever he hoped that the birth of their child would distract her from these bitter accounts. However their son Nikifor was unable to play the role of conciliator. The opposite—he became the focus of savage arguments.

Anton would try to keep his voice calm.

"Explain to me why you want to raise him the way they raised you back in Kon-Kolodets," he said. "Why do you want to lead him along the exact same paths that your Granny Pelageia led you along? You grew up to be so happy? You think you're a model of something, an example? Even if that were true, your son is another person. He might have a different character, other needs, other desires."

"No, no, no...you've got everything backwards. It's the other way around! I want him to become what I wasn't able to be, I want him to avoid all the pitfalls that I fell into."

"So how come every time he says 'I want' you have to say 'you can't?' What's the harm if he has strawberries first thing in the morning, instead of waiting until after breakfast? Why can't he turn the lights on and off? Why can't he suck on my ear? If he doesn't want to sleep yet, why force him? What, he's got to get up early to go to work?"

"A child has to have a regimen, he has to know the difference between what he can do and what he can't."

"But how come your 'can' is so little and your 'can't' is so incredibly huge? How is he going to learn to use a knife and fork or scissors and paste or soap dish and hairbrush if you take them all away from him, if they are always the other side of the 'can't' border?"

She couldn't stay calm and would begin to shout that he was erasing her, that nothing in the house belonged to her, that she couldn't even call the child hers or raise him thee way she wanted. Nikifor would begin to cry, hitting one or the other of them with his fists. The father was quick to get on his knees and answer the child with a series of extremely gentle uppercuts. The mother would break off the battle between two unequal weight divisions and carry the kicking fighter out beyond the ropes, into the safety of "can't".

She could take no pleasure in their wealth. She got no pleasure from their house, his blooming insurance business, the royalties on the book about their adventures on the Babylonia, the royalties on his radio and television appearances on behalf of Pirgoroy. (The refrigerator for travelling cat owners proved very popular, and Admiral Kozulin generously gave the inventor two cents for every can that the timer opened.) She began to pinch pennies. She would cut twenty-cent coupons out of the newspapers and magazines, and then proudly tot up her savings after every trip to the store. She conscientiously kept all the leftovers in the refrigerator. She would offer chicken leftovers, and left-over leftovers. A piece of bread had to be hard as a rock, a chunk of sausage had to sprout green spots before she would agree to throw them out.

She wanted to earn money of her own. Anton didn't object. She tried giving Russian lessons at home, and their friends tried hard to find pupils for her. For some reason the students never lasted very long. Anton called one of the students to ask straight out why she had stopped the lessons. After all, they surely didn't cost much.

"Your wife would get too upset at my mistakes," the woman answered frankly. "You'd have thought that the earth would stop turning if I said 'I heared' instead of 'I heard.' She would stop me and correct me almost every word. I'll never get ready for a trip to Moscow in a month like that."

"Here too it's the same," Anton thought. "It's all the same. The drive for absolute correctness, no matter what the cost. The correct words, the correct feelings, the correct regimen, the correct children..."

She tried to understand him.

"You want to say that I should be more spontaneous? That I have to be freer with myself and with others? That I have the right to act as my emotions tell me whenever I want? That all my emotions—all of them! every last one of them!—has the right to exist. Petty emotions, evil ones, fleeting ones, base ones, selfish ones? All of them? You want me to say everything I think right now, give you both emotional barrels in the face? Then you better go to the other side of the kitchen, and take away that big frying pan and that iron. And lock the knife drawer. And then get a great big pillow from the couch. Big enough to stop a flying soup bowl."

He could see that she wasn't kidding. Her sense of offense was growing day by day. Crowding love out. Sometimes it began to seem to him that her offense was infused with love, becoming a sign of special closeness. After all, she never got angry at other people, at strangers. Only at him. His words and actions couldn't be what was causing the offense, because the words and actions were all different, and the offense lived on forever, unchanging, save sometimes to be weaker, sometimes stronger. Offense that we are in the same room, but you aren't with me. That I'm next to you, but you are looking away. That you are looking at me, but not smiling. That you are smiling, but you aren't coming over to me. That you are coming over to me, but not hugging me. That you are hugging me, but not undressing me. That you are undressing me, but aren't trembling with happiness. That you are trembling with happiness but it will all end in a minute. That it all ended, and that you are no longer in me, but going away somewhere again.

Maybe she was waiting for him to answer her in kind somehow? To get offended at her for something, deeply, bitterly offended, to the point of tears? And their offenses would fling themselves at one another, and so flow together in an eternally indissoluble embrace? Perhaps, for her, offense had become the only form of spiritual closeness, of loving touch, of which she was capable? But how then could he help her with it?

THE LITTLE BLUE TOYOTA WITH THE TWO CHILDREN AND THE WOMAN DRIVING IS IN THE CENTER LANE OF A SIX-LANE HIGHWAY. RIGHT AND LEFT ARE THE WHEELED PLAY-THINGS OF ADULTS: MOTORBOATS, MOBILE HOMES, HORSE TRAILERS, MOBILE SWIMMING POOLS. THE TOYOTA INCHES CAREFULLY RIGHT, LEAVES THE ROAD. TURNS INTO A MOTEL. STOPS. A GIRL IN A BRIGHT DRESS COMES OUT OF THE MOTEL. SHE HAS A LITTLE WHITE SUITCASE. SHE IS WEARING A BROAD-BRIMMED HAT. SHE WAVES A DOLL-LIKE HAND AT THE TOYOTA. A PUFF OF BREEZE ALMOST CARRIES HER HAT OFF. THE GIRL GETS IN THE BACK DOOR, SLAMMING IT CARE-LESSLY, SO THAT THE HEM OF HER DRESS STICKS OUT. THE TOYOTA GETS BACK ON THE HIGHWAY, THE BRIGHTLY COLORED SCRAP OF CLOTH FLAPPING IN THE WIND.

The salon was empty. The tired guests had gone back to their cabins. They all wanted to rest up for the next day. Tempting pastimes to suit everybody had been planned. Horseback rides, a concert by a famous violinist, roulette, water-jetting, golf, fishing, the debut of a new comedy film sent from Hollywood as a gift, and then, the evening banquet.

Before leaving Melada brought the sleepy children to Anton. He kissed them, wished them a good night, promised them a ride the next day on the snow-white llama that had come down from the high Andes just to meet them. Melada permitted him to hug her as well, then offered her cheek. Yet when he touched her shoulders he could feel how tense she was, exactly as if suppressing her instinctive desire to jerk away.

Which meant things still had not healed in her. When she had left she thought that she only needed a couple of weeks. A few weeks in the wilds of Pennsylvania ("People say that the mountains in the north are a lot like the Carpathians") to think things over, get in touch with herself. She asked him not to pay for the cabin in advance, so she could come home at a moment's notice. But then she hadn't. Seven months in a row, and apparently it still hurt. But why seven? In fact it was a lot more. Almost eighteen. Because it was a year and half since his trip to Albany. After which he had come in and approached her, arms wide, to kiss and joke as if nothing had happened.

But it didn't work.

How could she feel that something had happened? What lessons taught her by the witches of Pskov had so sharpened the acuity of her sense of jealousy? He had not given himself away in anything. The trip was as usual as could be, planned well in advance, and he had in fact taken part in an evening television debate, which she could have watched herself, on channel 20. There was no way she could have found out that the night before Daughter #5.3 had called him at work for some advice, and during the conversation it had come out—a simple coincidence!—that they were also going to Albany that day, to visit their sick Aunt-Mother-Grandmother Clarence. How could daddy not come round to see them all? She needed his advice so badly right now! Because she had absolutely no idea how she should behave with that awful Peter Leroy. Who thinks that just because he's good at basketball that gives him the right to look down on his old friends. And not even come to rehearsals of the school play. And anyway in general...

Of course he couldn't say no to his daughter, and came to Albany a couple of hours early. And went to grandmother Clarence's house. And sitting on the couch with his arm around Daughter#5.3 while they worked out a strategy for dealing with the stuck-up basketball star he suddenly felt the glistening gaze of familiar eyes upon himself. Which still could, as they had many years before, in the roar of landing airplanes, melt with joy at meeting a stranger. And the berry of love suddenly ballooned in his throat with such belated strength that he choked. And asked for a glass of juice. And Wife #5 left, fussing for ages in the unfamiliar kitchen. So that he had gone after her. And there, in a tight corner behind the refrigerator, they leapt at each other like teenagers. Hugging one another as if they had not had behind them painful discoveries and adulteries and insults, not family routine, not the bitterness of parting.

"How are you? How's everything? You remember me? Yes, yes, yes! And you? I always remember... Always... Oh, what are we doing, what are we doing? We'll regret it later...You're older.. I listen to all your shows... Don't... Don't let that get out... Oh, my God! You haven't changed... That's not for nothing...it isn't just chance that brought us together...today...let's get together today. Your hotel? Maybe no... Our cabin in the mountains... I'll be free at nine... You remember? The woodpeckers' treasury? It's an hour away. You remember? You can find the way? I'll get there ahead of you. Oh, I can hardly wait to see you."

He lost every point of the television debate. He could scarcely wait until the end of the broadcast. In pitch black he sought out the road to the forest castle as if he had lived there all his life. Candle flames multiplied on the glasses, the knives, the grapes, on the beads of Wife #5. He looked at her high cheekbones, her eyes shining with fear and awe, and could not understand how he had ever been able to leave this woman. Who did not believe that happiness was possible for her, but who waited for it constantly. A woman closer and more necessary than any other in the world.

Just as ten years before, they felt like criminals on the lam, who had made a brief escape from under the never-sleeping watch of the tireless "have-to"s. And just as before they thought they could feel detectives hidden out in the dark, their lenses focusing on them. And just as he had then he felt the fluttering of butterflies of fear beneath his fingertips as they rested on her stomach. And the thankful astonishment was the same when she said afterwards, "How you can shout, sweetheart, how you can shout..."

But the next day though they turned obediently back, each to his own "have-to"—without plans, no words said about how they might some-time, somewhere steal themselves another such meeting.

Anton showered in his hotel, checked that no one had called him in the night, bought the kids souvenirs at the gift shop, a silver and agate ring for Melada and then he went home feeling tender, loving, and guiltless.

But she knew everything.

Guessed it at the first glance.

Apparently the night in the Woodpeckers' Castle had marked him somehow, remaining as a cloud of happiness which no sponge or shampoo could wash away.

She jerked back, almost jumped.

He thought he heard the scrape of closing bars, bolts, latches.

He hoped that it would pass, sooner or later. But it didn't pass in a week, not in two, not in a month. She stayed alone almost all the time, completely alone, a volunteer in her own prison. She came out to him for short appointments. Speaking as if through glass. She accused him of nothing, asked him about nothing. She showed not the slightest desire to come out to freedom. It was as though he were being offered the only possible route by which to bring her back, or to come back to her—to join her in her life sentence of secret incarceration.

Which he didn't wish to do. His patience wore thin. He also began to rebel.

THE TOYOTA STOPS AT THE DRIVE-UP WINDOW OF AN ICE CREAM STAND. BEHIND IT THERE ARE THREE ROWS OF COLORED PHOTOS OF SUNDAES, FLOATS, GLASSES WITH ORANGE SLICES, MELON SLICES, BANANAS ON THE RIMS. THE WOMAN DRIVING ROLLS HER WINDOW DOWN, GETS A MENU FROM THE WOMAN INSIDE. THE GIRL IN THE BRIGHT DRESS POINTS DECISIVELY AT A PHOTO OF STRAWBERRIES AND WHIPPED CREAM. THE SON TAKES COFFEE ICE CREAM. THE DAUGHTER FUSSES, REFUSING TO CHOOSE, POINTING AT THE PASSENGER'S WHITE BAG INSTEAD OF AT THE MENU. THE PASSENGER DOESN'T UNDERSTAND AT FIRST BUT THEN OPENS THE ZIPPER WIDE. "YES, YES," THE LITTLE FUSSER NODS HER HEAD. SHE WANTS WHAT IS IN THE RED THERMOS INSIDE THE BAG. THE PASSENGER LAUGHS, SHAKES HER HEAD. NO, YOU CAN'T HAVE THAT.

Undressing in his cabin Anton tried again to recall that anxious alarmed sensation that had flashed by during the day. The shadow of the Miserymaker was sliding past somewhere close by—of that he was sure. But where? Yes, it had been that morning, during the stop in Cleveland. The guests coming aboard Babylonia 2 had had to go through a metal detector gate. Naturally there had been an element of awkwardness in that sort of mistrust, which cast a bit of a shadow on the holiday. But the insurance company had insisted. A ship loaded with so many rich people and such works of art was too great a temptation for bandits. A well-trained handsome guard greeted everyone with a smile, gave the women a helping hand, and tried to make a joke of the whole thing.

Yes, perhaps it was for the best that Pablo-Pedro had refused to take the job of head of security for the Pirgoroy empire. His coarseness would definitely have ruined the mood of at least someone among the guests. He was completely satisfied with his work as a night watchman in the giant cosmetics plant, which paid him a double salary. Double because he allowed them to test new male deodorants on him. The only thing he had to do was promise not to wash for weeks. At night the stinking watchman didn't bother anyone and so could devote the long hours of his watch to his new favorite activity, translating the cost of luxury goods into the cost of good deeds. A small radical newspaper had published the results of his investigations. "The money that the billionaire Sophargys paid for the new limousine designed especially for him could have built three hospitals in Bangladesh, provided housing for 319 homeless in Chicago, given textbooks and clothes to 92,836 schoolchildren in Mozambique..."

Lin Chan, sent to negotiate with him, returned in alarm. She found her ex-husband leafing through fresh newspapers and magazines. His eyes were racing greedily through the social pages and the photographs in search of new victims.

"What are you keeping it a secret for?" he tapped his nail on the picture of a British princess. "You should know that you've been on my list a long time. Just try and buy yourself that new race horse. I'll be slinging mud at you real soon! And as for this one, just look at this one! Look how she's looking around. But it's not all just humping around buck naked on the screen and getting new husbands. You don't think I know how much your latest villa cost? Precisely two shiploads of rice for starving Ethiopians. You'll be reading about yourself real soon, don't you worry..."

Ah, Pablo-Pedro, poor Pablo-Pedro, an honest soldier in the hopeless battle for equality! Have you never heard that people kill themselves in despair in luxurious villas? That even in a castle with a marble swimming pool it is possible to be deeply and hopelessly unhappy? It is only hunger of the belly that can be stilled with a simple handful of rice, identical for all. People are not equal in the hunger of their souls, however, and there is nothing you can do about it, nothing Leo Tolstoy can do about it, nor Karl Marx, nor Jean-Jacques Rousseau, nor all the twelve apostles.

Pacing back and forth before the doors behind which Wife #7 had hidden in the prison of her secrecy, Anton composed speeches. Not the speeches of a man justifying himself however. They were attacks.

Yes, I did everything I could not to hurt you. And it isn't my fault that I wasn't able to conceal the main thing. That sense of renewal that remained in me after that night in the Woodpeckers' Castle. As if I had had a bracing swim in a warm forest lake. And you with your sorceress's senses immediately recognized it, discovered my feeling. So what? Go ahead and say again that I am an eternal nomad, that I carry off my boards and bricks, that I am chasing after other people's pastures and leave ruins behind.

And what if I don't want to go anywhere? How could you know, maybe I just feel cramped in your house? Maybe I'm just meant always to be building a newer and more roomy house? That would have room for all my wives and all my children and all the people I love? Because I do not have the strength to stop loving anyone and can not believe that this was sent me as a curse, instead of a blessing.

Of course he tried out snatches of these speeches in his television sermons.

The producer grabbed his head and ran to him from all the way across the studio, shaking his papers at him.

"Tony, you want to kill me? Tony, you want to ruin me? What is all this blather about Bible patriarchs with many wives? What's Jacob got to do with it and Deuteronomy and King Solomon? This is the 20th century we're living in! Who is going to 'remember our times as...' how did you put it? Oh yeah, 'as a benighted and evil era of compulsory monogamy?' That's 'no better than the kind of barbarism that obligates people to bury living wives and horses along with the tribal leader when he dies!'"

"Jack, enough. You know that I'm always speaking from the point of view of an imaginary person, an almost crazy prophet..."

"That's enough! Quit kidding yourself. The days are gone when some unknown Anthony Sebich can blather on about whatever comes into his head and then hide behind someone else's back. Now all your viewers, all your listeners know you down to your socks. How many wives you've had, how many children, how many divorces, they know everything! And you think that they're going to believe in some sort of made-up violator of the family bond? Have you ever seen the form that an immigrant to this country has to fill out? Nobody gets asked whether he's a thief or a heretic or a drug addict or a killer. No! The only thing that he is obligated to swear to is that he hasn't professed and will not profess polygamy. And if he swears it, come right on it! If not, then you can't come in! A broadcast like that one they won't buy from me even in Utah!"

"My weirdo isn't spreading polygamy! He's just talking about the unnecessary sufferings of millions of lonely people. Who hate loneliness and are filled with love they can't use, who are ready to share it with others. To live with a person they love, man or woman, in threes, in fours. But they can't. Because society will immediately hold them up to shame."

"And what do you want instead? Bands of hippies in clouds of marijuana smoke again? Separate towns for the 'liberated' types who look for each other through newspaper ads? Or just that someone starts a Society of Postlapsarian Sinners?"

"No, not at all. He recognizes the sanctity of marriage. Let people who value uniqueness above all live as they wish, their entire lives together, or alone in proud solitude. But for the others, to whom the words 'I love you' are more important than 'I own you,' let them live as their hearts demand. Modern, so-called civilized society, my eccentric would say, was created by property owners. They knew how to value property, but not how to value love. They knew nothing about love. So they also created the family on the principles which they revered. 'You are mine and I am yours. Forever. Inalienably. Irretractably. With all pursuant interest payments. With all inevitable losses.' History has not always done things that way, though. And in life there are only a certain number of people who are able to submit themselves fully to that principle. Reread the biographies of the people to whom we have raised monuments in the civilized countries. Are there many among them capable of living an entire life in a good marriage? Read the statistics, flip through the court reports of divorces and adultery. My eccentric is simply expressing the idea that love is like talent. Some people have it in abundance, others are without it. It is possible to live happily without talent and without love. There are many other pleasures in life. But living with unexploited talent and with unsatisfied love, that's torment. Can you imagine the society in which no person was allowed to write more than one book in his life, paint more than one picture, compose one sonnet? What my eccentric is saying is that all your Raphaels, Beethovens, and Faulkners would become outlaws in such a society. Just the way the good-hearted Casanova was made into an outlaw."

Outraged Producer Jack jammed the wadded-up sheets of paper into the waste basket and ran out of the office shouting, "Not me! Do what you want to do, but I'm not putting my name on it! I've had enough family scandals as it is! Somebody else try to break it to this blockhead that there's got to be a limit in everything!"

Anton backed off, putting the dangerous topic off for some other time. But inwardly he didn't surrender. A man must do what he's fated to do. To follow the faint cry. Even if he doesn't precisely know where it's leading him.

He didn't know. He didn't know what forced him again and again to sneak a day, an evening, a night, to jump in the car and dash to some motel in the middle of nowhere, halfway to Pittsburgh. Believing that coming toward him raced a car with a purple flag from another planet. The fields of love converged with the fields of danger, and at their point of intersection was an unbearably seductive radiance. The radiance surrounded Jill as she came to him through the door of the modest room, hanging on the outer knob the unhonorable request to "Please Do Not Disturb." Even to her he could promise nothing more than himself, that instant. And he was happy that she asked him to be no other. And that she raced to meet him, no matter when he called.

Who was to know, perhaps he was meant to spend the rest of his days with her? Or perhaps he was meant to begin with her and then go back along the entire path, returning in turn to each of his former wives. Perhaps instead he had to go only forward, even to a twelfth wife, and end his cruise through life on a ship packed with wives and children, who loved him and each other without jealousy, brought together by his love. This cruise on the Babylonia 2 that had brought so many people together who, had it not been for him, would never have found out whether they might like each other—might that not be a rehearsal for that future, final triumph? Perhaps his entire task was to have a great deal of love, enough for everybody?

THE TOYOTA STOPS AT A SPOT NEAR THE DOCK. BOTH WOMEN GET OUT, HELP THE CHILDREN OUT. THE PASSENGER TAKES THE BOY'S HAND. HIS MOTHER PUTS THE LITTLE SUITCASE IN A CART THAT ALSO HAS A SEAT FOR THE GIRL. THEY GO TOWARD THE GLIT-

TERING BABYLONIA 2. THEY SUDDENLY STOP
AND TURN, WAVING TO THE CAMERAMAN.
THE CAMERAMAN'S HAND APPEARS IN THE
PICTURE FOR A SECOND, WAVING BACK. IT IS
FUZZY, UNFOCUSSED. HOWEVER THE RINGS
AND LACE CUFF MAKE IT OBVIOUS THAT THE
CAMERAMAN IS A WOMAN. THE NEW ARRIV-
ALS GO UP THE GANGPLANK. THE JOVIAL SE-
CURITY MAN GREETS THE CHILDREN, CAR-
RIES THEM ONE AFTER THE OTHER THROUGH
THE METAL DETECTOR. HE OFFERS HIS HAND
TO THE WOMEN. THE PASSENGER IN THE
BRIGHT DRESS GETS THE RED THERMOS OUT
OF THE BAG, APOLOGETICALLY SHOWS IT TO
THE GUARD, TAPPING HER FINGER ON THE
METAL CASE. THE GUARD NODS UNDER-
STANDINGLY, HELPS PUT THE THERMOS BACK
INTO THE WHITE BAG. HE LETS THEM ONTO
THE SHIP.

A strangled cry woke Anton. He started up, sat on the bed, goggling at the darkness of the cabin. He understood immediately that it was he who had shouted.

"Just a bad dream," he thought. "Thank heaven it was just a night-mare. That I can wake up and save myself."

But the fear wouldn't go away.

He understood what had happened: in a dream his memory had finally been able to find the worrisome spot that had tormented him all day. The red thermos that he had glimpsed in the open bag.

Scores of other insignificant impressions instantly flared, focussing on that burning spot.

How?! How could he have forgotten about her?

Melada's friend! Where had Melada's friend gone to? And who was she? Wasn't she the one who had left the dock during the final, short stop in Windsor? True, that woman had been wearing a brown pant suit. But couldn't she simply have changed clothes, leaving the bright dress in the cabin? He had briefly noticed the woman as she left, but didn't recognize her. Now he remembered, there had been something familiar in her doll-like walk. Someone had distracted him at just that moment. He had never seen her face. In the evening she had not had a hat on. And he remembered a little detail—the ear lobe of the woman as she left had looked strangely deformed to him, as if squashed.

As he sank deeper into his abyss of unspeakable horror, he remembered too the strange expression on Melada's face this evening. And instead of saying 'good-night' as usual, she had spoken in Russian, 'farewell.' And the children? They hadn't been in the hall at first. Had she woken them? Brought them in to say farewell?

He shrieked again, this time awake.

He began to fight his way free of the bonds of blankets and sheets. Barefoot, dishevelled, half-naked, he dashed out into the corridor and dashed along it, shouting and banging on doors.

The frightened passengers woke one after another, stuck their heads out their doors, asking what had happened.

The alarm went off.

Blind with horror Anthony Sebich raced down the stairs and passages of the unfamiliar ship, unable to find the entrance to the hold.

"The fuel tank!" he shouted. "Where's the fuel tank?! Find the fuel tank! Hurry! There still might be time!"

Here we will leave him.

Czech explosives are not nearly as reliable as most people think. There have been instances, one in five hundred maybe, when they have even failed to respond to the electronic injection from the detonator.

The batteries in the detonator could be bad too. Their expiration date is unknown. Nor do we know how long they lay around, waiting for their hour. We don't even know the hour, or the moment, when the electrical contacts are set to touch.

Melada might realize what she is doing, and be horrified by what she has planned to do. She might dash out of her cabin, take him by the hand, drag him down a secret stair into the hold, show him the place—if she knows it—where the diabolical machine is taped to a fuel line on the bottom of the fuel tank.

He may have time because all of us, through Your unspoken mercy, have the saving refuge of existence. Where the seconds are so long that a barefoot runner can outstrip electrons coursing down a wire. Even if he does not have time, though—even if he loses his last race with the Miserymaker—we still may take the place of the Solitary Islander in front of his television. When we see the terrible pictures of the catastrophe on Lake Huron on our morning news shows, we can praise, in spite of everything, Your explosive power and incomprehensible wisdom.

Like hopeless left-back second graders do we not still have the right to raise our hands over and over, always to ask You the same questions? What is the meaning of these shattered bodies floating in a mix of diesel fuel and blood? How are we to understand the child's ribbon stuck to the fragment of a bed? What way marker for us is the face of a rescued woman, her eyes blown out?

Are we to continue improving our methods of self-defense and self-preservation for all eternity?

Or are we simply to respond to Your call each day, not waiting for the terrible shouts to remind us?

But why then must Your call stay so torturously obscure? If You wished, You might make its meaning plain even to ones so dense as we. What would it cost You to say simply and firmly: "Go there. Do that."? We would understand that, obey it, rush gratefully to do as told. But You don't want that? You get no pleasure from the fabric of Creation if the glittering thread of freedom is plucked from it? Our chance to be free even of Your commandments?

Of course there are those among us who hear Your call clearer and sharper than others. They strain onwards and upwards, towards You, always towards You. Yet even they halt, puzzled and melancholy, to look at the drowning passengers of Babylonia 2, old, young, and infant.

"This can't be the condition You set," they say. "It can't be that we are to run towards You as hard as we can, and as we do so not let the laggards fall behind? Can you be asking that not a single wounded heart remain behind? Ask us, rather, to order all the books of the world according to all alphabets of all languages, of all ancient and modern Towers of Babel."

But You are silent. And You let sick hearts shriek their unbearable terrible truth with a bloody uprooted tongue until we hear.

Are we meant to have time?

On what hour, day, month, year, century is Your detonator set?